THE HISTORY OF
TAMMANY HALL

THE HISTORY OF
TAMMANY HALL

BY

GUSTAVUS MYERS

WITH

A NEW INTRODUCTION BY

ALEXANDER B. CALLOW, JR.

DEPARTMENT OF HISTORY
UNIVERSITY OF CALIFORNIA
SANTA BARBARA

SECOND EDITION
REVISED AND ENLARGED

DOVER PUBLICATIONS, INC.

NEW YORK

Published in Canada by General Publishing Company, Ltd., 30 Lesmill Road, Don Mills, Toronto,
Ontario.
Published in the United Kingdom by Constable
and Company, Ltd., 10 Orange Street, London WC 2.

This Dover edition, first published in 1971, is an
unabridged and unaltered republication of the second
edition of the work originally published by Boni &
Liveright, Inc., N. Y., in 1917 (the first edition was
1901). A new Introduction has been written specially
for the present edition by Alexander B. Callow, Jr.

International Standard Book Number: 0-486-21554-4
Library of Congress Catalog Card Number: 78-164733

Manufactured in the United States of America
Dover Publications, Inc.
180 Varick Street
New York, N. Y. 10014

INTRODUCTION
TO THE DOVER EDITION

Tammany, Tammany,
Swamp 'em swamp 'em, get the "wumpum," Tammany
Tammany, Tammany, your policemen can't be beat.
They can sleep on any street . . . .
When Reformers think it's time to show activity,
They blame everything that's bad on poor old Tammany . . . .
They say when a bad man dies he goes to Tammany Hall . . . .
On the level you're a devil, Tammany.

> *From the song "Tammany, A Pale-Face Pow-Wow"*
> *by Vincent Bryan and Gustave Edwards*

Gustavus Myers died on December 7, 1942 at the age of seventy. If by some uncanny triumph over old age he had lived until today, he would have considered the reprinting of *The History of Tammany Hall* a delicious irony, indeed. Few books have had such a treacherous publishing history; it is, in fact, a saga that resembles the crafty political infighting of a Tammany Hall meeting itself. Myers brought out both editions when Tammany warriors were on a rampage: the first during the Seth Low campaign of 1901, the second during the John F. Hylan campaign of 1917. On both occasions the book came very close to not appearing at all. On both occasions the success of the book was threatened by the subject of the book, the most powerful, efficient, corrupt political machine in the history of urban America, New York's Tammany Hall.

The test of a city machine's power is not always limited to the political arena; Tammany could also reach the rarefied level of publishing. After years of bone-hard work, Myers could not find a publisher for his history in 1901. It had nothing to do with the quality of his work. The book was

simply too "hot," too embarrassing, too revealing about the
past and present of the New York Democracy. Tammany
threatened one publisher with higher assessments on his building if he published the book. Myers was forced to bring it out
by private subscription in a modest edition of only 1,000
copies. Almost immediately the books started to vanish. It
was said that Tammany ordered booksellers to buy and retire
all copies. *The History of Tammany Hall* became a suppressed
book. For sixteen years it was a collector's item.

By 1917 it was almost the same story all over again. Publishers feared the wrath of a Tammany Hall scorned. Finally,
Boni & Liveright had the courage to publish the second edition,
and from that time on it became required reading for any
serious student of the city machine in American history. Now
with this third edition, fifty-four years later, Myers' history
has passed the final test, in some ways the most difficult one
—the test of time—to become recognized as a classic of its
kind. For good reasons.

This is the best history of Tammany Hall in the literature.
There have been others, usually of two varieties: the effusive
whitewash, written to applaud the Hall and to hail its chiefs,
laced with the sentimental rhetoric of a Chamber of Commerce tract; or the fiery denunciation, crowded with moral
platitudes, depicting Tammany sachems as a kind of Satan's
Rogue Gallery. Perhaps the closest to Myers in quality is
M. R. Werner, *Tammany Hall* (New York, 1928), which differs
in approach with its emphasis on personalities rather than
political organization, but it lacks Myers' vigorous sense of
historical continuity and, above all, his dedication to accuracy.
For Myers' history is not only a brave and invaluable book,
it is also solid history—accurate, painstaking, thoroughly re-
searched. It is as an historian that Gustavus Myers shines.

Louis Filler, in fact, has argued that more than Raymond
Baker, Lincoln Steffens or even Ida Tarbell, Gustavus Myers
was *the* historian of the Progressive movement.[1] A pioneer

---

[1] *Crusaders For Modern Liberalism* (1950), 118.

of the muckraking tradition, Myers was unique, with the possible exception of Ida Tarbell, in method, approach and passion. Where the muckrakers mounted an almost myopically
present-minded attack upon evils ranging from corrupt trusts
and insufferable working conditions to impure food and
prostitution, Myers dove for depth into history. This "indefatigable mole," this "fact-worshipping reporter of Philadelphia
and Manhattan," dug deep into faded, dusty and often dull
records of the past: old newspapers, magazines, pamphlets,
municipal and state government journals and documents.
Where the literature of protest boomed with the thunder of
moral indignation and paraded characters colorful and flam-
boyant, Myers was quiet and chilly, piling up his evidence in
huge drifts of icy facts. His palette consisted of somber grays
and blacks. What emerged were no sermons on sin, like those
of William Allen White, no yeasty account of bad old New
York, as Alfred Lewis would have it; no adventures of generous, thoughtful, humorous political buccaneers such as
Lincoln Steffens found, but rather the numbing argument that
the history of Tammany Hall was the history of greedy, cold,
calculating thieves who, long on sagacity, short on honor,
manipulated the organization to plunder the public treasury.
It was a history of deception, broken promises, hypocrisy and
greed; above all, it was an orgy of corruption. The grandeur
of the larceny was staggering, whether committed by William
Mooney, the founder of the Wigwam; or Matthew Davis, who
stole $80,000 as City Treasurer; or Samuel Swartwout, who,
as Collector of the Port of New York, collected over a million
dollars and skipped; or Fernando Wood, who sold public
offices as Mayor; or Napthali Judah, who made tens of thousands in one day by tinkering with the Medical Science
Lottery; or the most notorious of all, the Tweed Ring, who
stole over two hundred million dollars.

This is the thesis of the book. What gives it a stunning
and enduring impact, what has made it persuasive to so many
readers for so many years, is the style of presentation: a
straightforward account, buttressed by the seemingly objective

tactic of let-the-facts-speak-for-themselves, all resting upon patient and exhaustive research.

Does this make Myers what in some quarters is seen as a model historian: aloof from the din of events, scrupulously objective, letting the hard facts and not bias reveal his subject? Myers claimed he was non-partisan. He was not. No historian is or can be. Objectivity is violated at the very start when the historian selects one fact over another. Gustavus Myers was intensely partisan, intensely anti-Tammany, convinced its history was an evil one. Like other muckrakers, he was passionate, but his passion was poured into his research, not his prose. He claimed he avoided moral platitudes. He did. He was a very moral man who did not moralize. He was shocked by the corruptions of Tammany, but restraint, not cajoling, was his method.

Throughout his career, he was passionately and morally committed to exposing injustices in American society. Unlike many crusading authors, Myers did not write from a comfortable middle-class background. Born in the industrial ugliness of Trenton, N. J., he endured a childhood of desperate poverty. Abandoned at seven, a factory worker at fourteen, he became a Populist, a Socialist (after five years he quit the party in 1912), a newspaperman, and finally a professional writer. In a dozen books, from 1900, with his scholarly exposé *The History of Public Franchises in New York*, to 1942, when he collapsed and eventually died from his labors on *The History of Bigotry in the United States*, he was a gadfly to American consciences.[2]

Gustavus Myers, then, was a committed partisan, and it affected his estimation of Tammany's growth and success. The modern urban historian, for example, would argue that he placed too much emphasis upon greed and corruption in accounting for the rise of Tammany. There was simply more to it than that. The rise of Tammany Hall was tightly stitched

---

[2] His monumental three-volume *History of the Great American Fortunes* also had trouble finding a publisher. After its publication in 1910, it was banned for a while in many college libraries.

to the political, economic and social development of Manhattan, the State of New York and national history itself. Tammany Hall was successful fundamentally because it offered services and satisfied needs that city and state government would not or could not. Through the years, formal municipal government became increasingly chaotic, its functions decentralized, its jurisdictions overlapping, its responsibilities diffused. The old ruling elite of middle and upper class "respectabilities" turned from public service to more profitable pursuits. The vacuum was filled by Tammany Hall and its professional politicians, who catered to the needs of a diverse group ranging from enterprising businessmen, ambitious politicians and criminals to the struggling poor, native and immigrant. Tammany especially offered the poor a means of social mobility, a primitive kind of social welfare, in which jobs, patronage and food were traded for a vote.

If Myers did not see all of these implications, perhaps it was because he was a man of his own time, growing up in the Gilded Age when Tammany, under such celebrated leaders as Big Bill Tweed, Honest John Kelly and the imperial Richard Croker, reached the nadir of corruption. Anyone writing at this time would be struck by the theme of graft, and while Myers highlights it, he was not overwhelmed by it. His historical judgment, the intensity of his research and his sense of fairness saved the book from becoming just another diatribe. For example, he squares the record by showing that Tammany had no monopoly on political sin. When in power its enemies, such as the Whigs, could be as venial as Tammany itself.

One of Myers' most significant roles, aside from that of a meticulous portrayer of a political machine in action, was that of historical revisionist, destroyer of myths. One myth, hoary with age, was the notion that despite its adventures in graft, historically Tammany Hall was an organization for the people, the little people—foreign and domestic—which repeatedly and successfully fought for their rights and their chance to seize a piece of the American bonanza. Myers shattered this myth by demonstrating that time and time again Tammany fought for the unprogressive and undemocratic side of critical public issues until forced to change by the pressure of public opinion. Thus, for years Tammany opposed manhood suffrage. Moreover, it was not always the haven of the immigrant. Before the 1840's, when Tammany sensed the political advantage of supporting the foreign-born, it had fought against reducing the naturalization period for citizenship; indeed, it had attempted to keep immigrants out of public office. It opposed the abolition of imprisonment for debt and the popular election of the Mayor; it denounced the registration of voters for the prevention of ballot frauds as un-American, tyrannical and unjust. Only at the last moment and under great pressure did it support a mechanics' lien law to protect workingmen against corrupt contractors. And until the Civil War, few organizations defended slavery as vigorously as Tammany Hall.

In his precise, matter-of-fact way, Gustavus Myers presents a story that in some ways, though on less heroic a scale, was happening in other great cities of America. Our heritage of big city machines is as American as a black derby, a fat cigar and a kind word at Mr. O'Higgins' wake. In a day when Americans are terribly concerned about their cities, it is fitting that this book about our greatest city should be reprinted, read—and pondered.

ALEXANDER B. CALLOW, JR.

PREFACE TO THE FIRST EDITION (1901)

In most men's minds a certain spell of wonder attaches to the career and character of the Tammany Society and Tammany Hall. The long continuance of this dual power; its control of the city, infrequently interrupted, throughout the century; the nature of its principles, the method of its practices and the character of its personnel — all these combine to furnish a spectacle which exerts over the general mind a peculiar and strong fascination.

It was under the sway of this mood that I began the investigation which has resulted in this volume. I had no thought, on beginning, to carry the work so far: I sought merely to satisfy my curiosity regarding the more important particulars of Tammany's history. But I soon learned that what I sought was not easily to be obtained. The few narratives already published were generally found to be either extravagant panegyrics, printed under the patronage of the Tammany Society, or else partisan attacks, violent in style and untruthful in statement. Usually both were characterized by their paucity of real information no less than by the number of their palpable errors of fact.

Turning from these, I determined to find the facts for myself. My search led me first through the files of all the available newspapers from 1789 to the present time, and thence — for origins and contributory causes — through publications as far back as 1783; thence through State and city histories, and a great number of biographies, sketches, essays, political pamphlets and broadsides. The fragmentary matter gleaned from these sources was found to be extremely valuable in helping to form the continuous thread of a narrative, and in deter-

mining contemporary spirit; but the statements and
conclusions, particularly with regard to the character
and conduct of public men, were generally contradictory
and inconclusive. Realizing this, I began the last phase
of my search — a task that has led me through numberless dreary pages of the Minutes and Documents of the
Common Council (which for the years previous to 1831
exist only in manuscript), Journals and Documents of the
Senate and Assembly, including the reports of various
legislative committees; Congressional and Executive Records, Treasury Reports, Records of the Police, Common
Pleas, Superior and Supreme Courts; Minutes of the Oyer
and Terminer; Grand Jury Presentments, and Records
of the Board of Supervisors. Finally, I have had the
good fortune, in developing the story of the middle and
later periods, of having secured many valuable interviews
with a number of men who actively participated in the stirring events of thirty, forty and even fifty years ago.

The purpose to write a book became fixed as my search
progressed. The work is finished, and the result is now
to be given to the public. What I have sought to produce is a narrative history — plain, compact and impartial. I have sought to avoid an indulgence, on the one
hand, in political speculation, and on the other, in moral-
izing platitudes. Such deductions and generalizations as
from time to time I have made, seem to me necessary in
elucidating the narrative; without them the story would
prove to the reader a mere chronology of unrelated facts.

If my narrative furnishes a sad story for the leaders
and chieftains of the Tammany Society and the Tammany Hall political organization, the fault is not mine,
but that of a multitude of incontestible public records.
It was in no partizan spirit that I began the work, and
in none that I now conclude it. I have always been an
independent in politics; and I have even voted, when
there seemed to me ample reason for doing so, a Tammany
ticket. I have tried to set down nothing in malice, nor

with such exceptions as are obviously necessary with regard to living men, to extenuate anything whatever.
Those who may be tempted to consider my work partial
and partizan, on account of the showing that it makes of
Tammany corruption and inefficiency, will do well to read
carefully the pages relating to the Whigs and to some
other opponents of Tammany Hall.

The records show that a succession of prominent Tammany leaders were involved in some theft or swindle,
public or private. These peculations or frauds ranged, in
point of time, from 1799 and 1805–6 to the later decades;
in the matter of persons, from the founder of the Tammany Society to some of the subsequent " bosses," and
in gradation of amount, from the petty thousands taken
by Mooney, Stagg and Page, in the first decade of the
century, to the $1,220,000 taken by Swartwout in 1830–
38, and the undetermined millions taken by Wood and
Tweed in the fifties, sixties and first two years of the
seventies. From nearly the beginning of its active political career, Tammany leaders, with generally brief interruptions, thus continued to abstract money from the city,
the State and the nation — the interruptions to the
practice generally coinciding with the periods when Tammany in those years was deprived of political power.

My search has shown me the absurdity of the pretense
that any vital distinction exists between the Tammany
Society and the Tammany Hall political organization.
Tammany members industriously propagate this pretense, but it has neither a historic nor an actual basis.
From 1805, the date of the apparent separation of the
organization from the society, the Sachems of the latter
have ruled the policies of the former. Repeatedly, as in
1828, 1838, 1853, and 1857, they have determined the
" regularity " of contending factions in the organization,
and have shut the hall to members of the faction against
which they have decided. The Sachems have at all times

been the leaders in the political body, and the control of the society in every year that Tammany has held control of the city, has determined the division of plunder for the ensuing year. The Tammany Society and the Tammany political organization constitute a dual power — but, unlike Ormuzd and Ahrimanes, a duality working by identical means for an identical end.

The records show that Tammany was thus, from the beginning, an evil force in politics. Its characteristics were formed by its first great leader, Aaron Burr, and his chief lieutenant, Matthew L. Davis; and whatever is distinctive of Tammany methods and policies in 1900 is, for the most part, but the development of features initiated by these two men one hundred years ago. It is curious to recall, on looking back to the time when my researches began, the abundant evidences of misapprehension regarding Tammany's earlier history. " No especial discredit attached to Tammany Hall before Tweed's time," wrote, in effect, Mr. E. L. Godkin in an essay published a few years ago. State Senator Fassett, in 1890, made a similar statement in his report on the investigation of conditions in New York City. " Down to the time," he says, " that the Tammany ' ring,' under the leadership of William M. Tweed, took possession of the government of New York City . . . the office [of Alderman] was held in credit and esteem." The exact reverse of both statements is true; and abundant proof of my contention, I believe, will be found in the pages of this book. Another instance may be given — though the opinion expressed, instead of being founded upon misapprehension, may charitably be set down as one of misjudgment. " I was a Sachem of Tammany," said a one-time noted politician recently, before the Society for the Reformation of Juvenile Delinquents, " in the days when it was *an honor to be a Sachem.*" The precise time he did not specify; and it would be difficult to identify it from the description he has given. Certainly, since 1805, the office of Sachem has been one ill calculated, of itself, to bring particular honor to the incumbent.

It would be dishonest to pretend for a moment that Tammany has been alone in its evil-doing; it has been simply the most ingenious and the most pretentious; and its practices have a historic continuity and persistence not shared by any of its rivals. The Whigs, for instance, sought in every possible way to outdo Tammany in election frauds; they stuffed ballot boxes, colonized voters, employed rowdies and thugs at the polls and distributed thousands of deceptive ballots for the use of their opponents. In fiscal frauds, likewise, they left a record well-nigh equaling that of Tammany. The Native Americans imitated both Whigs and Tammany men, and the Republicans have given instances at Albany of a wholesale venality unapproached in the history of legislative bodies. Among the few exceptions, during the earlier half of the century, to the general prostitution of civic ideals, was the career of the Workingmen's party (1829–31) and of its successor, the Equal Rights party (1834–38). The principles of both these parties were far in advance of their time; and though the effect tended somewhat to the temporary heightening of political standards, a reaction followed, which again brought in a long period of fraud and corruption.

But shameful as this record is, it is one which, viewed in the light of present practises and present ideals, gives the basis for a robust faith in the future. The hiding of vice and the employment of indirect methods in cheating and plundering, are themselves an evidence of the existence of moral standards; and it is unquestionable that Tammany to-day outwardly conforms to ethical demands which would have been scoffed at a half century ago. No one can read the details of political history without acknowledging a growing betterment in political methods. " Hardly a man [before the Civil War] could be found," says Jesse Macy in his recent *History of Political Parties*

in the United States, " who felt himself too virtuous to
go into politics. The sensitively moral were not repelled
by political methods which to-day are regarded as disgraceful." And further along he says: " It is easy to
forget that, from the very nature of moral progress, it
often happens that intelligent moral leaders of one generation will in all good conscience say and do things which
only the conscious hypocrite or the knave of a later generation can do." Pessimism as to political progress secures
no support from real research.

It may be asked, and with some show of reason, how
it has been possible for New York City to achieve its present rank in population, in wealth, in commerce and in
transportation facilities; how it has acquired its splendid
libraries, its magnificent buildings, its museums, its parks,
its benevolent institutions, in the face of this continued
dominancy of corruption, violence and fraud. The answer is simple: the city has grown *despite* these adverse
influences. The harbor of New York is one factor; the
Erie Canal (constructed notwithstanding the opposition
of the dominant political party of the city) is another;
the tremendous growth of the nation, and the thousand
external influences that determined the location of the
nation's metropolis, are yet other factors. The city has
grown to magnificence and world-wide influence; but it has
paid dear tribute for every forward step it has taken.
Imagination fails at picturing the metropolis that might
have been, could the city throughout the century have
been guided and controlled in the light of present-day civic
ideals.

The difficulties of securing the publication of this work
by any of the regular publishing houses proved insur-
mountable. Two of the best known firms wrote that they
could not encourage me to submit the manuscript to them
for consideration. Four others considered its publication
" inadvisable," though their readers had returned favor-

able recommendations. One other declined it without giving reasons. More recently, when the offer of certain responsible persons who had read the manuscript, to guarantee the expense of its publication, was made to a certain house, the firm replied: " . . . we should hardly feel warranted in locking horns with Tammany Hall . . ." It was thought that perhaps an out-of-town house might issue it, but here again declinations were forthcoming. Finally it was decided to attempt its publication by private subscription. To this end I solicited individual advances to a publication fund, from a number of the city's public-spirited citizens. The appearance of the work at this time is due to the kindly interests of these men.

Acknowledgments for the courtesies tendered me, and for material aid rendered in the project of issuing the work, are due to a number of persons: To the public-spirited citizens of different political faiths, who, while familiar with the scope of the work, contributed the funds for its publication without insisting upon a censorship of the manuscript or its alteration in any way for political purposes; and particularly to Mr. James B. Reynolds, Mr. James W. Pryor and Milo R. Maltbie, Ph. D.

GUSTAVUS MYERS.

New York City, January, 1901.

FOREWORD TO THE NEW EDITION (1917)

Since the original publication of this work, a large number of inquiries have appeared in the *Publisher's Weekly* and have come from other quarters requesting information as to where copies of *The History of Tammany Hall* could be obtained. For the last ten years this work has been in continuous demand but unavailable. For reasons fully set forth in the preface to that issue, the edition of 1901 was brought out in the face of difficulties. Not the least of these was the self-expressed dread of certain publishing houses to bring out a work which (as some of them frankly admitted in their letters of declination) might bring reprisals to them in some unexplained form or other.

Hence to all intents and purposes, that edition was in the nature of a restricted private edition. Denied the usual and almost indispensable publication and distribution facilities by the publishing houses, the work necessarily was subject to obvious disadvantages, and, so far as circulation went, practically took rank as a suppressed book — not, it is true, suppressed by any particular agency, but by the circumstances of the case.

In 1913 Mr. Edward Kellogg Baird, a public-spirited attorney in New York City, kindly undertook, in behalf of the author (who was absent in another country at the time) to see whether some one of the publishing houses would not bring out a new edition of *The History of Tammany Hall*, brought down to date. In his letters to these publishers, Mr. Baird pointed out that there never had been any lack of general interest in this work, and referred to the extremely large number of reviews in important publications in many countries treating the book at

length and commending its purpose and scope. Mr.
Baird also called the attention of publishers to the fact
that the book was recognized as the only authority on the
subject; that it had been tested by time; that there had
never been a libel suit arising from any of the statements
made therein; and that, therefore, there could be no valid
objection on the part of any publisher that publication of
further editions would lead to any legal trouble.

With such possible objections thus disposed of in advance, Mr. Baird confidently expected that he would find
at least one of the old-established publishers who would
not be deterred by such considerations as influenced them to
refuse publication in 1901. But the replies were virtually
repetitions of those received twelve years previously. One
of the first replies, dated February 24, 1913, from the
senior member of a New York publishing house, read as
follows:

"For the very same reason that the author of *The
History of Tammany Hall* was unable to obtain a publisher for the original edition, leads us to decide unfavor-
ably so far as we are concerned. The policy of publishing the book was the first question raised by one of my
partners, before he had a chance even to read the preface,
and we as a firm have decided that the objection is too
strong to permit us to bring the book out over our imprint. I am sorry that we must be so cowardly, for the
book itself is worthy of reissue, and I personally should be
glad to see it published by my firm. . . ."

At about the same time, the head of another prominent
and older New York publishing house — a citizen, by the
way, who had served as foreman of a noted grand jury
exposing Tammany corruption — wrote this reply:

"I have given due consideration, with my partners, to
the suggestion you are so kind to submit to us in regard
to the publication of a new edition of *The History of Tammany Hall* brought down to date. . . . I must report
that our judgment is adverse to the desirability of re-

issuing such a book with the imprint of our house. I should be individually interested in obtaining a copy for my own library in case you may be able to secure for the work a satisfactory arrangement with some other house."

An equally well-known New York publishing house sent this declination: "We have looked over with interest *The History of Tammany Hall*, which you were good enough to submit to us, but are sorry to say that after a careful examination we are unable to persuade ourselves that we could successfully undertake its publication." The head of still another old-established New York publishing house wrote, on March 4, 1913, a long apologetic letter giving his reasons for not caring to undertake the publication of the work, the principal of those reasons being the plea that there was not sufficient prospect of gain " to compensate for some of the unpleasantness its publishers would have to endure." Yet a year later a magazine published by this identical house contained a laudatory reference to " Myers's excellent *History of Tammany Hall*."

On April 10, 1913, Mr. Baird wrote to a prominent Boston publishing house. " Before offering the book," Mr. Baird wrote in part, " I want to tell you frankly that it has been turned down by other publishers, not because of any lack of excellence or authenticity, but simply because, as several of the publishers have frankly acknowledged, they ' are afraid of reprisals from Tammany Hall.'

" Your house has been suggested by a publisher as one which is probably not so timid as some others, and as you are located out of town you are therefore not subject to local influences, and I write to ask if you would be interested in having the publication submitted to you.

" I might add that I have been lecturing on this subject at the City Club and other prominent clubs in the city, and the subject itself seemed to bring out record audiences wherever the lecture was given, and it is because so many people have asked me where they can obtain copies of Mr.

Myers's book, that I am prompted to endeavor to have a reprint of it."

The reply of the Boston publishing house was a curt declination.

Subsequently the following letter was received by the author from a prominent New York City attorney:

" I have been endeavoring to purchase a copy of *The History of Tammany Hall* published by you, but as yet have been unable to find a copy in any of the book stores. I shall appreciate it very much if you can tell me where I can obtain a copy.

" You may be interested to know that a few months ago a number of booksellers were given instructions to purchase and retire all outstanding copies of the book. For whose account this order was given I do not know. I am told by the booksellers that an advertisement for the book resulted in their being able to purchase only a few copies."

To the present publishers the author gives all due appreciation for their unqualified recognition of the need of the publication of this work.

GUSTAVUS MYERS.

March, 1917.

CONTENTS

CHAPTER I
RESISTANCE TO ARISTOCRACY — 1789–1798 1

CHAPTER II
AARON BURR AT THE HELM — 1798–1802 11

CHAPTER III
TAMMANY QUARRELS WITH DE WITT CLINTON — 1802–1809 17

CHAPTER IV
SLOW RECOVERY FROM DISASTER — 1809–1815 . . . 29

CHAPTER V
TAMMANY IN ABSOLUTE CONTROL — 1815–1817 . . 37

CHAPTER VI
CLINTON MAINTAINS HIS SUPREMACY — 1817–1820 . 47

CHAPTER VII
THE SUFFRAGE CONTEST — 1820–1822 56

CHAPTER VIII
STRUGGLES OF THE PRESIDENTIAL FACTIONS — 1822–1825 60

CONTENTS

CHAPTER IX

PAGE

THE JACKSON ELEMENT VICTORIOUS — 1825–1828 . . 69

CHAPTER X

THE WORKINGMEN'S PARTY — 1829–1830 77

CHAPTER XI

TAMMANY AND THE BANK CONTEST — 1831–1834 . . 85

CHAPTER XII

THE EQUAL RIGHTS PARTY — 1834–1837 94

CHAPTER XIII

TAMMANY "PURIFIED" — 1837–1838 112

CHAPTER XIV

WHIG FAILURE RESTORES TAMMANY TO POWER — 1838–
1840 117

CHAPTER XV

RISE AND PROGRESS OF THE "GANGS" — 1840–1846 . 128

CHAPTER XVI

"BARNBURNERS" AND "HUNKERS" — 1846–1850 . . 140

CHAPTER XVII

DEFEAT AND VICTORY — 1850–1852 150

CHAPTER XVIII

"HARDSHELLS" AND "SOFTSHELLS" — 1852–1853 . . 161

CHAPTER XIX

A CHAPTER OF DISCLOSURES — 1853–1854 167

CHAPTER XX

FERNANDO WOOD'S FIRST ADMINISTRATION — 1854–1856 174

CHAPTER XXI   PAGE

WOOD'S SECOND ADMINISTRATION — 1856–1859 . . 181

CHAPTER XXII

THE CIVIL WAR AND AFTER — 1859–1867 194

CHAPTER XXIII

THE TWEED "RING" — 1867–1870 211

CHAPTER XXIV

TWEED IN HIS GLORY — 1870–1871 225

CHAPTER XXV

COLLAPSE AND DISPERSION OF THE "RING" — 1871–1872 237

CHAPTER XXVI

TAMMANY RISES FROM THE ASHES — 1872–1874 . . 250

CHAPTER XXVII

THE DICTATORSHIP OF JOHN KELLY — 1874–1886 . 258

CHAPTER XXVIII

THE DICTATORSHIP OF RICHARD CROKER — 1886–1897 . 267

CHAPTER XXIX

THE DICTATORSHIP OF RICHARD CROKER (*Concluded*) —
1897–1901 284

CHAPTER XXX

TAMMANY UNDER ABSENTEE DIRECTION — 1901–1902 . 290

CHAPTER XXXI

CHARLES F. MURPHY'S AUTOCRACY — 1902–1903 . . 299

CHAPTER XXXII

THE SWAY OF BRIBERY AND "HONEST GRAFT" — 1903–
1905 307

CONTENTS

CHAPTER XXXIII

PAGE

TAMMANY'S CONTROL UNDER LEADER MURPHY — 1906–
1909 324

CHAPTER XXXIV

ANOTHER ERA OF LEGISLATIVE CORRUPTION — 1909–1911 342

CHAPTER XXXV

"CHIEF" MURPHY'S LEADERSHIP — FURTHER DETAILS
1912–1913 356

CHAPTER XXXVI

GOVERNOR SULZER'S IMPEACHMENT AND TAMMANY'S DE-
FEAT — 1913–1914 375

CHAPTER XXXVII

TAMMANY'S PRESENT STATUS — 1914–1917 392

THE HISTORY OF
TAMMANY HALL

HISTORY OF TAMMANY HALL

CHAPTER I

RESISTANCE TO ARISTOCRACY

1789–1798

THE Society of St. Tammany, or Columbian Order, was founded on May 12, 1789, a fortnight later than the establishment of the National Government, by William Mooney.[1] " His object," says Judah Hammond,[2] an early member of Tammany, " was to fill the country with institutions designed, and men determined, to preserve the just balance of power. His purpose was patriotic and purely republican. The constitution·provided by his care contained, among other things, a solemn asseveration, which every member at his initiation was required to repeat and subscribe to, that he would sustain the State institutions and resist a consolidation of power in the general Government."

Before the Revolution, societies variously known as the " Sons of Liberty " and the " Sons of St. Tammany " had been formed to aid the cause of independence. Tammany,

---

[1] Mooney was an ex-soldier, who at this time kept a small upholstery shop at 23 Nassau street. He was charged with having deserted the American Army, September 16, 1776, and with joining the British forces in New York, where for a year he wore the King's uniform. The truth or falsity of this charge cannot be ascertained.

[2] Hammond, *Political History of the State of New York*, Vol. I, p. 341.

1

or Tamanend, was an Indian chief, of whom fanciful legends have been woven, but of whose real life little can be told. Some maintain that he lived in the neighborhood of Scranton, Pa., when William Penn arrived, and that he was present at the great council under the elm tree. His name is said to have been on Penn's first treaty with the Indians, April 23, 1683. He is also described as a great chief of the Delaware nation, and his wigwam is said to have stood on the grounds now occupied by Princeton University. The fame of his wisdom, benevolence and love of liberty spreading to the colonists, they adopted his name for their patriotic lodges. When societies sprang up bearing the names of St. George, St. Andrew or St. David and proclaiming their fealty to King George, the Separatists dubbed Tammany a saint in ridicule of the imported saints. The Revolution over, the " Sons of Liberty " and the " Sons of St. Tammany " dissolved.

The controversy over the adoption of the Federal constitution had the effect of re-uniting the patriotic lodges. The rich and influential classes favored Hamilton's design of a republic having a President and a Senate chosen for life, and State governments elected by Congress. Opposed to this attempt toward a highly centralized government were the forces which afterward organized the Anti-Federalist party. Their leader in New York was Governor George Clinton. The greater number of the old members of the Liberty and Tammany societies, now familiarly known as " Liberty boys," belonged to this opposition.

During this agitation Hamilton managed to strengthen his party, by causing to be removed, in 1787, the political disabilities bearing upon the Tories. New York was noted for its Tories, more numerous in proportion than in any other colony, since here, under the Crown, offices were dispensed more liberally than elsewhere. In the heat of the Revolutionary War and the times immediately following it, popular indignation struck at them in severe laws. In all places held by the patriot army a Tory refusing to renounce his allegiance to King George ran considerable danger not only of mob visit, but of confiscation of property, exile, imprisonment, or, in flagrant cases of adherence to the enemy, death. From 1783 to 1787 the " Liberty boys " of the Revolution, who formed the bulk of the middle and working classes, governed New York City politics. In freeing the Tories from oppressive laws, and opening political life to them, Hamilton at once secured the support of a propertied class (for many of them had succeeded in retaining their estates) numerous enough to form a balance of power and to enable him to wrest the control of the city from the " Liberty boys."

The elevation to office of many of the hated, aristocratic supporters of Great Britain inflamed the minds of the " Liberty boys " and their followers, and made the chasm between the classes, already wide, yet wider. The bitterest feeling cropped out. Hamilton, put upon the defensive, took pains in his addresses to assure the people of the baselessness of the accusation that he aimed to keep the rich families in power. That result, however, had been partially assured by the State constitution of 1777. Gaging sound citizenship by the ownership of property, the draughtsmen of that instrument allowed only actual residents having freeholds to the value of £100, free of all debts, to vote for Governor, Lieutenant-Governor and State Senators, while a vote for the humbler office of Assemblyman was given only to those having freeholds of £20 in the county or paying forty shillings rent yearly. Poor soldiers who had nobly sustained the Revolutionary cause were justly embittered at being disqualified by reason of their poverty, while full political power was given to the property-owning Tories.

" The inequality," wrote one who lived in those days,

" was greatly added to by the social and business customs of the times. . . . There was an aristocracy and a democracy whose limits

were as clearly marked by manner and dress as by legal enactment.
. . . The aristocracy controlled capital in trade, monopolized banks
and banking privileges, which they did not hesitate to employ as a
means of perpetuating their power."

Dr. John W. Francis tells, in his *Reminiscences,* of
the prevalence in New York for years after the Revolution of a supercilious class that missed no opportunity of
sneering at the demand for political equality made by
the leather-breeched mechanic with his few shillings a
day.

Permeated with democratic doctrines, the populace de-
tested the landed class. The founding of the Society of
the Cincinnati was an additional irritant. Formed by
the officers of the Continental army before disbandment,
this society adopted one clause especially obnoxious to the
radicals. It provided that the eldest male descendant of
an original member should be entitled to wear the insignia
of the order and enjoy the privileges of the society, which,
it was argued, would be best perpetuated in that way.
Jefferson saw a danger to the liberties of the people in
this provision, since it would tend to give rise to a race
of hereditary nobles, founded on the military, and breeding in turn other subordinate orders. At Washington's
suggestion the clause was modified, but an ugly feeling
rankled in the public mind, due to the existence of an
active party supposedly bent on the establishment of a
disguised form of monarchy.

It was at such a juncture of movements and tendencies
that the Society of St. Tammany or Columbian Order was
formed. The new organization constituted a formal protest against aristocratic influences, and stood for the
widest democratization in political life.

As a contrast to the old-world distinctions of the Cincinnati and other societies, the Tammany Society adopted
aboriginal forms and usages. The officers held Indian
titles. The head, or president, chosen from thirteen
Sachems, corresponding to trustees, elected annually, was

styled Grand Sachem. In its early years the society had
a custom, now obsolete, of conferring the honorary office
of Kitchi Okemaw, or Great Grand Sachem, upon the
President of the United States. Washington, John Adams, Jefferson, Madison, Monroe, John Quincy Adams
and Jackson were hailed successively as the Great Grand
Sachems of Tammany. After the Sachems came the Sagamore, or Master of Ceremonies, a Scribe, or secretary,
and a Wiskinskie,[3] or doorkeeper. Instead of using the
ordinary calendar designations, the society divided the
year into seasons and these into moons. Its notices bore
reckoning from the year Columbus discovered America,
that of the Declaration of American Independence and of
its own organization. Instead of inscribing: " New York,
July, 1800," there would appear: " Manhattan, Season
of Fruits, Seventh Moon, Year of Discovery three hundred and eighth; of Independence twenty-fourth, and of
the Institution the twelfth." In early times the society
was divided into tribes, one for each of the thirteen original States; there were the Eagle, Otter, Panther, Beaver,
Bear, Tortoise, Rattlesnake, Tiger, Fox, Deer, Buffalo,
Raccoon and Wolf tribes, which stood respectively for
New York, New Hampshire, Massachusetts, Rhode Island,
Connecticut, New Jersey, Pennsylvania, Delaware, Maryland, Virginia, North Carolina, South Carolina and Geor-
gia. A new member of the Tammany Society had the
choice of saying to which of these tribes he cared to be
attached. Frequently the members dressed in Indian
garb and carried papooses in their public parades. They
introduced the distinction between " long talks " and
" short talks " in their public addresses. The name
" Wigwam " was given to their meeting-place, and Barden's Tavern was selected as their first home.

At the initiation of the Grand Sachem a song beginning, " Brothers, Our Council Fire Shines Bright, et-

[3] So spelled in all the earlier records. Later, the *s* in the penulti-
mate syllable came to be dropped.

hoh!" was sung, and at the initiation of a member another song was sung, beginning:

> " Sacred's the ground where Freedom's found,
> And Virtue stamps her Name."

The society contemplated founding a chain of Tam⸍many societies over the country, and accordingly designated itself as Tammany Society, No. 1. A number sprang into life, but only a few — those in Philadelphia, Providence, Brooklyn and Lexington, Ky., continued for any time, and even these disappeared about the year 1818 or a few years later.

The society showed its Indian ceremonies to advantage and gained much prestige by aiding in the conciliation of the Creek Indians. After useless attempts to make a treaty with them, the Government undertook, as a last resort, in February, 1790, to influence Alexander McGillivray, their half-breed chief, to visit New York, where he might be induced to sign a treaty. To Col. Marinus Willett, a brave soldier of the Revolution, and later Mayor of New York City, the mission was intrusted. In July, 1790, Willett started North accompanied by McGillivray and twenty-eight Creek chiefs and warriors. Upon their arrival in New York, then the seat of the National Government, the members of the Tammany Society, in full Indian costume, welcomed them. One phase of the tale has it that the Creeks set up a wild whoop, at whose terrifying sound the Tammany make-believe red-faces fled in dismay. Another version tells that the Tammany Society and the military escorted the Indians to Secretary Knox's house, introduced them to Washington and then led them to the Wigwam at Barden's Tavern, where seductive drink was served. On August 2 the Creeks were entertained at a Tammany banquet. A treaty was signed on August 13.

In June of the same year Tammany had established, in the old City Hall, a museum " for the preservation of Indian relics." For a brief while the society devoted itself with assiduity to this department, but the practical men grew tired of it. On June 25, 1795, the museum was given over to Gardiner Baker, its curator, on condition that it was to be known for all time as the Tammany Museum and that each member of the society and his family were to have entrance free. Baker dying, the museum eventually passed into the hands of a professional museum-owner.

Tammany's chief functions at first seem to have been the celebration of its anniversary day, May 12; the Fourth of July and Evacuation Day. The society's parades were events in old New York. On May 12, 1789, the day of organization, two marquees were built two miles above the city, whither the Tammany brethren went to hold their banquet. Thirteen discharges of cannon followed each toast. The first one read: "May Honor, Virtue and Patriotism ever be the distinguishing characteristics of the sons of St. Tammany." John Pintard,[4] Tammany's first Sagamore, wrote an account[5] of the society's celebration of May 12, 1791. "The day," he says,

"was ushered in by a Federal salute from the battery and welcomed by a discharge of 13 guns from the brig Grand Sachem, lying in the stream. The society assembled at the great Wigwam, in Broad street, five hours after the rising of the sun, and was conducted from there in an elegant procession to the brick meeting house in Beekman street. Before them was borne the cap of liberty; after following seven hunters in Tammanial dress, then the great standard of the society, in the rear of which was the Grand Sachem and other officers. On either side of these were formed the members in tribes, each headed by its standard bearers and Sachem in full dress. At the brick meeting house an oration was delivered by their brother, Josiah Ogden Hoffman, to the society and to a most respectable and crowded audience. In the most brilliant and pathetic language he traced the origin of the Columbian Order and the Society of the Cincinnati. From the meeting house the procession proceeded (as before) to Campbell's

[4] John Pintard was one of the founders of the New York Historical Society, the Academy of Design and other institutions. He was a very rich man at one time, but subsequently failed in business.
[5] *Dunlap's American Daily Register*, May 16, 1791.

grounds, where upwards of two hundred people partook of a handsome and plentiful repast. The dinner was honored by his Excellency [George Clinton] and many of the most respectable citizens."

The toasts, that now seem so quaint, mirror the spirit of the diners. "The Grand Sachem of the Thirteen United Fires," ran the first, "may his declining sun be precious in the sight of the Great Spirit that the mild luster of his departing beams may prove no less glorious than the effulgence of the rising or transcendent splendor of his meridian greatness." The second: "The head men and chiefs of the Grand Council of the Thirteen United Fires — may they convince our foes not only of their courage to lift, prudence to direct and clemency to withhold the hatchet, but of their power to inflict it in their country's cause."

Up to 1835, at least, toasts were an important feature in public dinners, as they were supposed to disclose the sentiments, political or otherwise, of the person or body from whom they came. In this fashion the Tammany Society announced its instant sympathy with the French Revolution in all its stages. On May 12, 1793, the sixth toast read: "Success to the *Armies* of France, and Wisdom, Concord and Firmness to the Convention." "The first sentence was hardly articulated," a newspaper [6] records, "when *as one* the whole company *arose* and gave three cheers, continued by roars of applause for several minutes; the toast was then given in whole and the applauses re-iterated."

At ten o'clock that morning, the same account relates, "the society had assembled at Tammanial Hall, in Broad street, and marched to St. Paul's Church, where Brother Cadwallader D. Colden delivered to a crowded and brilliant audience an animated talk on the excellence of the Government and situation of the United States when contrasted with those of despotic countries." In the proces-

[6] *New York Journal and Patriotic Register*, May 15, 1793.

sion were about 400 members in civilian dress. From each hat flowed a bucktail — the symbol of Liberty — and the standard and cap of Liberty were carried in front of the line. From the church " the Tammanials went to their Hall, where some 150 of them partook of an elegant dinner."

Public feeling ran high in discussing the French Revolution, and there were many personal collisions. The Tammany Society was in the vanguard of the American sympathizers and bore the brunt of abuse. The pamphlets and newspapers were filled with anonymous threats from both sides. " An Oneida Chief " writes in the *New York Journal and Patriotic Register*, June 8, 1793:

" A Hint to the Whigs of New York: To hear our Brethren of France villified (with all that low Scurrility of which their enemies the English are so well stocked) in our streets and on the wharves; nay, in our new and elegant Coffee House; but more particularly in that den of ingrates, called Belvidere Club House, where at this very moment *those enemies to liberty* are swallowing potent draughts to the destruction and *annihilation of Liberty, Equality* and the *Rights of Man*, is not to be borne by freemen and I am fully of opinion that if some method is not adopted to suppress such daring and presumptuous insults, a band of determined Mohawks, Oneidas and Senekas will take upon themselves that necessary duty."

There is no record of the carrying out of this threat.

Despite its original composition of men of both parties, the Tammany Society drifted year by year into being the principal upholder of the doctrines of which Jefferson was the chief exponent. Toward the end of Washington's administration political feelings developed into violent party divisions, and the Tammany Society became largely Anti-Federalist, or Republican, the Federalist members either withdrawing or being reduced to a harmless minority. It toasted the Republican leaders vociferously to show the world its sympathies and principles. On May 12, 1796, the glasses ascended to " Citizen " Thomas Jefferson, whose name was received with three cheers, and to " Citizen " Edward Livingston, for whom nine cheers were given. " The people," ran one toast, " may they ever at the risk of life and liberty support their equal rights in opposition to Ambition, Tyranny, to Sophistry and Deception, to Bribery and Corruption and to an enthusiastic fondness and implicit confidence in their fellow-fallible mortals."

Tammany had become, by 1796–97, a powerful and an extremely partizan body. But it came near being snuffed out of existence in the last year of Washington's presidency. Judah Hammond writes that when Washington, before the close of his second term,

> " rebuked self-creative societies from an apprehension that their ultimate tendency would be hostile to the public tranquillity, the members of Tammany supposed their institution to be included in the reproof, and they almost all forsook it. The founder, William Mooney, and a few others continued steadfast. At one anniversary they were reduced so low that but three persons attended its festival.[7] From this time it became a political institution and took ground with Thomas Jefferson."

To such straits was driven the society which, a short time after, secured absolute control of New York City, and which has held that grasp, with but few and brief intermissions, ever since. The contrast between that sorry festival, with its trio of lonesome celebrators, and the Tammany Society of a few years afterwards presents one of the most striking pictures in American politics.

[7] This statement of Hammond probably refers to May 12, 1797.

CHAPTER II

1798–1802

THE second period of the Tammany Society began about 1798. Relieved of its Federalist members, it became purely partizan. As yet it was not an " organization," in the modern political sense; it did not seek the enrollment and regimentation of voters. Its nature was more that of a private political club, which sought to influence elections by speeches, pamphlets and social means. It shifted its quarters from Barden's Tavern to the " Long Room," a place kept by a sometime Sachem, Abraham or " Brom " Martling,[1] at the corner of Nassau and Spruce streets. This Wigwam was a forlorn, one-story wooden building attached to Martling's Tavern, near, or partly overlapping, the spot where subsequently Tammany Hall erected its first building — recently the *Sun* newspaper building. No larger than a good-sized room the Wigwam was contemptuously styled by the Federalists " the Pig Pen." In that year New York City had only 58,000 inhabitants. The Wigwam stood on the very outskirts of the city. But it formed a social rendezvous very popular with the " Bucktails " of the time. Every night men gathered there to drink, smoke and " swap " stories. Fitz-Greene Halleck has written of a later time:

[1] Martling was several times elected a Sachem. Like most of the Republican politicians of the day he had a habit of settling his disputes in person. Taking offense, one day, at the remarks of one John Richard Huggins, a hair-dresser, he called at Huggins's shop, 104 Broadway, and administered to him a sound thrashing with a rope. When he grew old Tammany took care of him by appointing him to an obscure office (Keeper of the City Hall).

11

" There's a barrel of porter at Tammany Hall,
And the Bucktails are swigging it all the night long;
In the time of my boyhood 'twas pleasant to call
For a seat and cigar mid the jovial throng."

This social custom was begun early in the life of the
society, and was maintained for several decades.

Aaron Burr was the first real leader of the Tammany
Society. He was never Grand Sachem or even Sachem;
it is doubtful whether he ever set foot in the Wigwam;
it is known that it was never his habit to attend caucuses;
but he controlled the society through his friends and protégés. The transition of Tammany from an effusive,
speech-making society to an active political club was
mainly through his instrumentality. Mooney [2] was a
mediocre man, delighting in extravagant language and
Indian ceremonials, and was merely a tool in the hands
of far abler men. " Burr was our chief," [3] said Matthew
L. Davis, Burr's friend and biographer, and several times
Grand Sachem of the society.

Davis's influence on the early career of Tammany was
second only to that of Burr himself. He was reputed to
be the originator of the time-honored modes of manufacturing public opinion, carrying primary meetings, obtaining the nomination of certain candidates, carrying a ward,
a city, a county or even a State. During one period of
his activity, it is related, meetings were held on different
nights in every ward in New York City. The most for-
cible and spirited resolutions and addresses were passed
and published. Not only the city, but the entire country,
was aroused. It was some time before the secret was
known — that at each of these meetings but three persons
were present, Davis and two friends.

Though Davis was credited with the authorship of these
methods, it is not so certain that he did not receive his les-

[2] Mooney was a life-long admirer of Burr, but was ill-requited in
his friendship. At Mooney's death, in 1831, a heap of unpaid bills
for goods charged to Burr was found.
[3] *American Citizen,* July 18, 1809.

sons from Burr.   Besides Davis, Burr's chief protégés, all
of whom became persons of importance in early New York,
were Jacob Barker, John and Robert Swartwout, John and
William P. Van Ness; Benjamin Romaine, Isaac Pierson,
John P. Haff and Jacob Hayes.[4]   When Burr was in disgrace William P. Van Ness, at that time the patron of the
law student Martin Van Buren, wrote a long pamphlet defending him.   At the time of his duel with Hamilton these
men supported him.   They made Tammany his machine;
and it is clear that they were attached to him sincerely,
for long after his trial for treason, Tammany Hall, under
their influence, tried unsuccessfully to restore him to some
degree of political power.   Burr controlled Tammany
Hall from 1797 until even after his fall.   From then on
to about 1835 his protégés either controlled it or were its
influential men.   The phrase, " the old Burr faction still
active," is met with as late as 1832, and the Burrites were
a considerable factor in politics for several years thereafter.   Nearly every one of the Burr leaders, as will be
shown, was guilty of some act of official or private pecula-
tion.

These were the men Burr used in changing the character of the Tammany Society.   The leader and his satellites were quite content to have the Tammany rank and
file parade in Indian garb and use savage ceremonies; such
forms gave the people an idea of pristine simplicity which
was a good enough cloak for election scheming.   Audacious to a degree and working through others, Burr was
exceedingly adroit.   One of his most important moves was
the chartering of the Manhattan Bank.   Without this institution Tammany would have been quite ineffective.   In
those days banks had a mightier influence over politics
than is now thought.   New York had only one bank, and
that one was violently Federalist.   Its affairs were admin-

4 Hayes, as High Constable of the city from 1800 to 1850, was a
character in old New York. He was so devoted to Burr that he
named his second son for him.

istered always with a view to contributing to Federalist success. The directors loaned money to their personal and party friends with gross partiality and for questionable purposes. If a merchant dared help the opposite party or offended the directors he was taught to repent his' independence by a rejection of his paper when he most needed cash.

Burr needed this means of monopoly and favoritism to make his political machine complete, as well as to amass funds. He, therefore, had introduced into the Legislature (1799) a bill, apparently for the purpose of diminishing the future possibility of yellow fever in New York City, incorporating a company, styled the Manhattan Company, to supply pure, wholesome water. Supposing the charter granted nothing more than this, the legislators passed it. They were much surprised later to hear that it contained a carefully worded clause vesting the Manhattan Company with banking powers.[5] The Manhattan Bank speedily adopted the prevailing partizan tactics.

The campaign of 1800 was full of personal and party bitterness and was contested hotly. To evade the election laws disqualifying the poor, and working to the advantage of the Federalists, Tammany had recourse to artifice. Poor Republicans, being unable individually to meet the property qualification, clubbed together and bought property. On the three election days [6] Hamilton made speeches at the polls for the Federalists, and Burr directed political affairs for the Republicans. Tammany used every influence, social and political, to carry the city for Jefferson.

Assemblymen then were not elected by wards, but in bulk, the Legislature in turn selecting the Presidential

[5] Hammond, Vol. I, pp. 129–30.

[6] Until 1840 three days were required for elections in the city and State. In the earlier period ballots were invariably written. The first one-day election held in the city was that of April 14, 1840. For the rest of the State, however, the change from three-day elections was not made until several years later.

electors. The Republican Assembly candidates in New York City were elected [7] by a majority of *one*, the vote of a butcher, Thomas Winship, being the decisive ballot. The Legislature selected Republican electors. This threw the Presidential contest into the House of Representatives, insuring Jefferson's success. Though Burr was the choice of the Tammany chiefs, Jefferson was a favored second. Tammany claimed to have brought about the result; and the claim was generally allowed.[8]

The success of the Republicans in 1800 opened new possibilities to the members of the Tammany Society. Jefferson richly rewarded some of them with offices. In 1801 they advanced their sway further. The society had declared that one of its objects was the repeal of the odious election laws. For the present, however, it schemed to circumvent them. The practise of the previous year of the collective buying of property to meet the voting qualifications was continued. Under the society's encouragement, and with money probably furnished by it, thirty-nine poor Republicans in November, 1801, bought a house and lot of ground in the Fifth Ward. Their votes turned the ward election. The thirty-nine were mainly penniless students and mechanics; among them were such men as Daniel D. Tompkins, future Governor of New York and Vice-President of the United States; Richard Riker, coming Recorder of New York City; William P. Van Ness, United States Judge to be, Teunis Wortman, William

---

[7] During the greater part of the first quarter of the century members of the Legislature, Governor and certain other State officers were elected in April, the Aldermen being elected in November.

[8] Shortly after Jefferson's inauguration Matthew L. Davis called upon the President at Washington and talked in a boastful spirit of the immense influence New York had exerted, telling Jefferson that his elevation was brought about solely by the power and management of the Tammany Society. Jefferson listened. Then reaching out his hand and catching a large fly, he requested Davis to note the remarkable disproportion in size between one portion of the insect and its body. The hint was not lost on Davis, who, though not knowing whether Jefferson referred to New York or to him, ceased to talk on the subject.

A. Davis, Robert Swartwout and John L. Broome, all of whom became men of power.

The result in the Fifth Ward, and in the Fourth Ward, where seventy Tammany votes had been secured through the joint purchase of a house and lot at 50 Dey street, gave the society a majority in the Common Council.[9]   The Federalist Aldermen decided to throw out these votes, as being against the spirit of the law, and to seat their own party candidates.   The Republican Mayor, Edward Livingston, who presided over the deliberations, maintained that he had a right to vote.[10]   His vote made a tie.   The Tammany, or Republican, men were arbitrarily seated, upon which, on December 14, 1801, eight Federalists seceded to prevent a quorum; [11] they did not return until the following March.

The Tammany Society members, or as they were called until 1813 or 1814, the Martling Men (from their meeting place), soon had a far more interesting task than fighting Federalists.   This was the long, bitter warfare, extending over twenty-six years, which they waged against De Witt Clinton, one of the ablest politicians New York has known, and remembered by a grateful posterity as the creator of the Erie Canal.

[9] The Common Council from 1730 to 1830 consisted of Aldermen and Assistant Aldermen, *sitting as one board*.   The terms " Board of Aldermen " and " Common Council " are used interchangeably.
[10] *Ms. Minutes of the Common Council*, Vol. 13, pp. 351–52.
[11] *Ibid.*, pp. 353–56.

CHAPTER III

1802–1809

THE quarrel between Tammany and De Witt Clinton arose from Clinton's charge in 1802 that Burr was a traitor to the Republican party and had conspired to defeat Jefferson. De Witt Clinton was a nephew of George Clinton. When a very young man he was Scribe of the Tammany Society. Owing to the influence of his powerful relative, backed by his own ability, he had become a United States Senator, at the promising age of thirty-three. His principal fault was his unbridled temper, which led him to speak harshly of those who displeased him. George Clinton thought himself, on account of his age and long public service, entitled to the place and honors heaped upon Burr, whom he despised as an unprincipled usurper. He was too old, however, to carry on a contest, and De Witt Clinton undertook to shatter the Burr faction for him. To oppose the Tammany Society, which embraced in itself nearly all there was of the Republican party in New York City, was no slight matter. But De Witt Clinton, with the confidence that comes of steady, rapid advancement, went about it aggressively. He had extraordinary qualities of mind and heart which raised him far above the mere politicians of his day.

Such of the elective offices as were allowed the city were filled by the Tammany Republicans from 1800 to 1809. State Senators, Assemblymen and Aldermen were elective, but the Mayor, Sheriff, Recorder, Justices of the Peace of counties — in fact, nearly all civil and military officers from the heads of departments and Judgeships of the Supreme Court down to even auctioneers — were appointed by a body at Albany known as the Council of Appointment, which was one of the old constitutional devices for centralizing political power. Four State Senators, chosen by the Assembly, comprised, with the Governor, this Council. Gov. Clinton, as president of this board, claimed the exclusive right of nomination, and effectually concentrated in himself all the immense power it yielded. He had De Witt Clinton transferred from the post of United States Senator to that of Mayor of New York City in 1803, and filled offices in all the counties with his relatives or partizans. The spoils system was in full force, as exemplified by the Council's sudden and frequent changes. Though swaying New York City, Tammany could get only a few State and city offices, the Clintons holding the power elsewhere throughout the State and in the Council of Appointment. Hence in fighting the Clintons, Tammany confronted a power much superior in resources.

One of the first moves of the Clintons was to get control of the Manhattan Bank. They caused John Swartwout, Burr's associate director, to be turned out. Some words ensued, and De Witt Clinton styled Swartwout a liar, a scoundrel and a villain. Swartwout set about resenting the insult in the gentlemanly mode of the day. Clinton readily accepted a challenge, and five shots were fired, two of which hit Swartwout, who, upon being asked whether he had had enough said that he had not; but the duel was stopped by the seconds.

While the Clintons were searching for a good pretext to overthrow Burr, the latter injudiciously supplied it himself when in 1804 he opposed the election of Morgan Lewis, his own party's nominee for Governor. Burr's action gave rise to much acrimony; and from that time he was ostracized by every part of the Republican party in New York except the chiefs of the Tammany Society, or Martling Men. He fell altogether into disgrace with the gen-

eral public when he shot Alexander Hamilton in a duel,
July 11, 1804. Tammany, however, still clung to him.
Two of Tammany's chiefs — Nathaniel Pendleton and
William P. Van Ness — accompanied Burr to the field;
John Swartwout, another chief, was at Burr's house awaiting his return. The Tammany men looked upon much of
the excitement over Hamilton's death as manufactured.
But as if to yield to public opinion, the society on July 13
issued a notice to its members to join in the procession to
pay the " last tribute of respect to the *manes* of Hamilton."

In the inflamed state of public feeling which condemned
everything connected with Burr and caused his indictment
in two States, the Sachems knew it would be unwise for a
time to make any attempt to restore him to political power.
They found their opportunity in December, 1805, when,
strangely enough, De Witt Clinton, forced by the exigen-
cies of politics, made overtures to form a union with the
Burrites in order to resist the powerful Livingston family,
which, with Gov. Morgan Lewis at its head, was threatening the Clinton family. The Burrites thought they would
get the better of the bargain and be able to reinstate their
chief.

The negotiators met secretly February 20, 1806, at
Dyde's Hotel. John Swartwout and the other Tammany
chiefs insisted as conditions of the union that Burr should
be recognized as a Republican; that his friends should be
well cared for in the distribution of offices, and that
" Burrism " should never be urged as an objection against
them. The Clintons, anxious to beat down the Livingstons, were ready to agree to these terms, knowing that
Burr's prestige was utterly swept away and that any effort of his followers to thrust him forward again would
be a failure. Clintonites and Burrites set to drinking
hilariously as a token of good will. But their joy was
premature.

When the body of the Tammany men learned of the

arrangement they were aroused. The Sachems drew off, and the Tammany Society continued to revile Clinton and to be reviled in return.

It was just before this that the Tammany Hall political organization, as apparently distinct from the Tammany Society, was created. In 1805 the society made application for, and obtained from the Legislature, the charter, which still remains in force, incorporating it as a benevolent and charitable body " for the purpose of affording relief to the indigent and distressed members of said association, their widows and orphans and others who may be proper objects of their charity."

The wording of the charter deluded only the simple. Everybody knew that the society was the center around which the Republican politics of the city revolved. It had its public and its secret aspects. " This society," says *Longworth's American Almanac, New York Register and City Directory* for 1807–1808, in a description of Tammany, " has a constitution in two parts — public and private — the public relates to all external or public matters ; and the private, to the arcana and all transactions which do not meet the public eye, and on which its code of laws are founded."

The Sachems knew that to continue appearing as a political club would be most impolitic. Year after year since 1798 the criticisms directed at the self-appointed task of providing candidates for the popular suffrage grew louder. In 1806 these murmurings extended to Tammany's own voters. Honest Republicans began to voice their suspicions of caucuses which never met and public meetings called by nobody knew whom. The Sachems, though perfectly satisfied with the established forms which gave them such direct authority, wisely recognized the need of a change.

It was agreed that the Republicans should assemble in each ward to choose a ward committee of three and that these ward committees should constitute a general com-

mittee, which should have the power of convening all public
meetings of the party and of making preparatory arrangements for approaching elections. This was the origin of
the Tammany Hall General Committee, which, consisting
then of thirty members, has been expanded in present times
to over five thousand members.

At about the same time each of the ten wards began
sending seven delegates to Martling's, the seventy forming a nominating committee, which alone had the right to
nominate candidates. The seventy met in open convention. At times each member would have a candidate for
the Assembly, to which the city then sent eleven members.
These improvements on the old method gave, naturally, an
air of real democracy to the proceedings of the Tammany
faction in the city and had the effect of softening public
criticism. Yet behind the scenes the former leaders contrived to bring things about pretty much as they planned.

The action of the nominating committee was not final,
however. It was a strict rule that the committee's nominations be submitted to the wards and to a later meeting
of all the Republican electors who chose to attend and who
would vote their approval or disapproval. If a name
were voted down, another candidate was substituted by
the meeting itself. This was called the " great popular
meeting," and its design was supposed to vest fully in the
Republican voters the choice of the candidates for whom
they were to vote. But in those days, as has always been
the case, most voters were so engrossed in their ordinary
occupations that they gave little more attention to politics
than to vote; and the leaders, except on special occasions,
found it easy to fill the great popular meeting, as well as
other meetings, with their friends and creatures, sending
out runners, and often in the winter, sleighs, for the dila-
tory. To the general and nominating committees was
added, several years later, a correspondence committee,
which was empowered to call meetings of the party when
necessary, the leaders having found the general committee

too slow and cumbersome a means through which to reach that important end.

To hold public favor, the Tammany Society thought prudent to make it appear that it was animated by patriotic motives instead of the desire for offices. That the people might see how dearly above all things Tammany prized its Revolutionary traditions, the society on April 13, 1808, marched in rank to Wallabout, where it laid the cornerstone of a vault in which were to be placed the bones of 11,500 patriots who had died on board the British prison ships. On April 26, the vault being completed, the remains were laid in it. The Tammany Society, headed by Benjamin Romaine and the military; the municipal officials, Gov. Daniel D. Tompkins, members of Congress, Army and Navy officers, and many other detachments of men of lesser note participated in the ceremony.

The Federalists maintained that Tammany's patriotic show was merely an election maneuver. Subsequent developments did not help to disprove the charge. The society proclaimed far and wide its intention of building a monument over the vault, and induced the Legislature to make a grant of land worth $1,000 for the purpose. Associations and individuals likewise contributed. The political ceremonies connected with the burial having their expected effect, Tammany forgot altogether about its project until ugly rumors, pointing to the misuse of the money collected, forced the society in 1821 to petition the Legislature for further aid in erecting the monument. On that occasion the Tammany Society was denounced bitterly. It was brought out that such was Tammany's interest in the monument that no request was ever made for the land granted by the Legislature in 1808. The Legislature, however, granted $1,000 in cash.[1] This sum was not enough; and as Tammany did not swell the amount, though its Sachems were rich with the spoils of office, a

[1] *Journal of the Assembly,* 1821, p. 532, also p. 758.

resolution was introduced in the Assembly, March 4, 1826,[2] stating that as the $1,000 appropriated February 27, 1821, had not been used for the purpose but remained in the hands of Benjamin Romaine, the society's treasurer, it should be returned, and threatening legal proceedings in case it was not. This resolution, slightly amended, was passed on a close vote. There is, however, no available record of what became of the $1,000.

During three years, culminating in 1809, a series of disclosures regarding the corruption of Tammany officials astounded the city. Rumors grew so persistent that the Common Council was forced by public opinion to investigate. In the resultant revelations many Tammany chiefs suffered.

Benjamin Romaine, variously Sachem and Grand Sachem, was removed in 1806 from the office of City Controller for malfeasance, though the Common Council was controlled by his own party.[3] As a trustee of corporation property he had fraudulently obtained valuable land in the heart of the city, without paying for it. The affair caused a very considerable scandal. The Common Council had repeatedly passed strong resolutions calling on him to explain. Romaine must have settled in some fashion; for there is no evidence that he was prosecuted.

On January 26, 1807, Philip I. Arcularius, Superintendent of the Almshouse, and Cornelius Warner, Superintendent of Public Repairs, were removed summarily.[4] It was shown that Warner had defrauded the city as well as the men who worked under him.[5]

Jonas Humbert, Inspector of Bread and sometime Sachem, was proved to have extorted a third of the fees collected by Flour Inspector Jones, under the threat of having Jones put out of office. In consequence of

2 *Ibid.*, 1826, p. 750.
3 *MS. Minutes of the Common Council*, Vol. 16, pp. 239–40 and 405.
4 *MS. Minutes of the Common Council*, Vol. 16, pp. 288–89.
5 *Ibid.*, p. 316.

the facts becoming known, Humbert and his associate Inspector, Christian Nestell, discreetly resigned their offices—probably to avert official investigation.[6]

Abraham Stagg, another of the dynasty of Grand Sachems, as Collector of Assessments failed, it was disclosed in 1808, to account for about $1,000.[7] Two other Assessment Collectors, Samuel L. Page (for a long time prominent in Tammany councils), and Simon Ackerman, were likewise found to be embezzlers.[8] Stagg and Page managed to make good their deficit by turning over to the city certain property, but Ackerman disappeared.

John Bingham, at times Sachem, and a noted politician of the day, managed, through his position as an Alderman, to wheedle the city into selling to his brother-in-law land which later he influenced the corporation to buy back at an exorbitant price. The Common Council, spurred by public opinion, demanded its reconveyance.[9] Even Bingham's powerful friend, Matthew L. Davis, could not silence the scandal, for Davis himself had to meet a charge that while defending the Embargo at Martling's he was caught smuggling out flour in quantities that yielded him a desirable income.

But worse than these disclosures was that affecting the society's founder, William Mooney. The Common Council in 1808 appointed him Superintendent of the Almshouse, at an annual recompense of $1,000 and the support of his family in the place, provided that this latter item should not amount to over $500. Mooney had a more exalted idea of how he and his family ought to live. In the summer of 1809 the city fathers appointed a committee to investigate. The outcome was surprising. Mooney had spent nearly $4,000 on himself and family in addition to his salary; he had taken from the city supplies about $1,000 worth of articles, and moreover had expended various sums for " trifles for

6 *Ibid.*, p. 50.
7 *Ibid.*, Vol. 18, p. 194.
8 *Ibid.*
9 *Ibid.*, Vol. 20, pp. 355–56.

Mrs. Mooney" — a term which survived for many years in local politics. The ofttimes Grand Sachem of the Tammany Society could not explain his indulgences satisfactorily, and the Common Council relieved him of the cares of office, only one Alderman voting for his retention.[10]

Most of these leaders were only momentarily incommoded, the Tammany Society continuing many of them, for years after, in positions of trust and influence. Mooney subsequently was repeatedly chosen Grand Sachem and Father of the Council; Romaine was elected Grand Sachem in 1808, again in 1813, and frequently Sachem; Matthew L. Davis was elected Grand Sachem in 1814 and reelected in 1815 [11] and was a Sachem for years later; Abraham Stagg remained a leader and continued to get contracts for street paving and regulating, and neither Jonas Humbert nor John Bingham suffered a loss of influence with the Wigwam men.

Meanwhile the Sachems were professing the highest virtue. The society's calls for meetings ran like this:

"Tammany Society, or Columbian Order — Brothers, You are requested to assemble around the council fire in the Great Wigwam, No. 1, on Saturday, the 12th inst., at 9 o'clock A. M. (wearing a bucktail in your hat), to celebrate the anniversary of the Columbian Order and recount to each other the deeds of our departed chiefs and warriors in order that it may stimulate us *to imitate them in whatever is virtuous and just.*" [12]

The public, however, took another view of the matter. These scandals, and the showing of a deficit in the city's accounts of $250,000, hurt Tammany's prestige considerably. The Republican strength in the city at the election of April, 1809, showed a decrease of six hundred votes, the majority being only 116, while the Federalists carried

10 *Ibid.,* Vol. 20, p. 303. The full report on Mooney's administration appears in *Ibid.,* pp. 376–92.

11 Although the subsequent laws of the Tammany Society forbade the successive reelection of a Grand Sachem, the incumbent of the office was frequently permitted to "hold over."

12 Advertisement in the *Columbian,* May 14, 1810.

the State, and thus secured control of the Council of Appointment.

The lesson was lost on the leaders. The society at this time was led by various men, of whom Teunis Wortman[13] was considered the chief power. Wortman was as enraged at the defection of these few hundred voters as his successors were at a later day at an adverse majority of tens of thousands. He caused a meeting to be held at Martling's on May 19, and secured the appointment of a committee, with one member from each of the ten wards, instructed to inquire into the causes contributing to lessen Tammany's usual majority. The committee was further instructed to call a general meeting of the Republican citizens of the county, on the completion of its investigation, and to report to them, that it might be known who were their friends and who their enemies. Here is to be seen the first manifestation of that systematic discipline which Tammany Hall thereafter exercised. Wortman's plan excited both Clintonites and Federalists. The committee was called "the committee of spies," and was regarded generally as the beginning of a system of intimidation and proscription.

In the passionate acrimony of the struggle between Tammany and the Clintons, the Federalists seemed to be well-nigh forgotten. The speakers and writers of each side assailed the other with great fury. One of these was James Cheetham, a Clinton supporter and editor of the *American Citizen*. Goaded by his strictures, the Tammany Society on the night of February 28, 1809, expelled him from membership on the grounds that he had assailed the general Government and vilified Jefferson.

In the *American Citizen* of March 1, Cheetham replied that the resolution was carried by trickery. " Tammany Society," Cheetham continued, " was chartered by the

[13] Wortman had been a follower of Clinton and had been generously aided by him. He suddenly shifted to Tammany, on seeing better opportunities of advancement with that body.

Legislature of the State for *charitable purposes*. Not a member of the Legislature, when it was chartered, imagined, I dare to say, that it would be thus perverted to the worst purposes of faction." On May 1 he sent this note to the Grand Sachem:

> "Sir, I decline membership in Tammany Society. Originally national and Republican, it has degenerated into a savage barbarity."

Cheetham then wrote to Grand Sachem Cowdrey for a certified copy of the proceedings, saying he wanted it to base an action which he would bring for the annulment of the charter of the Tammany Society for misuser. Cowdrey expressed regret at not being able to accommodate him. "Tammany Society," wrote Cowdrey,

> "is an institution that has done much good and may and undoubtedly will do more. . . . I do not think one error can or ought to cancel its long list of good actions and wrest from it its charter of incorporation, the basis of its stability and existence."

The *American Citizen* thereupon bristled with fiercer attacks upon Tammany. "Jacobin clubs," says "A Disciple of Washington," in this newspaper, July 29, 1809,

> "are becoming organized to overawe, not only the electors but the elected under our government; such are the Washington and the Tammany Societies. The latter was originally instituted for harmless purposes and long remained harmless in its acts; members from all parties were admitted to it; but we have seen it become a tremendous political machine. . . . The Washington Jacobin Club, it is said, consists of at least two thousand rank and file, and the Tammany Jacobins to perhaps as many. . . . The time will come, and that speedily, when the Legislature, the Governor and the Council of Appointment shall not dare to disobey their edicts."

Tammany retaliated upon Cheetham by having a bill passed by the Legislature taking away from him the position of State Printer, which paid $3,000 a year.

Tammany's comparative weakness in the city, as shown in the recent vote, prompted Clinton to suggest a compromise and union of forces. Overtures were made by his agents, and on July 13, 1809, twenty-eight of the leaders of the Clinton, Madison, Burr and Lewis factions met in a private room at Coleman's Fair House. Matthew L. Davis told them the chiefs ought to unite; experience demonstrated that if they did they would lead the rest — meaning the voters. Tammany, he said, welcomed a union of the Republican forces so as to prevent the election of a Federalist Council of Appointment. Davis and Wortman proposed that they unite to prevent any removals from office; that the two opposition Republican clubs in turn should be destroyed and that their members should go back to the Tammany Society, which, being on the decline, must be reenforced. Or, if it should be thought advisable to put down the Tammany Society, "considering its prevailing disrepute," then a new society should be organized in which Burrites, Lewisites, Clintonites and Madisonians were to be admitted members under the general family and brotherly name of Republican.

De Witt Clinton cautiously kept away from this meeting, allowing his lieutenants to do the work of outwitting Tammany. A committee of ten was appointed to consider whether a coalition of the chiefs were practicable; whether, if it were, the people would agree to it; whether the Whig (opposition Republican) clubs should be destroyed and whether the Tammany Society should be reenforced.

The meeting came to naught. In this effort to win over the Tammany chiefs, De Witt Clinton abandoned his protégé and dependent, Cheetham, who had made himself obnoxious to them. Finding Clinton's political and financial support withdrawn, Cheetham, out of revenge, published the proceedings of this secret meeting in the *American Citizen,* and, awakening public indignation, closed the bargaining. A few nights later a Tammany mob threw brickbats in the windows of Cheetham's house. By his death, on September 19, 1810, Tammany was freed from one of its earliest and most vindictive assailants.

CHAPTER IV

1809–1815

THE Tammany men fared badly for a time. During 1809 the Council of Appointment removed numbers of them from office. In November the Federalists elected a majority of their Aldermanic ticket, and in April, 1810, they elected their Assembly ticket by the close majority of 36. Even when the Federalists were beaten the following year, it brought no good to Tammany, for a Clintonite Council of Appointment dispensed the offices. Clinton, though ousted from the Mayoralty in 1810 to make room for the Federalist Jacob Radcliff, was again made Mayor in the Spring of 1811.

But before long affairs took another turn. Tammany was the only real Republican organization in the city. It stood for the national party. As men were inclined to vote more for party success than for particular local nominees, Tammany's candidates were certain to be swept in at some time on the strength of party adherence. While the rank and file of the organization were concerned in seeing its candidates successful only inasmuch as that meant the success of democratic principles, the leaders intrigued constantly for spoils at the expense of principles. But whatever their conduct might be, they were sure of success when the next wave of Republican feeling carried the party to victory.

De Witt Clinton's following was largely personal. Drawing, it was estimated, from $10,000 to $20,000 a year in salary and fees as Mayor, he lived in high style

and distributed bounty liberally among his supporters.
His income aroused the wonder of his contemporaries.
The President of the United States received $25,000
annually; the Mayor of Philadelphia, $2,000. " Poster-
ity," said one observer, " will read with astonishment
that a Mayor of New York should make the enormous
sum of $15,000 out of his office." This was no inconse-
quential salary at a time when a man worth $50,000 was
thought rich; when a good house could be rented for $350
a year, and $750 or $800 would meet the expenses of the
average family. Many of those whom Clinton helped
picked a quarrel with him later, in order to have a pretext
for the repudiation of their debts, and joined Tammany.

Tammany had the party machine, but Clinton had a
powerful hold on the lower classes, especially the Irish.
As United States Senator he had been foremost in having the naturalization period reduced from fourteen to
five years, and he made himself popular with them in other
ways. He, himself, was of Irish descent.

The Irish were bitter opponents of Tammany Hall.
The prejudice against allowing " adopted citizens " to
mingle in politics was deep; and Tammany claimed to
be a thoroughly native body. As early as May 12, 1791,
at Campbell's Tavern, Greenwich, the Tammany Society
had announced that being a national body, it consisted
of Americans born, who would fill all offices; though
adopted Americans were eligible to honorary posts, such
as warriors and hunters. An " adopted citizen " was
looked upon as an " exotic." Religious feeling, too, was
conspicuous. It was only after repeated hostile demon-
strations that Tammany would consent, in 1809, for the
first time to place a Catholic — Patrick McKay — upon
its Assembly ticket.

The accession of the Livingston family had helped the
society, adding the support of a considerable faction and
" respectability." The Livingstons, intent on supersed-
ing the Clintons, seized on Tammany as a good lever.

Above all, it was necessary to have a full application of
" respectability," and to further that end the society
put up a pretentious building — the recent *Sun* newspaper building. In 1802 the Tammany Society had
tried by subscription to build a fine Wigwam, but was
unsuccessful. The unwisdom of staying in such a place
as Martling's, which subjected them to gibes, and which
was described as " the Den where the Wolves and Bears
and Panthers assemble and drink down large potations
of beer," was impressed upon the Sachems who, led by
Jacob Barker, the largest shipbuilder in the country at
the time, raised the sum of $28,000. The new Wigwam
was opened in 1811, with the peculiar Indian ceremonies.
Sachem Abraham M. Valentine — the same man who, for
malfeasance, was afterward (May 26, 1830) removed
from the office of Police Magistrate[1] — was the grand
marshal of the day.

From 1811 the Tammany, or Martling, men came
under the general term of the Tammany Hall party or
Tammany Hall; the general committee was called technically the Democratic-Republican General Committee.
The Tammany Society, with its eleven hundred members, now more than ever *appeared* distinct from the
Tammany Hall political body. Though the general committee was supplied with the use of rooms and the hall in
the building, it met on different nights from the society,
and to all appearances acted independently of it. But
the society, in fact, was and continued to be, the secret
ruler of the political organization. Its Sachems were
chosen yearly from the most influential of the local Tammany political leaders.

De Witt Clinton aimed to be President of the United
States and schemed for his nomination by the Republican

[1] *MS. Minutes of the Common Council,* Vol. 72, p. 137. Judge
Irving and an Aldermanic committee, after a searching investigation, found Valentine guilty of receiving from prisoners money for
which he did not account to the city.

Legislative caucus. Early in 1811 he sought and received from the caucus the nomination for Lieutenant-Governor. He purposed to hold both the offices of Mayor and Lieutenant-Governor, while spending as much time as he could at Albany so as to bring his direct influence to bear in person. As a State officer he could do this without loss of dignity. He would have preferred the post of State Senator, but he feared if he stood for election in New York City Tammany would defeat him. The chiefs, regarding his nomination as treachery toward Madison, immediately held a meeting and issued a notice that they ceased to consider him a member of the Republican party; that he was not only opposing Madison but was bent on establishing a pernicious family aristocracy.

When the Clinton men tried to hold a counter meeting at the Union Hotel a few days later, the Tammany men rushed in and put them to flight.[2] Tammany was so anxious to defeat Clinton that it supported the Federalist candidate for Lieutenant-Governor, defeating the aggressive Mayor. But Clinton obtained the caucus nomination for President. His partizans voted the Federalist Assembly ticket (1812) rather than aid the Republican ticket of Tammany Hall. Assisted by the Federalists, Clinton received the electoral vote of New York State, but was overwhelmed by Madison. His course seemed precisely that with which Tammany had charged him — treason to the party to which he professed to belong. In a short time the Wigwam succeeded in influencing nearly all the Republicans in New York City against him.

One other event helped to bring back strength and prestige to Tammany Hall. This was the War of 1812, which Tammany called for and supported. On February 26, four months before war was declared, the Tammany

2 Hammond, Vol. I, p. 294.

Society passed resolutions recommending immediate war
with Great Britain unless she should repeal her " Orders
in Council." The members pledged themselves to support the Government " in that just and necessary war"
with their " lives, fortunes and sacred honor." The conservative element execrated Tammany, but the supporters
of the war came to look upon it more favorably, and about
a thousand persons, some of whom had been members before but had ceased attendance, applied for membership.
Throughout the conflict Tammany Hall was the resort of
the war-party. At the news of each victory the flag was
hoisted to the breeze and a celebration followed. The successful military and naval men were banqueted there, while
hundreds of candles illumined every window in the building. On August 31, 1814, 1150 members of the society
marched to build defenses in Brooklyn; but this was not
done until public pressure forced it, for by August 15 at
least twenty other societies, civil and trades, had volun-
teered, and Tammany had to make good its pretensions.

The leaders prospered by Madison's favor. From one
contract alone Matthew L. Davis reaped $80,000, and
Nathan Sanford was credited with making his office of
United States District Attorney at New York yield as
high as $30,000 a year. The lesser political workers were
rewarded proportionately. Having a direct and considerable interest in the success of Madison's administration,
they were indefatigable partizans. Some of the Tammany leaders proved their devotion to their country's
cause by doing service in the Quartermaster's Department. Among these were the two Swartwouts (John and
Robert), who became Generals, and Romaine, who became
a Colonel.

This war had the effect of causing the society to aban-
don its custom of marching in Indian garb.[3] In 1813
the Indians in the Northwest, incited by British agents,

[3] R. S. Guernsey, *New York City During the War of 1812.*

went on the war-path, torturing and scalping, devastating settlements and killing defenseless men, women and children. Their very name became repulsive to the whites. The society seemed to be callous to this feeling, and began preparations for its annual parades, in the usual Indian costumes, with painted faces, wearing bearskins and carrying papooses. The Federalists declared that these exhibitions, at all times ridiculous and absurd, would be little short of criminal after the cruelties which were being committed by the Tammany men of the wilderness. These attacks affected the Tammany Society so much that a majority of the members, consisting mainly of the politicians and young men, held a secret meeting and abolished all imitations of the Indians, in dress and manners as well as in name, and resolved that the officers should thereafter bear plain English titles.

Mooney opposed the change.[4] He would not listen to having those picturesque and native ceremonies, which he himself had ordained, wiped out. He resigned as Grand Sachem, and many of the Sachems went with him. On May 1, 1813, Benjamin Romaine was elected Grand Sachem, and other " reformers " were chosen as Sachems. On July 4 the Tammany Society marched with reduced numbers in ordinary civilian garb. From that time the society contented itself with civilian costume until 1825, when its parades ceased.

The attitude of the political parties to the war had the effect of making Tammany Hall the predominant force in the State, and of disorganizing the Federalist party beyond hope of recovery. Tammany began in 1813 to organize for the control of the State and to put down for all time De Witt Clinton, whom it denounced as having tried to paralyze the energies of Madison's administration. Meanwhile the Federalist leaders in the city, with a singular lack of tact, were constantly offending the

4 Mooney had now become opulent, being the owner of three or four houses and lots.

popular feeling with their political doctrines and their
haughty airs of superior citizenship.   To such an extent
was this carried that at times they were mobbed, as on
June 29, 1814, for celebrating the return of the Bourbons
to the French throne.

The organization of Tammany Hall, begun, as has
been seen, by the formation of the general, nominating
and correspondence committees, in 1806 and 1808, was
now further elaborated.   A finance committee, whose duty
it was to gather for the leaders a suitable campaign fund,
was created, and this was followed by the creation of the
Republican Young Men's General Committee,[5] which was
a sort of auxiliary to the general committee, having limited
powers, and serving as a province for the ambitions of the
young men.   The Democratic-Republican General Committee was supposed to comprise only the trusted ward
leaders, ripe with years and experience.   About the beginning of the War of 1812, it added to its duties the
issuing of long public addresses on political topics.   These
general committees were made self-perpetuating.   At the
close of every year they would issue a notice to the voters
when and where to meet for the election of their successors.
No sooner did the committee of one year step out than the
newly elected committee instantly took its place.   There
were also ward or vigilance committees, which were expected to bring every Tammany-Republican voter to the
polls, to see that no Federalist intimidation was attempted
and to campaign for the party.   The Tammany Hall organization was in a superb state by the year 1814, and in
active operation ceaselessly.   The Federalists, on the contrary, were scarcely organized, and the Clintonites had
declined to a mere faction.

The Tammany leaders, moreover, were shrewd and
conciliating.   About forty Federalists — disgusted, they

[5] The moving spirit in this committee for some years was Samuel
L. Berrian, who had been indicted in August, 1811, for instigating
a riot in Trinity Church, convicted and fined $100.

said, with their party's opposition to the war — joined the
Tammany Society. They were led by Gulian C. Verplanck, who severely assailed Clinton, much to the Wigwam's delight. Tammany Hall not only received them
with warmth, but advanced nearly all of them, such as
Jacob Radcliff, Richard Hadfelt, Richard Riker and
Hugh Maxwell, to the first public positions. This was
about the beginning of that policy, never since abandoned, by which Tammany Hall has frequently broken
up opposing parties or factions. The winning over of
leaders from the other side and conferring upon them rewards in the form of profitable public office or contracts
has been one of the most notable methods of Tammany's
diplomacy.

CHAPTER V

B Y 1815 Tammany Hall obtained control of the State, and in 1816 completely regained that of the city. The Common Council and its dependent offices since 1809 had been more or less under Federalist rule, and from the beginning of the century the city had had a succession of Clintonite office-holders in those posts controlled by the Council of Appointment.

At the close of the War of 1812 the population of the city approached 100,000, and there were 13,941 voters in all. The total expenses of the municipality reached a little over a million dollars. The city had but one public school, which was maintained by public subscription. Water was supplied chiefly by the Manhattan Company, by means of bored wooden logs laid underground from the reservoir in Chambers street. No fire department was dreamed of, and every blaze had the city at its mercy. The streets were uncleaned; only two or three thoroughfares were fit for the passage of carriages, though until 1834 the law required the inhabitants to clean the streets in front of their houses. Many of those elaborate departments which we now associate with political control were then either in an embryo state or not thought of.

The Aldermen were not overburdened with public anxieties. No salary was attached to the office, yet none the less, it was sought industriously. In early days it was regarded as a post of honor and filled as such, but with the beginning of the century it was made a means of profit. The professional politician of the type of to-day was rare. The Aldermen had business, as a rule, upon which they depended and to which they attended in the day, holding sessions of the board sporadically at night. The only exception to this routine was when the Alderman performed, some judicial office. Under the law, as soon as an Alderman entered office he became a judge of some of the most important courts, being obliged to preside with the Mayor at the trial of criminals. This system entailed upon the Aldermen the trial of offenses against laws many of which they themselves made, and it had an increasingly pernicious influence upon politics. Otherwise the sole legal perquisites and compensation of the Aldermen consisted in their power and custom of making appropriations, including those for elaborate public dinners for themselves. It was commonly known that they awarded contracts for city necessaries either to themselves or to their relatives.

The backward state of the city, its filthy and neglected condition and the chaotic state of public improvements and expenditures, excited little public discussion. The Common Councils were composed of men of inferior mind. It is told of one of them that hearing that the King of France had taken umbrage he ran home post haste to get his atlas and find out the location of that particular spot. In the exclusive charge of such a body New York City would have struggled along but slowly had it not been for the courage and genius of the man who at one stroke started it on a dazzling career of prosperity. This was De Witt Clinton.

No sooner did a Republican Council of Appointment step into office, early in 1815, than Tammany Hall pressed for the removal of Clinton as Mayor and announced that John Ferguson, the Grand Sachem of the Society, would have to be appointed in his place.[1] The

[1] Hammond, Vol. I, p. 399.

Council, at the head of which was Gov. Tompkins, wavered and delayed, Tompkins not caring to offend the friends of Clinton by the latter's summary removal. At this the entire Tammany representation, which had gone to Albany for the purpose, grew furious and threatened that not only would they nominate no ticket the next Spring, but would see that none of their friends should accept office under the Council, did it fail to remove Clinton. This action implied the turning out of the Council of Appointment at the next election. Yielding to these menaces, the Council removed Clinton. Then by a compromise, Ferguson was made Mayor until the National Government should appoint him Naval Officer when Jacob Radcliff (Mayor 1810–1811) was to succeed him — an arrangement which was carried out.[2]

The Wigwam was overjoyed at having struck down Clinton, and now expected many years of supremacy. From youth Clinton's sole occupation had been politics. He had spent his yearly salaries and was deeply in debt. His political aspirations seemed doomed. Stripped, as he appeared, of a party or even a fraction of one, the Sachems felt sure of his retirement to private life forever. In this belief they were as much animated by personal as by political enmity. Clinton had sneered at or ridiculed nearly all of them, and he spoke of them habitually in withering terms.

Besides, to enlarge their power in the city they needed the Mayor's office. The Mayor had the right to appoint a Deputy Mayor from among the Aldermen, the Deputy Mayor acting with full power in his absence. The Mayor could convene the Common Council, and he appointed and licensed marshals, porters, carriers, cartmen, carmen, cryers, scullers and scavengers, and removed them at

---

[2] Valentine in his *Manual of the Common Council of New York*, for 1842–44, p. 163, states that Ferguson held on to both offices until President Monroe required him to say which office he preferred. Ferguson soon after resigned the Mayoralty. He held the other post until his death in 1832.

pleasure.   He licensed tavern-keepers and all who sold ex-
cisable liquors by retail.   The Mayor, the Deputy Mayor,
Recorder and Aldermen were ex-officio Justices of the
Peace, and were empowered to hold Courts of General Sessions.   The Mayor, Recorder and Aldermen were also
Justices of Oyer and Terminer; and the Mayor, Deputy
Mayor and Recorder could preside over the Court of Common Pleas with or without the Aldermen.   The gathering
of all this power into its own control gave further strength
to Tammany Hall.

But the expressions of regret at Clinton's removal were
so spontaneous and sincere that Tammany feigned participation in them and took the utmost pains to represent
the removal as only a political exigency.   The Common
Council (which was now Federalist) passed, on March 21,
1815, a vote of thanks to Clinton for his able administration.[3]   Curiously, the very Wigwam men who had made it
their business to undertake the tedious travel over bad
roads to Albany to effect his removal (Aldermen Smith,
George Buckmaster, Mann and Burtis) voted loudest in
favor of the resolution.

Out of office, Clinton found time to agitate for the
building of a navigable canal between the great western
lakes and the tide waters of the Hudson.   The idea of
this enterprise was not original with him.   It had been
suggested over thirty years before, but it was he who
carried it forward to success.   The bigotry and animus
with which it was assailed were amazing.   Tammany Hall
frequently passed resolutions denouncing the project as
impracticable and chimerical, declaring that the canal
would make a ditch fit to bury its author in.   At Albany
the Tammany representatives greeted the project with a
burst of mockery, and placed obstacle after obstacle in its
path.

In the intervals of warring upon Clinton, Tammany

[3] *MS. Minutes of the Common Council,* Vol. 29, p. 150.

was adroitly seizing every post of vantage in the city. The Burr men ruled its councils and directed the policy and nominations of the Republican, or, as it was getting to be more generally known, the Democratic-Republican party. Three men, in particular, were foremost as leaders — George Buckmaster, a boat builder; Roger Strong and Benjamin Prince, a druggist and physician. Teunis Wortman, one of the energetic leaders in 1807–10, was now not quite so conspicuous. What the Wigwam lacked to make its rule in the city complete was a majority in the Common Council. The committees of the Council not only had the exclusive power of expenditures, but they invariably refused an acceptable accounting.[4] The Federalists, though vanishing as a party owing to their attitude in the recent war, still managed, through local dissensions among the Republicans, to retain control of the Common Council. The Federalists, therefore, held the key to the purse. It had always been customary for the Mayor to appoint the Common Council committees from the party which happened to be dominant.

Established forms meant nothing to Mayor Radcliff and to Buckmaster[5] and other Tammany Aldermen, who late in December, 1815, decided to turn out the Federalist chairmen of committees and put Tammany men in their

[4] As late as July 28, 1829, the Common Council refused such an accounting. Charles King, a prominent citizen, memorialized the Council, through Alderman Lozier, to furnish an itemized statement of the expenditure of over half a million dollars for the previous fiscal year. By a vote of 15 to 6 the Council refused to grant the request. A public agitation on the question following, the board later rescinded its action, and supplied the statement.

[5] Buckmaster had a record. On October 9, 1815, the Common Council passed a secret resolution to sell $440,000 of United States bonds it held at 97 — the stock being then under par. About $30,000 worth was disposed of at that figure, when the officials found that not a dollar's worth more could be sold. Investigation followed. Gould Hoyt proved that Buckmaster had disclosed the secret to certain Wall street men, who, taking advantage of the city's plight, forced the sale of the stock at 95. Buckmaster was chairman of the general commitee in 1815 and at other times, and chairman of the nominating committee in 1820.

places. Radcliff imprudently printed a handbill of officers he intended appointing, copies of which he sent to his partizans. A copy fell into a Federalist's hands. At the next meeting, before the Mayor could get a chance to act, the Federalist majority altered the rules so as to vest in future the appointment of all committees in a majority of the board. The Sachems were so enraged at Radcliff's bungling that they declared they would have him removed from office. About a year afterward they carried out their threat.

In 1816 Tammany elected not only its Congress and Assembly ticket, but a Common Council, by over 1000 majority out of 9000 votes. This victory was the result of the wily policy of further disrupting the Federalist party by nominating its most popular men. Walter Bowne, a late Federalist, an enemy of Clinton and a man of standing in the community, was one of those nominated by Tammany Hall for State Senator, and the support of the wealthy was solicited by the selection of men of their own class, such as Col. Rutgers, said to be the richest man in the State.

Most of Tammany's early members, certainly the leaders, were now rich and had stepped into the upper middle class; but their wealth could not quite secure them admittance to that stiff aristocracy above them, which demanded something more of a passport than the possession of money. Another body of members were the small tradesmen and the like, to whom denunciations of the aristocracy were extremely palatable. A third class, that of the mechanics and laborers, believed that Tammany Hall exclusively represented them in its onslaughts on the aristocracy. From the demands of these various interests arose the singular sight of Tammany Hall winning the support of the rich by systematically catering to them; of the middle class, which it reflected, and of the poor, in whose interests it claimed to work. The spirit of the Tammany Society was well illustrated in its odd

address on public affairs in 1817, wherein it lamented the
spread of the foreign. game of billiards among the aristocratic youth and the prevalence of vice among the lower
classes. Again, in May, 1817, the Tammany majority of
the Common Council, under pressure from the religious
element, passed an ordinance fining every person $5 who
should hunt, shoot, fish, spar or play on Sunday — a law
which cut off from the poor their favorite pastimes.

Here, too, another of the secrets by which the organization was enabled to thrive, should be mentioned. This
was the " regularity " of its nominations. Teunis Wortman, a few years before, had disclosed the real substance
of the principle of " regularity " when he wrote: " The
nominating power is an omnipotent one. Though it approaches us in the humble attitude of the *recommendation*, its influence is irresistible. Every year's experience
demonstrates that its recommendations are commands.
That instead of presenting a choice it deprives us of all
option." [6] The plain meaning was that, regardless of the
candidate's character, the mass of the party would vote
for him once he happened to be put forth on the "regular "
ticket. Fully alive to the value of this particular power,
the Tammany Hall General Committee, successively and
unfailingly, would invite in its calls for all meetings
" those friendly to regular nominations." Its answer to
charges of dictatorship was plain and direct. Discipline
was necessary, its leaders said, to prevent aristocrats from
disrupting their party by inciting a variety of
nominations.

It was through this fertile agency that " bossism " became an easy possibility. With the voters in such a
receptive state of mind it was not difficult to dictate
nominations. The general commitee was composed of
thirty members; its meetings were secret and attended
seldom by more than fourteen members. So, substan-

---

[6] *New York Public Advertiser*, April 13, 1809. This journal was
secretly supported for a time by the funds of the Tammany Society.

tially, fourteen men were acting for over five thousand Republican voters, and eight members of the fourteen composed a majority. Yet the system had all the pretense of being pure democracy; the wards were called upon at regular intervals to elect delegates; the latter chose candidates or made party rules; and the " great popular meeting " accepted or rejected nominees; it all seemed to spring directly from the people.

This exquisitely working machine was in full order when the organization secured a firm hold upon the city in 1816. The newly elected Common Council removed every Federalist possible and put a stanch Tammany man in his place. The Federalist Captains of Police and the heads and subordinates of many departments whose appointments and removal were vested in the Common Council were all ejected. This frequent practice of changes in the police force, solely because of political considerations, had a demoralizing effect upon the welfare of the city.

Both parties were as responsible for this state of affairs as they were for the increase in the city's debt. To provide revenue the Aldermen repeatedly caused to be sold ground owned by the municipality in the heart of the city. This was one of their clumsy or fraudulent methods of concealing the squandering of city funds, on what no one knew. They were not ignorant that with the growth of the city the value of the land would increase vastly. It was perhaps for this very reason they sold it; for it was generally themselves or the Tammany leaders who were the buyers. One sale was of land fronting Bowling Green, among the purchasers being John Swartwout, Jacob Barker and John Sharpe. A hint as to the fraudulent ways in which the Tammany leaders became rich is furnished by a report made to the Common Council respecting land in Hamilton Square, bought from the city by Jacob Barker, John S. Hunn and others. The report stated that repeated applications for the payment of principal and interest had been made without effect.[7]

By 1817 the Federalists in New York City were crushed, quite beyond hope of resurrection as a winning party. The only remaining fear was Clinton, whose political death the organization celebrated prematurely. Public opinion was one factor Tammany had not conquered.

This inclined more and more daily to the support of Clinton. Notwithstanding all the opposition which narrow-mindedness and hatred could invent, Clinton's grand project of the Erie Canal became popular — distinctively so throughout the State, then so greatly agricultural. On April 15, 1817, the bill pledging the State to the building of the canal became a law, the Tammany delegation and all their friends voting against it.

Gov. Tompkins becoming Vice-President, a special election to fill the gubernatorial vacancy became necessary. A new and powerful junction of Clinton's old friends and the disunited Federalists joined in nominating him to succeed Tompkins. This was bitter news to Tammany, which made heroic efforts to defeat him, nominating as its candidate Peter B. Porter, and sending tickets with his name into every county in the State.

Inopportunely for the Wigwam, the resentment of the Irish broke out against it at this time. Tammany's long-continued refusal to give the Irish proper representation among its nominations, either in the society or for public office, irritated them greatly. On February 7, a writer in a newspaper over the signature "Connal," averred in an open letter to Matthew L. Davis that on the evening of February 3, the Tammany Society had considered a resolution for the adoption of a new constitution, the object of which was to exclude foreigners entirely from holding office in the society. This may not have been strictly true, but the anti-foreign feeling in the organiza-

[7] *MS. Minutes of the Common Council,* Vol. 18, p. 359.

tion was unquestionably strong. The Irish had sought, some time before, to have the organization nominate for Congress Thomas Addis Emmett, an Irish orator and patriot and an ardent friend of Clinton. As Tammany Hall since 1802 had not only invariably excommunicated all Clintonites, but had broken up such Clinton meetings as were held, this demand was refused without discussion. The Irish grew to regard Tammany Hall as the home of bigotry; the Wigwam, in turn, was resolved not to alienate the prejudiced native support by recognizing foreigners; furthermore, the Irish were held to be Clintonites trying to get into Tammany Hall and control it.

The long-smouldering enmity burst out on the night of April 24, 1817, when the general committee was in session. Two hundred Irishmen, assembled at Dooley's Long Room, marched in rank to the Wigwam and broke into the meeting room. The intention of their leaders was to impress upon the committee the wisdom of nominating Emmett for Congress, as well as other Irish Catholics on the Tammany ticket in future, but the more fiery spirits at once started a fight. Eyes were blackened, noses and heads battered freely. The invaders broke the furniture, using it for weapons and shattering it maliciously; tore down the fixtures and shivered the windows. Reinforcements arriving, the intruders were driven out, but not before nearly all present had been bruised and beaten.[8]

Clinton received an overwhelming majority for Governor, Porter obtaining a ridiculously small vote in both New York City and the rest of the State.[9] Thus in the feud between Tammany Hall and DeWitt Clinton, the latter, lacking a political machine and basing his contest solely on a political idea — that of internal improvements—emerged triumphant.

[8] *The National Advocate,* May 10, asserted that the Irish entered Tammany Hall, shouting "Down with the Natives!" but the assertion was denied.

[9] Clinton's vote was nearly 44,000; Porter's not quite 1,400.

CHAPTER VI

CLINTON MAINTAINS HIS SUPREMACY

1817–1820

WITH Gov. Clinton at the head of the Council of Appointment, Tammany men expected the force of his vengeance. They were not disappointed. He removed many of them for no other reason than that they belonged to the organization.

Hoping to make terms with him, the Wigwam Assemblymen, early in 1818, presented to the Council of Appointment a petition praying for the removal of Mayor Radcliff and the appointment in his place of William Paulding, Jr. "Radcliff," the paper read, "is an unfit person longer to fill that honorable and respectful office." Clinton smiled at this ambidexterity. It was rumored that he intended to award the honor to Cadwallader D. Colden, a Federalist supporter of the War of 1812, and one of the Federalists Tammany Hall had sent to the Assembly in 1817, as a means of breaking up that party. Colden now let it be understood that he sided with Clinton.

The whole Tammany delegation lived in a single house at Albany and met in a large room, No. 10, in Eagle Tavern. "This system of acting as a separate body," admitted Tammany's own organ,[1] "was very injudicious to our city. It created suspicion and distrust among country members; it looked like a separate interest; a combination of a powerful delegation to frown down or over-

---

[1] *National Advocate*, October 7, 1822. A circumstantial account of the meeting referred to on the following page appears in this issue. The paper was edited and owned by M. M. Noah, who became Grand Sachem in 1824.

power the delegation of a smaller county." Colden did not join in these nightly meetings. One day he was coaxed in to take a glass of wine. To his surprise, upon opening the door of No. 10, he found the delegation in caucus. The meeting seemed to be waiting for him before transacting business. He had scarcely taken a seat, when one of the members arose, and in a long speech protested against any member of the city delegation accepting an office, and suggested that each member should pledge himself not to do so. Colden saw at once that the resolution was directed against himself. He exclaimed energetically against the trickery, declaring that he had not asked for the office of Mayor, but would accept it if offered. The meeting broke up; Colden was appointed Mayor, and Tammany Hall from that time denounced him.

In Albany, Clinton was vigorously pushing forward the Erie Canal project; the Tammany men were as aggressively combatting it.[2]   While Clinton was thus absorbed in this great public enterprise the Wigwam was enriching its leaders in manifold ways. An instance of this was the noted Barker episode. Jacob Barker was a Sachem, a leader of great influence in the political organization, and such a power in financial and business circles that at one time he defied the United States Bank. He and Matthew L. Davis were Burr's firmest friends to the hour of Burr's death. Early in 1818 a bill prohibiting private banking, prepared at the instance of the incorporated banks, which sought a monopoly, passed the Senate; though as a special favor to Barker the Senate exempted from its provisions the latter's Exchange Bank for three years. But Barker desired an indefinite lease. To create a show of public sentiment he had the hall packed with his friends and creatures on April 14, when resolutions were passed stating that the proposed bill would destroy all competition with the incorporated banks, " benefit the rich, oppress

2 Hammond, Vol. I, p. 450.

the poor, extend the power of existing aristocracies, and terminate the banking transactions of an individual whose loans have been highly advantageous to many laborious and industrious mechanics and neighboring farmers." The Legislature granted the privileges Barker asked. A few years later (1826) the sequel to this legislative favoritism appeared in the form of one of the most sensational trials witnessed in early New York.

The year 1818 saw Tammany Hall in the unusual position of advocating a protective tariff. The War of 1812 having injured domestic manufacturing, the demand for such a measure was general. Party asperity had softened, and Republicans, or Democrats — as they were coming to be known — and Federalists alike favored it. The society made the best of this popular wave. It issued an address, advising moderate protective duties on foreign goods. But New York then, and until after the Civil War, was a great shipbuilding center; and the shipbuilders and owners and the importing merchants soon influenced Tammany to revert to the stanch advocacy of free trade.

The almost complete extinction of national party lines under Monroe caused the disappearance of violent partizan recriminations and brought municipal affairs more to public attention. From 1817 onward public bodies agitated much more forcibly and persistently than before for the correction of certain local evils. Chief among these were the high taxes. In 1817 the city tax levy was $180,000; in 1818 it rose to $250,000, " an enormous amount," one newspaper said. Though the city received annually $200,000 in rents from houses and lots, for wharves, slips and piers, and also a considerable amount from fines, yet there was a constantly increasing deficit. The city expenses were thought to be too slight to devour the ordinary revenue. The Democratic, or Tammany, officials made attempts to explain that much of the debt was contracted under Federalist Common Councils, and said that sufficient money must be provided or " the poor would starve."

At almost the identical time this plea was entered, E. C. Genet was laying before the Grand Jury a statement to this effect: that although it was known that the aggregate capital of the incorporated banks, insurance and commission companies in New York City, exclusive of one branch of the United States Bank, amounted in 1817 to about $22,000,000, in addition to the shares in those companies, yet the city and States taxes combined " on all that vast personal estate in New York City are only a paltry $97,000."

The explanation of the blindness of the Wigwam officials to the escape of the rich from taxation is simple. The Tammany Hall of 1818 was not the Tammany Hall of 1800. In that interval the poor young men who once had to club together in order to vote had become directors in banking, insurance and various other corporations, which as members of the Legislature or as city officials they themselves had helped to form. Being such, they exerted all the influence of their political machinery to save their property from taxation. From about 1805 to 1837 Tammany Hall was ruled directly by about one-third bankers, one-third merchants and the remaining third politicians of various pursuits. The masses formed — except at rare times — the easily wielded body. The leaders safeguarded their own interests at every point, however they might profess at election times an abhorrence of the aristocracy; and the Grand Jury being of them, ignored Genet's complaint.

A new series of revelations concerning the conduct of Tammany chieftains was made public during 1817–18. Ruggles Hubbard, a one-time Sachem and at the time Sheriff of the county, absconded from the city August 15, 1817, leaving a gap in the treasury.[3]   John L. Broome,

---

[3] In what year Hubbard was Sachem is uncertain. His name is included in Horton's list. He was one of the chiefs in the nominat-

another Sachem, was shortly after removed from the office
of City Clerk by the Council of Appointment for having
neglected to take the necessary securities from Hubbard.
John P. Haff, a one-time Grand Sachem and long a power
in the organization, was removed by President Monroe on
November 14, 1818, from the office of Surveyor of the
Port, for corruption and general unfitness.[4]

But the most sensational of these exposures was that
concerning the swindling of the Medical Science Lottery,
by which Naphthali Judah [5] and others profited hand-
somely. The testimony brought out before Mayor Colden, November 10, 1818, showed that a corrupt understanding existed between Judah and one of the lottery's
managers, by which the former was enabled to have a
knowledge of the state of the wheel. Not less than
$100,000 was drawn on the first day, of which Judah re-
ceived a large share. Further affidavits were submitted
tending to show a corrupt understanding between Judah
and Alderman Isaac Denniston in the drawing of the
Owego Lottery, by which Denniston won $35,000. John
L. Broome was also implicated in the scandal, and Teunis
Wortman, while not directly concerned in it, was considered involved by the public, and suffered a complete loss
of popular favor,[6] though retaining for some time a cer-

ing committee from 1815 to 1817. It is worthy of note that only
a short time before his flight a committee of the Common Council had
examined his accounts and approved them as correct.

[4] That Haff was removed is certain, though the author has been
unable to find a record of the fact in the available papers of the
Treasury Department. The Tammany organ, the *National Advocate,*
November 19, 1818, commented as follows: " The rumors which, for
several days past, have been afloat and which we treated as idle and
interested, are confirmed — Captain Haff has been removed from
office." Many evidences of public gratification were shown. In
one instance, eighty citizens dragged a field piece from the Arsenal
to the Battery and fired a salute.

[5] Naphthali Judah had been Sachem of the Maryland tribe in 1808,
and continued for some time to be a leader in the party's councils.
He was again elected a Sachem in 1819.

[6] How deeply the people of New York were concerned in lotteries
may be gathered from the fact that in 1826 there were 190 lottery

tain degree of influence in the society and organization.

Always as popular criticism began to assert itself, Tammany would make a sudden display of patriotism, accompanied by the pronouncement of high-sounding toasts and other exalted utterances. Such it did in 1817, when the society took part in the interment of the remains of Gen. Montgomery in St. Paul's Church. And now the Sachems prepared to entertain Andrew Jackson at a banquet, and also indirectly signify that he was their choice for President. William Mooney, again elected Grand Sachem, sent to Gen. Jackson, under date of February 15, 1819, a grandiloquent letter of invitation which, referring to the battle of New Orleans, said in part:

> "Columbia's voice, in peals of iron thunder, proclaimed the dread fiat of that eventful morn! Terra was drenched with human gore! The perturbed elements were hushed! Mars and Bellona retired from the ensanguined field! and godlike Hera resumed her gentle reign. . . . We approbate your noble deeds and greet you hero. Scourge of British insolence, Spanish perfidy and Indian cruelty — these, sir, are the sentiments of the Sons of Liberty in New York who compose the National Institution of Tammany Society No. 1 of the United States. Here, sir, we guard the patriot flame —'preserved by concord'— its effulgence, in a blaze of glory, shall surround and accompany you to the temple of interminable fame and honor."

Jackson accepted the invitation. Cadwallader D. Colden, who had been re-appointed Mayor a few days before, was asked to preside. When, on February 23, the banquet was held and Jackson was called for his toast, Colden arose, and to the consternation of the Tammany men proposed: "De Witt Clinton, the Governor of the great and patriotic State of New York." This surprising move made it appear that Jackson favored the Clinton party. To counteract the impression, the General in-

offices legalized by statute in New York City. A saying obtained that "one-half the citizens got their living by affording the opportunity of gambling to the rest." Many State institutions were in part supported from the proceeds of the lotteries. These swindles, therefore, became a matter for legislative investigation. A great number of pages of the Journal of the Assembly for 1819 are taken up with the testimony.

stantly left the room, " amidst reiterated applauses," and
a dead silence ensued for three minutes. This incident, it
may well be believed, did not dampen the society's enthusiasm for Jackson; it continued to champion him
ardently.

Colden was re-appointed Mayor for the third time in
February, 1820. Municipal issues were dividing the public consideration with Tammany's renewed efforts to overthrow Clinton. The report of the Common Council
Finance Committee, January 10, 1820, showed that the
city would soon be $1,300,000 in debt. An attempt was
made to show how the money had been spent on the new
City Hall and Bellevue Hospital, but it proved nothing.
Although the law expressly prohibited Aldermen from being directly or indirectly interested in any contract or
job, violations were common. It was alleged that streets
were sunk, raised and sunk again, to enable the contractors
to make large claims against the city. To soothe public
clamor, the Aldermen made a show of reducing city expenses. The salary of Colden — he being a Clintonite —
was reduced $2,500, and the pay of various other city
officers was cut down. The salaries of the Wigwam men
were not interfered with.

The wholesome criticism of municipal affairs was soon
obscured again by the reviving tumult of the contest between Tammany and Clinton. The Governor stood for
re-election against Daniel D. Tompkins in April, 1820.
Tompkins had long been the idol of the Tammany men and
for a time was one of the society's Sachems. In 1818 he
had been practically charged with being a public defaulter. State Controller Archibald M'Intyre submitted
to the Legislature a mass of his vouchers, public and
private (for the time Tompkins was Governor), which
showed a balance against him of $197,297.64. In this
balance, however, was included the sum of $142,763.60
which was not allowed to Tompkins's credit because the
vouchers were insufficient. Allowing Tompkins this

amount, the balance against him was $54,533.44. Tompkins, on the other hand, claimed the State owed him $120,000. His partisans in the Senate in 1819 passed a bill to re-imburse him, but it was voted down in the Assembly.[7]

The statements of both sides during the campaign of 1820 were filled with epithets and strings of accusations. Tammany contrasted Clinton's alleged going over to the British with Tompkins's patriotism in the War of 1812. Party lines were broken down, and Federalists and Tammany men acted together, as they had done the year before (1819), when their Legislative ticket won over the Clintonites by 2,500 majority. The Clintonites were tauntingly invited to visit the Wigwam, because in that " stronghold of Democracy would be found no ' Swiss ' Federalism, no British partizans, no opponents of the late war, no bribers or bribed for bank charters, no trimming politicians, no lobby members or legislative brokers." In Tammany Hall they would see a body of independent yeomen, of steady and unerring Republicans and men who rallied around their country in the hour of danger.[8]

While Clinton's adherents in New York City on election day were inactive, his opponents, ever on the lookout, carried the city by 675 majority. The popularity of the Erie Canal, however, which was fast nearing completion, carried the rest of the State for Clinton.[9] "Heads up! tails down," shouted the exuberant, successful Clintonites some days after, pointing to the disappointed, discomfited Bucktails. For Tammany had been so sure of Tompkins's

---

[7] *Journal of the Assembly*, 1819, pp. 222–45, and *Ibid.*, pp. 1046–53. Tompkins, now Vice President, made this race for " vindication." It is altogether likely that this particular charge against Tompkins was made for political effect in a campaign in which each side sought to blacken the other by fierce personal attacks.

[8] *National Advocate*, March 29, 1820.

[9] Tammany charged that in the construction of the Erie Canal, land had been cut up in slips to make additional voters for Clinton and cited the county of Genesee, which, though polling but 750 freehold votes in 1815, gave nearly 5,000 votes in this election.

election that it had procured, at considerable expense, a
painting of him which was to be exhibited in the hall when
the news of his election should arrive. By way of consolation the Sachems drank to this toast at their anniversary on May 12:

> " De Witt Clinton, our lean Governor —
> ————— May he never get fat,
> While he wears two faces under one hat."

CHAPTER VII

TAMMANY HALL now entered upon a step destined to change its composition and career, and greatly affect the political course of the State and nation. From its inception the society had declared among its objects the acomplishment of two special reforms — the securing of manhood suffrage and the abolition of the law for the imprisonment of debtors. No steps so far had been taken by either the organization or the society toward the promotion of these reforms; first, because the leaders were engaged too busily in the contest for office, and second, because Tammany Hall, though professing itself devoted to the welfare of the poor, was, to repeat, essentially a middle-class institution. Having property themselves, the men who controlled and influenced the organization were well satisfied with the laws under which Tammany had grown powerful and they rich; they could not see why so blissful a state of affairs should be changed for something the outcome of which was doubtful. The farmer, the independent blacksmith, the shoemaker with an apprentice or two, the grocer—these had votes, and though they looked with envy on the aristocratic class above them, yet they were not willing that the man with the spade should be placed on a political equality with themselves. In addition, most of the aristocratic rich were opposed to these reforms, and the Tammany leaders were either ambitious to enter that class or desirous of not estranging it. Lastly, the lower classes had sided with

Clinton generally; they regarded him as their best friend; to place the ballot unrestrictedly in their hands, Tammany Hall reckoned, would be fatuous. As to the debtors' law, the tradesmen that thronged Tammany were only too well satisfied with a statute that allowed them to throw their debtors, no matter for how small an amount, into jail indefinitely.

Agitation for these two reforms, begun by a few radicals, gradually made headway with the public. The demand for manhood suffrage made the greater progress, until in 1820 it overshadowed all other questions. The movement took an such force and popularity that Tammany Hall was forced, for its own preservation, to join. Agreeable to instructions, the *National Advocate*, September 13, 1820, began to urge the extension of the right of suffrage and the abolition of those cumbersome relics of old centralizing methods, the Council of Appointment and the Council of Revision — the latter a body passing finally on all laws enacted by the Legislature. On October 7, a meeting of Democrats from all parts of the State was held in the Wigwam, Stephen Allen presiding, and the Legislature was called upon to provide for a constitutional convention for the adoption of the amendments.

The aristocracy and all the powers at its command assailed the proposed reforms with passionate bitterness. " Would you admit the populace, the patron's coachman to vote? " asked one Federalist writer. " His excellency (the Governor) cannot retain the gentry, the Judges, and the 'manors' in his interest without he opposes either openly or clandestinely every attempt to enlarge the elective franchise." " We would rather be ruled by a *man* without an estate than by an estate without a *man*," replied one reform writer. The Legislature passed a bill providing for the holding of a constitutional convention, and the Council of Revision, by the deciding vote of Clinton, promptly rejected it. Doubtless this action was due to the declared intention of the advocates of the constitutional convention to abolish this body. Again an assemblage gathered at Tammany Hall (December 1) and resolved that as the "distinction of the electorial rights, the mode of appointment to office and the union of the judiciary and legislative functions were objectional and highly pernicious," the next Legislature should pass the pending bill.

Upon this issue a Legislature overwhelmingly favorable to the extension of suffrage and other projected reforms was elected. The aristocratic party opened a still fiercer onslaught. But when the Legislature re-passed the convention bill, the Council of Revision did not dare to veto it. The convention bill was promptly submitted to the people and ratified. On the news of its success the Democratic voters celebrated the event in the Wigwam, June 14, 1821.

Beaten so far, the Federalists tried to form a union with the reactionary element in Tammany Hall by which they could elect delegates opposed to the projected reforms. All opposition was unavailing, however; the reformers had a clear majority in the convention, and the new amendments, embodying the reforms, were submitted to the people. They were adopted in January, 1822, the city alone giving them 4608 majority.[1] When the Legislature took oath under the revised constitution on March 4, the bells of the city churches were rung; flags were flung on the shipping and public buildings; " a grand salute " was fired by a corps of artillery from the Battery; the City Hall was illuminated at night, and the municipality held a popular reception there. In Tammany Hall a

[1] A considerable increase in the number of voters was made by the suffrage reform. The last remnant of the property qualification was abolished in the State in 1826 by a vote of 104,900 to 3,901.

The abolition of the Council of Appointment carried with it a clause vesting the Appointment of the Mayor in the Common Council. It was not until 1834 that the Mayor was elected by the people. By the Constitutional Amendments the gubernatorial term was changed to two years and the election time to November.

gala banquet was spread, one toast of which ran: " The
right of suffrage — Corruption in its exercise most to be
apprehended from its limitation to a few." After that
pronouncement, so edifying in view of later developments,
came another as instructive: " The young and rising politician — May integrity and principle guide him — study-
ing the public good, not popularity."

So Tammany Hall built for itself a vast political
following, which soon made it practically invincible.

CHAPTER VIII

1822–1825

INEVITABLY the greater part of the newly created voters gravitated to Tammany Hall, but they did not instantly overrun and rule it.

A new set of leaders came in view. Wortman and Judah had been forced from public life through the lottery exposures of 1818, and Broome had lost prestige. Hubbard had fled; Haff, Buckmaster, Strong and Prince were no longer powerful, and Jonas Humbert, who until 1820 had been a person of some authority, was now no longer in public notice. Stephen Allen and Mordecai M. Noah, with a following of some of the old Burrites, were now regarded as being at the helm.

The pro-Tammany Council of Appointment chosen late in 1820, before the new constitutional amendments were adopted, had removed Colden and appointed Allen (Grand Sachem about this time) Mayor [1] in his place. Noah was made Sheriff, and all the other offices were filled with Wigwam men.

The new voting element coming into the organization had to be impressed with the traditional principle of discipline. Otherwise there might be all kinds of nominations, whose effect upon the machine-made " regular " nominations of the organization would be disastrous, if not destructive. To this end the different ward commit-

---

[1] The first election for Mayor by the Common Council, under the new constitution, resulted in the choice of William Paulding, Jr., 1823–25).

tees passed resolutions (April 27 and 28, 1822) declaring in nearly identical terms that the sense of a majority, fairly expressed, ought always to govern, and that no party, however actuated by principle, could be truly useful without organization. " Therefore, that the discipline of the Republican party, as established and practised for the last twenty-five years, has, by experience, been found conducive to the general good and success of the party."[2]

In 1822 Clinton declined to stand for re-election. Tammany Hall was considered so invincible in the city that the Clintonites and the remnant of the Federalists refused to nominate contesting candidates for Congress and the Legislature. Experience demonstrating that almost all the voters cast their ballots for the " regular " ticket without asking questions, competition for a place on that ticket, which now was equivalent to election, became sharp. When, on October 30, the nominating committee reported the name of M. M. Noah for the office of Sheriff, Benjamin Romaine moved to have that of Peter H. Wendover substituted. Two factors were at work here; one was religious prejudice against Noah, who was a Jew; the other and greater, was the struggle between the partizans of Andrew Jackson, John Quincy Adams and William H. Crawford to get control of Tammany Hall, as a necessary preliminary to the efforts of each for the nomination for President.[3] Romaine was an Adams supporter and could easily have nominated a ticket independent of Tammany Hall, but it would have lacked " regularity," and hence popular support. A row ensued; and while Noah's party rushed out of Tammany Hall claiming the " regular " nomination, the other faction, by the light of a solitary candle, passed resolutions denounc-

[2] Advertisements of the ward committees in the *National Advocate,* April 29, 1822.
[3] It is a convincing commentary on the absolute disruption of party lines at this epoch that a contest could arise in such an organization as Tammany Hall between supporters of men of such diverse political beliefs as Andrew Jackson and John Quincy Adams.

ing Noah and claiming that Wendover was the "regular" nominee.

Each of the candidates put himself before the people, declaring that a majority of the nominating committee favored him as " regular." The leaders of the organization inclined to Noah, as one of its heads, but Wendover skillfully appealed to Anti-Semitic bigotry and gathered a large following. The Sachems dared not interfere between them, and each in consequence had a room in Tammany Hall, where his tickets were distributed and his agents made their headquarters. Noah was defeated at the polls; but his defeat did not impair his influence in Tammany Hall. He was a person of singular ability. A facile writer and effective manipulator, he maintained his hold.

" Regularity," then, was the agency by which the leaders imposed their candidates upon the thousands of voters who, from their stores and benches, offices and farms, went to the polls to deposit a list of names prepared for them. The voters were expected only to vote; the leaders assumed the burden of determining for whom the voting should be done. An instance of the general recognition of this fact was given in 1820 when the counties of Suffolk, Queens, Kings and Dutchess voted to discontinue the practice of holding Senatorial conventions in Tammany Hall because a fair expression of the wishes of a great proportion of the Democratic-Republican electors was not obtainable there. At the same time, and for years later, complaints were frequent that the ward meetings had long since become an object of so little interest that they were nearly neglected; and that a small knot of six or eight men managed them for their own purposes.

In 1823 attempts were made by different factions to obtain the invaluable " regular" nominations. Seemingly a local election, the real point turned on whether partisans of Jackson, Adams or Crawford should be chosen. Upon this question Tammany Hall was still

divided. The nominating committee, however, was for
Jackson. The voters were bidden to assemble in the
hall at 7 o'clock on the evening of October 30 to hear
that committee's report. When they tried to enter, they
found the hall occupied by the committee and its friends.
This was a new departure in Tammany practices. Since
the building of the hall the nominating commitee had always waited in a lower room for the opening of the great
popular meeting, and had then marched up stairs and reported. To head off expected hostile action by the Adams
men, the committee this time started proceedings before
the appointed hour. The names of its candidates were
called and affirmed in haste. Gen. Robert Swartwout, a
corrupt but skillful politician and an Adams supporter,
proposed a substitute list of names, upon which the chairman declared that the meeting stood adjourned. A general fist-fight followed, in the excitement of which Swartwout took the chair, read off a list of names and declared
it adopted. Epithets, among which " liar " and
" traitor " figured most, were distributed freely. Both
tickets went to the people under the claim of " regularity,"
and each carried five of the ten wards.

Though Robert Swartwout [4] was for Adams, another
Swartwout (Samuel), an even shrewder politician, was
Jackson's direct representative in the task of securing
the organization's support for President. A third and
less important group were the Crawford advocates. They
were led by Gen. John P. Van Ness, an adroit intriguer

---

[4] When United States Navy Agent in 1820, Robert Swartwout became indebted to the Government in the sum of $68,000, a defalcation
he could not make good. The Government took a mortgage on his
property for $75,000. This and political influence saved him from
prison. It was because of Adams's efforts in his behalf that his extraordinary devotion to the sixth President was credited. Tammany
Hall, considerate of human infirmity, continued him in full favor as
a leader. These facts were brought out in the suit of the United
States Government against Francis H. Nicholl, one of Robert Swartwout's sureties, before Judge Van Ness in the United States District
Court, April 8, 1824.

and one of the old Burr chieftains of Tammany. In 1821 Adams, then Secretary of State, ascertaining that Van Ness, as president of the Bank of the Metropolis, was indebted to that institution to the amount of $60,000 and that its affairs were in bad condition, transferred the account of the State Department to another bank. From that time Van Ness bore deep hatred against Adams, and supported Crawford, Secretary of the Treasury, for President. Crawford had deposited as a standing balance with Van Ness about the same sum Adams had withdrawn, notwithstanding the bank's suspicious character. The Crawford men went first about the business of obtaining complete ascendency in the Tammany Society. With that end in view they tried in 1823 to elect a Grand Sachem favoring Crawford. The old Burr faction now brought forth a Presidential candidate of its own in the person of John C. Calhoun, and taking advantage of the absence of most of the society's members, dexterously managed to elect William Todd, a partisan of Calhoun, Grand Sachem.

The popular voice for Jackson becoming daily stronger, some of the Adams leaders changed about. Perhaps having a premonition that Adams would be chosen President by the House of Representatives, the general committee of Tammany Hall, on October 3, 1823, resolved that the election of President by that branch of Congress was " an event to be deprecated," and that the constitution ought to be so amended as to give the election directly to the people without the intervention of electors. The ward committees passed similar resolutions. This action was on a line with that of a few years before when the Wigwam, fearing the nomination of Clinton for Governor by legislative caucus, recommended that State nominations be made by a State convention of delegates. In the following April (1824) Jackson's friends filled Tammany Hall and nominated him for President.

Before the election came on, however, the organiza-

tion, in the full swing of power, again brought public
odium upon itself. De Witt Clinton, having filled his
gubernatorial term, was now serving in the modest post
of a Canal Commissioner, without pay and utterly without political power. Yet Tammany carried its hatred of
him so far as to cause the Legislature to remove him
(April 12, 1824), despite the protests of a few of its more
sagacious members.[5]

Naturally, this petty act caused an immediate and
strong reaction in a community endeared to Clinton by
that splendid creation of his energy — the Erie Canal.
No sooner did the news reach New York City than 10,000
persons held an indignation meeting in the City Hall Park
and in front of Tammany Hall. Throughout the State
similar meetings were held. In spite of the politicians,
the cyclonic popular movement forced Clinton to be again
a candidate for Governor.

The chiefs regretted their folly. At the same time
they were subjected to public criticism in another direction. One of them, William P. Van Ness, Burr's companion at the Hamilton duel, a Judge of the United States
District Court, took it upon himself to select Tammany
Hall permanently for a court-room, his object being to
have the Government pay rent to the Tammany Society.
His colleague, Judge Thompson, a scrupulous official,
indignantly asked why the courts were not to be held in
the City Hall, as usual. Judge Van Ness defiantly held
court in Tammany Hall, Judge Thompson going to the
City Hall. Public digust asserting itself, an investigation
was set afoot. Van Ness tried to throw the blame on
his marshal. But this officer, as was conclusively shown,
acted under written instructions from Van Ness in refusing
to consider any other place than Tammany Hall, and he
agreed to pay to the society $1,500 a year rent. The
lease, which was made under the plea that no room was

5 *Journal of the Senate,* 1824, p. 409.

available in the City Hall, contained a stipulation that not only should the tavern be allowed in Tammany Hall but that the court-room should be used, when required, as the meeting place of the society or of the political conventions. The citizens assembled in the wards and denounced the proceeding. The Aldermen decided to shift the responsibility which Van Ness attempted to place upon them. Their committee reported (October 24, 1824),[6] that the City Hall always had been and would be at the service of the United States Court Judges, and that a room had been set apart especially for their use. Judge Van Ness was forced to return to the City Hall to hold court.[7]

Tammany now had recourse to its customary devices in endeavoring to bring out its usual vote in the coming election. The general committee announced that at no period in the last twenty years had the welfare and perpetuity of the party more imperiously required a rigid adherence to ancient usages and discipline. This was meant to play on the partizan emotions of the Democrats. It was likewise a threat to punish any man of independent views who disobeyed the orders of the general committee. Such summary, veiled notifications of the general committee were seldom disregarded by those who profited or expected to profit by politics. After toasting their " squaws and papooses " on July 4 the society impressively made this toast: " May regular nominations ever prevail " — a thrust at the method of Clinton's nomination and a warning for the future guidance of all Tammany men.

Tammany further attempted to counteract the impetus of the Clinton movement by touching at length upon its own patriotism in the past and by stirring up class hatreds. On the vital issues the Wigwam was silent; but in another long fulmination it recalled the " sins " and

6 *MS. Minutes of the Common Council*, Vol. 52, pp. 75–78.

7 During this agitation Jacob Barker, Judge Van Ness and M. M. Noah repeatedly presented, in the public prints, arguments in favor of using Tammany Hall as a court-room. We shall have need to refer to Barker again on another page.

" treason " of Clinton against the Democratic party.
" He is haughty in his manners," it went on, " and a friend
of the aristrocracy — cold and distant to all who cannot
boast of wealth and family distinctions and selfish in all the
ends he aims at."

The partizans of Jackson carried the city. Presidential
electors were still selected by the Legislature, and it is
therefore impossible to determine Jackson's vote. A
fusion between the Clintonites and the People's party
caused the defeat of most of Tammany's Assembly candidates, but the victors were Jackson men, and Clinton
himself had declared for Old Hickory. The full Jackson
strength was shown in the vote for the three Tammany
candidates for Congress, who were elected.

Clinton's victory was sweeping. The near completion
of the Erie Canal, for which he had labored so zealously
and which Tammany had opposed so pertinaciously, made
him the idol of the people, and he was again elected Governor, carrying even New York City by 1,031 majority.
That eye was blind which could not see in the opening of
the canal the incalculable benefits Clinton had estimated
from the first. This great work secured as a virtual gift
to New York City the inland commerce of the vast empire
west of the mountains, no rival being able to contend for it.
The trade of the canal almost immediately increased the
city's business $60,000,000 annually, and year by year the
amount grew. Along its course a hundred new and thrifty
villages sprang into existence, and the State's wealth and
population went upward by leaps and bounds.

Compared with this illustrious achievement, a summary of the record of Clinton's antagonists, the Tammany leaders, makes but a poor showing. Contributing
to the development of democracy, for the most part, only
so far as it benefited themselves; declining to take up even
the question of manhood suffrage until forced to, they
did little or nothing, even in the closer domain of the city,
for the good of their own time or of posterity. In the

years when Clinton was engaged in projecting and building the canal, they were too busy wrangling over offices or cribbing at the public treasury to improve city conditions. The streets were an abomination of filth. The local authorities long refused, despite public pressure, to take steps to have the city furnished with pure water. As a result of the bad water of a private corporation and the uncleanliness of the streets, yellow fever and cholera had several times devastated the city, and in one year (1822) it was so deserted that grass grew in the streets. To make up for municipal deficits the city fathers continued selling the public land, that might have been made into parks or retained for future uses, buying it in as individuals. Between 1813 and 1819, according to the admission of the Tammany organ in the latter year, $440,347 worth of land, whose present value probably amounts to tens of millions of dollars, was thus fraudulently disposed of.[8] In a word, their records, public and private, furnish an extreme contrast to the record of Clinton, who, while a politician when need be, gave his years and his talents to the completion of a public work of the greatest utility and importance.

   [8] For a part of this time, it should be stated, the Federalists were in power.

CHAPTER IX

1825–1828

FACTIONAL strife had not entirely smothered the demand for improvement in the city government.[1] The arbitrary powers of the Common Council, composed, as it was, of one Board in which sat both Aldermen and Assistant Aldermen, excited general dissatisfaction. Having the power of making assessments, ordering public improvements, and disposing of the public property at will, the Aldermen made no detailed account of their expenditures. One writer advised the Aldermen to curtail some of their own extravagances: "Why not stop," he wrote,

> "in their career of eating the most unreasonable and costly suppers every time they meet on public business and drinking such wines as they never in the course of their lives tasted before; choice wines that cost $40 a dozen? O! but I will soon tell a tale that will make our citizens stare. I understand that our city expenses are now nearly $2,000 a day."

The State constitution of 1821–22 had granted the Common Council greater powers than before in vacating and filling important offices in the city. In 1823 the city debt was rising, and though the Common Council professed to attempt retrenchment, no real effort was made, the fathers being loth to give over the voting of pretended improvements out of which they benefited as individual contractors. The agitation continuing, the Legislature,

[1] William Paulding was succeeded by Philip Hone (1825–26), who in turn was followed by Paulding (1826–29).

in April, 1824, had passed a law to " erect " two separate
chambers — a Board of Aldermen to be elected from
among the freeholders for two years, and a Board of
Assistants for one year, with concurrent powers. The
opponents of the new branch termed it derisively the,
" House of Lords " and denounced its aristocratic nature.
The amendment was defeated by the radicals in June,
though the interest in it was slight. Over 8,000 electors
failed to vote.

Other schemes for municipal reform dissolved in talk,
and by the Spring of 1825 public attention became concentrated again on the matter of Jackson's candidacy
for the office of President. Barely had John Quincy
Adams been inaugurated when Tammany set about to
make Jackson his successor. On May 12 Sachem
Nicholas Schureman, at the anniversary celebration of
the society, gave this toast: " Jackson, the Hero of
New Orleans, our next President." Again, on July 4, the
principal toast was to Jackson.[2]

The Jackson campaign went energetically on. But it
was rudely interrupted during the following Autumn by a
fresh series of revelations regarding certain Tammany
chieftains. The legislative favoritism by which Jacob
Barker was enabled to secure advantages for his Exchange Bank (1818)[3] now culminated in a grave public
scandal. In September, 1826, Barker, Henry Eckford,
another of the line of Sachems; Matthew L. Davis, lately
Grand Sachem, and several other accomplices were prin-
cipals in one of the most extended and sensational trials
which the city had known. They stood charged with
swindles aggregating several million dollars. The Grand
Jury's indictment of September 15 charged them, and also

[2] This anniversary was the first on which the society, since its formation, did not march in the streets and go to church. Each
" brother," wearing a bucktail in front of his hat, went instead to the
great council chamber, where the Declaration of Independence was
read by Matthew L. Davis.

[3] See Chapter vi.

Mark Spencer, William P. Rathbone, Thomas Vermilyea
and others, with defrauding the Mechanics' Fire Insurance
Company of 1,000 shares of its own capital stock, 1,000
shares of United States Bank stock and $50,000; the Ful-
ton Bank of 2,000 shares of its own capital stock and
$50,000; the Tradesmen's Bank of 2,000 shares of its
own capital stock and $50,000; the Morris Canal and
Banking Company of 2,000 shares of its own capital
stock and $50,000; and the Life and Fire Insurance Com-
pany of 2,000 shares of its own capital stock. The indictment further charged these men with obtaining
fraudulently 1,000 promissory notes for the amount of
nearly $100 each, belonging to the Fulton Bank; and the
same number of notes for similar sums belonging respectively to the Tradesmen's Bank, the Morris Canal and
Banking Company, and the Life and Fire Insurance Company, and with additionally obtaining by fraud the sum
of $50,000, the property of Henry Barclay, George Bar-
clay and others.[4]

A disagreement of the jury marked the first trial; the
second brought a conviction of the prisoners. Tammany
Hall was unwilling to see any of its leaders go to prison.
As soon as the storm of popular indignation blew over, a
new trial was had for Davis, and owing to strong political
influence his acquittal was the outcome. Barker was again
convicted, but, thanks to the discreet use of his money,
never saw a cell. He went South and lived on till over
ninety years of age.[5] Eckford fled to the Orient and died
in Syria. The severity of the law fell on the minor
offenders, two of whom, Mowatt and Hyatt, went to prison
for two years, and the Lambert brothers for one year.

The trial over, public interest again centered on the
Presidential struggle. Alive to the necessity of winning

[4] *Minutes of the Oyer and Terminer*, Vol. 6, pp. 3–137.

[5] Barker maintained that a conspiracy had been formed against him.
A pamphlet entitled, *Jacob Barker's Letters Developing the Conspiracy Formed in 1826 for His Ruin*, was extensively circulated about
this time or later.

Tammany to his interest, President Adams chose most of his New York appointees from its organization, thereby creating in that body an alert clique of devoted partizans. If the leaders had been able to direct the organization absolutely, Adams might have bribed nearly all of them with offices, favors or promises, but there were other deciding factors. The first was the mass of the Democrats who favored Jackson and forced most of the leaders to his support. The second was the organizing genius of Martin Van Buren. He was a member of the Tammany Society, and in September, 1827, he visited New York to compose the discord in the general committee, which was divided equally on the question of the Presidency, although in the society itself a majority was for Jackson. The Jackson men quickly gained predominant influence. On September 27 the general committee recommended in a public address to its " fellow-citizens " that when they met in their wards, they should elect such citizens *only*, to represent them in their different committees, as were favorable to Jackson. The Adams men were enraged.[6] Col. James Fairlie, a veteran of the Revolution; Benjamin Romaine, Peter Sharpe, William Todd, W. H. Ireland, Abraham Stagg, Peter Stagg and John L. Lawrence, known as " the elite " of Tammany Hall, and others, denounced this action. " Was such a power of proscription and dictation ever delegated to or practised by any other general committee? " they asked in an address.

The ward primary elections on the night of October 3 were tumultuous. The Jackson men took possession of the meeting rooms, installed their own chairmen and passed resolutions, without allowing the Adams supporters a chance to be heard. Both factions then alternately

---

[6] The action of the general committee had a sweeping national importance. "The State of New York represents the Democracy of the Union; the City of New York gives tone to the State; the General Committee govern the City." Quoted by " A Journalist " as applying to these years in his *Memoirs of James Gordon Bennett and His Times*, New York, 1855.

held meetings in Tammany Hall. So determined was the
struggle to get possession of the Wigwam that the Adams
men contrived to expel their opponents from it for one
day, and the Jackson men had to make their nominations
in the cellar called " the Coal Hole." At a later meeting
of the Adams faction, embracing a group of old Federalists, Col. Marinus Willett, a venerable Revolutionary
patriot, who presided, spoke of " the danger and absurdity
of confiding the destinies of the country to a mere arbitrary
soldier." The meeting passed resolutions denouncing the
general committee majority and reiterating its support of
Adams. The Jackson men rallied to the Wigwam in force
and approved the ticket nominated in " the Coal Hole."
The nominees were for local offices and were themselves of
no particular importance. The great question was
whether New York City favored Jackson or Adams, and
the coming election was the accepted test.

The Jackson men made desperate efforts to carry the
city. Now were observable the effects brought about by
the suffrage changes of 1822 and 1826. The formerly dis-
inherited class had become attached to Tammany Hall,
and the organization, entirely reversing its exclusive native
policy, declared for a reduction of the five-year naturalization period. From that time forth the patronage of aliens
became a settled policy of Tammany. In this election
these aliens exercised a powerful influence, materially aiding Jackson.

Cases of fraud and violence had hitherto been frequent;
but nothing like the exhibition at the primaries and polls
in November, 1827, had ever been known. Cart-loads of
voters, many of whom had been in the country less than
three years, were used as repeaters in the different wards.
An instance was known of one cart-load of six men voting
at six different places. Other men boasted of having voted
three and four times. In an upper ward, where the
foreign population had full sway, an American found it
almost impossible to appear or vote at all. If he tried the

experiment, he was arrested immediately, his votes were taken from him and Jackson votes put in his hands. Many of the polling places had no challengers, and most of the inspectors did duty for the Jackson ticket by a display of stout hickory branches. By such means the Jackson men rolled up in the city a majority of nearly five thousand.

Reflective citizens of both parties were alarmed and humiliated by the events of the election. The public conscience was not used to the indiscriminate stuffing of ballot boxes. To the revelations of this election can be traced the origin of the Native American party, whose cry that "political privileges should belong exclusively to the natives of the country" even now was heard.

Though a year before the time for choosing a President, the result of this election strongly indicated the choice of Jackson and caused great exultation and encouragement among his supporters in other cities. In the Winter of 1827, Tammany sent a delegation to visit him at New Orleans, ostensibly to present an address on the anniversary of the battle of New Orleans, but in reality, it was supposed, to confer with him on the work to be done in his behalf. By the beginning of 1828 the organization was controlled wholly by Jackson men. Not a nomination, however petty, was made of a man not known to be his partizan. The great body of Democrats approved this course on the ground that Jackson's election was the real issue, and that local issues were subordinate for the time. When the Adams men tried to hold anti-Jackson meetings in the Wigwam, the Sachems stepped forward and exercised a long dormant power — a power which explains the real connection between the society and the organization, and which it frequently used later against hostile factions. Through pressure, the lessee of Tammany Hall sold to the society his lease. This secured, the society put in charge of the building

(which was fitted in part as a hotel as well as a hall) another person, instructed not to let any room to the Adams
committee. The Adams men asked by what right a
" charitable and benevolent society " interfered in politics.
But, being excluded, they could no longer claim they represented Tammany Hall — a fatal loss to them and an important advantage to the Jackson men, who now were the
only Tammany organization. The Adams committees
were thus shut off from holding any meetings in the hall.

With the Adams committees put out, the Jackson men
began to quarrel among themselves for local and State
nominations. The Wigwam's inveterate foe, De Witt
Clinton, was out of the way, he having died on February
11, 1828, while still Governor. As nominations continued
to be looked upon as almost certainly resulting in election,
there was a swarm of candidates.[7] The ambitions of few
of these were gratified. The nominations were settled be-
forehand by a small clique, headed, it was said, by M. M.
Noah.

Of a voting population of 25,000, Tammany Hall secured a majority of 5,831 for Jackson[8] and elected
all its candidates except one. That hundreds, if not
thousands, of illegal votes were counted was admitted.
Boys of 19 and 20 years of age voted and were employed
to electioneer for the Jackson ticket. On the other hand,
raftsmen just arrived from the interior and men who had
no homes were gathered in bunches and sent to swell the

---

[7] " Should the Independent electors," wrote one of them, Aaron
Sergeant, " give me a nomination (for Sheriff) (as there will be
several candidates for the office) I shall succeed by a handsome majority. The Sons of Erin are my most particular friends. I rely with
confidence on their support.
" Knowing the office to be one worth $10,000 per annum, should I be
elected, I shall give one-third of the income of this office to be divided
equally to [among] the several charitable Religious Societies in the
city. My claims for the office are, that I am a citizen born, and my
father one of the *Patriots of the Revolution for seven long years* . . ."
[8] This was the first election in the State in which Presidential electors were voted on by the people.

Adams vote, though it is doubtful whether their votes were counted. For the first time in city elections money was used to influence voting.

The Common Council soon after removed every office-holder not of the Jackson faith. As a matter of course, Jackson rewarded his friends. He made Samuel Swartwout Collector of the Port and filled every Federal local post with his Tammany adherents.

CHAPTER X

IN 1829 the indignation against the Tammany leaders
crystallized in a " purifying " movement. Under the
direction of its banker, merchant and lawyer leaders,
Tammany Hall had been made a medium for either coerc-
ing or bribing the Legislature or the Common Council into
passing dozens of bank charters and franchises with
scarcely any provision for compensation to either State
or city.[1] In 1819 the Tammany Society, in one of its
pompous addresses, had recited the speculative spirit and
consequent distress brought about by the multiplication
of incorporated banks, and suggested that the Legislature
adopt a prompt and decisive remedy tending to the abolition of those institutions. This sounded well; but at that
very time, as before and after, the Sachems were lobby-
ing at Albany for charters of banks of which they became
presidents or directors. By one means or another these
banks yielded fortunes to their owners; but the currency
issued by them almost invariably depreciated. The laboring classes on whom this bad private money was imposed
complained of suffering severely. Each year, besides, wit-

[1] " The members [of the Legislature] themselves sometimes participated in the benefits growing out of charters created by their own
votes; . . . if ten banks were chartered at one session, twenty must
be chartered the next and thirty the next. The cormorants could
never be gorged. If at one session you bought off a pack of greedy
lobby agents . . . they returned with increased numbers and more
voracious appetite."— Hammond, Vol. II, pp. 447–48.

Four conspicuous " charter dealers " at Albany were Sachems Samuel B. Romaine, Michael Ulshoeffer, Peter Sharpe and Abraham
Stagg, all powerful organization leaders.

nessed an increase in the number of chartered monopolies, armed with formidable powers for long periods, or practically in perpetuity.[2]   To the first gas company, in May, 1823, the Common Council had granted the exclusive right to light all the streets south of Grand street for thirty years, without returns of any kind to the city.[3] At the rate at which the city was expanding, this was a concession of immense value, and formed one of the subjects of complaint in 1829.

While laws were instituted to create a money aristocracy, the old debt and other laws bearing on the working classes were not changed.   No attempt was made to improve a condition which allowed a dishonest contractor to put up a building or a series of buildings, collect his money and then swindle his laborers out of their wages. The local administration, moreover, continued corrupt.   It was freely charged at this time that $250,000 of city money was being stolen outright every year.   The city charter drafted and adopted in 1829–30 contained provisions which, it was thought, might remedy matters. It created two bodies of the Common Council — the Aldermen and Assistant Aldermen — and gave each a negative upon the propositions of the other, vesting a supreme veto power in the Mayor.   It again separated the election of the Common Council from the general election. It abolished secret contracts and compelled all resolutions involving appropriations of public money or placing taxes or assessments to be advertised, and included other precautionary measures against corruption.   But it opposed the public wish in still vesting the appointment of the Mayor in the Common Council.

To battle against the prevailing injustices the Mechanics' or Workingmen's party was formed.   Its chief inspiration was Robert Dale Owen, son of the famous Robert Owen.   " Dale " Owen, as he was familiarly

[2] Hammond, Vol. II, pp. 447–48.
[3] *MS. Minutes of the Common Council*, Vol. 48, pp. 59–60.

known, and others had recently returned to the city after
an unsuccessful experiment at cooperative colonizing at
New Harmony, Indiana, and a number of bright and
ardent intellects gathered about him. Boldly declaring
against the private and exclusive possession of the soil
and against the hereditary transmission of property, the
new party won over a large part of the laboring element.
" Resolved," ran its resolutions adopted at Military Hall,
October 19, 1829,

> " in the opinion of this meeting, that the first appropriation of the
> soil of the State to private and exclusive possession was eminently
> and barbarously unjust. That it was substantially feudal in its
> character, inasmuch as those who received enormous and unequal
> possessions were *lords* and those who received little or nothing were
> *vassals*. That hereditary transmission of wealth on the one hand
> and poverty on the other, has brought down to the present genera-
> tion all the evils of the feudal system, and that, in our opinion, is
> the prime source of all our calamities."

After declaring that the Workingmen's party would
oppose all exclusive privileges, monopolies and exemp-
tions, the resolutions proceeded:

> " We consider it an exclusive privilege for one portion of the com-
> munity to have the *means of education in colleges* while another is
> restricted to common schools, or perhaps, by extreme poverty, even
> deprived of the limited education to be acquired in those establish-
> ments. Our voice, therefore, shall be raised in favor of a system
> of education which shall be equally open to *all,* as in a real republic
> it should be."

The banks, too, came in for a share of the denunciation.
The bankers were styled " the greatest knaves, impostors
and paupers of the age." The resolutions continued:

> " As banking is now conducted, the owners of the banks receive
> annually of the people of this State not less than two millions of
> dollars in their paper money (and it might as well be pewter money)
> for which there is and can be nothing provided for its redemption
> on demand . . ."

The Workingmen put a full ticket in the field.

Tammany Hall, dominated by some of the same men
and interests denounced by the Workingmen's party,

opened a campaign of abuse. Commercial and banking men outside the Wigwam joined ardently in the campaign. The new movement was declared to be a mushroom party, led by designing men, whose motives were destructive. The *Evening Post*, which represented the commercial element and which sided with Tammany in opposition to the new party, said that it remained for the really worthy mechanics who might have associated accidentally with that party, to separate themselves from it, now that its designs and doctrines were known. The *Courier and Enquirer*, partly owned and edited by Noah,[4] styled the Workingmen's party an infidel ticket, hostile to the morals, to the institutions of society and the rights of property. The Tammany Hall, or to speak more technically, the Democratic-Republican General Committee, declaiming on the virtues of Jackson and Democracy, advised all good men, and especially all self-respecting laborers, not to vote the Workingmen's ticket.

Nevertheless, its principles made such an impression that in November it polled over 6,000 votes, while Tammany, with its compact organization, could claim little more than 11,000 votes. It was well settled that numbers of Whig workingmen voted the new party's ticket; and that the rich Whigs secretly worked for the success of Tammany Hall, whose ticket was almost entirely successful, though the Workingmen elected Ebenezer Ford to the Assembly.

Tammany was dismayed at the new party's strength, and determined to destroy it by championing one of the reform measures demanded. In January, 1830, a bill for the better security of mechanics and other laborers of New York City was introduced by Silas M. Stillwell. The Tammany men immediately took it up as if it were their

---

[4] Noah, after falling into financial difficulties, had been ousted from the editorship of the *National Advocate* and had now become associated with his former political enemy, James Watson Webb, in the conduct of the *Courier and Enquirer*.

own, urged its passage and secured the credit of its adoption, when in April, much emasculated, it became a law. It required, under penalties, the owner of a building to retain from the contractor the amount due to the mechanics employed thereon. By exploiting this performance to the utmost, Tammany succeeded in making some inroads on the Workingmen's party. The organization leaders had recognized that it was time they did something for the laboring classes. They were fast losing caste with even independent Democrats of means, because of their subservience to the aristocracy and of the common knowledge of the illegitimate ways in which they were amassing wealth.

One result of the Workingmen's movement was the failure of the Wigwam to secure a majority in the Common Council. This seemed to frustrate the design to reelect, as Mayor, Walter Bowne (Grand Sachem in 1820 and 1831). Fourteen Aldermen and Assistants were opposed to Bowne, and thirteen favored him. There was but one expedient calculated to reelect him, and to this Tammany Hall resorted. Bowne, as presiding officer of the Council, held that the constitution permitted him to vote for the office of Mayor. " I will persist in this opinion even though the board decide against me," he said. To prevent a vote being taken, seven of Bowne's opponents withdrew on December 28, 1829. They went back on January 6, 1830, when Tammany managed to reelect Bowne by one vote. How this vote was obtained was a mystery. Fourteen members declared under oath that they had voted for Thomas R. Smith, Bowne's opponent.[5] Charges of bribery were made, and an investigating committee was appointed on January 11; but as this committee was com-

[5] *MS. Minutes of the Common Council*, Vol. 70, p. 311. Shortly after this the Wigwam men removed Smith from his post of Commissioner of the Almshouse for opposing Bowne. So great was the haste to oust him, before the Aldermen went out of office, that one of the board seconded the motion for his removal before the motion was made.

posed of Bowne's own partizans, it announced its inability
to find proofs. Meanwhile the general committee [6] had
issued a loftily worded manifesto saying that it (the
committee) was established and was maintained to watch
over the political interests of the Democratic-Republicans
of the city and "to expose and repel the insidious and
open machinations of their enemies," that it could not
discover anything wrong in the conduct of the Chief
Magistrate of the city, and that it "repelled the accusations of his enemies."

The Workingmen's party continued its agitation, and
prepared for another campaign. In the meantime the
Wigwam's agents skilfully went about fomenting divisions,
with the result that three tickets, all purporting to be
the genuine Workingmen's, were put into the field in
October, 1830. One was that of the "Clay Workingmen"; it was composed of a medley of admirers of Clay,
the owners of stock in various great manufacturing establishments, workingmen who believed in a protective tariff,
Whigs,[7] and a bunch of hack politicians who had taken
up the Workingmen's movement for selfish ends. The
second was that of a fragment of the Workingmen's
party of the year before, standing resolutely for their
principles and containing no suspicious politicians or
monopolists. The third was that of the Agrarian party,
embracing a few individuals of views too advanced even
for the Workingmen's party.

[6] The general committee was now composed of thirty-six members,
mainly the directors in banking and other companies. Remonstrances
at this time were frequent that its important proceedings were a
sealed book to the electors. Among other things it dictated to the
wards not only when, but where, they should meet.

[7] The term "Whig" had now come to have a definite party meaning,
being used as a popular designation of the group led by John Quincy
Adams and Henry Clay, officially known (1828–36) as the National
Republican party. The term is first found in American politics applied to the Separatists during the Revolution. About 1808 it was
taken by the anti-Burr faction of the Democratic-Republican party.

To the Clay Workingmen's party [8] Tammany Hall
gave little attention, since it was made up mainly of Whigs
who had always, under different names, been opposed to
the organization. But the genuine movement Tammany
Hall covered with abuse. " Look, fellow-citizens," said
the address of the " general nominating committee,"

> " upon the political horizon and mark the fatal signs prognosticating
> evils of a dire and fatal nature! Associations and political sects
> of a new and dangerous character have lately stalked into existence,
> menacing the welfare and good order of society. These associa-
> tions . . . have assumed to represent two of the most useful and
> respectable classes of our citizens — our *Workingmen and Mechan-
> ics*. . . . Confide in them, and when they have gained their ends they
> will treat you with derision and scorn! Then rally round your an-
> cient and trusty friends and remember that honest men and good
> citizens never assume false names nor fight under borrowed ban-
> ners! "

To display its devotion to the cause of Democracy,
Tammany Hall celebrated, on November 26, the revolution in France. It persuaded former President James
Monroe to preside in Tammany Hall at the preliminary
arrangements, and made a studied parade of its zeal.
There was a procession, Samuel Swartwout acting as
grand marshal. Monroe, in a feeble state of health, was
brought in a stage to Washington Square, where for ten
minutes he looked on. A banquet, the usual high-flown
speeches, and fireworks followed.

The election was favorable to Tammany. About 3,800
workingmen who had supported the independent movement the previous year, went back to Tammany, because
of its advocacy of the mechanics' lien law. The average
Tammany plurality was 3,000. The real Workingmen's
ticket polled a vote of about 2,200; the Clay Workingmen's ticket a little above 7,000, and the Agrarian, 116.

---

[8] The men of this party, as a rule, voted the Anti-Masonic State
ticket. While the Anti-Masonic party occasioned political commo-
tion in the State, there is no evidence that it had any perceptible effect
on Tammany's career.

For the next few years the contest of Jackson with the
United States Bank drew together the energies of all
Democrats supporting .him. Dropping local contests,
they united to renew his power. For the time, the Workingmen's movement ceased to exist.

CHAPTER XI

1831–1834

TAMMANY lost no time in announcing its intention to support the renomination of Jackson. The general committee, on March 3, 1831, unanimously passed a resolution approving of his renomination by the Democratic members of the Legislature. Seven days later the General Committee of Democratic Young Men and the ward committees acted likewise.

Since the campaign of 1800 there had not been a Presidential contest in which the masses joined with such enthusiasm. Although the national election was more than 18 months distant, the excitement was intense. The late Workingmen's party and Tammany men fraternized. The ward resolutions were full of fire, the meetings spirited. The Democratic electors of the Sixth Ward "friendly to regular nominations" resolved, on March 15:

". . . That aristocracy in all its forms is odious to us as Democratic-Republicans, and that of all aristocracies an aristocracy of wealth, grinding the faces of the poor and devouring the substance of the people, is the most alarming. That we regard an incorporated association of rich men wielding the whole monied capital of the country as dangerous to our rights and liberties. That we consider the next Presidential election as substantially a contest between the people on one side and the monied aristocracy of the country on the other." [1]

The organization's first object was to gain a majority of the local offices in the Spring election of 1831 on the Jackson issue. The National Republican party, recently

[1] Advertisement in the New York *Evening Post,* March 17, 1831.

organized in New York City on the same general lines as Tammany Hall, and headed by Clarkson Crolius, a former Grand Sachem, set out to crush the Jackson movement. If a defeat could be administered to it at this time, the practical effect would be great; New York would possibly influence the entire Union. To accomplish this, the National Republicans tried to divert the issue to local lines and agitated for the election of the Mayor by the people. The Tammany men joined issue at once, and in February, 1831, the Common Council committee on application, composed chiefly of Tammany men, reported adversely on a motion to suggest to the Legislature a revision of the charter. The time was declared to be inexpedient for such an innovation, one Tammany Alderman, Thomas T. Woodruff, declaring, when the matter again came up, on April 8, that the people could not be trusted with the choice of that important official. The National Republicans replied by denouncing the Common Council for its lavish expenditures of public money, its distribution of favors in the shape of " jobs " and contracts among a few retainers whose sole merits lay in their close relationship to certain managing members of the board, and for its efforts to prevent the people from having the right to elect their own Mayor.[2]

The opposition to Tammany was ineffectual. In the ensuing election, not less than 22 of the 28 members chosen for the new double-chamber Common Council were Tammany men, elected solely upon their pledge of allegiance to the national and State administrations. The first trial of the new charter, therefore, showed that the separation of municipal from general elections did not prevent the division of the voters on national party lines. The extent of this preliminary Jackson victory made a sensation throughout the Union and caused gloom among the United States Bank supporters.

[2] Resolutions of the Sixth Ward Anti-Tammany Republicans, March 24, 1831.

The prestige of Tammany Hall was now overwhelming; its influence upon the Democratic party, great before, became greater. No aspirant for public favor could ignore its demands and decrees. When, on May 12, the society held an imposing celebration of the forty-second anniversary of its founding, politicians from the highest to the lowest, national and local, four hundred and over, crowded there with words of flattery. Lewis Cass, Nathaniel P. Tallmadge, the Governor and Lieutenant-Governor of the State of New York; members of the National Senate and of the House of Representatives — these and the rest were glad to avail themselves of the invitation. William Mooney was there, very old and feeble, beaming with pride at the power of the institution he had founded.[3] After the banquet, which was described in the old Indian terms, as consisting " of the game of the forest, the fish of the lakes, the fruits of the season and the waters of the great spring," came the reading of letters. Jackson wrote: " Nothing could afford me greater gratification than to participate with your ancient and honorable society of Republicans on such an occasion," but that press of official duties kept him away. A letter of regret, in high-flown and laudatory diction, from Secretary of State Martin Van Buren followed. James Watson Webb proposed this toast: " Martin Van Buren, the Grand Sachem of the Eagle Tribe — The Great Spirit is pleased with his faithful support of the Great Grand Sachem of the Nation and smiles graciously upon the sages and warriors of the tribe who aim to elevate their chief in 1836 to the highest station in the country." This was greeted by nine cheers, and instantly disclosed Tammany's choice for Jackson's successor in 1836. The only troublous note was furnished by Duff Green, who sprang this toast upon the surprised

---

[3] Mooney passed away the following November. Tammany passed panegyric resolutions on his character, and organized a large funeral procession which escorted his body to the grave.

gathering: "De Witt Clinton — His friends honor his memory — his enemies dare not assail it!" By "enemies" he referred to those present; they retorted that he was an intruder, was not invited, and had not paid for his ticket.[4] Mayor Bowne was then installed as Grand Sachem in place of Stephen Allen, the former Mayor.

The Fall election of 1831 also turned upon national issues. Upon Jackson's popularity nearly every Democratic candidate in New York city was elected by an average majority of 6,000. There were rumors of illegal voting, but no proof was submitted. The Wigwam was so overjoyed at the result that a banquet was held on November 21, presided over by Benjamin Bailey, who for a dozen years had been chairman of the general committee. He had reached his seventy-second year and could claim little political influence. But as a captain in the Revolutionary army, and as one of those confined in the Jersey prison ships, the Tammany chiefs considered him a valuable figurehead. Gen. Wool, Cols. Twiggs and Crogham and five hundred men of various importance spent the night in the Wigwam drinking to Jackson, Tammany Hall and coming victory.

Not only did Tammany take the initiative in supporting Jackson, but it was the first body to nominate Van Buren for Vice-President. On the news of the Senate's rejection of Van Buren as Minister to England, an indignation meeting was held in Tammany Hall, January 30, 1832, this being the opening expression of public opinion. Van Buren was suggested for Vice-President, and the Wigwam gathering showed its satisfaction by repeated cheers.[5] Twenty-four leading Tammany men drew up a

[4] Green was an influential and intimate friend of Jackson and a member of his "Kitchen Cabinet." He had come up from Washington to attend the banquet as one of Jackson's personal representatives.

[5] The *Courier and Enquirer*, owned by Webb and Noah, promptly came out with this ticket in large black type upon its editorial page: For President, Andrew Jackson. For Vice-President, Martin Van Buren.

letter containing their sentiments on Van Buren's rejection, and on May 31 an outpouring in the Wigwam approved his nomination.

Then followed a striking revelation, showing the venality of some of Tammany's leaders. The United States Bank officials began bargaining for the betrayal of Jackson. The *Courier and Enquirer* suddenly abandoned him for the support of the bank candidates, giving as a reason the fear of the " fearful consequences of revolution, anarchy and despotism," which assuredly would ensue if Jackson were reelected. The real reason was that Webb and Noah, as revealed by a Congressional investigation,[6] had borrowed directly and indirectly $50,000 from the United States Bank, which had now called them to time. Mayor Bowne was their sponsor to Nicholas Biddle, head of the bank. Some of the other Tammany leaders, it appeared, had been for years the bank's retainers. Representative Churchill C. Cambreleng enjoyed a place on its pay rolls. Gulian C. Verplanck, another of the Wigwam's representatives in Congress, had voted in its behalf, and Stephen Allen, in the State Senate, had voted for a resolution in its favor. Peter Sharpe, Ogden Edwards,[7] William H. Ireland, John Morss — all influential men in times past — now vigorously opposed Jackson, and the services of other Tammany chiefs were secured.

Two influences, however, prevented the organization leaders from betraying the Democratic cause — one the common people, the other the owners of the State banks,

[6] *The First Session of the Twenty-Second Congress*, Vol. IV., containing reports from Nos. 460 to 463, Washington, 1831.

[7] Edwards was for many years a person of great power in the organization. In 1821, while Counsel to the Board of Aldermen, a salaried office, he was specifically charged with having mulcted the city out of $5,414 as a payment for a few hours' service in arranging the details of a delinquent tax sale. Further charges credited him with having cleaned up more than $50,000 in five years, through various pickings connected with his office. Such, however, was his influence, that he not only escaped prosecution, but retained an unimpaired prestige in the organization.

whose self-interest called for the speedy downfall of the United States Bank. Finding that they could not control the Wigwam, the Tammany agents of that bank seceded, and joined the National Republicans. The State Bank men remained in the organization and labored for Jackson, with no other idea than that their institutions would benefit in the distribution of Government funds if the United States Bank were put down. The course of the leaders remaining in Tammany smacked of double dealing. Refusing to renominate Verplanck, they put in his place Dudley Selden, who had borrowed $8,000 from the United States Bank, but who had professed to support Jackson's veto. It looked as though certain potent influences were operating in Tammany Hall for the election of a pro-bank Congress, whoever might be chosen President.

The Tammany ward organizations, assisted by the men of the late Workingmen's party, appointed vigilance committees to undo any mischief the leaders might attempt, and to electioneer for Jackson's success. So enthusiastic was the Jackson feeling that many politicians of note, understanding its depth and having a care for their political futures, made haste to change front. Almost daily the people were rallied to the Wigwam by the beating of drums. A few years before, a hickory tree had been planted in front of the Wigwam; now, on October 30, a second was put there, and a barrel of beer was used to moisten its roots.

Both sides were guilty of election frauds. Votes were bought at the rate of $5 each, most of the buying being done by the National Republicans, who were supplied with abundant resources. The National Republicans, moreover, had sought to bribe certain men with the promise of offices, and on the three election days they foisted upon the voters a Jackson electoral ticket containing forty-three names, instead of the legal number, forty-two, thereby invalidating each of these ballots voted. This trick, it was calculated, lost to Jackson more than a thousand votes. Of a total of 30,474 votes, Tammany carried the city by 5,620 majority. The Wigwam for many successive nights was filled with celebrating crowds. Jackson gave a conspicuously public display of his recognition of Tammany's invaluable services, when, on the evening of June 13, 1833, he visited the society, attended by the Vice-President, Secretary Woodbury, Gov. William L. Marcy, the Mayor, and the members of the Common Council.

The United States Bank supporters did not surrender with Jackson's reelection. They exerted themselves to influence Congress by means of a defeat for the anti-bank forces in New York City in the Fall election of 1833. Tammany Hall during the campaign sent out runners ordering every office-holder to his electioneering post. Vigorous meetings were held, and all the secret influences of the general committee were employed. On the other hand, merchants laid aside their ruffled shirts and broadcloth coats, put on their roundabouts and worked at the polls on the three election days for the Whig ticket. Tammany carried the city by between 2,000 and 3,000 majority. Touching this and previous elections a committee of Assistant Aldermen reported on February 10, 1834: "That frauds have been practised at the polls, the committee are convinced. At any rate, a universal and deep conviction prevails among our citizens that tricks have been resorted to for the purpose of defeating the election of one candidate and securing that of another." It was further set forth that persons were brought up to vote who were not citizens of the United States nor qualified to vote in the State. Others voted in more than one ward. Voters also were transferred overnight from a sure to a doubtful ward.[8] No remedy followed the report.

[8] *Documents of the Board of Aldermen and Assistant Aldermen,* 1834, No. 82.

The Spring election of 1834, though local, again turned upon national issues. For the first time in the history of the city, the Mayor was to be elected by the people. The growth of public opinion had been such that the Legislature was forced, in 1833, to grant this reform.

The contending hosts were swayed, first, by the question of the United States Bank, and second, by the spoils. The merchants shut their shops and sent their whole body of clerks and laboring men to surround the polls and influence voters against Tammany Hall. The United States Bank spread abroad the cry of "panic." If its directors could show that public opinion in the foremost city in the Union had altered so as to favor the continuation of the bank charter, then they could use that as a good basis for influencing Congress. There was no concealment of coercion of voters; the weak, the timid, the fearful were overawed by the increasing clamor of paid newspapers that the destruction of the United States Bank meant " widespread revulsion of trade and everlasting injury to the poor." In fact, a general depression of business was produced. A row began in the " bloody ould Sixth," by the breaking of some ballot boxes. Both parties armed with stones and bludgeons, and turned the scene into one of violence. The riot became general. A crowd, composed chiefly of Whigs, ransacked gun-shops in Broadway and made for the State arsenal at Elm and Franklin streets. Rumors of their intentions spreading, a gathering of peaceably inclined citizens arrived before them and held the arsenal until the militia hastened there and restored order.[9]

Cornelius W. Lawrence, the Tammany candidate, was declared elected by 181 votes out of a total of nearly 35,000 [10] over Gulian G. Verplanck, who had gone over to the Whigs. Verplanck never ceased to contend that he

[9] *Documents of the Board of Alderman*, 1839, No. 29.
[10] Lawrence, 17,576; Verplanck, 17,395; blank and scattering, 18; total, 34,989.

had been defrauded of the office. The Whigs obtained a majority in the Common Council, 17 members to the Wigwam's 15, and joyfully said that Tammany Hall in electing the Mayor had the shadow; while they, in securing the corporation, had the substance. With the Common Council they could carry the whole patronage of the city, amounting to more than $1,000,000 a year.

This election demonstrated clearly that the propertied classes as a whole were combined against the laborers, mechanics, farmers and producing classes generally, and that they were as much concerned over the spoils of office as was the most rabid Tammany man. As a protest against the indifference of the local leaders of both parties to the real interests of the people, and to put a stop to the granting of special privileges, the Equal Rights party now came into existence.

CHAPTER XII

1834–1837

THE Equal Rights movement, which began its activity inside the Tammany organization, was virtually a moral, then a political, revival of the Workingmen's movement. Its principles, however, were less radical, and its demands more moderate. It advocated the equal rights of every citizen in his person and property and in their management; declared unqualified and uncompromising opposition to bank notes as a circulating medium, because gold and silver were the only safe and constitutional currency, and a like opposition to all monopolies by legislation. It also announced hostility "to the dangerous and unconstitutional creation of vested rights by legislation, because these were a usurpation of the people's sovereign rights," and asserted that all laws or acts of incorporation passed by the Legislature could be rightfully altered or repealed by its successors. The Equal Rights movement comprised men of various classes. Moses Jacques and Levi D. Slamm were its principal leaders. To comprehend its nature, a brief review of the causes which conspired to bring it into being will be necessary.

Up to 1831 the repeal of the law for the imprisonment of debtors had been a subject of almost constant agitation by reformers and workingmen. Under this law more than 10,000 persons, mainly unfortunate laborers, were imprisoned annually in loathsome prisons, without inquiry as to their innocence or guilt, lying there at their creditors' will, unsupplied by the city with any of the necessities of life.[1] Tammany Hall had taken no action until 1831, when its leaders gave a belated approval to a bill introduced in the Assembly, abolishing imprisonment for debts of any sum except in the cases of non-residents.[2]

This bill had become a law in that year; yet by 1833 the interest of Tammany's chiefs in the workingman had died away to such an extent that the Assembly was allowed to pass a measure entitled " a law abolishing imprisonment for debt," but reinstituting imprisonment on all debts under $50, thus completely nullifying the law so far as the poor were concerned.

The measure failed to become a law; but the sharp practise shown in its wording, and in the means taken to push it through the Assembly, disgusted the Equal Rights men, and in their meetings they passed resolutions denouncing the chiefs responsible therefor. Their resolutions furthermore declared that the proceedings at Tammany Hall were a sealed book; that a few men — William Paxen Hallett, Elisha Tibbits, J. J. Roosevelt and John Y. Cebra — made up important nominations in Wall street after the bankers had decided upon the candidates and then had the nominating committee accept them.

Popular disaffection was increased by the manner in which the Legislature and the Aldermen continued to create corporations with enormous grants. The scandals over the procurement of legislative charters, particularly bank charters, had for more than 25 years aroused a growing indignation among the people. In

---

[1] The minutes of the Common Council covering these years show continuous records of petitions from imprisoned debtors, praying for fuel and the patching up of windows in the dead of Winter. Charitable societies were in existence to supply the jailed debtors with food.

[2] This singular provision, by which non-residents were liable to imprisonment for debt, while the natives of the city were exempted, was erased in 1840.

1805, shortly after the passage of the Merchants' Bank charter, Peter Betts, an Assemblyman, declared in open session of the lower house, that Luke Metcalfe, a fellow-member, had sought to bribe him to vote for the measure. The price promised was 15 shares of the bank's stock, valued at $50 each. Conflicting testimony was given on the matter, and a motion was made to expel Metcalfe; the house, however, retained him in his seat by a vote of 37 to 16.[3]

Charges of the same kind, affecting practically every session of the Legislature, were common, though only occasionally were they made the subject of official investigation. In 1812, however, shortly after the Assembly, forced by public criticism, had passed a resolution compelling each member to pledge himself that he had neither taken nor would take, " any reward or profit, direct or indirect, for any vote on any measure," [4] another scandal arose. The Bank of America, with very moderate assets of any sort, received a charter on a stated capitalization of $6,000,000, an enormous sum in those days. Charges of corruption were bandied about, one Assemblyman, Silas Holmes, declaring under oath that the sum of $500, " besides a handsome present," had been offered him. A committee of the lower house listened to testimony in the case, and then, by a decisive majority, voted that the body was above suspicion.[5] But in a pronunciamento to Gov. Tompkins during the same year the same house graciously reported: " We are well aware that the number of charters for banking institutions already granted has awakened general solicitude and anxiety."

The Chemical Bank was a more modern instance. The report of the joint legislative committee in 1824 had shown that its promoters set apart $50,000 worth of

[3] *Journal of the Senate and Assembly*, 1805, pp. 351 and 399.
[4] *Ibid.*, 1812, p. 134.
[5] *Journal of the Senate and Assembly*, 1812, pp. 259–60.

stock at par value [6] to buy the votes of members, Gen.
Robert Swartwout — he who had defaulted for $68,000
in 1820 — acting as one of the lobbyists and claiming
$5,000 for his services.[7] Other scandals throwing strong
light on legislative practises were those of the Ætna and
Chatham Fire Insurance Companies. The testimony
brought out in the investigation of these companies in
1826 showed that William J. Waldron (one of the line
of Grand Sachems) gave $20,000 in certificates of stock
to Gen. Jasper Ward, a State Senator, and $20,000 more
to various other persons to get the Ætna charter through
the Legislature.[8] The Chatham charter, passed in 1822,
cost $20,000 in stock at par value, additional sums being
paid for the passage of certain amendments in 1824.[9]
Ward wrote from Albany to a friend in the city, com-
plaining that the Jefferson Fire Insurance Company,
which secured a charter at the same time (1824), had
paid only 5 per cent. of what it had promised, giving
notes for the remainder.[10] These were but a few examples of the general legislative corruption. The men
who profited by these charters brought about, in 1830,
the exemption of bank stock in the city from taxation.
That nearly every Tammany leader held bank stock
was proved by the testimony before an investigating committee in June, 1833, which set forth how the organizers of the newly founded Seventh Ward Bank had distributed thousands of shares among over one hundred
State and city office-holders, both Tammany and Anti-
Masonic. Every Tammany Senator was involved.

[6] Stock given at par value meant an almost immediate rise in value
to the legislator. Most stocks went upward from 10 to 15 per cent.
on the passage of the charter, and in the case of the more profitable
and exploitative corporations, far higher advances were scored in a
short time.

[7] *Journal of the Senate*, 1824, pp. 498–532.

[8] *Journal of the Senate*, 1826, Vol. 6, Appendix B. A considerable
part of the money and stock promised the members of the Legislature
for their votes was withheld owing to the expected investigation.

[9] *Ibid.*   [10] *Ibid.*

James Perkins, the principal lobbyist for the charter, swore repeatedly that $5,000 in stock at par value had been taken directly by State Senators and from $10,000 to $25,000 in stock distributed indirectly.[11] Perkins charged Thurlow Weed with accepting a $500 bribe.[12] The investigating committee reported finally that it could find no proof involving any but one of the accused.[13] As the bill for the charter had originally passed the Senate by a vote of 27 to 2,[14] and as the members of the investigating committee had been chosen from this majority, its conclusions were naturally viewed with a good deal of suspicion.

The Equal Rights men complained that 75 per cent. of the whole of the bank notes circulating in New York City consisted of depreciated paper. The circulation of these in notes of $5 or under amounted by March, 1835, to nearly $1,500,000. One establishment alone, whose weekly pay-roll in 1834 amounted to $40,000, paid the greater part of this sum in depreciated notes. The wage-earner was in constant fear that any morning he might wake to hear that the bank whose notes he held had failed. Frequently the worst deceptions on the public were connived at by the officials. The Hudson Insurance Company, for instance, with a nominal capital of $200,000, was permitted to issue bonds to the amount of $800,000, upon the most fictitious resources. This was far from being an isolated instance. The law allowed a bank with only $100,000 capital to loan $250,000, thus receiving interest on more than twice the capital actually invested.[15]

The Council was more than ever a hotbed of venality. Numberless small " jobs " were perpetrated without public notice; but when it was proposed in October, 1831,

---

[11] *Senate Documents*, 1834, No. 47, and *Ibid.*, No. 94. Walter Bowne was the bank's president.   [12] *Ibid.*, No. 94.   [13] *Ibid.*, No. 47.
[14] *Journal of the Senate*, 1833, p. 396.
[15] *Documents of the Senate*, 1834, No. 108.

to give the Harlem Railroad Company the franchise for
the perpetual and exclusive use of Fourth avenue, free
of all payment to the city, Alderman George Sharp,
one of the few public-spirited members, drew general
attention to the matter by an energetic denunciation.
After every other means had been resorted to without
success to influence his vote, he was told that he would
be excluded from the party by certain persons at Tammany Hall. Alderman Stevens, who declared that he
had seen stock given to members of the board and to the
" corps editorial " to secure their influence, was also
threatened. The words of these two men proved conclusively the truth of what for a long time was common
report: that the group of Tammany leaders not only
controlled the party nominations but threatened public
officials with their displeasure, with all which that implied — exile from public life, loss of political influence,
perhaps ruin of fortune — in case they did not vote
for certain measures whose " merits " were recommended
to them.

The laborer had other grievances. For seventeen
years the Council had refused to grant any additional
ferries between New York City and Brooklyn. During
that period the population of New York had increased
150,000 and that of Brooklyn 15,000. This growth
involved a vast amount of marketing and increased the
business intercourse between the two places more than
fourfold. The lessees of the Fulton Ferry — the sole
ferry — had made an agreement in 1811, it was alleged,
with the New York City Corporation, by which the latter undertook to bind itself not to establish any additional ferries from south of Catherine street to the
Village of Brooklyn for twenty-five years. The large
landholders influenced the Common Council to continue
this monopoly, their aim being to force the people to
stay in New York, where rents were 35 per cent. higher
than in any other city in the Union. The exactions of

the water, gas and steamboat monopolies likewise had a share in causing the formation of the Equal Rights party.

Besides the dispensing to favored knots of citizens of trading privileges and immunities which were withheld from the great body of the community, the laboring element believed that there was a gross inequality of taxation in the interests of the rich. Taxes rose from $550,000 in 1832 to $850,000 in 1833, but the increase fell upon the poor. The Merchants' Bank was assessed at $6,000; the lot and building had cost that sum twenty years before, and were now worth at least twice as much. The Merchants' Exchange was assessed at $115,000, yet it was known that the land and building had cost $300,000. Dozens of like instances were cited by the reformers and they now determined upon a concerted effort looking to better government.

A powerful influence came to the aid of the Equal Rights men when William Cullen Bryant and William Leggett assumed the editorship of the *Evening Post*. This journal now advocated industrial and political reforms with singular independence and ability. It revived the original conception of the nominating committee's functions. It urged the electors to remember that the nomination by a nominating committee was but a recommendation to the people of certain candidates whose merits and qualifications were as fair a matter of discussion as any under Heaven; and that it was for this very purpose that nominations were made so long before the great popular meeting was convened. Besides his editorial support of the movement, Leggett participated in the practical work of its organization and management. The clear thought and definite expression shown in most of the Equal Rights manifestoes and resolutions are perhaps directly due to him.

The Equal Rights faction became especially active in the Fall of 1834. Its orators raised such a stir that both

Tammany Hall and the Whigs suddenly developed an astonishing care for the workingmen. To conciliate them, the Tammany Nominating Committee exacted a written pledge from every one of its candidates requiring an expression of his sentiments on the monopoly question. To counteract the Wigwam, the Whigs gathered a meeting of "Whig Mechanics" at Masonic Hall, October 14, at which opposition to monopolies, especially banking monopolies, was declared. Not to be outdone, the Wigwam got together a meeting of "Democratic Mechanics," who resolved to oppose monopolies and to restore the constitutional currency. Tammany also began to recognize, even more liberally than before, the naturalized citizens. As a consequence, it won the Fall (1834) election by over 2,300 majority, most of the Equal Rights men voting with it. One-third of its 18,000 voters were estimated at this time to be of foreign birth.

Nearly all the Tammany Assemblymen proceeded to forget their pledges, only four of the delegation voting in the February following against the bill giving exclusive privileges to the Peaconic Company.

The first clash between the Equal Rights faction and the Tammany monopolists occurred at a meeting at the Wigwam on March 31, 1835. Certain that the Aldermen would never grant additional ferries, the Equal Rights men favored a measure, then pending in the Legislature, for the establishment of a State Board of Commissioners clothed with that power. Gideon Lee,[16] a Wall Street banker, called the meeting to order and nominated Preserved Fish for chairman. Many objections were uttered, and Fish retired. The radicals howled down the Tammany speakers and ran the meeting themselves, adopting resolutions prepared by Joel P. Seaver, declaring for the creation of the State board.

[16] Lee was the last Mayor elected by the Common Council (1833-34).

A bill for a new ferry — the present South Ferry — was passed the same year.

The Equal Rights men still hoped to gain their ends inside the organization. When Cornelius W. Lawrence [17] stood for reelection as Mayor in April, 1835, there was scarcely any opposition to him from any quarter, he receiving 17,696 votes out of a total of 20,196.

In the Fall of 1835, however, the Tammany Nominating Committee recommended for State offices candidates of a character most obnoxious to the Equal Rights men, and called a meeting for the evening of October 29, to ratify its nominations. Barely were the doors opened when the Equal Rights men rushed in and frustrated an attempt to place Isaac L. Varian in the chair. In the mêlée, the Bank Democrats, finding themselves unable to control the meeting, withdrew, but in doing so turned off the gas, leaving the Equal Rights men in total darkness. The trick must have been anticipated; for each man drew forth a candle and a lucifer, or " loco foco " match, and in a twinkling the hall was resplendent with dancing lights. The Equal Rights men adopted resolutions and a suitable ticket of their own. [18]

Three sets of candidates stood for election. The Native Americans, who opposed the election of foreigners to office and urged the repeal of the naturalization laws, took the place of the Whigs. In the face of this strong sentiment, Tammany Hall acted with its usual diplomacy. The general committee boasted that the regular Tammany ticket was composed of only native Americans, which was true, the naturalized citizens having been cajoled on the promise of receiving the usual

[17] Lawrence had a curious habit of strolling the streets carrying his spectacles in his hand behind his back, and ogling all the pretty girls he met, a habit which was broken later when one winsome lass tangled him in a plot, much to his financial and mental distress.

[18] The next day the Equal Rights men were dubbed " Locofocos," a name afterward applied by the Whigs to the entire Democratic party.

quota among nominations the next year. Of the nearly
23,000 votes cast at the election, Tammany Hall obtained an average majority of about 800. The Native
Americans polled 9,000 votes, and the Equal Rights
men, or Anti-Monopolists, over 3,500. It was estimated
that 2,000 Whigs voted the Tammany ticket to defeat
the Anti-Monopolists, and that about 5,500 Whig votes
were divided between Tammany Hall and the Native
Americans.

The news of its slight plurality was hailed with anything but pleasure at the Wigwam, where the Anti-
Monopolists were denounced as political swindlers and
adventurers. Instead, however, of making a show of
outward fairness, the organization leaders blindly took
the course most adapted to fan the flame of opposition to
themselves. After the great fire of 1835, which destroyed
$20,000,000 worth of property, and the extent of which
was due to the refusal of the corrupt Aldermen to give
the city a proper water supply, the Common Council
agreed to loan $6,000,000 at 5 per cent. interest for the
relief of insurance companies and banks which had suffered from the fire.[19]   Nothing was said or done for the
relief of the poor sufferers whom the Wigwam claimed to
have under its especial protection. The Council allowed
pawnbrokers 25 per cent. interest and prohibited them
from loaning more than $25 on a single pledge.[20]   The
city institutions were in a melancholy state.[21]   Most
serious of all on the public mind were the disclosures
concerning the Commercial Bank, from which funds were
embezzled in the scheme of cornering the stock of the
Harlem Railroad. As a step towards this end, Samuel
Swartwout and Garrit Gilbert (a sometime Sachem) lobbied for the passage of a bill to increase the capital stock
of this road, which in turn, it was thought, would in-

---

[19] *Documents of the Board of Aldermen,* 1836, Nos. 65 and 100.
[20] *Ibid.,* 1837, No. 48.   [21] *Ibid.,* 1837, No. 32.

crease the price of all the stock — two Senators agreeing to raise objections temporarily " so as to blind the
eyes of the New Yorkers." [22]

The leaders made no effort to stop the granting of
charters, or to curtail the monopolist privileges already
granted. It was admitted generally that no legislation
even remotely affecting the interests of the banks could
pass without the consent of those institutions. Tradesmen also had their combinations. But combinations,
legal enough when organized by capital, were declared
illegal when formed by workingmen. At this time the
Supreme Court of the State of New York decided that
combinations to raise the wages of any class of laborers
amounted to a misdemeanor, on the ground that they
were injurious to trade. Later, in June, 1836, twenty
tailors were found guilty of conspiracy under that decision and fined by Judge Edwards $1,150 in the aggregate
for engaging in a strike for higher wages.

The mechanics prepared to hold an indignation meeting and applied for permission to use Tammany Hall.
This was refused by the Sachems.[23] In defiance of the
Wigwam, the meeting, a gathering of 20,000 persons,
was held in the park fronting Tammany Hall. " Are
workingmen," read the address of the committee of this
meeting,

" free in reality when they dare not obey the first instinct of all
animated beings; when our courts pronounce it criminal to exercise

[22] *Documents of the Senate*, 1836, Vol. II, No. 94.
[23] A short time before, at an Anti-Monopolist meeting, Chairman
Job Haskell had represented that the Tammany Society — the secret
body, responsible to no one and enforcing its demands through the
Tammany Hall political organization — was to blame for the political
corruption. Resolutions were then passed setting forth that whereas
the self-constituted, self-perpetuating Tammany Society had assumed
a dictatorial attitude and by usages made by itself endeavored to rule
the people as with a rod of iron; and as they (the Equal Rights men)
believed the people were capable of managing their own affairs without the aid of said inquisitorial society, " that we deem the Tammany
Society an excrescence upon the body politic and dangerous to its
rights and liberties."

nature's paramount law of self-preservation? Trades unions and mechanick societies are only self-protective against the *countless combinations of aristocracy;* boards of bank and other chartered directories; boards of brokers; boards of trade and commerce; combinations of landlords; coal and wood dealers; monopolists and all those who grasp at everything and produce nothing. If *all these combinations* are suffered to exist, why are trades unions and combinations of workingmen denounced? Should they not have an equal chance in the pursuit of life, liberty and happiness? Should they not have an equal right with the other classes of society, in their person, in their property or labor, and in their management?"

The meeting, in strong resolutions, condemned the Supreme Court decision and that of Judge Edwards.

At this moment the peculiar Wigwam methods were being displayed in another direction to an edified public. In the first days of May, 1836, the Board of Aldermen found itself divided equally, Tammany Hall and the Whigs each having eight votes, precluding either from electing a president. The Tammany members, in the tea-room downstairs, made merry over refreshments. The Whigs could not muster a quorum, and sent word to the organization men to appear; the Wigwam men replied that they didn't choose, and bade the Whigs come to them. Meanwhile the public business stood still. Finally the balloting was begun. On May 23, seventeen votes were found to have been cast, although there were only sixteen voting Aldermen.[24] By the end of May more than 120 ballots were had. At last, on July 1, the Tammany men persuaded Alderman Ward, a Whig, to offer a resolution electing Isaac L. Varian, a Wigwam candidate, for the first six months, which was done.

Taking these proceedings as a cue, the Equal Rights party, on June 6, at Military Hall, adopted a long series of resolutions stating that the aristocracy of the Democracy, or in other words, the monopolists, the papercurrency Democrats, the partizans of the " usages," had long deceived and misguided the great body of the Democrats. Through these " usages," the tools of the

[24] *Proceedings of the Board of Aldermen,* Vol XI, p. 16.

banks and other incorporated and speculative interests were enabled to take advantage of the unsuspicious self-security of the people, both before and at primary meetings.   By the aristocracy and through secret caucuses, candidates were chosen, proceedings were cut and dried, and committees were packed.   When committees could not be packed without opposition, the resolutions further read, two sets of committeemen were usually elected, and that set whose political complexion best suited the packed majority of the general committee was always accepted without any regard to the majorities of the people.   The Union did not furnish a more dangerous usurpation upon the sovereignty of the people than the fact of the Tammany Hall Nominating Committee sending recently a petition to the Legislature in favor of chartering more banks and banking paper capital and designating themselves, not as citizens, but as members of the nominating committee, notwithstanding the very nominees of such a committee had given their written pledge to oppose new banks and monopolies.

The "usages," the Equal Rights party next resolved, so productive of secret caucuses, intrigues and abuses, furnished the avenue through which one portion of the Democracy had been corrupted, and the other portion — the great mass — led astray.   The latter was taught to believe that "usages" alone made men Democrats, and that to keep Federalists and Whigs out of office was the very essence of Democracy.[25]

The Equal Rights party then nominated Isaac L. Smith, of Buffalo, for Governor, and Moses L. Jacques, of New York City, for Lieutenant-Governor.

To draw from the strength of the new party, some of Tammany's leaders — Samuel Swartwout, Jesse Hoyt, Stephen Allen, Saul Alley and a few others — professed to favor the repeal of the Restraining law, which

[25] These resolutions were published officially in the New York *Evening Post,* June 8, 1836.

in effect prohibited private banking and gave the incorporated institutions a monopoly. The Anti-Monopolists
were not to be deluded. On September 21 they declared
that in the recent *professions* of the Tammany corrup-
tionists in advocating this repeal and in favoring some
other few *minor* democratic measures, they beheld the
stale expedient of luring the bone and sinew of the country to the support of their monopoly and banking men
and measures and that they had no faith in Tammany
" usages," policy or its incorrigible Sachems.

The characters of most of the Wigwam nominations
were so tainted that it seemed as if the candidates were
put forward in defiance of the best public sentiment. It
is not so certain that outside the Equal Rights party the
voters were repelled by the current methods of buying
legislation and dictating nominations. A low tone of
public morals was manifested. Men were bent on money-
making. He who could get rich by grace of the Legislature was thought " smart " and worthy of emulation.
The successful in politics were likewise to be envied, and,
if possible, imitated. A large part of the community
bowed in respect to the person of wealth, no matter
whence came his riches; and the bank lobbyists were the
recipients of a due share of this reverence.

From these men the Tammany leaders selected candidates. One of the Assembly nominees was Prosper M.
Wetmore, who had lobbied for the notorious State Bank
charter. This bank, according to the charter, was to
have $10,000,000 capital, although its organizers did not
have more than a mere fraction of that sum. This was
going too far, even for Albany, though upon modifying
their application, the charter was granted.[26] Reuben
Withers and James C. Stoneall, bank lobbyists; Benjamin Ringgold, a bank and legislative " go-between," and
Morgan L. Smith, preeminent among lobbyists, were

[26] Cornelius W. Lawrence, the Tammany Mayor, became the bank's
first president.

other Tammany nominees. Notwithstanding the low standards of public morals, these men were so unpopular, that when the form of submitting their names for ratification to the great popular meeting at the Wigwam on November 1, was carried out, a hostile demonstration followed. The names of Wetmore, Smith and Ringgold especially were hooted. But the leaders had groups of "whippers-in" brought in hurriedly to vote affirmatively, and the presiding officer declared all the nominees duly accepted by the people.

Only six of the organization's thirteen Assembly nominees survived the popular wrath, and the nominees for nearly all the other offices were beaten, notwithstanding the expectation that the Presidential election would carry them in on the party ticket. A number of Tammany men of principle refused to vote. The Whigs, the Native Americans and some "Locofocos" joined forces. They were aided by the panic, which, breaking out shortly before election, reacted against the Democrats. The Equal Rights men as a rule voted for Van Buren. Tammany Hall and the Whigs both committed frauds. Van Buren received 1,124 majority in New York City, which in 1832 had given Jackson nearly 6,000 majority.

Made wiser by defeat, the organization leaders realized the importance of the Equal Rights movement, and caused, as a sop, the passage, in February, 1837, of the bill repealing the Restraining act. The Common Council likewise modified the Pawnbrokers' act by cutting down the interest to a more reasonable percentage.[27]

Their providence stopped at this point, however,[28] and during the panic Winter following neither Legislature nor Common Council did anything to alleviate the miseries of the poor. On the contrary, the poor complained that the tendency more and more was to use the power of the law to make the rich richer. While the suffering

[27] *Documents of the Board of Aldermen,* 1837, No. 48.
[28] Excepting some instances of private charity by Tammany leaders.

was greatest, Alderman Aaron Clark, a Whig, who had
made his fortune from lotteries, proposed that the city
spend several millions of dollars to surround its water
front with a line of still-water ponds for shipping purposes, his justification for this expenditure being that the
North River piers would " raise the price of every lot
25 x 100 feet west of Broadway $5,000 at a jump." [29]
" Millions to benefit landowners and shippers, but not
a dollar for the unemployed hungry! " exclaimed the
Anti-Monopolists. Alderman Bruen, another Whig, at
a time when the fall in the value of real estate in New
York City alone exceeded $50,000,000, suggested the
underwriting by the city to the speculators for the sum
of $5,000,000, to take in pledge the lands they had
bought and to give them the bonds of the city for two-
thirds their value. To the Equal Rights men there was
not much difference between the Tammany Hall and the
Whig leaders. Both, it was plain, sweated the people
for their own private interests, although the Whigs,
inheriting the Federalist idea that property was the sole
test of merit, did not flaunt their undying concern for
the laborer so persistently as did the Wigwam.

The city in 1837 was filled with the homeless and unemployed. Rent was high, and provisions were dear.
Cattle speculators had possession of nearly all the stock,
and a barrel of flour cost $12. On February 12 a crowd
met in the City Hall Park, after which over 200 of them
sped to the flour warehouse of Eli Hart & Co., on Washington street. This firm and that of S. B. Herrick &
Son, it was known, held a monopoly in the scarce supply
of flour and wheat. The doors of Hart's place were
battered down, and nearly 500 barrels of flour and 1,000
bushels of wheat were taken out and strewed in the street.
Herrick's place likewise was mobbed.[30] On May 10,
when the banks suspended specie payments, a vast and

29 *Documents of the Board of Aldermen*, 1836, No. 80.
30 *Documents of the Board of Alderman*, 1839, No. 29.

excited crowd gathered in Wall Street, and a riot was narrowly averted.[31]

The Equal Rights party could not be bought out or snuffed out. To deprive it of its best leaders Tammany Hall resorted to petty persecution. Jacques and Slamm had headed a petition to the Legislature protesting against the appointment of a certain suspicious bank investigating committee. The Wigwam men in the Legislature immediately secured the passage of a resolution for the appointment of a committee to investigate this petition, and this committee instantly haled Jacques and Slamm to appear at Albany and give testimony.[32] The purpose was plain. The Tammany men sought to have the Equal Rights leaders at Albany, which was not as accessible from the city as now, and there keep them under various pretexts while the Spring campaign for Mayor was going on. Jacques and Slamm did not appear and were adjudged guilty of contempt. When they were most needed in New York City they were arrested and arraigned before the Legislature. William Leggett also was threatened, but escaped arrest.

The Equal Rights party, however, was soon to demonstrate its capacity to do harm to Tammany. The organization nominated John J. Morgan for Mayor; the Whigs named Aaron Clark, and the Equal Rights party opposed them with Jacques. The 3,911 votes Jacques received were enough to defeat Morgan, with his 12,974 votes, against Clark's 16,140. Worst blow of all, Tammany Hall lost the Common Council. When the new body came in it removed all of the Wigwam's office-holders that it could. The spoils in the form of annual salaries paid by the city, amounting to $468,000; the perquisites and contracts — such as that for the Croton Aqueduct, in favor of which the people had voted some years before — and other improvements, all went to the Whigs.

[31] *Ibid.*
[32] *Documents of the Assembly*, 1837, Nos. 198 and 327.

The Tammany men, regarding the Equal Rights men responsible for this loss of power, were now disposed to treat with them and willing enough to throw over the banker-corporation element.

CHAPTER XIII

1837–1838

ONE of the important changes in the composition of Tammany Hall came in 1837. The United States Bank dependents, lobbyists and supporters had left the Wigwam, as has been noted, in 1832, but the State Bank men, well satisfied with the destruction of the great rival corporation, had remained. Finding the organization no longer subservient to them they, in turn, quit Tammany during Van Buren's administration.

This happened in the Fall of 1837. The Tammany General Committee, whose membership had recently been increased from thirty-six to fifty-one members, held a meeting on September 7, thirty-six members being present. Resolutions were offered upholding Van Buren's scheme of placing the United States funds in sub-treasuries. This was a bitter dose to the State Bank men who, wanting to retain Government deposits, opposed the sub-treasury plan. The " bank conservatives " vainly tried to put off a vote on the resolutions, but being repeatedly outvoted, all but one of them left the room before the main question was put. Nineteen members remained. As seventeen formed a quorum, the question was put and the resolutions were adopted by a vote of 18 to 1. The bank men pretended that the resolutions were passed clandestinely, and they so deviously managed things that in a few days they regained control of the general committee, which at their behest refused to call a public meeting to act on the resolutions.

112

But the Democratic-Republican Young Men's Committee was saturated with Equal Rights ideas and rebelled at the policy which allowed the acts of the bankers to antagonize Democrats of principle and bring defeat to Tammany Hall. This committee met in the Wigwam on September 11 and passed a series of resolutions with which the Anti-Monopolists were as pleased as the bankers were angry. The resolution declared the public satisfaction in anticipating the separation of bank and state, and welcomed the approach of an era when legislation should not be perverted to the enrichment of a few and the depression of the many. The Young Men resolved that the crisis was sufficient reason for their committee assuming to recommend a public meeting of those who approved Van Buren's recent message, to be held in Tammany Hall, on September 21.

The bank men were angry that the Young Men's committee should dare to act independently of the elder, the general committee. The latter, meeting on September 14, disapproved of the manner in which the Young Men's meeting had been called, declined cooperation with it, and by a vote of 21 to 16 ordered the Young Men's General Committee to withdraw the recommendation for that meeting. The Young Men ignored the order and held their meeting. Van Buren and his prospective subtreasuries were indorsed and fiery resolutions adopted denouncing the incorporated banks.

Coming, as this denunciation did, from Tammany Hall, which had a far-reaching influence over the Union, the " bank conservatives " grew even more exasperated, for they had come to look upon the organization as almost their private property. As two-thirds of the Sachems belonged to their clique, they held a meeting in the Wigwam, on September 25, to disapprove of the subtreasury scheme. In rushed the progressive Democrats in overwhelming force, and for an hour the place was a fighting arena. The bank men were forced to leave, and the progressives organized and carried out the meeting.

Regarding Tammany as having ceased to be the tool of the exploiting interests, the Anti-Monopolists were disposed to a union with the advanced organization party. When the Equal Rights men met at Military Hall on October 27, Col. Alexander Ming, Jr., one of the party's organizers, said that one of the chief purposes of the Equal Rights party was to effect reform in Tammany Hall; this having been accomplished, it was the duty of every Democrat to unite on one ticket against the " high-toned Federalists, Whigs and aristocrats." A fusion Assembly ticket was made up, composed of both Tammany and Equal Rights men, each Tammanyite subscribing in writing to the Equal Rights principles. A small contingent of the Equal Rights party, however, accused their comrades of selling out to the Wigwam, and nominated their own candidates — Job Haskell, Daniel Gorham, William E. Skidmore and others.

The " bank conservatives " allied themselves with the Whigs. They were credited with raising an election fund of $60,000, a sum which at that time could do great execution. By raising the cries of " agrarianism " and " infidelity," ascribing the effects of the panic of 1837 to the Democrats, coercing laborers and using illegal votes, the combined conservatives wrested nearly 3,000 majority out of a total of 33,093 votes.

Stimulated by this victory, the bank men attempted to regain control of Tammany and called a meeting for January 2, 1838, at 7 o'clock, in the Wigwam. The Anti-Bank Democrats then issued a call for a meeting on the same night, but one hour earlier. The Council of Sachems were mostly either " bank conservatives " themselves or sympathizers; but they feared to alienate the dominant progressives. As the best solution, they agreed that neither party should meet in the Wigwam. On January 1 they resolved that both calls were unauthorized and that neither had been sanctioned by any act of the general

committee. " The lease of Tammany Hall," read their
resolution, " reserves to the Council of Sachems of the
Tammany Society the right to decide on all questions of
doubt, arising out of the rooms being occupied by or let
to a person or persons as a committee or otherwise for
political purposes! " The Council sent a copy of these
resolutions to Lovejoy and Howard, the lessees [1] of Tammany Hall, forbidding them to " rent, hire to, or allow
either of the assemblages named on the premises." Identical with this decree, Lovejoy and Howard issued a notice
(which was published in the public prints) that their lease
of Tammany Hall " contained covenants " that they would
not permit any persons to assemble in the hall " whose
political opinions the Council of Sachems of Tammany
Society should declare not to be in accordance with the
political views of the general committee of said Tammany
Society," and they (Lovejoy and Howard) therefore could
not permit either meeting.[2] The conservatives then met
in the City Hall Park, where they were assaulted and mal-
treated.[3]

The Anti-Bank men won over the general committee,
which gave the necessary permission for their meeting in
the Wigwam on January 9. The policy of Jackson and of
Van Buren was upheld, and it was set forth that while the
Democracy, unlike its calumniators, did not arrogate to
itself " the possession of all the decency, the virtue, the
morals and the wealth of the community," it felt no more
disturbed at being called " Agrarians," " Locofocos " or

[1] It will be remembered that in 1828 the Sachems had bought back a
lease on the building in order to shut out the Adams men. The lease
had again been let, but under restrictions which left the Sachems the
power to determine what faction should be entitled to the use of the
hall.

[2] These details are of the greatest importance as revealing the
methods by which the society asserted its absolute ascendency over
the organization. They proved the absurdity of the claim that the two
bodies were distinct and separate from each other.

[3] The *New Yorker* (magazine), January 13, 1838. This journal was
edited and published by Horace Greeley.

"Radicals" than it did at being abused in the days of Jefferson.

That foremost Equal Rights advocate, the *Evening Post*, now acknowledged the purification of Tammany Hall; [4] saying that the spurious Democrats who had infested the party for their own selfish purposes had either been drummed out of the ranks, had left voluntarily, or had acquiesced sullenly in the decision of the majority.

[4] January 11, 1838. The credit for this temporary purification must in considerable measure be given to the *Evening Post's* editors, William Cullen Bryant and William Leggett.

CHAPTER XIV

1838–1840

THE course of the Whig city administration served only to strengthen Tammany and was responsible for the conviction, which later so often prevailed, that if Tammany Hall was bad the Whigs were no better, and were perhaps worse. At this time of general distress complaints were numerous that the sum of $1,300,000 was exacted from the rentpayers in a single year. In the early part of 1838 one-third of all the persons in New York City who subsisted by manual labor was substantially or wholly without employment.[1] Not less than 10,000 persons were in utter poverty and had no other means of surviving the Winter than those afforded by the charity of neighbors. The Almshouse and all charitable institutions were full to overflowing; the usual agencies of charity were exhausted or insufficient, and 10,000 sufferers were still uncared for. The great panic of 1837 had cut down the city's trade one-half. Notwithstanding the fall of prices, the rents for tenements in New York were greater than were paid in any other city or village upon the globe.[2] So exorbitant were the demands of the landlords that the tenants found it impossible to meet them. The landowners were the backbone of the Whig party; it was not unnatural, therefore, that

[1] The *New Yorker*, January 20, 1838.
[2] *Ibid.*, February 17, 1838. James Parton, in his biography of Horace Greeley, attributes the latter's conversion and life-long devotion to Socialist principles in large part to the frightful sufferings which he witnessed in New York City, in the Winter of 1838.

their rapacity developed among the people at large a profound distrust of Whig men and principles.

The Whig officials, so far as can be discovered, took no adequate steps to relieve the widespread suffering. The Tammany ward committees, on the other hand, were active in relief work. This was another of the secrets of Tammany Hall's usual success in holding the body of voters. The Whigs made fine speeches over champagne banquets, but kept at a distance from the poor, among whom the Wigwam workers mingled, and distributed clothing, fuel and food and often money. The leaders set the example. One of these was John M. Bloodgood,[3] who frequently went among the charitable citizens, collecting, in a large basket, cakes, pies, meat and other eatables, and distributing them among the needy.

In the Spring of 1838 Tammany nominated Isaac L. Varian for Mayor, and the Whigs renominated Aaron Clark. The Whigs used the panic as an example of the result of Democratic rule. Controlling the city, they employed all its machinery to win. It was reasonably certain that they did not stop at fraud. In some wards canvassing was delayed until other wards were heard from. In still other wards the Whigs refused to administer the oath to naturalized citizens. With all this they obtained a plurality of only 519 out of 39,341 votes. Had it not been for dissensions in the tumultuous Sixth Ward, Tammany would have won.

In the Fall election of 1838 the Whig frauds were enormous and indisputable. The Whigs raised large sums of money, which were handed to ward workers for the procuring of votes. About two hundred roughs were brought from Philadelphia, in different divisions, each man receiving $22. Gen. Robert Swartwout, now a Whig, at the

---

[3] Bloodgood was the son of Abraham Bloodgood, one of the earliest Tammany politicians. The son likewise achieved considerable influence in the organization. He was for a long time a Police Justice. He will be met with again toward the end of this chapter.

instance of such men as Moses H. Grinnell, Robert C.
Wetmore and Noah Cook, former Wigwam lights, who left
the Hall because the " destructionist " Anti-Monopolists
captured it, arranged for the trip of these fraudulent
voters. After having voted in as many wards as possible,
each was to receive the additional compensation of $5.
They were also to pass around spurious tickets purporting
to be Democratic. The aggregate Whig vote, it was
approximated, was swelled through the operations of this
band by at least five to six hundred.[4] One repeater,
Charles Swint, voted in sixteen wards. Such inmates of
the House of Detention as could be persuaded or bullied
into voting the Whig ticket were set at large. Merritt, a
police officer, was seen boldly leading a crowd of them to
the polls. Ex-convicts distributed Whig tickets and busily
electioneered. The cabins of all the vessels along the
wharves were ransacked, and every man, whether or not a
citizen or resident of New York, who could be wheedled
into voting a Whig ballot, was rushed to the polls and his
vote was smuggled in. The Whigs were successful, their
candidate for Governor, William H. Seward, receiving
20,179 votes, to 19,377 for William L. Marcy.

Departing from its custom of seeking local victory on
national issues, Tammany, in April, 1839, issued an address expatiating on the increase of the city expenses
from a little over $1,000,000 in 1830 to above $5,000,000
in 1838. Deducting about $1,500,000 for the Croton
works, there would still remain the enormous increase of
$2,500,000. The city population had not trebled in that
time, nor had there been any extraordinary cause for expenditure. Where had all this money gone?

Tammany further pointed out that, unlike the Whigs,
it had never stooped so low as to discharge the humble
laborers in the public service, when it (Tammany) held

4 Confession of Hart Marks, one of the leaders, before Justice
Lowndes in the lower Police Court, November 6, 1838, and of Jonathan
D. Stevenson and others in the Recorder's Court, October 20, 1840.

the Common Council.   Nor had it ever been so abject as
to provide them with colored tickets, as the Whigs had
done, so that the laborers might be detected if they voted
contrary to their masters.   Tammany further charged
that the Whigs in the previous election had taken the Almshouse paupers, with embossed satin voting tickets in their
hands, to the polls, and were planning to do it again.

Tammany made good use of this charge.   But the practise was not exclusively a Whig industry.   In those years
both Democrats and Whigs, according to which held power,
forced Almshouse paupers to vote.   For a fortnight before the election the paupers were put in training.   On the
morning of election they were disguised with new clothing,
so that the public might not see their gray uniforms.
They were given tickets to vote " and tickets for grog,
silver coin and also good advice as to their conduct at the
polls."   Then they were carried to the polls in stages, with
an officer on each step to see that none escaped.   Many
would return to the Almshouse drunk and with torn clothing, or after having exchanged their new garments for
liquor.[5]   There were usually about 300 paupers.   In the
Fall and Winter of 1838 a quarter of the population was
relieved at the Almshouse.

Clark and Varian were both renominated for Mayor in
the Spring of 1839.   Preparations for fraud on a large
scale were made by both parties.   The newspapers supporting Varian admitted that Tammany thought proper to
follow the Whigs' example, and to counteract its effects,
by colonizing the doubtful wards with Democratic voters.
On both sides repeating was general.   An Albany police
officer named Coulson brought twenty-three persons, one of
whom was only seventeen years old, to New York City,
where they voted the Whig ticket in the different wards.
For this they received $5 in advance, and $1 a day.

Of the 41,113 votes Varian [6] received 21,072, and Clark

[5] *Documents of the Board of Aldermen*, 1844-45, XI, No. 51.
[6] Varian was a rugged, popular, but not over-educated man.   Sir

20,005. The Wigwam secured a majority of 12 in the Common Council.

Fearing that Tammany in power would use the administration machinery in elections even more than had the Whigs, the latter now made a great outcry for a registry law,[7] proclaiming it the only fraud preventive. The sudden conversion of the Whig leaders to civic purity called forth derision. But the people at large, the non-politicians, ashamed of such barefaced frauds in their city, took up the agitation. The Registry bill was introduced in the Legislature in May, 1839. It provided for the registration of voters in New York City, and made fraudulent voting a felony, with severe penalties.

After the frauds of 1834 the Wigwam leaders had given out that they would take serious steps to obtain from the Legislature a law causing voters to be registered, but had done nothing. They now opened a campaign against the Whig bill. In the Spring of 1840 the ward committees declared against it on the pretext that it interfered with constitutional rights; that it was an insidious attempt to take from the poor man either his right of suffrage or to make the exercise of that right so inconvenient as practically to debar him from voting. The Common Council, on March 16, 1840, denounced the proposed law as inquisitorial,

Charles Lyell, the noted British geologist, once asked him questions as to the formation of Manhattan Island. Varian said he had dug a well on his farm at Murray Hill and after going through " a stratagem of sand and a stratagem of clay they struck a stratagem of red rock." At another time, while reading a New York newspaper at the Stanwix House in Albany, Varian remarked to Walter Bowne, then Mayor, that they had a new Street Inspector in New York City. "Indeed! who is he?" "A perfect stranger," replied Varian; and he read from the paper: "'Last evening the wind suddenly changed to the north, and this morning, thanks to Old Boreas, our streets are in a passable condition.' Old Boreas," said Varian, reflectively, " I thought I knew every Democrat in New York, but I never heard of him."

[7] In 1834 the Board of Assistant Aldermen had passed a resolution in favor of the registry of voters, and the Native American Association, early in 1838, had petitioned the Legislature similarly. The Whigs seized hold of the movement as political capital for themselves.

tyrannical and disfranchising in its effect, as well as unjust, because they (the Aldermen) " know of no sin which
she (New York City) has committed to make her worthy
of the signal reproach now sought to be cast upon her." [8]
A few days later the Common Council on joint ballot delivered itself of a solemn protest against the constitutionality
of the Registry bill, and on the night of March 24 an
assemblage in the Wigwam did likewise. It was in this
year that the full account of the Whig frauds of 1838 was
made public. Commenting upon this, the Tammany Nominating Committee, with characteristic naïveté, said in its
address: " It is with shame that we record these dark
transactions and proclaim them to the people. We would,
if we could, blot out their existence, for it brings disgrace
on our whole country and will make the enemies of civil
freedom laugh with joy."

The Registry bill became a law, but Tammany continued to protest against it. When, in 1841, the Legislature increased the penalties for its violation, Acting Mayor
Elijah F. Purdy commented upon it severely.[9]

The able, sincere and high-minded William Leggett, the
guiding spirit of the Equal Rights party, died on May 29,
1839, not quite forty years old. The Tammany Young
Men's General Committee eulogized his virtues and talents,
proclaimed him amongst the purest of politicians and announced the purpose of raising a monument to his memory.
Of this committee, curious to relate, the chairman was
Fernando Wood and the secretary Richard B. Connolly —
two men who became known for anything but devotion to
the virtues they here exalted.

Leggett, some years before this, had become a radical
Abolitionist. By this time the anti-slavery movement in
the city and State had grown to considerable proportions,
though as yet it had exercised but little influence on politics. Several riots had taken place in the streets of the

[8] *Proceedings of the Board of Aldermen,* Vol. XVIII, pp. 404–5.
[9] *Ibid.,* Vol. XX, pp. 229–30.

city, two rather serious ones happening on July 9 and 10, 1834, and June 21, 1835, and Lewis Tappan, an anti-slavery propagandist, had been mobbed. The local move-ment gradually acquired new adherents, and constantly increased its propaganda. At this period, however, it was more in the nature of a growing moral force.

During this period another great series of disclosures regarding Tammany chieftains was made public. Samuel Swartwout, whom Jackson had made Collector of the Port shortly after coming into office in 1829, fled from the city late in 1838. He had long been a power in the organiza-tion. His name had been mentioned unpleasantly when he, with M. M. Noah and Henry Ogden,[10] contrived by means of their official positions to get $10,000 reward for the recovery of the jewels stolen from the Prince of Orange, though the recovery had been made by others. And in 1833 he had threatened, as Collector of the Port, to remove the Custom House uptown because the merchants would not lend him more than $7,000 on the strength of some worthless " Jersey meadows." Three years later he was connected with the unsavory Harlem Railroad stock corner and the manipulation of the funds of the Com-mercial Bank. Early in 1838 he joined forces with the notorious politicians of the Seventh Ward Bank for the defeat of William Leggett for the Democratic nomination for Congress, securing the nomination of Isaac L. Varian in his stead. A few months later the city was astounded to learn that since 1830 he had been systematically rob-bing the Government, through the manipulation of Custom House receipts, and that the total of his thefts amounted to nearly $1,250,000.[11] Fleeing to Europe, he wandered

[10] Ogden was a Tammany politician of considerable importance. At the time of Swartwout's flight he was the Cashier of the Custom House, a post which he had held for several years. He was also a director of the Seventh Ward Bank.

[11] The exact amount was $1,222,705.69. *House Executive Docu-ment, No. 13, Twenty-fifth Congress, Third Session;* also *House Re-port, No. 313.*

aimlessly about [12] for many years.[13]   The community was
so impressed with the size of this defalcation that a verb,
" to Swartwout," was coined, remaining in general use for
many years thereafter.   A defaulter was generally spoken
of as having " Swartwouted."

A lesser figure in Tammany circles, though a person of
considerable consequence, followed Swartwout in flight.
This was William M. Price, at the time District Attorney
for the Southern District of New York.   It was discovered
that he had defaulted to the Government in the sum of
$75,000.   Price, like so many other Tammany politicians
of his time, had been mixed up with Seventh Ward Bank
politics.   During the latter part of his career he had been
known as the personal representative in the city of President Van Buren.

During the following Spring, William Paxen Hallett,
a member of the " Big Four " against whom the Equal
Rights party had so energetically protested in 1836, was
made the defendant in a civil suit involving grave fraud.
As referee in a suit for damages of one John A. Manning
against one Charles J. Morris, Hallett had wrongfully reported that only trifling judgments remained outstanding
against Morris, and the court had accordingly given the
latter a year's time in which to make good a judgment for
$3,496 rendered in favor of Manning.   It appeared, how-
ever, in the proceedings before the Superior Court, May
20, 1839, that Hallett knew, or should have known, of a
previous judgment against the defendant for $15,014.44
in favor of one Nathan Davis, who during the year of

[12] A pathetic tale is told of an American meeting Swartwout in
Algiers, several years after this episode, and of the defaulter crying
like a child over his enforced exile from the land of his birth.

[13] Jesse Hoyt, another Sachem, succeeded Swartwout as Collector of
the Port.   Hoyt was charged, about this time, with having defaulted
in the sum of $30,000 in dealings with certain Wall street brokers.
The Superior Court Judgment Roll for 1839–40 records two judgments against him, secured by Effingham H. Warner, one for $10,000
and one for $5,747.72.   Both judgments were satisfied within a few
years after his assumption of the Collectorship of the Port.

grace seized upon all of Morris's property, thus defrauding Manning. The testimony was so convincing that Hallett was forced to compromise the suit by paying the damages asked for. Through the influence of the organization, however, he escaped prosecution.

The "ring" of Police Justices had for several years been a crying scandal. Whig and Tammany magistrates were equally involved. Public clamor fixed upon John M. Bloodgood, despite his private charities, as the first victim. The Assistant Aldermen impeached him in January, 1839,[14] and submitted the case to the Court of Common Pleas, by whom he was tried.[15] Testimony was brought out tending to show that the Police Justices, by means of an understanding with policemen and jailers, extorted money from prisoners and shielded counterfeiters, thieves, street walkers and other malefactors from arrest or conviction. The charges were dismissed.[16] Stronger testimony of the same kind was brought out in May, 1840, on the trial of Police Justice Henry W. Merritt, and other testimony involved in the same way Special Justice Oliver M. Lowndes. The case, however, was dismissed.[17]

14 See "Articles of Impeachment," *Journal and Documents of the Board of Assistant Aldermen*, 1839, Vol. XIII, No. 12 and No. 25.

15 *Court Minutes, New York Common Pleas*, record of February 19 and 20, 1839. (These records are neither paged nor indexed.) The Common Pleas of this time was popularly known as the Mayor's Court; and the Judges were the Mayor, Recorder and certain Aldermen. The later Court of Common Pleas was not established until 1856.

16 A curious reason for the dismissal was given in the decision of the Judges. It was that the charges had not been individually sworn to. It appeared, therefore, that the Board of Assistant Aldermen, acting in its official capacity in formulating impeachment proceedings, was not a recognizable party before the Court of Common Pleas.

17 *Journal and Documents of the Board of Assistant Aldermen*, 1839–40, Vol. XV, No. 71. The reason for dismissing these charges was identical with that given in the case of Bloodgood. A statement of the case is given in the report of District Attorney James R. Whiting to the Board of Aldermen during this year. See *Proceedings of the Board of Aldermen*, 1840, Vol. XIX, pp. 135–37. The Common Pleas volume for 1840 is missing from its place in the County Court Building.

A strong public agitation had been waged for the re-organization of the criminal courts. The *Weekly Herald* of February 1, 1840, had made the statement that the farce of conducting the correctional machinery of the city involved a yearly sum of $1,360,564 — this sum being the total of judges', policemen's and court attendants' salaries (about $50,000), added to the blackmail exacted from offenders, and various "pickings and stealings." The statement was an extravagant one; $700,000 would have been nearer the mark. But whatever the sum, the acquittal of the Police Justices by their fellows in judicial evil-doing indicated that the carnival was to continue. The Tammany leaders had been "out" for the two years 1837–38, and were now vigorously making hay while the sun shone, while such of their Whig contemporaries as still held office were vying with the chiefs in systematic and organized plundering.

The Manhattan Bank scandals were made public in February, 1840. This was the bank whose charter Aaron Burr had so ingeniously secured in 1799. It had been a Tammany institution from the beginning, and Tammany politicians had ruled its policies. It was now generally regarded as the leading financial institution in the city, rivaled only by the Bank of America. It carried $600,000 of Government funds on deposit, and, of course, a large city and State fund.

It was now shown that for years it had loaned large sums to Tammany leaders and to family connections of its directors and officials, and that it had spent other large sums for political purposes. The total of its worthless loans and political expenditures reached the enormous sum of $1,344,266.99. Cashier Campbell P. White, tried on the technical charge of stealing several of the bank's books, was freed through the disagreement of the jury,[18] but on a second trial, charged with assaulting Jonathan Thomp-

[18] *Session Minutes,* 1840.

son, a Tammany director of the bank who had criticized
his management, he was fined $250 and imprisoned for fif-
teen days.[19]   In the midst of the excitement Colin G. Newcomb, the teller, disappeared with $50,000.   That the
bank weathered the storm well-nigh reaches the dimensions
of a miracle.   Paulding, twice a Tammany Mayor; Bowne,
another Tammany ex-Mayor; and Robert H. Morris, at
that time Recorder, appeared as the defendant's witnesses
in the first trial.   White was an influential Wigwam chief,
and in 1832 had been elected to Congress on the Tammany
ticket.

19 *Ibid.*

CHAPTER XV

1840–1846

ABOUT the year 1840 the change in the personnel and the policy of the Wigwam became distinctly evident. After its absorption of the Equal Rights party, the organization had remained "purified" for a year or so, and then, as usual, had relapsed. But a new power and new ideas prevailed. No longer did the bankers and merchants who once held the Wigwam in their grasp, venture to meet in the secret chamber of the hall and order nominations, command policies or determine the punishment of refractory individuals. Tammany from this time forward began to be ruled from the bottom of the social stratum, instead of from the top.

Something had to be done to offset the disclosures of 1838–40. Accordingly, the policy of encouraging the foreigners, first rather mildly started in 1823, was now developed into a system. The Whigs antagonized the entrance of foreign-born citizens into politics, and the Native American party was organized expressly to bar them almost entirely from the enjoyment of political rights. The immigrant had no place to which to turn but Tammany Hall. In part to assure to itself this vote the organization opened a bureau, a modest beginning of what became a colossal department. An office was established in the Wigwam, to which specially paid agents or organization runners brought the immigrant, drilled into him the advantages of joining Tammany and furnished him with

128

the means and legal machinery needed to take out his naturalization papers. Between January 14 and April 1, 1840, 895 of these men were taken before Tammany Marine Court Judges and naturalized. Judges of other courts helped to swell the total. Nearly every one of these aliens became and remained an inveterate organization voter. Tammany took the immigrant in charge, cared for him, made him feel that he was a human being with distinct political rights, and converted him into a citizen. How sagacious this was, each year revealed. Immigration soon poured in heavily, and there came a time when the foreign vote outnumbered that of the native-born citizens.[1]

The Whigs were bewildered at this systematic gathering in of the naturalized citizens. After the election of April, 1840,[2] when Tammany reelected Varian Mayor and carried the Common Council, the Committee of Whig Young Men [3] issued a long address on the subject. After specifically charging that prisoners had been marched from their cells in the City Prison by their jailers to the polls to vote the Tammany ticket, the address declared that during the week previous to, and on election-day, naturalization papers had been granted at the Marine Court on tickets from Tammany Hall, under circumstances of great abuse.

In the campaign of 1840 the so-called best elements of the town were for General Harrison. The Wigwam men had much at stake in Van Buren's candidature and exerted themselves to reelect him. Tammany now elaborated its naturalization bureau. A committee sat daily at the Wigwam, assisting in the naturalization process, free of charge

[1] The statement was made at a reform meeting in City Hall Park on April 11, 1844, that from 1841 to 1844 not less than 11,000 foreigners had been naturalized at $1 a head, though the legal fee was $5. The Judges, the speaker said on the authority of Judge Vanderpoel, signed their names to the papers without asking questions.

[2] This was the first election in the city occupying only one day. Before 1840 three days were used. The vote stood: Varian, 21,243; J. Phillips Phoenix (Whig), 19,622; scattering, 36; total, 40,901.

[3] The Whigs had formed committees in imitation of the Tammany organization.

to the applicant. The allegiance of foreign-born citizens
was further assured by humoring their national pride in the
holding of Irish, German and French meetings in the hall,
where each nationality was addressed in its own language.
The more influential foreigners were rewarded with places
on the Assembly or local ticket, and to the lesser workers
of foreign birth were given petty jobs in the department
offices, or contract work.

The outcome was, that in the face of especially strong
opposition Tammany harvested 982 plurality in the city
for Van Buren, though the vote of the Western counties
gave Harrison the electoral vote of the State.   It was such
instances as this — demonstrating its capacity of swaying
New York City even if the rest of the State voted op-
positely — that continued to give Tammany Hall a powerful hold on the Democratic party of the nation, notwithstanding the discredit that so often attached to Tammany
men and measures.

Another example of the change in the personnel of
Tammany was shown in the rise and progress of the " ward
heeler " and his " gangs."   The " gangs " were not conspicuous in 1841, when the organization elected Robert H.
Morris Mayor.[4]   In April, 1842, when Morris was reelected,[5] the " gangs " were still modestly in the background.   But in the Fall of that year they came forth in
their might.

One of their leaders was " Mike " Walsh, who became a
sort of example for the professional " ward heelers " that
followed in his wake.   Walsh had no claim at all on the
ruling politicians at the Wigwam, and would have been
unnoticed by them.   But he was ambitious, did not lack
ability of a certain kind, and had a retinue of devoted
" plug-ugly " followers.   He spoke with a homely elo-

---

[4] Election of 1841:   Robert H. Morris (Tammany), 18,605; J. Phillips Phoenix (Whig), 18,206; Samuel F. B. Morse, 77; scattering, 45;
total, 36,933.
[5] Election of 1842; Morris, 20,633; Phoenix, 18,755; total, 39,388.

quence, which captivated the poor of his ward. The turbulent he won over with his fists. On November 1 the
Tammany Nominating Committee reported to the great
popular meeting. Walsh, with the express purpose of
forcing his own nomination for the Assembly, went there
with such a band of shouters and fighters as never before
had been seen in the hall. His " shoulder-hitters "— men,
as a rule, of formidable appearance — did such hearty execution and so overawed the men assembled there, that
upon the question being put to a vote the general committee decided in his favor and placed his name on the regular
ticket. While in the ensuing election he received not quite
3,000 votes to the nearly 20,000 cast for his opponent (the
nominee first reported by the committee), he eventually was
successful in his aim. Seeing how easy it was to force
nominations at the Wigwam if backed by force, other men
began to imitate him and get together " gangs " of their
own.

This was the kind of men who, with their " gangs,"
superseded the former Democratic ward committees, nearly
every member of which kept a shop or earned his living in
some legitimate calling. By helping one another in intro-
ducing " gangs " of repeaters from one ward to another at
the primary elections, the " ward heelers " became the masters of the wards and were then graduated into leaders,
whose support was sought by the most dignified and illustrious politicians.

In fact, the city was frequently in a state of turmoil.
Since 1834 there had been half a dozen riots.[6] There were
constant fights between rival volunteer engine companies,
to which lawless and abandoned characters attached themselves. Engines were stolen, clubs, pipes, wrenches and
other weapons were used, and the affrays generally closed

[6] *Documents of the Board of Aldermen*, 1839, No. 29. The *Weekly
Herald*, February 15, 1840, stated that official documents showed, for
the previous ten months, a total of nineteen riots, twenty-three mur-
ders and nearly 150 fires, the latter involving a loss of about $7,000,000.

with stabbings and broken skulls.[7]   There was no police force to speak of ; even Mayor Morris, whom the " gangs " called " Bob " and tapped familiarly on the shoulder, described it as " lamentably defective." [8]   One out of every twenty-one white persons in the city could not read and write.[9]   From so large a population of illiterates, the " ward heelers " easily recruited great numbers of followers.   Morris allowed the " gangs " full sway, and was popular accordingly.   Naturally, with this encouragement, the " gangs " grew and became ever bolder.

General disgust at the low character of politics was felt by the independents, who rightly held both Tammany and the Whigs responsible.   During the time each party held power affairs had gone from bad to worse.   A joint special committee of Aldermen, appointed under public pressure, reported, in 1842, that dishonest office-holders had recently robbed the city of little short of $100,000.[10] A street cleaning contract was awarded for $64,500 a year, for five years, when other responsible persons offered to take it for not quite $25,000 a year.[11]   The fraudulent selling of city land to cover up the increasing debt was continued.[12]   The city office-holders sold real estate for unpaid assessments, frequently without giving notice to the owner, and bought it in themselves and so " possessed themselves of estates." [13]   Heavy and oppressive assessments for improvements never actually made were laid on the taxpayers.[14]   Hundreds of thousands of dollars were expended uselessly and extravagantly.[15]   Mayor Morris complained that he had no power over expenditures; that he knew nothing of legislative action on public works until

---

[7] See *Documents of the Board of Aldermen,* Vol. VIII, No. 35, and No. 41, 1843–44, for extended accounts.

[8] Mayor Morris's *Message,* July, 1842.

[9] *Documents of the Board of Aldermen,* Vol. VIII, No. 22.

[10] *Ibid.,* 1842–43, No. 5.

[11] *Ibid.,* Vol. IX, No. 69.   [12] *Ibid.,* Vol. X, part 1, No. 46.

[13] *Senate Documents,* 1842, Vol. IV, No. 100.

[14] *Ibid.*

[15] *Message* of Mayor Morris, 1843.

the warrants for payment were sent to him.[16]   In violation
of the charter, the Aldermen participated in all the profitable " jobs." [17]

Convicts were allowed to escape from Blackwell's Island
on condition that they voted as their keepers ordered
them.[18]   Prisoners whose terms had expired were kept at
the public expense until election day, to get their votes.
The inmates of the Almshouse and the Penitentiary were
forced to manufacture articles for the use and profit of the
officers of those departments.   " It is a well-known fact
to all who have been familiar with those establishments,"
declared the Almshouse Commissioners, " that large quantities of cabinet furniture, clothing and sometimes elegant
carriages, cut-glass decanters, punch-bowls, and other
articles have been made at the expense of the city ; and this
has been carried on more or less for years." [19]   It was the
custom of the officers " to expend large sums in sumptuous
and costly dinners for the entertainment of partizans."
Persons confined in the City Prison were frequently
swindled out of their money or effects by the officers, or
by " shyster " lawyers, acting in connivance with the jailers ; and to get a mere note or message delivered to friends
they had to pay an exorbitant price.[20]

Despite the disclosures, Tammany again elected Morris,
in April, 1843, by nearly 5,000 plurality, he receiving
24,395 votes to 19,516 for Robert Smith, the Whig candidate.   The storm, however, was gathering, both in and out
of Tammany.   Inside the organization, charges were common of monstrous frauds in the primaries.   Frauds
against the Whigs were acceptable enough, but by Democrats against Democrats were intolerable.   So pronounced
was the outcry over these frauds that the Tammany General Committee, in the Fall of 1843, directed that in future

---

[16] *Message* of Mayor Morris, 1843.   [17] *Ibid.*
[18] *Report of Commissioners of the Almshouse, Documents of the
Board of Aldermen,* Vol. XI, No. 40.   [19] *Ibid.:* 400.
[20] *Ibid.;* see also *Presentment of Grand Jury, Ibid.,* Vol. X, part 1,
No. 53.

the ward meetings should be held on the same night and that only those whose names appeared on the poll lists should be allowed to vote.[21]

Outside criticism materialized in an independent reform movement. It found a rallying point in the Native American or American Republican party, which previously had polled about 9,000 votes. It resented the intrusion of foreigners into politics, large numbers of whom had secured office. It was partially industrial in its character and following; numbers of American workingmen believed that with 100,000 immigrants [22] pouring into this country every year they would soon have to be satisfied with a shilling or twenty cents a day for their labor, instead of $1.50 they were receiving. The native element also complained of the organization of the Irish into a distinct and separate element, with a high Roman Catholic prelate at its head, in order to get part of the public school funds. The discussion of the public school question only the more accentuated hatreds, bringing to the surface the most delicate questions touching the religious feelings and prejudices of the major part of the community.

Tammany nominated Jonathan I. Coddington for Mayor, and placed very few naturalized citizens on its ticket. The Native American candidate was James Harper, and the Whig, Morris Franklin.

Mayor Morris called a meeting in Tammany Hall at which resolutions were passed denouncing the Common Council for its corruption and its failure to carry out reform. The advocates of the new party declared that they were not to be deceived. Their campaign was carried on with vigor. Honest men generally were roused against both Tammany and the Whigs. Religious and racial vituperation were partially cast aside and forgotten for

[21] About this time the general committee was enlarged. Until now the delegates had been selected from each ward. In 1843 the practise was begun of sending them from each election district.

[22] Sixty thousand of these entered the port of New York yearly. The total immigration rose to 154,000 in 1846 and to 427,000 in 1854.

the time when the reform men took hold of the movement;
not wholly so, however, for we find one of the chief native
orators declaring in a campaign speech that " the American Republicans will not be found with Roman Catholics
in the same ranks." This bigotry was overlooked, inasmuch as the Native Americans promised city reform, good
police, reductions in taxes, clean streets and economical
expenditure of the public money. The community was
pervaded by a profound sense of the corruption and inefficiency of the old parties, and ordinary political lines
were forgotten.

Tammany made desperate efforts to carry the election.
On the preceding night, convicts in batches of twenty and
thirty were taken from Blackwell's Island to New York,
where they were lodged, and the next day given Democratic
ballots, free lunch and in some instances were employed to
electioneer.[23]

The Native Americans won, however, the vote standing:
Harper, 24,606; Coddington, 20,726; Franklin, 5,207.

The new administration was a distinct disappointment.
Though it had a majority in the Common Council, it
accomplished few or none of the reforms its supporters had
promised. The scramble for office continued as before;
municipal improvements progressed slowly, and though salaries and appropriations were cut to some extent, taxes
and expenditures increased. A part of this increase was
doubtless justified, but the people had been promised reduction, and they refused to take into account the fiscal needs
of a rapidly growing city. The administration further
weakened its hold by passing and enforcing stringent " blue
laws." Not only were the unfortunate women of the
streets warred upon and quiet drinking places raided, but
irritating measures, such as the prohibiting of fireworks
on the Fourth of July and the driving of apple women and
other vendors from the streets, were taken. The result
was a public reaction.

[23] *Documents of the Board of Aldermen*, 1844-45, Vol. XI, No. 40.

Mayor Harper was a quaint character, and his odd rulings when presiding in Special Sessions were the talk of the town.   If a shoemaker, for instance, was arraigned before him, he would say: " Well, we want shoemakers on the island, so we'll send you up for three months, and be smart while you *last*, John, be smart."   Or, in the instance of a man who claimed to be " a sort of carpenter ":   " Well, we'll send you up for two months to round your apprenticeship, and the city will take care of your lodging and board, Matthew."

In the reaction that set in, many voters swung back to Tammany on the general belief that it was no worse than the other parties.   This change of sentiment put the organization in good form to carry the city for James K. Polk in November, 1844.   A short time before this there had come into distinction one of the most effective auxiliaries of the Wigwam.   This was the Empire Club,[24] of No. 28 Park Row.   Its chief was Captain Isaiah Rynders, and its membership was made up of a choice variety of picked worthies who could argue a mooted point to a finish with knuckles.   Rynders had a most varied career before entering New York politics.   A gambler in New Orleans, he mixed in some bowie and pistol fights there in which he was cut severely on the head and elsewhere, and his hat was perforated by a bullet.   On a Mississippi steamboat he drove O'Rourke, a pugilist, out of the saloon with a red-hot poker, after O'Rourke had lost at faro and had attempted to kill the winner.   These were but a few of his many diversions.   In Washington he was arrested with Breedlove and Jewell on suspicion of being connected with the theft of a large sum in Treasury notes, though no proof was found against him.   He was a very considerable

[24] Within a few months after its organization the Empire Club had thirty-three parades and had been hired to go to Albany, Trenton, Tarrytown and other cities to help the Democracy.   Whenever the Empire Club met a rival political club, a fight was sure to follow.

power in the Wigwam for over twenty years, frequently officiating at meetings there. Chief among the club's other members of like proclivities were such noted fighters and "unterrified Democrats" as "Country McCleester" (McClusky), "Bill" Ford, "Manny" Kelly, John Ling, "Mike" Phillips, "Bill" Miner, "Denny" McGuire, "Ike" Austin, "Tom" McGuire, "Tom" Freeman and "Dave" Scandlin. After the nomination of Henry Clay, "Johnny" Austin — a common report of the day had it — was offered the sum of $2,000 to bring himself and five of his associates — McClusky, Kelly, Ford, Scandlin and Phillips — into the Unionist Club (a Whig organization) with the hope that they could secure success to the Whigs in the city. Offices also were promised, but the offers were refused; whether because the Wigwam held forth greater inducements is not clear.

Aided by these worthies, and by the popular indignation against the reform administration, the Wigwam men grew confident. They were now heard boasting that they intended electing their entire ticket. There being no longer fear of the Registry law (which the Wigwam had recently influenced a friendly Legislature to repeal on the ground of its discriminative application to New York City alone), fraud was open and general. The vote on its face proved this; since, while New York City could claim a legitimate vote of only 45,000, the Polk electors were credited with 28,216, and the Clay electors with 26,870 votes. For James G. Birney, the Abolition candidate, but 118 votes were polled, or at least counted.

The Tammany General Committee, on January 13, 1845, passed resolutions favoring the annexation of Texas and calling a public meeting. With a view of glorifying John Tyler — to whom they owed their positions — and at the same time of winning the good will of the incoming administration, the Custom House officers tried to anticipate the committee's action, but were not allowed to use the hall.

Resolved, at any rate, to control the meeting regularly called, they crowded two thousand of their creatures, under the leadership of Rynders, into the Wigwam. The meeting was soon one of uproar, turbulence and some fighting. Rynders had his resolutions adopted " amid yells, shouts, screams, oaths, cheers, blasphemy, hisses and an uproar never before known in the pandemonium of politics." It was the generally expressed opinion that the time had come when the proceedings of a meeting at Tammany Hall were no longer to be considered as any certain indication of the opinions of the Democratic party; that a class of men who chose to organize themselves for the purpose, by being early on the ground, acting in concert and clamoring according to certain understood signals, could carry any set of resolutions they pleased, in the very teeth of the large majority of the Democratic party.

In the local campaign of 1845 Tammany acted sagaciously. It nominated William F. Havemeyer for Mayor, laying stress on the fact that he was a " native New Yorker." The Native Americans renominated Harper, and the Whigs, Dudley Selden. The vote stood: Havemeyer, 24,183; Harper, 17,472; Selden, 7,082. Tammany secured a majority of 26 on joint ballot in the Common Council — the real power.

Mayor Havemeyer sincerely tried to effect reforms. In the beginning of his term he urged the fact that the Common Council united in itself nearly all the executive with all the legislative power, and declared that its main business was to collect and distribute, through the various forms of patronage, nearly a million and a half dollars a year.[25] His attacks upon the arbitrary powers and corrupt practises of the Common Council made so little impression upon that body that on May 13, the very first day of convening, the Aldermen, immediately after the reading of the Mayor's message, removed not less than

[25] *Annual Message,* 1845.

seventy officials, from the heads of departments to Street Inspectors; [26] and on subsequent days the process was continued until every post was filled with a Tammany man.

But the effect upon the public mind was such that in 1846 a new charter was drafted and adopted, which deprived the Common Council of the power which it hitherto had enjoyed of appointing the heads of departments, and gave their election direct to the people.

Mayor Havemeyer not being pliable enough for the Wigwam leaders, they nominated and elected, in the Spring of 1846, Andrew H. Mickle, by a vote of 21,675, the Whigs receiving 15,111, and the Native Americans 8,301.[27] Mayor Mickle was regarded as " one of the people." He was born in a shanty in the " bloody ould Sixth," in the attic of which a dozen pigs made their habitation. Marrying the daughter of the owner of a large tobacco house, he later became its proprietor. He improved his opportunities, business and official, so well that he died worth over a million dollars.

[26] *Proceedings of the Board of Aldermen,* Vol. XXIX, pp. 1–55.

[27] Tammany won by a minority vote both in 1845 and in 1846. That neither Tammany nor the Native Americans had enacted any competent reforms in the matter of the taxation of property was conclusively shown in an Aldermanic report of 1846. It appeared from this report that thirty million dollars' worth of assessable property escaped taxation every year, and that no bona fide efforts were being made by the officials to remedy this state of affairs. *Proceedings of the Board of Assistant Aldermen,* Vol. XXIX, Document No. 24.

CHAPTER XVI

" BARNBURNERS " AND " HUNKERS "

1846–1850

TWO factions had lately arisen in Tammany Hall — the " Barnburners " and the " Hunkers." Differences in principle had at first caused the division, but it was characterized, nevertheless, by a lively race for office.

The " Barnburners " were the radical Democrats who believed, among other things that slavery should not be extended to free territory. The nickname was occasioned by the saying of a contractor, a few years before: " These men are incendiaries; they are mad; they are like the farmer, who, to get the rats out of his granary, sets fire to his own barn."

The " Hunkers " were the office-holding conservatives, very unwilling to have anything disturb their repose, and above all, opposed to the agitation of the slavery question. Their influence was thrown wherever possible with the slaveholding States. The term " Hunkers " arose from their characteristic of striving to keep their offices to the exclusion of everybody else —" to get all they can and keep all they can get." [1]

The quarrel was as sharply defined throughout the State as in New York City. Such men as Samuel J. Tilden, C. C. Cambreleng, William F. Havemeyer and Minthorne Tompkins were the local leaders of the " Barn-

[1] The Century Dictionary derives the word from the Dutch *honk*, post, goal or home. The transition in meaning from " goal " to " office " is easy and natural.

140

burners"; John McKeon, Lorenzo B. Shepard,[2] a brilliant young leader who was a noted orator at the early
age of 19; Edward Strahan and Emanuel B. Hart were
some of the chiefs of the "Hunkers." This factional
struggle, together with the dissatisfaction given by the
city administration, weakened Tammany, whose nominee,
in the Spring election of 1847, J. Sherman Brownell, was
defeated by the Whig candidate, William V. Brady. The
vote stood: Brady, 21,310; Brownell, 19,877; Ellis G.
Drake (Independent), 2,078. This was the first time in
nine years that the city had been carried by the Whigs
proper, though they were aided somewhat by the Native
Americans.

"Barnburners" and "Hunkers" laid aside their differences momentarily when President Polk visited the city
in June, 1847, one of his objects being to be initiated a
member of the Tammany Society. On June 26 he was
waited upon at the Astor House by a deputation of the
society, headed by Elijah F. Purdy. Quite worn out
after a torrid day of handshaking, Polk accompanied his
escorts to the large room in the Wigwam, where members
of the society were usually initiated. Later, the President emerged, looking happy at having availed himself
of membership in a political society which could sway
Presidential choices and elections and perhaps determine
his own future political fate.

This incident past, the factions resumed their quarrel
and warred so effectually that in the general election of
November, 1847, the Whigs again won, by more than
3,000 votes. But Tammany, in its darkest moments, was
fertile in expedients. It now arranged a great meeting
for February 5, 1848, in commendation of the Mexican
War. Sam Houston and General Foote made speeches,

---

[2] Shepard became Grand Sachem at an early age. He was one of
the very few influential men achieving prominence in the society or
organization against whose character, public or private, no charges
were ever brought.

and one of the Tammany orators assured the audience that though Tammany Hall "erred sometimes," its "patriotic ardor was never cooled." The success of this war brought thousands of voters back to the Democratic ranks in the city. Besides, "Barnburners" and "Hunkers" were tiring of defeat. Neither relished exile from office all the time. They agreed on the nomination of former Mayor Havemeyer, who personally was popular, though the Wigwam leaders had caused his administration to be discredited. Havemeyer was elected by the slender majority of 928 over the Whig candidate, Mayor Brady. The Native American party had now about gone out of existence.

But the factions soon disagreed again on national questions, and sent conflicting Tammany delegations to the national convention in Baltimore, in May, 1848. After tedious debate and much acrimony both were allowed a half vote to each delegate. When, however, it was seen that the "Barnburners" voted with some other States in support of the principle against the extension of slavery to free territory, a movement was started to reject them. The prospect of losing the all-important electoral vote of New York State was not pleasant to the convention. To avoid the arbitrary rejection of either faction the committee on credentials suggested a compromise by which it refused to open the discussion as to which faction ought to be accepted until both had pledged themselves to abide by the decision of the convention. Knowing that this would be pro-slavery, the "Barnburners" declared that "the Democracy of New York must be admitted unconditionally or not at all," and withdrew. The "Hunkers" took the required pledge.

Arriving home, the "Barnburner" delegates issued an address saying that a faction existed among them whose object was the perpetuation and the extension of human servitude. Bold, unscrupulous and active, it wielded to a great degree the patronage of the Federal Government.

It addressed itself to the fears of some, to the cupidity of others. By these means it had got possession of the late national convention and had proclaimed a candidate for the Presidency — a man who obtained his nomination only as the price of the most abject subserviency to the slave power. The " Barnburners " then took steps to name candidates in opposition to Lewis Cass and Gen. W. O. Butler, the Baltimore nominees, who had been promptly approved by the " Hunker " element in the Wigwam. Calling Martin Van Buren from obscurity, they nominated him for President, anticipating the action of the Free Soil convention at Buffalo in August.

Throughout the slavery agitation up to the firing on Fort Sumter, the South had no firmer supporter than Tammany. In the hall Southern representatives spoke and spread broadcast their doctrines on every available occasion; however ultra those doctrines might be, the Wigwam audiences never missed applauding them enthusiastically.

The " Hunkers " immediately opened a series of Cass meetings. " All the South asks," said Gen. Stevenson at one of them in Tammany Hall, on June 9, 1848, " is non-interference." He was cheered wildly. As usual, the " regular " Democratic nominations were supported by the backbone of the Democracy in New York City — those who clung to the mere name and forms of the party as well as the active men who lived in office and luxuriated on the spoils. The " Barnburners," otherwise now styled the Free Soilers, were quite as active as the " Hunkers," and their defection on election day enabled Gen. Taylor to carry the city — the supposed Democratic stronghold — by 9,883 votes.

The dissensions in the Wigwam were as pronounced in the Spring of 1849 — at least outwardly. The two factions held separate Mayoralty conventions on the same night. The " Barnburners " were naturally eager for Havemeyer, one of themselves, but he would not have the honor. Hearing that the "Hunkers" were proposing Myndert Van Schaick, an extremely popular man, the "Barnburners" resolved to steal the "Hunkers'" thunder by nominating him themselves. This they accordingly did, and the bewildered public was treated to the spectacle of Van Schaick standing as the candidate of both the recriminating factions. There were not wanting those who professed to see in this action an agreement between the leaders on the matter of the local offices. The Whigs elected Caleb S. Woodhull by 4,121 plurality, and secured over two-thirds of the members of the Common Council. The Democrats of the "Old School,"— the unyielding "Hunkers"— would not vote for a candidate the Free Soilers approved of; they either did not vote at all or voted for Woodhull.

The "Barnburners," practically driven out of Tammany Hall by the "Hunkers," had been meeting elsewhere. Tiring of defeats, however, overtures for reunion were made during the Fall campaign. A fusion resulted, not only in the city but in other parts of the State, and candidates were agreed upon.[3] But no sooner had the reunion been declared than a number of irreconcilable "Hunkers" and certain other politicians — including Daniel E. Sickles, James T. Brady, "Mike" Walsh and John M. Bloodgood — formed a self-constituted "Democratic-Republican Executive Committee" to oppose the deal. On the day before election they sent out a circular denouncing the fusion, and declaring that though it promised much it was really only a means of engrafting upon Democratic time-honored principles a set of aboli-

[3] New York *Weekly Herald,* November 3, 1849. James Gordon Bennett, editor and owner of this newspaper, "was a recognized member of the Tammany party." ("Memoirs of James Gordon Bennett and His Times," 1855, p. 80.) When Bennett first contemplated starting a newspaper, it was to the Young Men's General Committee that he applied for funds. Though professing to be independent, the Herald nearly always supported Tammany Hall. In 1837–39, however, it had supported Aaron Clark.

tion doctrines, "hostile to the peace and welfare of the Republic and repugnant to the sympathies and intelligence of the Democratic party." [4]

This circular was misleading. Neither the "Barnburners" nor the "Hunkers" had imposed any sacrifice of principle upon the other. They merely agreed for the time being to suspend their differences in order to get a controlling influence over the disbursement of municipal finances. The opinion of each voter on the slavery question was left untouched.

The election was hotly contested, for by the new State constitution the selection of minor State offices had been taken from the Governor and Legislature and given to the people. [5] Owing to this defection of a strong Tammany group the Whigs carried the city. The excitement in the Wigwam, when the result became known, was intense. Four thousand Tammany men, looking either for office or party triumph, were in a frenzy. W. D. Wallach, a politician of some note, mounted the rostrum, and under the stimulus of disappointment, held forth in a long and remarkable harangue, to which his auditors listened in comparative silence, though the same utterances at another time might have provoked a riot in the Wigwam. Men of downright dishonesty, Wallach said, had crept into the organization by the aid of bullies and loafers. These men of late years had managed to wield great power at Tammany primary elections, where, as everybody knew, matters long had been arranged "upon the assumption that by a free application of money, violence and roguery, the people could and should be controlled." What wonder was it, he asked, that thousands of quiet and respectable Democrats had ceased to bow to the authority of regular nominations, however

[4] The committee advertised the stand it had taken in the Democratic journals of the city on November 5.

[5] The city charter of 1846 had likewise increased the number of elective offices in the municipality.

worthy the candidates, when they found more or less of the Tammany nominating committees returned in part notoriously by violence, if not by fraud?

The breach between the " Barnburners " and the extreme " Hunkers " was reopened and widened by this self-constituted committee's action. It led to the formation of two bodies, each claiming to be the genuine general committee of Tammany Hall. One was led by Fernando Wood, who was suspected of being a " Hunker," but was too much of a politician to be active against the " Barnburners." This general committee was of a compromising disposition. In brief, it was composed mainly of what were known as political " trimmers "— men willing to make any sacrifices of principle for individual or party success. The other committee, of which Henry M. Western was the head, was composed of " Hunkers " and took up the interests of the self-formed " Democratic-Republican Executive Committee." It was the first body in the North to call a meeting to denounce the Wilmot proviso. To all intents standing for principle, each committee sought the tremendous advantages of the possession of Tammany Hall and its political machinery. By being recognized as the " regular " general committee, its nominations would be " regular " and as such would command the votes of the great mass of Democrats. To obtain that recognition both committees realized the necessity of obtaining a majority of the Council of Sachems, which, in critical moments, had so thoroughly demonstrated its legal right to eject from the Wigwam any man or body of men it pleased.

The opening struggle between the factions for mastery took place at the annual election of the society on April 15, 1850. Each body made desperate efforts to elect its list of Sachems. The ticket in favor of a union of the factions and of reorganizing the " Wood committee " was headed by Elijah F. Purdy, then Grand Sachem, and contained the names of Isaac V. Fowler, John A.

Bogert, John J. Manning and others. Former Mayor Mickle, Charles O'Conor, Francis B. Cutting and M. M. Noah led the rival ticket.

The " Hunkers " brought to the polls many men, who, though still members of the society, long since had gone over to the Whigs and had lost the habit of attending the society's meetings. These men claimed the right to vote, and it was unquestionably theirs. In law the Tammany Society was merely a charitable and benevolent corporation. No member in good standing could be debarred from voting. With cheerful alacrity these Whig members lent their aid in distracting the Democratic party into keeping up a double organization. Officeholders and other men openly attached to the Whig party voted.[6] When it seemed that most of the Purdy ticket was elected, the two " Hunker " inspectors suddenly found three more " Hunker " tickets in the ballot box. Previously this box had been examined, emptied and exposed publicly. These three ballots, if counted, would have elected one more Sachem of the " Hunker " stripe, giving that faction six of the thirteen Sachems — one short of a majority. The two " Barnburner " inspectors refused to count them. The result of the election being disputed, Purdy promptly took possession of the books and papers of the society.

As the best solution of the troubles, the Sachems, on April 26, determined to forbid both committees admittance to the Wigwam. The Sachems did not acknowledge accountability to any one for their actions, not even to the society which elected them.[7] Representing themselves as the supreme judges of which was the real Democratic General Committee or whether there was any,[8] the Sachems let it be understood that they would act as mediators. By a vote of 10 to 1,[9] they " recom-

6 New York *Evening Post* (Democratic), April 16, 1850.
7 New York *Weekly Herald,* May 4, 1850.   8 *Ibid.*
9 *Evening Post,* May 2, 1850.

mended "— an action equivalent to an arbitrary order
— that the "Wood committee" provide for the election
of delegates to a convention in Tammany Hall "to re-
organize the New York City Democracy." From the
substance of the invitation sent out by the society to
various conspicuous personages it was evident that,
though the "Wood committee" had been favored, somehow a majority of the "Hunker," or pro-slavery Sachems was installed.[10]

The plan of a convention was accepted by both factions. But by manipulating the primary elections for
delegates Fernando Wood succeeded in filling the convention with his own creatures, allowing, for form's sake,
a sprinkling of opponents. Wood, whose aim was to get
the nomination for Mayor, was the chief "trimmer,"
though each side made concessions. Various equivocal
resolutions touching the slavery question were adopted,
and a new Tammany General Committee, comprising
"Barnburners," mild "Hunkers" and ultra-"Hunkers,"
was formed.

The "Barnburners" and "Hunkers" then agreed
upon a coalition in State and city, uniting on Horatio
Seymour for Governor. Despite the diplomacy of Wood,
who had arranged this pact, an explosion was narrowly
averted a few weeks later. Finding themselves in a majority at a slimly attended meeting of the general
committee in the latter part of September, 1850, the
uncompromising "Hunkers" denounced parleying with
Free Soilers, and by a vote of 16 to 11 refused to sustain
Seymour. As soon as their action became known there

10 Seven Sachems signed the letter of invitation, which read in part:
"Brothers of this society look with deep concern at the present critical state of the country and are not unmindful of the services of those
who are laboring to thwart the designs of the fanatics and demagogues
who are waging an unholy crusade against a union of independent
sovereignties, which union has done much to advance and perpetuate
the principles of American liberty throughout the world. . . . We
have no sympathy with those who war upon the South and its institutions."

was a burst of indignation. The threat was made that
if the committee did not rescind it, the Council of Sachems, most of whom, it seems, Wood had won over to
his plans, would turn it out of Tammany Hall. The
members of the committee hastened to meet, the ultra-
" Hunkers " were routed, and the State candidates
strongly indorsed.

CHAPTER XVII

1850–1852

UNDER a new charter the Mayor's term was extended to two years, and the time of election, with that of the other city officers, was changed to November. The latter change gave great satisfaction to the leaders, for it enabled them to trade votes. Trading grew to such an extent that charges become common of this or that nominee for President, Governor, State Senator and so on being "sold out" by the leaders to insure their own election.

The Tammany organization, too, had made a change. It had adopted the convention system of nominating. This new method was much more satisfactory to the leaders, because the election of delegates to the conventions could easily be controlled, and the risk of having prearranged nominations overruled by an influx of "gangs" into the great popular meeting was eliminated.

A show of opposition to the proposed program was, however, still necessary. The first general convention was held in October, 1850. Fernando Wood was the leading candidate for Mayor, and it was certain that he would be nominated. But the first ballot showed a half-dozen competitors. The second ballot, however, disclosed the real situation, and Wood was chosen by 29 votes, to 22 for John J. Cisco.

Wood was a remarkable man. As a tactician and organizer he was the superior both of his distant predecessor Burr and of his successors Tweed and Sweeny. He was born in Philadelphia, in June, 1812, of Quaker parents. At the age of thirteen, he was earning $2 a week as a clerk. Later, he became a cigarmaker and tobacco dealer, and still later, a grocer. As a lad he was pugnacious; in a Harrisburg bar-room he once floored with a chair a State Senator who had attacked him. But he seems to have been amenable to good advice; for once when a Quaker reprimanded him for his excessive use of tobacco with the observation, " Friend, thee smokes a good deal," he at once threw away his cigar, and gave up the habit.

Coming to New York, he engaged in several business enterprises, all the while taking a considerable interest in politics. He was elected to Congress in 1840, serving one term. Gradually he came to make politics his vocation. Political manipulation before his day was, at the best, clumsy and crude. Under his facile genius and painstaking care, it developed to the rank of an exact science. He devoted himself for years to ingratiating himself with the factors needed in carrying elections.[1] He curried favor with the petty criminals of the Five Points, the boisterous roughs of the river edge, and the swarms of immigrants, as well as with the peaceable and industrious mechanics and laborers; and he won a following even among the business men. All these he marshaled systematically in the Tammany organization. Politics was his science, and the " fixing " of primaries his specialty; in this he was perhaps without a peer.

His unscrupulousness was not confined to politics. During this brief campaign he was repeatedly charged with commercial frauds as well as with bribery and dishonest practises at the primaries. A year later he was shown to have been guilty before this time of having

[1] Wood's was an attractive personality. He was a handsome man, six feet high, slender and straight, with keen blue eyes, and regular features. His manner was kindly and engaging.

defrauded a partner of $8,000, and he escaped conviction by the merest technicality.[2]

Political standards in the fifties were not high. But the rowdy character of a great part of Tammany's membership, and the personal character of many of its nominees, particularly that of Wood, proved too much to bear, even for those days, and a strong revulsion followed. Former Mayors Havemeyer and Mickle; John McKeon, a leader of note, and other prominent Democrats revolted. The election resulted in a Whig victory, Ambrose C. Kingsland securing 22,546 votes to 17,973 for Wood. A great Democratic defection was shown by the fact that Horatio Seymour carried the city by only 705 plurality.

So general were the expressions of contempt for the character of the Wigwam that the Sachems resolved to invoke again the spirit of patriotism, and consequently fixed upon a revival of the old custom of Independence Day celebrations. In 1851 the ruling Council of Sachems was a mixture of compromise " Barnburners " and " Hunkers." The committee of arrangements — Elijah F. Purdy, Daniel E. Delavan, Richard B. Connolly, Stephen C. Duryea and three others — sent invitations, filled with lofty and patriotic sentiments, to various national politicians. " Barnburners " also were invited, the conciliatory Sachems being sincerely tired of a warfare which threatened to exile them all from the sinecures of city and State offices.

The Society of Tammany, or Columbian Order, the

---

[2] Wood was charged with having obtained about $8,000 on false representations from his partner, Edward E. Marvine, in a transaction. Marvine brought suit against Wood in the Superior Court, and three referees gave a unanimous decision in the plaintiff's favor. The Grand Jury, on November 7, 1851, indicted Wood for obtaining money under false pretenses, but he pleaded the Statute of Limitations. A friendly Recorder decided that as his offense had been committed three years previously (on November 7, 1848), the period required by the statute had been fully covered. The indictment, therefore, was quashed, and Wood escaped by *one* day.

circular said, had originated "in a fraternity of patriots, solemnly consecrated to the independence, the
popular liberty and the federal union of the country."
Tammany's councils were "ever vigilant for the preservation of those great national treasures from the grasp
alike of the treacherous and the open spoiler." It had
"enrolled in its brotherhood many of the most illustrious statesmen, patriots and heroes that had constel-
lated the historic banners of the past and present age.
. . . And it remained to the present hour," the glowing
lines read on, "instinct with its primitive spirit and true
to the same sacred trust."

The rhetoric delivered at the celebration was quite as
pretentious and high-flown. But the phrases made no
impression on the public mind. No impartial observer
denied that the Wigwam's moral prestige with the State
and national party was for the time gone. Throughout the country the belief prevailed that the politicians
of the metropolis deserved no respect, merit or consideration; and that they were purchasable and transfer-
able like any stock in Wall street.

If before 1846 nominations were sold it was not an
open transaction. Since then the practise of selling them
had gradually grown, and now the bargaining was unconcealed. Upon the highest bidder the honors generally
fell. Whigs and Tammany men were alike guilty. If
one aspirant offered $1,000, another offered $2,000. But
these sums were merely a beginning; committees would
impress upon the candidate the fact that a campaign
costs money; more of the "boys" would have to be
"seen"; such and such a "ward heeler" needed "pacify-
ing"; a band was a proper embellishment, with a parade
to boot, and voters needed "persuading." And at the
last moment a dummy candidate would be brought forward as a man who had offered much more for the nomination. Then the bidder at $2,000 would have to pay
the difference, and if the office sought was a profitable

one, the candidate would be a lucky man if he did not have to disgorge as much as $15,000 before securing the nomination. Some candidates were bled for as much as $20,000, and even this was a moderate sum compared to the prices which obtained a few years later.

The primaries were attended by " gangs " more rowdy and corrupt than ever; Whig ward committees often sold over to Tammany,[3] and Whig votes, bought or traded, swelled the ballot boxes at the Wigwam primaries. Nearly every saloon was the headquarters of a " gang " whose energies and votes could be bought. In Tammany Hall an independent Democrat dared not speak unless he had previously made terms with the controlling factions, according to a relatively fixed tariff of rates. The primaries of both parties had become so scandalously corrupt as to command no respect.

The discoveries of gold in California and Australia created in all classes a feverish desire for wealth. Vessel after vessel was arriving in the harbor with millions of dollars' worth of gold dust. Newspapers and magazines were filled with glowing accounts of how poor men became rich in a dazzlingly short period. The desire for wealth became a mania, and seized upon all callings. The effect was a still further lowering of the public tone; standards were generally lost sight of, and all means of " getting ahead " came to be considered legitimate. Politicians, trafficking in nominations and political influence, found it a most auspicious time.

This condition was intensified by the influx of the hordes of immigrants driven by famine and oppression from Ireland, Germany and other European countries. From over 129,000 arriving at the port of New York in 1847, the number increased to 189,000 in 1848, 220,000 in 1849, 212,000 in 1850, 289,000 in 1851 and 300,000 in 1852. Some of these sought homes in other States,

[3] New York *Tribune*, May 5, 1852. (This admission on the part of a Whig journal caused a great stir.)

but a large portion remained in the city. Though many of these were thrifty and honest, numbers were ignorant and vicious, and the pauper and criminal classes of the metropolis grew larger than ever. The sharper-witted among them soon mended their poverty by making a livelihood of politics. To them political rights meant the obtaining of money or the receiving of jobs under the city, State or national government, in return for the marshaling of voters at the polls. Regarding issues they bothered little, and knew less.

The effects of the Whig and Native American denunciation of the alien vote were now seen. The naturalized citizens almost invariably sided with Tammany Hall, although there were times when, by outbidding the Wigwam, the Whigs were enabled to use them in considerable numbers.

Despite an unusual degree of public condemnation, Tammany managed, by a temporary pacification of the factions and a general use of illegal votes, to carry the city in the Fall of 1851 by nearly 2,000 majority. But it could not hold the regular Democratic strength, for Wright, the candidate for Governor, received over 3,000 majority. Frauds were notorious. In one of the polling places of the Nineteenth Ward, the Wigwam's candidates for Alderman and Assistant Alderman were counted in after a mob invaded it and forced the Whig inspectors to flee for their lives. When the votes for the Assembly ticket were counted 532 were announced, although there were only 503 names on the poll list. This was but an instance of the widespread repeating and violence.

With its large majority in the Common Council Tammany at first made a feint at curtailing city expenses. The taxpayers complained that the taxes were upwards of $3,500,000, for which there was little apparent benefit. The new Common Council made professions of giving a spotless administration; but before its term was over it had generally earned the expressive title of " the

Forty Thieves." [4]   This was the body that with lavish
promises of reform replaced the Whig Common Council.
William M. Tweed, an Alderman in the " Forty Thieves "
Common Council, was busy in the Fall of this year indignantly defending, in speeches and public writings, the
Aldermen from the numerous charges of corruption; but,
as will be seen, these charges were by no means ground-
less.

Since the passings of the Equal Rights party, the
mechanics and laborers had taken no concerted part in
politics, not even as a faction.   But at this period they
were far from being lethargic.   The recent discoveries of
gold and silver had given a quickened pulse to business.
enormously increasing the number of transactions and
the aggregate of profits.   The workers were determined
to have their share of this prosperity, and acted accordingly.   Old trade-unions were rapidly strengthened and
new ones formed.   More pay and shorter hours of work
were demanded.   Between the Spring of 1850 and the
Spring of 1853 nearly every trade in the city engaged
in one or more strikes, with almost invariable success.

Having now no sincere leaders to prompt them to concerted political action, the workers oscillated listlessly
between the two parties.   They had lost the tremendous
influence secured in the thirties, and the business element
had again become dominant.   Legislature and Common
Council vied with each other in granting exploitative
charters, and the persons who secured these, generally
by bribery, were considered the leaders of public opinion.
Every company demanding special privileges of the State
maintained its lobby at Albany.   The City Council was
more easily reached, and was generally dealt with personally.   Fortunes were made by plundering the city
and State, and while the conduct of the agents and actual
performers in this wholesale brigandage — the lobbyists,

[4] There was another " Forty Thieves " Council five or six years later,
which must not be confounded with the earlier and more notorious one.

Legislators and Aldermen — was looked upon somewhat doubtfully, their employers stood before the world as the representatives of virtue and respectability. The one force which might have stood as a bulwark against this system of pillage had been so completely demoralized by its political experiences that it could now only look on and let matters drift as they would.

In the Baltimore Democratic convention the Wigwam was represented by so boisterous a delegation that its speakers were denied a hearing. Among the delegates were Capt. Rynders, "Mike" Walsh and a number of the same kind. Cass was their favorite, and they shouted for him lustily; but on attempting to speak for him they were invariably howled down, despite the fact that Cass had a majority of the convention almost to the end of the balloting.

The Wigwam, however, lost no time in indorsing the nomination of Franklin Pierce. In this ratification the "Barnburners" joined, ardently urging the election of candidates on a platform which held that Congress had no power under the Constitution "to interfere with the domestic institutions of the States"; which advocated compromise measures, the execution of the Fugitive Slave law, and which opposed all attempts to agitate the slavery question.

The election of November, 1852, was not only for President and Congressmen, but for a long list of officials, city and State. Each of the Wigwam factions began playing for advantage. On July 16 a portion of the general committee met, apparently to accept an invitation to attend the funeral of Henry Clay. The "Barnburners," finding themselves in a majority, sprang a trick upon the "Hunkers" by adopting a plan of primary elections favorable to their side. Later the general committee, in full meeting, substituted another plan, and a great hubbub followed. A "committee of conciliation," composed of members of both factions, was appointed. When it met, on August 20, the halls, lobbies and entrances of Tammany Hall were filled with a vicious assortment of persons, chiefly inimical to the general committee. " The bar-room," wrote a chronicler, " was the scene of several encounters and knockdowns. It was only necessary for a man to express himself strongly on any point, when down he went, by the hammer-fist of one of the fighting men." Even members of the committee, while passing in and out of the room, were intimidated. Daniel E. Sickles was threatened with personal violence, and it might have gone hard with him had he not taken the precaution of arming himself with a bowie and revolver. Members' lives were constantly threatened; the scenes of uproar and confusion were indescribable. Mr. Sickles, for his own safety, had to jump from a window to Frankfort street, and other members were forced to retreat through secret byways.[5] It was near day-break when the factions consented to leave the Wigwam.

The anxiety of each was explained by the proceedings at the primaries. The faction having a majority of the inspectors secured by far the greater number of votes, and consequently the delegates who had the power of making nominations. At the primaries of August, 1852, fraud and violence occurred at nearly every voting place. In some instances one faction took possession of the polls and prevented the other from voting; in others, both factions had control by turns, and fighting was desperate. One party ran away with a ballot box and carried it off to the police station. Many ballot boxes, it was alleged, were half filled with votes before the election was opened. Wards containing less than 1,000 legal Democratic voters yielded 2,000 votes, and a ticket which not a hundred voters of the ward had seen was elected by 600 or 700 majority. Whigs, boys and pau-

---

[5] The *Herald*, which, as usual, supported Tammany this year, described (August 24, 1852) these violences in detail.

pers voted; the purchasable, who flocked to either party according to the price, came out in force, and ruffianism dominated the whole.

The police dared not interfere. Their appointment was made by the Aldermen and Assistant Aldermen, with the nominal consent of the Mayor, exclusively on political grounds and for one year. The policeman's livelihood depended upon the whims of those most concerned in the ward turmoils. A hard lot was the policeman's. On the one hand, public opinion demanded that he arrest offenders. On the other, most of the Aldermen had their " gangs " of lawbreakers at the polls, and to arrest one of these might mean his dismissal.[6] But this was not all. The politics of the Common Council changed frequently; and to insure himself his position the guardian of the peace must conduct himself according to the difficult mean of aiding his own party to victory and yet of giving no offense to the politicians of the other party. Hence, whenever a political disturbance took place the policeman instantly, it was a saying, became "deaf and blind, and generally invisible." [7]

The necessity of uniting to displace the Whigs from the millions of city patronage and profit brought the factions to an understanding. Jacob A. Westervelt, a moderate " Hunker," and a shipbuilder of wealth, who was considered the very essence of " respectability," and a contrast to Wood, was nominated for Mayor. Tammany planned to have its candidates swept in on the Presidential current. National issues were made dominant, and the city responded by giving the Pierce

[6] The political lawbreaker had a final immunity from punishment in the fact that Aldermen sat as Justices in the Mayor's Court, which tried such culprits, if ever they happened to be arrested.

[7] See Report of Chief of Police Matsell, *Documents of the Board of Aldermen*, Vol. XXX, part 1, No. 17. The extreme turbulence of the city at this time may be judged from the fact that, despite the comparative immunity of political lawbreakers, during the eight years 1846-54, 200,083 arrests were made, an average of 25,010 a year.

electors 11,159 plurality, and electing the whole organization ticket.[8] Fraud was common. No registry law was in force to hinder men from voting, as it was charged some did, as often as twenty times. On the other hand, 80,000 tickets purporting to be Democratic, intended for distribution by the Whigs, but not containing the name of a single Democrat, were seized at the post-office and carried in triumph to the Wigwam.

Tammany once more had full control of the city.

[8] The vote on Mayor stood: Westervelt, 33,251; Morgan Morgans, 23,719; Henry M. Western, 861; blank and scattering, 227; total, 58,058.

CHAPTER XVIII

THE "Barnburner"-"Hunker" factional fight was succeeded by that of the "Hardshells" and "Softshells." How the ludicrous nicknames originated it is not possible to say. The "Softshells" were composed of a remnant of the "Barnburners" [1] and that part of the "Hunkers" who believed in a full union with the "Barnburners," especially in the highly important matter of distributing offices. The "Hardshells" were the "Old Hunkers" who disavowed all connection with the "Barnburners," or Free Soilers, except so far as to get their votes. This division also extended to other parts of the State, where perhaps real differences of political principle were responsible for it; but in the city the fundamental point of contention was the booty of office.

The "Hardshells" boasted in 1852 of a majority of the Tammany General Committee which met on December 2 to choose inspectors for the ward elections of delegates to the general committee for 1853. The control of these inspectors was the keynote of the situation, for they would return such delegates as they pleased. Angered at the appointment of "Hardshell" inspectors, the "Softshells" broke in the door of the committee room, assaulted the members of the committee with chairs,

---

[1] Many of the "Barnburners" had finally broken with the Democratic party, and were now acting independently as Free Soilers. Afterward, in great part, these independents gravitated to the new Republican party.

fractured some heads and forced the " Hards " to flee for refuge to the Astor House.[2]

Agreeable to "usages," the departing general committee instructed the delegates of its successor to assemble in Tammany Hall on January 13, 1853, to be installed as the general committee for the ensuing year. Until this installation, the committee of the last year remained in power. In the interval the Sachems, who, in the peculiar mix of politics, were for the most part " Softshells," decided to take a hand in the game of getting control of the organization, and therefore called a meeting for the same night and at the same time.

The object of the old general committee was to allow only delegates whose seats were uncontested to vote on the organization, or the contest of seats, which would return a " Hardshell " committee. The Sachems, on the contrary, favored voting by those who had the indorsement of two of the three inspectors.

The " Hardshells " insisted that the Sachems had unwarrantably interfered; that this was the first time in the history of the society of any interference as to the manner of organizing the general committee; that the only power the Sachems had was to decide between contending parties for the use of the hall for political meetings, and that even then their power was doubtful.

The Grand Sachem ordered the doors of the meeting room locked till 7:30 o'clock, at which hour both factions streamed in. Soon there were two meetings in the same room, each with a chairman, and each vociferously trying to shout down the other. Neither accomplished anything, and both adjourned, and kept adjourning from day to day, awaiting positive action by the society.

The " Softshell " section of the general committee called a meeting for January 20, but it was prohibited by the Sachems. When doubt of their authority was

[2] This affair was exploited in the General Courts later. Seven rioters were arrested.

expressed, the Sachems produced a lease executed in 1842
to Howard, the lessee of the property, by the Tammany
Society, in which he agreed that he would not lease,
either directly or indirectly, the hall, or any part of the
building, to any other political party (or parties) whatever, calling themselves committees, whose general political principles did not appear to him or the Sachems
to be in accordance with the general political principles
of the Democratic-Republican General Committee of New
York City, of which Elijah F. Purdy was then chairman.
Howard had also agreed that

> " if there should be at any time a doubt arising in his mind or that
> of his assigns, or in the mind of the Grand Sachem of the Tammany
> Society for the time being, in ascertaining the political character of
> any political party that should be desirous of obtaining admission to
> Tammany Hall for the purpose of holding a political meeting, then
> either might give notice in writing to the Father of the Council of
> the Tammany Society, in which event it was the duty of the Father
> of the Council to assemble the Grand Council, who would determine
> in the matter and whose decision should be final, conclusive and
> binding."

Of the thirteen Sachems, eleven were " Softshells "—
a predominance due to the activity of the " Barnburners." The " Hardshells," without doubt, were in a majority in the Tammany Society and in Tammany Hall,
but they had taken no such pains as had their opponents to elect their men. The Sachems' meeting on January 20, professedly to decide the merits of the contest,
called for the ward representatives in turn. The " Hardshells " refused to answer or to acknowledge the Sachems'
authority to interfere with the primary elections of the
people. The Sachems then named by resolution the general committee they favored, thus deciding in favor of
the " Softshell " committee. There was no little suppressed excitement, since the members of the Tammany
Society, it was naïvely told, though allowed to be present, were not allowed to speak.

Alderman Thomas J. Barr, a member of the Tammany

Society and chairman of the " Hardshell " committee,
handed to the Sachems, on behalf of his associates, an
energetic protest. Summarized, it read as follows:

" Tammany Society is a private association, incorporated for charitable purposes. There is nothing in its charter, constitution or
by-laws making it a political organization in any sense of the term.'
The Democrats of New York City have never, in any manner or
by any act, vested in the society the right to prescribe the rules for
their government in matters of political organization.

" The society comprises among its members men belonging to all
the different political parties of the day. The only political test of
admission to membership is to be ' a Republican in favor of the
Constitution of the United States.' It is, besides, a secret society,
whose transactions are known only to its own officers and members,
except so far as might be the pleasure of the Council to make the
proceedings public. It can never be tolerated that a body which,
in the language of its charter, was created ' to carry into effect
the benevolent purpose of affording relief to the indigent and distressed,' and which is wholly independent of the great body of the
Democracy shall be permitted to sit in judgment upon the primary
organization of the Democratic-Republican party of the city of New
York; and such a state of things, if its absurdity be not too great
for serious consideration, would amount to a despotism of the most
repugnant character and render the Democratic party of the city an
object of contempt and ridicule everywhere. . . . Tammany Society
owns a portion of the premises known as Tammany Hall, which is let
to Mr. Howard and forms the plant of his hotel. This fact is all
that gives to the Tammany Society any, even the least political
significance.

" The general committee derives its powers from the people, who
alone can take them away. The committee in its objects, its organization and its responsibilities to a popular constituency is wholly
distinct from and independent of the Tammany Society, its council
or its officers, and to be efficient for any good purpose must always
so remain, leaving to the Tammany Society its legitimate duty of
excluding from Tammany Hall those who are hostile to the Democracy and its principles." [3]

In the bar-room many leaders of the excluded faction
were assembled, surrounded by their fighting men. When
the Sachems' adverse decision was announced, their anger
found vent in a sputter of oaths and threats, and the
sum of $15,000 was subscribed on the spot for the build-

[3] The statements of both sides were published officially in the New
York *Herald,* February 10, 1853, the bare facts covering more than an
entire page of solid print.

ing of a rival Tammany Hall. It is almost needless to
say that the rival hall was never built.

The Sachems later replied to the protest with the defense that their lease to Howard obliged them to act
as they did. By that lease the succession of Elijah F.
Purdy's committee alone was at liberty to meet as a
general committee in Tammany Hall; they (the Sachems)
had not recognized Barr's committee as such, and moreover did not admit the claim the " Hardshell " committee made of *their* right to hire a room separate from the
majority in a building in which they had no property
whatever. The Council of Sachems insisted that it had
exercised the right of excluding so-called general committees before; that Tammany was a benevolent society,
and that benevolent societies had the same right as others
to determine who should occupy their property.

The " Hardshells " attempted to rout the " Softshells "
at the regular meeting of the Tammany Society on February 12, but the Sachems' action was confirmed by a
vote of two hundred to less than a dozen. Each faction
then strained to elect a majority of the Sachems at the
annual election on April 18. Private circulars were distributed, that of the " Softshells " being signed by Isaac
V. Fowler, Fernando Wood, Nelson J. Waterbury, John
Cochrane and others. It breathed allegiance to the national and State administrations, the regular organization and to the Baltimore platform. The " Hardshell "
circular had the signatures of Richard B. Connolly, Cornelius Bogardus, Jacob Brush and others styling themselves the " Old Line Democrats."

The " Softshells " elected their ticket, and Isaac V.
Fowler, afterward postmaster, was chosen Grand Sachem.
This vote of a few score of private individuals decided
the control of Tammany Hall and the lot of those who
would share in the division of plunder for the next year.

" With the exception of some few quarrels," one
friendly account had it, " which fortunately did not result

in any personal damage to the disputants, the affair passed off very quietly. While the votes were counted upstairs some interesting scenes were presented in the bar-room, which was crowded with anxious expectants. Language of a rather exceptional character, such as ' political thieves,' ' swindlers,' etc., was employed unsparingly, but as the majority was peaceably inclined, there were no heads fractured."

CHAPTER XIX

A CHAPTER OF DISCLOSURES

1853–1854

NOW came an appalling series of disclosures regarding public officials. Acting on the affidavit of James E. Coulter, a lobbyist, charging that there was a private organization [1] in the Board of Aldermen formed to receive and distribute bribes, the Grand Jury, after investigation, handed down a presentment, on February 26, 1853, together with a vast mass of testimony.

"It was clearly shown," stated the presentment, "that enormous sums of money have been expended for and towards the procurement of railroad grants in the city, and that towards the decision and procurement of the Eighth Avenue Railroad grant a sum so large that would startle the most credulous was expended; but in consequence of the voluntary absence of important witnesses, the Grand Jury was left without direct testimony of the particular recipients of the different amounts." [2]

Solomon Kipp, one of the grantees of the Eighth and Ninth Avenue Railroad franchises, admitted frequently to a member of the Grand Jury that he had expended, in 1851, upwards of $50,000 in getting them. Five grantees of the Third Avenue Railroad franchise swore that upwards of $30,000 was paid for it in 1852 in bribes to both boards. [3] Of this sum Alderman Tweed received

[1] William H. Cornell, a sometime Sachem, was, according to the affidavit of Coulter, the head of this organization.

[2] *Documents of the Board of Aldermen*, Vol. XXI, part 2, No. 55.

[3] *Documents of the Board of Aldermen*, Vol. XXI, part 2, No. 55, pp. 1333–35, and p. 1573. See also *The History of Public Franchises*

$3,000. Chief among those who bribed the Aldermen were Elijah F. Purdy (one of the line of Grand Sachems) and Myndert Van Schaick, who only a few years before had been the Tammany candidate for Mayor. A franchise for a surface railroad on Broadway, with scarcely any provision for compensation and with permission to charge a five-cent fare, was given to Jacob Sharp, over five profitable bids from responsible persons. One applicant, Thomas E. Davies, had offered to give the city one cent for every fare charged. In another application, Davies, D. H. Haight and others had offered $100,000 a year and the payment of a license fee of $1,000 on each car (the prevailing fee being $20) for a ten-years' grant, on the agreement to charge a five-cent fare. There were two other offers equally favorable.[4] When Mayor Kingsland had vetoed the bill[5] the Aldermen had re-passed it, notwithstanding an injunction forbidding them to do so.[6]

Dr. William Cockroft had to pay, among other sums, $500 to Assistant Alderman Wesley Smith to get favorable action on his application for a lease of the Catherine Street Ferry. After the passage of the grant, Smith demanded $3,000 more, which Cockroft refused to pay.[7] Burtis Skidmore, a coal dealer, testified that in the Fall of 1851 James B. Taylor informed him that he had been an applicant for a ferry across the East River to Greenpoint, and that " he bribed members of the Common Council for the purpose of obtaining said grant, and that other applicants for the same ferry gave

in *New York City* by Gustavus Myers in which full details are given of the briberies attending the grants of the Eighth, Ninth and Third Avenue Railroad franchises, and other franchises.

4 *Proceedings of the Board of Aldermen,* Vol. XLVIII, pp. 530–37.
5 *Ibid.,* p. 532.
6 For violating this injunction one Alderman — Oscar W. Sturtevant (a Whig) — was sentenced to a nominal fifteen days in prison and to pay a fine of $350, and the other offending Aldermen were merely fined. The courts afterward annulled the Sharp franchise.
7 *Document No. 55,* p. 1219.

a larger bribe than he did, and obtained the grant, and
that all members of the Common Council whom he had
bribed returned to him the money he had paid them, with
the exception of Alderman Wood, who kept the money
from both parties." [8]

John Morrell swore that one of the applicants for the
lease of the ferry to Williamsburg applied to some of the
Aldermen and was told that it would cost about $5,000
" to get the grant through." But a Mr. Hicks, another
applicant, was so eager to " get it through " that he
gave more than $20,000. [9]

The lease of the Wall Street Ferry was similarly disposed of. Silas C. Herring testified that he with others
was told he could secure it by paying a certain Alderman $5,000. Herring declined. James B. Taylor was
another applicant, in 1852. He was informed that it
would cost him $15,000. He offered $10,000, but on
the same night " Jake " Sharp offered $20,000 and got
the grant. Taylor also testified that he additionally
applied for the Grand Street Ferry lease. Other parties,
however, paid more bribe money and obtained it, whereat
one Alderman said that " it was the damnedest fight that
was ever had in the Common Council; it cost them [Tay-
lor's rivals] from $20,000 to $25,000." [10]

The Aldermen extorted money in every possible way.
In defiance of the Mayor's veto they gave a $600,000
contract for the " Russ " street pavement, afterward
found to be worthless, and which had to be replaced at
additional cost. Russ had offered one Assistant Alderman $1,000 to help carry his election the next Fall if he
voted favorably. [11] Exorbitant prices were paid for land
on Ward's Island, several Aldermen and officials receiving for their influence and votes bribes of $10,000, and
others even larger sums. [12] The Common Council sold to
Reuben Lovejoy the Gansevoort Market property for

8 *Ibid.* p. 1310.   9 *Ibid.* p. 1403.   10 *Ibid.* pp. 1426-28.
11 *Document No. 55,* pp. 1575-76.   12 *Ibid.,* p. 1282.

$160,000 in the face of other bids of $225,000 and $300,-000. Lovejoy, who, it was disclosed, was merely a dummy for James B. Taylor and others, testified "that it would cost from $40,000 to $75,000 to get this operation — the purchase of the Gansevoort property — through the city government." [13]

A coal merchant had to pay money for a favorable vote on his application for a lease of the Jefferson Market property, and another merchant testified to having paid one Assistant Alderman about $1,700 to get a pier lease.[14] The Aldermen demanded and received bribes not only for passing measures but for suppressing them, and even invented many "strikes," as instanced by the case of Alderman Smith, who agreed for $250 to silence a resolution to reduce the Coroners' fees.[15] They demanded a share of every contract made by any city official, threatening, if it were not given, to stop his supplies and have his accounts investigated." [16] If a contractor or lessee refused to meet a "request," the Aldermen retaliated by imposing burdens upon him and reporting hostile resolutions.[17]

Applicants for the police force paid the Police Captains $40, and more to the Aldermen who appointed them. One man was reappointed Police Captain by Alderman Thomas J. Barr for $200, and another, assistant Captain for $100.[18]

Every city department was corrupt. It was found that one hundred and sixty-three conveyances were deeded

13 *Ibid.* p. 1445. In 1862 the Council resolved to buy back this same property for $533,437.50 and repassed the resolution over Mayor Opdyke's veto on January 3, 1863, thus, as the Mayor pointed out, entailing a new loss to the city of over $499,000, though the property had not increased in value. *Proceedings of the Board of Councilmen,* Vol. LXXXVIII, pp. 723-25.

14 *Document No. 55,* p. 1572.

15 *Document No. 55,* p. 1219.

16 *Ibid.,* pp. 1395-96.   17 *Ibid.,* pp. 1397-98.

18 *Documents of the Board of Aldermen,* Vol. XXII, No. 20, pp. 52-54.

to the Chief of Police, George W. Matsell, and his partner, Capt. Norris, in about a year.[19]   Matsell was mentioned also as receiving money from about one hundred
men who patronized the odious Madame Restell's establishment in Greenwich street.[20]   Both the police and
Aldermen collected money from saloons, though the Aldermen obtained the larger share, as they had the power
of granting licenses.

Within three or four years William B. Reynolds received over $200,000 from the city, under a five-years'
contract for removing dead animals, offal and bones,
though at the time the contract was made other persons
had offered to remove them free of expense, and one had
even offered to pay the city $50,000 a year for the ex-
clusive privilege.[21]   It was owing to Controller Flagg's
action that a contract to index certain city records at a
cost of between $200,000 and $300,000, despite the offer
of a well-known publisher to do it for $59,000, was can-
celed.[22]   Flimsy tenement houses, causing later much
fatality and disaster, were built in haste, there being no
supervisory authority over their erection.[23]   The lighting of the city was insufficient, thousands of oil lamps
still being used, and these, according to an old custom,
not being lighted on moonlit nights.[24]

Both Tammany and Whig Aldermen and officials were
implicated in these disclosures.   Such was the system of
city government that, though twenty-nine Aldermen were
at one time under judgment of contempt of court, and a
part of the same number under indictment for bribery,
yet under the law they continued acting as Judges in the
criminal courts.   According to Judge Vanderpoel, bribery was considered a joke.

A new reform movement sprang up, which quickly de-

[19] *Ibid.*, No. 43, p. 79.   [20] *Ibid.*
[21] *Documents of the Board of Aldermen*, Vol. XX, No. 32, and Vol.
XXII, No. 41.   [22] *Ibid.*, Vol. XXX, part 1, No. 16.
[23] *Ibid.*, Vol. XX, No. 5.   [24] *Ibid.*, No. 6.

veloped into the City Reform party. The reformers proposed, as a first step, to amend the charter. The granting of leases for more than ten years was to be prohibited, and the highest bidder was to get them. A two-thirds vote was to be required to pass a bill over the Mayor's veto. Work to be done and supplies furnished costing more than $250 were to be arranged for on contract to the lowest bidder. Any person guilty of bribery, directly or indirectly, was to be sentenced, upon conviction, to not above ten years in prison and fined not over $5,000, or both. The right to sit as Judges of the criminal courts was to be taken away from the Aldermen, as was also the power of appointing policemen. The Board of Assistant Aldermen was to be abolished, and a Board of Councilmen, consisting of sixty members, was to be instituted in its place, the collective title of the two boards to be " the Common Council." The Aldermen were to be elected for two years (as determined in the charter of 1849) and the Councilmen for one year. An efficient auditing· of accounts and claims against the city was called for, and only the more popular branch of the Common Council was to originate appropriations of money.

Tammany had grown suddenly virtuous again, and responding to the public clamor over the disclosures, had declared its devotion to pure government. At a " reform " meeting of the Young Men's Union Club, John Cochrane, one of Wood's lieutenants, who later announced that he would vote " for the devil incarnate if nominated by Tammany Hall," declared: " Reform is at home in Tammany Hall. Its birthplace is Tammany Hall." The purification movement advanced so unmistakably that Tammany approved the amendments, and the legislative bill embodying some of them was supported by the Tammany delegation in the Senate and Assembly.

The bill passed, and upon being submitted to the people

of the city, in June, 1853, was adopted by the significant vote of 36,000 to 3,000.

One of the benefits due to the City Reform party was the reorganization (1853) of the police under a separate department. The police were compelled to wear a uniform against which there had been bitter prejudice,[25] and the term of appointment was made dependent upon good behavior.

Fortunately for the City Reform party, the division between the " Hardshells " and " Softshells " extending throughout the State caused the nomination of separate Democratic tickets in the Fall of 1853. There seemed less than ever any vital difference between the professed principles of the two. Under the name of " National Democrats " the " Hardshells " met in City Hall Park on September 26, and resolved:

> " We regret that the Democracy of the city are prevented from holding this meeting in their accustomed hall. . . . The Democracy of the city waged in time past a successful war against a corporation which sought to control by money the political destinies of the country. We now from this time forward commence a campaign against another corporation known as the Tammany Society — a secret, self-elected and irresponsible body of men who have dared to usurp the right of determining who shall and who shall not meet in Tammany Hall. . . . The accidental ownership of a small equity of redemption of a small part of the ground upon which Tammany Hall stands may continue to enable the Sachems to prevent the Democracy from meeting within the hall, but we can meet in the park or in the open air or elsewhere."

The City Reform party nominated acceptable Whigs and Democrats pledged to reform, and obtained a decisive majority in the next Common Council.

25 The general extent of this prejudice may be judged from the fact that at this time a number of suits were pending in the courts, seeking to restrain the city from enforcing an earlier order compelling uniforms to be worn.

CHAPTER XX

THOUGH the City Reform party brought about some beneficial changes in the system of city government, its Common Council did not meet public expectations. The *Tribune*, the chief supporter of the party, admitted this (May 3, 1854), declaring that much feeling was manifested over the failure of the reformers to realize the public hopes, and attributing the failure " to the power of those representing the great political parties in the two boards to league together and sell out to each other the interests of the city as partizan or personal considerations might dictate."

Accordingly, preparations were made to overthrow the new party. Fernando Wood now secured the " Softshell " nomination for Mayor, by packing the convention with his henchmen. The " Hardshells " held a separate convention, which ended in a row, a part nominating Wood, and the rest Augustus Schell.

Wood successfully intrigued to cause the Whigs to separate from the City Reformers; and to further divide the opposition, Tammany nominated sham reformers for the lesser city and State offices. The Whigs nominated for Mayor, John J. Herrick; the City Reformers, Wilson G. Hunt, and the Native Americans, or " Know-Nothings," springing to life again, put forward James W. Barker. Schell, Wood's Tammany opponent, withdrew in favor of Hunt.

The disreputable classes, believing that his success

meant increased prosperity to themselves, energetically
supported Wood, and the liquor-dealers formally com-
mended him. In the city at this time were about 10,000
shiftless, unprincipled persons who lived by their wits
and the labor of others. The trade of a part of these
was turning primary elections, packing nominating conventions, repeating and breaking up meetings. Most of
these were Wood's active allies.

He needed them all on election day. With every re-
source strained to the utmost, he won by a close margin.
He was credited with 19,993 votes; Barker with 18,553;
Hunt, 15,386, and Herrick, 5,712. Tammany, therefore,
succeeded, though in a minority of over 17,000 votes.

Upon assuming office, Wood surprised his followers by
announcing that he would purge all offices of corruption
and give good government. His messages were filled with
flattering promises and lofty sentiments. At the outset
he seemed disposed for good. He closed the saloons on
Sunday, suppressed brothels, gambling houses and rowdy-
ism, had the streets cleaned, and opened a complaint book.
The religious part of the community for a time believed
in him. He assumed personal charge of the police, and
when a bill was introduced in the Legislature to strip him
of this power, the foremost citizens called a mass meeting
to support him.

The troubles between the " Hardshells " and " Softshells " continued throughout the year 1855. When the
latter held their county ratification meeting in the Wigwam and the name of their nominee for Street Commissioner was announced, the " Hardshells," who had come
thither with a nominee of their own, raised an uproar,
whereupon " the factions on both sides went to work and
pummeled each other pretty soundly and highly satisfactorily to the lookers, for at least ten minutes."

The election of 1855 was of little consequence. All
eyes were now turned to the coming contest of 1856.
Before the end of a year Wood had begun to reveal his

real nature. Many of the decent element that had for a time believed in him began to turn against him. He had also made himself unpopular with certain powerful Sachems by not giving them either a share, or a large enough share, in the spoils. His appointments were made wholly from a circle of personal friends who were more attached to him than to the Tammany organization. Knowing the folly of expecting a renomination from Tammany, as it was then constituted, he set about obtaining it by trickery.

Inducing Wilson Small, a Custom House officer holding a seat in the general committee, to resign, Wood had himself substituted. Then he personally assumed control of the primary election inspectors in every ward, so as to manipulate the election of convention delegates. He caused the appointment of an executive committee, which was to have the entire choice of inspectors in every instance in which the general committee failed to agree. This new committee was composed mainly of his friends, and he named himself chairman.

His henchmen incited divisions in such of the wards as were not under the control of his inspectors, and the contests, upon being referred to the " executive committee," were of course decided in Wood's favor. Thus he appropriated a great majority of the delegates to the nominating convention.

" It is well known," wrote Peter B. Sweeny and J. Y. Savage, secretaries of the Tammany General Committee, in a long statement denouncing Wood's thimble-rigging " that for many years this [primary] system has been degenerating until it has become so corrupt as to be a mere machine in the hands of unprincipled men, by which they foist themselves before the people as the nominees of a party for office in defiance of public sentiment." [1] Sweeny and Savage charged further than when the

[1] This statement was published officially in the New York newspapers, September 27, 1856.

primary elections took place under this patent process for cheating the people, the ballot boxes were stuffed and detachments of police were stationed at every poll to aid Wood's agents and bully his opponents. A sickening mass of evidence of corruption was at hand, Sweeny and Savage recounted.

Wood was renominated by the city convention, and at an hour when most of his opponents on the general committee were absent, he had that body endorse his nomination by a vote of 56 to 26, nearly all of those voting being office-holders by his grace.

He also arranged a reconciliation between the "Hardshells" and "Softshells." With a show of traditional Tammany custom, the "Softs" marched in Indian file to the Stuyvesant Institute, the headquarters of the "Hards," and the reunited leaders marched back to Tammany Hall — in pairs, arm-in-arm. The "Hardshell"-"Softshell" contention thus became a thing of the past.

But Wood's personal enemies in the Wigwam were not to be appeased, and they nominated a candidate to oppose him — James S. Libby. Bitter feelings were aroused. At the Wood ratification meeting in the Wigwam, October 22, both Wood and Anti-Wood men crowded in, and then ensued another of those clashes for which Tammany Hall had become so celebrated. When John Kelly mentioned Wood's name the Anti-Wood men raised a din and smothered the speaker's voice. The Wood men, growing enraged, " pitched into the Anti-Woodites hot and heavy, and for a time a scene of the wildest clamor ensued. A general fight took place in front of the speaker's stand and all round the room. Blows were given and exchanged with great spirit, and not a few faces were badly disfigured." After a few planks had been plucked from the stand and wielded with telling effect, the Wood men won. " The great body of the Libbyites were kicked out of the room and down the stairs with a velocity proportionate to the expelling force behind."

The City Reform party was far from being satisfied with Wood's administration. In fact, it is no exaggeration to say that by the time of his second year in office the blackness of his administration exceeded anything known before. Seasoned men fancied they knew something of corruption, extravagance and malfeasance in the City Hall, but by 1856 they better understood the growth of these under a reckless and unprincipled Mayor.

The saloon power had grown until it controlled the politics of the city. In every groggery could be found a crowd of loafers and bruisers who could always be relied upon to pack a primary or insure or defeat the election of certain nominees. In these saloons the ward politicians held their meetings, and the keepers were ready at all times to furnish persons to parade, carrying partizan banners they could not read, or to cheer at mass meetings at the drop of a handkerchief. The saloon-keepers also furnished cheap illegal voters, ballot-box stuffers and thorough-bred "shoulder-hitters," to intimidate peaceable citizens, or as a last resort, to smash the ballot boxes.

The saloon-keepers were largely above the law. A disingenuous bill, passed in 1855, ordered the saloons to be closed on Sunday, but made no provision for enforcement. They were accordingly kept open, likely enough through assurances from Wood that the owners would not be molested. Their support of the Mayor was well-nigh unanimous.

It was the domination of politics by this element that caused great irritation and disgust. But the opposition to Wood was hopelessly divided. It had to contend, moreover, with the adverse factor of the introduction into the campaign of national issues. The fear of the new Republican party was sure to bring out a heavy vote for Buchanan and Breckinridge, and on the strength of this wave Tammany reasonably expected to be again swept into power.

The City Reformers had greatly declined in numbers,

but they again came forward for the contest, nominating
Judge James R. Whiting.[2]   The Native American party,
still maintaining its bitterness against the control of pol-
itics by foreigners, chose Isaac O. Barker, and the Whigs,
Anthony J. Bleecker, making, with Wood and Libby, five
Mayoralty candidates.

Though backed by the dregs of the city on the one
hand, Wood did not neglect to secure some " respectability " on the other.   During the campaign he received
a testimonial signed by some of the leading bankers and
merchants, praising him and his administration and expressing the hope of his reelection.   Nearly all of the
signers, it was afterwards disclosed, profited by Wood's
placing of city funds or buying of city goods.

Wood sought to force every man on the police force to
subscribe to his election fund, one policeman, who refused
to contribute, being kept on duty twenty-four hours at a
stretch.   From this source alone he gathered in from
$8,500 to $10,000.

On election day the scum of the town shouted, repeated
and bruised for Wood.   Candidates were traded openly,
and bribing was unconcealed.[3]   The majority of the policemen were off on furlough, given by the Mayor as head
of the Police Department, assisting actively for his reelection.   At the polling places, so terrific was the competition for the millions of city plunder, that the Wood

[2] Whiting, according to the testimony of James Perkins, before the
Senate Investigating Committee in 1833, had been the chief lobbyist in
the task of securing the notorious Seventh Ward Bank charter in 1831.
It is a striking commentary on political standards of the day that
unrebutted charges of such a nature formed no bar to the advancement of a politician to such distinctions as those of Judge, District
Attorney and reform candidate for Mayor.

[3] Josiah Quincy related, in a lecture in Boston, that while in New
York City on this election day, he saw $25 given for a single vote for a
member of Congress.   Upon expressing his surprise, Quincy was told
that this man could afford to pay it.   If reelected, it would be a
money-making operation.   He had received $30,000 at the last session
for " getting a bill through," and at that rate could afford to pay a
good price.

and Anti-Wood men fought savagely. In the Sixth
Ward the Wood partizans, upon being attacked, retreated
for the while, and coming back, armed with brickbats,
clubs, axes and pistols, set upon and routed their foes.
The police meanwhile calmly looked on, until the riot was
at its height, when they made a show of concern by firing
fifteen or more shots, all of which fortunately went
astray. The Wood partizans then broke the ballot boxes
to pieces and carried off the fragments for kindling wood.
In the Seventeenth Ward the Anti-Wood men destroyed
some of the Wood boxes; and in the First, and most of
the other wards, the day was enlivened with assaults, riots
and stabbings.

The count of the vote gave Wood, 34,860; Barker,
25,209; Bleecker, 9,654; Libby, 4,764, and Whiting,
3,646. The Buchanan electors carried the city with
41,913 votes; Fillmore, the American candidate, and Fremont, Republican, were allowed respectively 19,924 and
17,771 votes. Tammany Hall obtained a serviceable majority in the Common Council.

The Republicans maintained that 10,000 fraudulent
Democratic votes were cast in New York City and Brooklyn, and credited Wood with having profited by the most
of those cast in this city. It was not an unreasonable
contention, in view of the enormous increase over the vote
of two years before.

A few days after the election a meeting in Tammany
Hall, called to celebrate Buchanan's triumph, resolved
that next to the success of Buchanan and Breckinridge,
" the brightest and most signal achievement of the Democratic party, at this election, was the triumphant election
of Fernando Wood! "

CHAPTER XXI

U NDER Wood's second administration city affairs went from bad to worse. The departments reeked with frauds. The city paid Robert W. Lowber $196,000 for a lot officially declared to be worth only $60,000 and to two-thirds of which, it was proved, Lowber had no title. Controller Flagg charged that both the Mayor and the Common Council were parties to it.[1] Fraudulent computations and illegitimate contracts were covered by false entries.[2] Amounts on the ledger were revised so as to steal considerable sums from the city outright.[3] To Bartlett Smith had been awarded a contract for grading certain streets. Before beginning work, however, the Legislature created Central Park out of that very territory.[4] Smith demanded $80,000 from the city " for trouble in arranging to do the grading "—

[1] *Documents of the Board of Aldermen*, 1859, No. 16. The courts decided later in favor of Lowber. As Controller Flagg refused to pay the claim on the ground of no funds being " applicable," Lowber caused the Sheriff to sell at auction, in October, 1858, the City Hall with its equipment and paintings to satisfy a judgment of $228,000, including damages, costs and interest. Mayor Tiemann bid the City Hall in for the sum of $50,000, and turned it over to the city when reimbursed. *Documents of the Board of Alderman*, 1859, Vol. XXVI, No. 1.

[2] *Ibid.*, Vol. XXIII, No. 42; also *Ibid.*, Vol. XXV, No. 10.

[3] *Ibid.*

[4] The Act was passed July 21, 1853. This was one of the very few public-spirited measures of the time. Tammany, however, immediately began to utilize the measure, through contracts for the clearing and improvement of the park, to the profit of its leaders and followers.

a claim the Common Council allowed, but Flagg refused to pay.

It was generally charged that Wood sold the office of Street Commissioner to the notorious Charles Devlin [5] for $50,000 cash, with certain reservations as to the patronage and profits. Devlin recouped himself; for an investigation revealed that he spent half a million dollars on contracts of which he was either the real contractor or surety, and on which he made the prices 75 per cent higher than they ought to have been.[6] Of how much the city was plundered it was impossible to find out, since no reliable accounts of expenditures were kept in the Finance Department.[7] Not a few officials, relinquishing offices paying about $2,500 a year, retired loaded with riches and surrounded by friends whom they had enriched. Wood himself was now reputed to be worth $400,000.

Even the Judiciary was held in general contempt. The Lowber fraud (see previous page) was promptly excused and the defendant exonerated by the courts. In November, 1855, a City Judge was tried for corruption in having entered a *nolle prosequi* in a certain case. The verdict was " not guilty," with this remarkable addition: " And the jury are unanimously of opinion that in the entry of the *nolle prosequi* by the City Judge he has been guilty of irregularity, and it is the unanimous recommendation of the jury that Judge ———— resign." He resigned.[8] In December, 1855, during a trial for murder in the Supreme Court, counsel for the defendant exclaimed: " I know the jury have too much intelligence

5 Devlin was appointed by Mayor Wood to succeed Joseph S. Taylor, deceased. At the same time Daniel D. Conover was selected for the post by the Governor, who claimed the right of appointment. The Mayor used inflammatory language, a turbulent mob gathered, and the militia had to be ordered out to prevent serious violence between the partizans of each. (*Assembly Documents*, 1858, No. 80.) The courts later decided in favor of Devlin.

6 Devlin was removed from office by Mayor Tiemann in April, 1858.

7 *Report of Special Common Council Committee*, October 22, 1857.

8 *Harper's New Monthly Magazine*, November, 1856.

to pay any regard to the assumptions of the Court." [9]
A man was killed at a prize fight. The Coroner, after
stating the evidence at the inquest, concluded: "If the
persons implicated are tried before our Court of Sessions
they will have reason to congratulate themselves, as it is
a difficult matter in this city to convict a person charged
with any other crime than theft." [10] In January, 1856,
the seat of one of the Judges of the Supreme Court was
contested by two candidates, both claiming to have been
elected by popular vote. Both asserted the right to sit;
in opposition to the opinions of the Judges sitting, one
of the contestants took and kept his seat by pure
" nerve." [11]

A new city charter, adopted in 1857, changed the date
of municipal elections to the first Tuesday in December,
and provided for an election for Mayor and Common
Council in December, 1857. The change was aimed
partly at Wood. He had probably expected severe opposition of some kind, for he had early begun planning for
the continued control of the Tammany General Committee, so as to secure a renomination.

In the primary elections, late in 1856, for delegates to
this committee for 1857, a majority favorable to Wood
had been elected, after violence and ballot-box stuffing in
every ward. The Wood men took possession of the Wigwam and elected Wilson Small chairman. The rival
party met in another place and organized a general committee. Each put forward the claim of " regularity."

As the " usages " of the party required that the " regular " committee should have legal possession of Tammany Hall, it was necessary to determine which that committee was. Then the Sachems stepped in. Seven of
them — a majority of one — were Wood's personal enemies. By a vote of seven to five the Sachems concluded
to order the election of a new general committee, which

[9] *Ibid.*   [10] *Ibid.*   [11] *Ibid.*

was to have all known Democrats enrolled into associations.

"Tammany Society," said the "seven Sachems'" report,

"is the undisputed owner of Tammany Hall; and the right to control the use of that building which is inherent in its ownership has been fully secured by the lease. The Council is determined that their action shall vindicate fully the rights and powers of the venerable society of which they are officers; and also, prove a safe and efficient barrier against the tide of corruption and fraud which is sapping the power of the great party to which the society has adhered during the whole period of its existence."

At the society's annual election, on May 20, the Isaac V. Fowler, or "reform" ticket, had the names of some men of note — Samuel J. Tilden, Elijah F. Purdy, Peter B. Sweeny, Edward Cooper, William H. Cornell, John McKeon and Emanuel B. Hart — while Wood's candidates were inferior hack politicians and nonentities. The "seven Sachems" had previously managed to get into the Wigwam unobserved by the Wood men, and had rapidly elected nearly sixty new members, all their own partizans, to the society.[12] These voted at the election, enabling Wood's opponents to beat him by a majority of sixty.[13] Then the "seven Sachems" turned Wood and his men out of the Wigwam.

In a public address, the Wood men thereupon declared the society an irresponsible body of less than four hundred members, one-third of whom held no communication with the Democratic party, and that of its thirteen Sachems seven were "Libby bolters." "What, then, is the issue?" asked the address. "Shall the Sachems rule

[12] Statement to the author by Douglas Taylor, one of the "seven Sachems."

[13] Of this action Talcott Williams (*Tammany Hall*, G. P. Putnam's Sons, 1898) says: "For the first time, the Tammany Society, which is only the landlord of the political body which leases its hall, exercised its singular power of deciding between rival organizations." This, of course, is a decided error. Repeated instances of the activity of the society in this direction have been given in this work.

the people; or shall the people rule themselves? Shall the Sachems of this close corporation, to procure offices for themselves and friends, be permitted, unrebuked by. the people, to exercise this omnipotent, dictatorial, supervisory power over the great Democratic party, its organization and interests, to rule out or rule in your general committees whenever it suits their caprice or selfish purposes?"

The control of the police force was considered as necessary as ever to success at the election. The changes of 1853, from which much was hoped, had proved of little benefit. The force was in a chaotic state. Political and pecuniary reasons alone guided the appointment of policemen. No record of merit was kept; there was no systematic instruction of policemen in their duties except as to drill. Some Captains wore uniforms, others refused. When an applicant appointed to the force was tested for qualifications in reading, a large newspaper was given to him, and he was told to read the title. Murder abounded, and the city was full of escaped convicts.[14] One of the most important provisions of a special act of 1857 was the transfer of the police from city control to that of the State. Unwilling to surrender so effective a hold, Wood resisted the Legislature's action. For a time there were two police departments — the Metropolitan force, under the State Commissioners, and the municipal police, under the Mayor — each contending for supremacy. One day a part of the two forces came into collision in the City Hall, and twelve men were wounded. It was found necessary to summon the militia to quell the disturbances, and Wood was arrested. Finding resistance useless, he submitted grudgingly to the new order.[15]

The police being so disorganized, the criminal classes

14 *Assembly Documents*, 1857, II, part 2, No. 127.
15 *Assembly Documents*, 1858, No. 80. The chaos produced during this dispute was extreme. Members of one force would seize and liberate prisoners taken by the other force, combats were frequent, and peaceable citizens were often unable to secure protection.

ran the town. Chief among Wood's supporters were the
" Dead Rabbits " or " Black Birds,"— a lawless " gang "
who overawed certain portions of the city and who had a
rival in the " Bowery Boys," whose sole profession seems
to have been to pack primaries, break ballot boxes and
fight the " Dead Rabbits." On July 4, 1857, the " Dead
Rabbits," presumably having nothing else to do, attacked
a body of police in Jackson street. A band of " Bowery
Boys " hurried to the front, and a pitched street battle
ensued, pistols and muskets being procured from neighboring places. Barricades were thrown up in the most
approved Parisian style. The result was the killing of
ten and the wounding of eighty persons, some of whom
were innocent bystanders. This was the most deadly of
the numerous collisions of these " gangs." As they had a
powerful political influence, the police did not molest
them.[16]

As a member of the Metropolitan Police Commission,
Mayor Wood about this time was instrumental in giving
out a contract for 4,000 glass ballot boxes, at $15 apiece.
It was disclosed in James Horner's affidavit before Judge
Davis, in the Supreme Court, in November of this year,
that the city needed no more than 1,200 of the boxes;
that Wood's brother had secured the 4,000 boxes at a
cost of less than $5 apiece and that the Mayor was to
share in the $40,000 of expected profits.

Wood neglected no means of ingratiating himself with
the masses. The panic of 1857 suddenly deprived over
30,000 mechanics and laborers in the city of employment.
Wood proposed the employment of the idle on public
works, and the buying by the city of 50,000 barrels of
flour and an equal amount of other provisions to be disposed of to the needy at cost.[17] The Common Council
failed to see the value of this plan, but did appropriate a
sum for public works in Central Park, the better share of

[16] This riot is briefly treated in Document No. 80.
[17] *Proceedings of the Board of Alderman*, Vol. LXVII, pp. 157–60.

which went to contractors and petty politicians. To win the good will of the Roman Catholics, becoming more and more a power, the Common Council gave over to the Roman Catholic Orphan Asylum a perpetual lease of the entire plot from Fifth to Fourth avenue, Fifty-first to Fifty-second street, at a rental of $1 a year.[18]

So resourceful was Wood and so remarkable his political ingenuity that though he and his general committee were driven out by the Tammany Society, he nevertheless brought things about so that the Democratic convention in Tammany Hall, on October 15, renominated him for Mayor, by 75 votes to 12. The Tammany General Committee thereupon openly repudiated him, and the curious complication was presented of a candidate who was the Tammany " regular " nominee, yet opposed by both the society and the general committee.

Instantly a determined citizen's movement to defeat him sprang up. The city taxes had nearly doubled in the three years of Wood's administration and were now over $8,000,000, of which over $5,000,000 had already been signed away in contracts or spent in advance of collection. Yet the Common Council had recently resolved to spend the exorbitant sum of $5,000,000 on a new City Hall. The Mayor vetoed the resolution only when the most intense public opposition was manifested.

A committee of citizens, representative of the Republicans, Democrats and Native Americans, nominated Daniel F. Tiemann, a paint dealer, and a member of Tammany Hall, but who was an Alderman and as Governor of the Almshouse had made a good record.

To Wood's support there concentrated the preponderance of the foreign born, the native rowdies and the usual mass blinded into voting for the " regular " ticket. The gamblers, brothel-keepers, immigrant runners and swindlers of every kind bought and cheated for him in the be-

18 *Ibid.*, Vol. LXVIII, p. 140.

lief that the reformers would drive them from the city. Wood had taken the precaution to manufacture thousands of voters. From the Wigwam, where the Wood partizans backed up their right to meet with fists, drummers-up were sent to bring in prospective citizens. Upon promising faithfully to vote the Tammany ticket, a card, valued at fifty cents, was furnished gratuitously to each. It was addressed to a Judge who owed his election to Tammany, and read:

> " Common Pleas:
>   " Please naturalize the bearer.
>   " N. Seagrist, chairman." [19]

From 3,000 to 4,000 voters, it was estimated, were turned out by this process.

The sentiment of certain politicians may be taken from John Cochrane's [20] remark that " he would vote for the devil incarnate if nominated by Tammany Hall." Meanwhile they took care to make out Wood to be a much-abused man. At the ratification meeting in Tammany Hall, on November 23, long resolutions were passed, fulsomely flattering Wood and asking voters to remember that if Wood was assailed, so Jefferson, Jackson and Daniel Webster were pursued to their graves by harpies. The voters were asked not to be deceived by the abuse of the graceless, godless characters and disappointed demagogues.

[19] This reference to Seagrist was handed down in an Aldermanic committee's report some years before: ". . . Thomas Munday, Nicholas Seagrist, Captain Norris, Mackellar and others were charged with *robbing the funeral pall of Henry Clay*, when his sacred person passed through this city." *Documents of the Board of Aldermen*, Vol. XXII: No. 43.

[20] Cochrane later followed Wood into Mozart Hall, but subsequently returned to Tammany Hall. He was elected to Congress, serving one term. He raised a regiment at the outbreak of the Civil War, and in June, 1862, was made a Brigadier-General. He was elected Attorney-General of the State in 1863. In 1872 he joined the Greeley movement. He held various local offices, both in 1872 and in 1883 being elected to the Presidency of the Board of Aldermen. As late as 1889 he was a Sachem. He died in 1898, in his 85th year.

Wood and his partizans strained every nerve for success. But it was a futile effort. The opposition won, Tiemann receiving 43,216 votes, to 40,889 for Wood. His large vote, however, showed the dangerous strength of the worst classes of the city, and boded ill for the years to come.

The opposition of the Tammany Society and the general committee having been responsible for his defeat, Wood made renewed efforts to regain sway over both. On their part, elated at his supposed downfall, the Anti-Wood members of the general committee decided to expel Daniel E. Sickles and C. Godfrey Gunther, two of his supporters, and met for that purpose in the Wigwam on December 9, 1857.

Wood's followers thought proper to impress upon the general committee a sense of their strength. Accordingly, their fighting men were present in full force, awaiting an opportunity to mingle in the proceedings. The probability of a violent row increasing momentarily, the Metropolitan police were summoned to Tammany Hall. For a time they kept the hostiles within bounds; but the bar was well patronized, and large delegations of the " Dead Rabbits " and " shoulder-hitters " from the wards were flowing in constantly.

At 9 o'clock a desperate fight was begun in the center of the bar-room, amid intense excitement. By using their clubs unsparingly, the forty policemen succeeded in separating the combatants, though not before a young man, Cornelius Woods, had been shot in the shoulder with a slug. Unwilling to draw upon themselves the resentment of the influential ward politicians, the police made no arrests. The meeting broke up without definite action being taken in the matter of expelling the two supporters of Wood.

The first and chief point in the struggle for the control of the organization was, as usual, the control of the Tammany Society. Both factions were alive to this necessity.

On April 13, 1858, 150 members of the society met at the Westchester House, Bowery and Broome streets, where it was announced that 212 members were pledged to vote for Anti-Wood Sachems. Some of these members were seeking the ascendency for their own benefit, while others were not active in politics at all, but had become disgusted with Wood's methods and men. At the election, six days later, the Anti-Wood ticket, headed by Isaac V. Fowler and Nelson J. Waterbury, won by a majority of nearly 100, 378 members voting. More than twenty members who had not been at an election of the society for twenty years or more, and a large number who had eschewed voting for ten years, hastened, some from distances, to deposit their votes. Three came from Hudson, a number from Albany, two from Washington, and one from Cincinnati.

The result was Wood's forced withdrawal from the organization. He immediately started a Democratic organization opposed to Tammany and upon the same lines. It was known generally as " Mozart Hall," from the name of the assembly room in which it met. Wood denounced Tammany, declaring that its nominees were chosen by five members of the Tammany Society, in a parlor, and ferociously expressed his determination to wage war upon the society as long as he lived until (this reservation was added) " it opened its doors."

Each hall, as a matter of political business, made the most virtuous and the strongest claims of being the true Democratic organization. Each execrated the other and announced itself as the sole, valiant, sincere upholder of Democracy.

Wood's enemies made haste to guarantee their ascendency when, on December 28, the Sachems ordered elections for the committees to be held on December 30, thus giving but *one day's* notice of the event. Moreover, they forced upon all persons accepting membership in the committees, a pledge that in case of their election they would support

the Tammany organization and all nominations made
under its authority, and disclaim allegiance to any other
organization, party or clique.

The election of delegates to the various nominating
conventions, in the Fall of 1858, was attended by the customary disorder. Wood's partizans were everywhere
inciting trouble. At O'Connell's Hall, on Mulberry street,
a crowd, seeing that the result was unfavorable to their
side, split the ballot boxes and threw them into the street.
The "Dead Rabbits," scenting trouble, appeared hastily,
and a fight ensued on Hester street, in which two of them
were shot.

This municipal election was the first in which the Democratic voters of Irish nativity or lineage insisted on a
full share of the best places on the party's ticket. Previously they had seldom been allowed any local office
above Coroner. Their dominance on the Tammany ticket
again roused the "Know-Nothing" sentiment, and a
combination of Native Americans, Republicans and independents resulted. The combination secured 16 of the
24 Councilmen.

The politicians were now confronted with a registry
act, which omitted the blunder of that of 1840 in applying only to New York City. This measure became a law
in 1859, despite the stubborn opposition of Tammany,
some of whose leaders, Isaac V. Fowler and others, issued
an address asking Democrats to arise and defeat it.
Failing to defeat it, they resolved to circumvent it by
means of the Board of Supervisors, which was required to
appoint the registry clerks. This body was by law divided
equally as to politics, the Legislature calculating that this
would insure fair dealing. But by the purchase of the vote
of one of the Republican Supervisors for $2,500,[21] the

21 Statement of William M. Tweed before a special investigating
committee of the Board of Aldermen, 1877 (*Document No. 8, Documents of the Board of Aldermen*, Vol. II, pp. 15–16). Isaac V. Fowler, Tweed testified, furnished the $2,500 which was paid to Peter R.
Voorhis, a Republican member. Tweed further stated, that besides

Tammany members were enabled not only to redistrict the city to their own advantage, but to appoint trusted tools as registrars. For appearances' sake they allowed a Republican registry clerk here and there. Of 609 registrars appointed, the Republicans secured about 75; and of the whole 609, 68 were liquor-sellers, 92 were petty office-holders, 34 were supposed gamblers, and 50 of the names were not in the city directory. The Tammany leaders held daily private caucuses, and made a list of henchmen with extreme care, in order to exclude Wood from any influence with the registry clerks. William M. Tweed, a member of the board, generally named the men, and Elijah F. Purdy boasted that Tammany demanded the appointment of none but Democrats, and that they (the Tammany Supervisors) meant to sustain their party at any and all hazards. Having the registry clerks, Tammany Hall could revel in false registry and repeating. Good citizens, dejected at the outlook, were sure of a repetition of the frauds of former years.

Seeking to satisfy all parties, Mayor Tiemann failed to satisfy any. He was accused of using the official patronage for the advantage of Tammany Hall, in the hope of getting a renomination from it in 1859. He and his chief office-holders appointed to the office the most notorious fighting men and ruffians in the city. The Tammany leaders did not favor him, possibly because they thought William F. Havemeyer a man of more weight, popularity and respectability.

Accordingly they nominated the latter. Wood had himself nominated by Mozart Hall, and the Republicans chose George P. Opdyke, a millionaire. In this triangular contest the Tammany men felt that the force of Havemeyer's good record would put them in power. Singularly, however, with all its manipulation of the registry lists, and the excellent character of its nominee, Tammany lost.

himself there were in the conspiracy Elijah F. Purdy, William C. Conner, Isaac Bell, Jr. (a Sachem) and John R. Briggs.

The Irish voters sided almost solidly with Wood, and the lowest classes of the city, fearing the election of a man so distasteful to them as Havemeyer or Opdyke, used all their effectiveness for Wood, who received 29,940 votes, against 26,913 for Havemeyer, and 21,417 for Opdyke.

It was conceded that much of the worst part of Tammany's strength had gone over to Wood. This fact was suggestive, to a degree, of Wood's assurance, considering the declaration in his letter of acceptance of the nomination that he favored " excluding the bullies and rowdies from public employment and of dealing summarily with that class of outlaws."

Although Tammany had nominated a good man, for the sake of sliding into power upon the strength of his reputation, its lesser candidates were generally incompetent or of bad character; half a dozen of its nominees for Councilmen were under indictment for various crimes.

CHAPTER XXII

THE CIVIL WAR AND AFTER

1859–1867

THE stirring years of the Civil War were drawing near. In this crisis, Tammany, ever pro-slavery, dealt in no equivocal phrases. On November 1, 1859, at a meeting called to order by Isaac V. Fowler, James T. Brady, acting as president, referred to John Brown's raid as " riot, treason and murder." Brady and others spoke dolefully of the dire consequences of a continuation of the abolition agitation and prophesied that if the " irrepressible conflict " ever came, it would result in an extermination of the black race.

But Grand Sachem Fowler was not to officiate at any more meetings. He had been living for several years at a rate far beyond his means. In one year his bill at the New York Hotel, which he made the Democratic headquarters, amounted to $25,000.[1] He had spent $50,000 toward the election of Buchanan. A social favorite, he gave frequent and lavish entertainments.[2] President Pierce had appointed him Postmaster, but the salary was only $2,500 a year, and he had long ago exhausted his private means and much of the property of his family. It was therefore a source of wonder whence his money

[1] Statement to the author by Douglas Taylor, then his private secretary.

[2] Fowler was an exception to the average run of the leaders who preceded him, in that he was a college graduate and moved in the best social circles. With a view of bettering the " tone " of the Wigwam, he had induced a number of rich young men to join the organization.

came. The problem was cleared up when, on May 10. 1860, he was removed from office, and an order was issued for his arrest under the accusation of having embezzled $155,000.[3] The filching, it appeared, had been going on since 1855.[4]

Isaiah Rynders, then United States Marshal at New York, upon receiving orders to arrest Fowler, went to his hotel, but tarried at the bar and by his loud announcement of his errand, allowed word to be taken to Fowler, who forthwith escaped. He subsequently made his way to Mexico. His brother, John Walker Fowler, who upon recommendation of the " seven Sachems " had been appointed clerk to Surrogate Gideon J. Tucker, subsequently absconded with $31,079.65 belonging to orphans and others.[5]

In 1860 Tammany was greatly instrumental in inducing the Democrats of New York State to agree upon a fusion Douglas-Bell-Breckinridge electoral ticket. On the registration and election days the frauds practised against the Lincoln electors surpassed anything the city had known. In the Third Ward 63 fictitious names were registered in a single election district. Five hundred of the 3,500 names of the Twelfth Ward register were found to be fraudulent. In the Seventeenth Ward 935 names on the registry books were spurious, no persons representing them being discoverable at the places given as their residences. An Irish widow's two boys, six and seven years old respectively, were registered, mother and sons, of course, knowing nothing of it — and so on *ad libitum*. Fictitious names, accredited to vacant lots or

[3] *Report of Postmaster-General Holt, Senate Documents, 1st Session, 36th Congress,* Vol. XI, No. 48. Also Postmaster-General Holt's communication to James J. Roosevelt, United States District Attorney, at New York, *Ibid.,* XIII, No. 91, p. 11.

[4] Nelson J. Waterbury, Grand Sachem (1862), was at this time, and had been for several years, Fowler's Assistant Postmaster.

[5] Statement by Mr. Tucker to the author. Confirmed by reference to report of Charles E. Wilbour to the Board of Supervisors, May 26, 1870.

uninhabited buildings, were voted by the thousands. The announcement of the result gave the Fusionists 62,611 votes, and Lincoln 33,311.

At the outbreak of the war, Mozart Hall, for purposes of political display, took a prompt position in favor of maintaining the Union, although Wood, its master spirit, advocated, in a public message, the detaching of New York City from the Union and transforming it into a free city on the Hamburg plan.[6] Tammany, perforce, had to follow the lead of Mozart Hall in parading its loyalist sentiments. The society raised a regiment, which was taken to the field in June, 1861, by Grand Sachem William D. Kennedy.[7] Tammany long dwelt upon this action as a crowning proof of its patriotism.

The real sentiments of the bulk of Tammany and of Mozart Hall were to the contrary. Both did their best to paralyze the energies of Lincoln's administration. In a speech to his Mozart Hall followers at the Volks Garden, on November 27, 1861, Wood charged the national administration with having provoked the war, and said that they (the administration) meant to prolong it while there was a dollar to be stolen from the national Treasury or a drop of Southern blood to be shed. At the Tammany celebration of July 4, 1862, Grand Sachem Nelson J. Waterbury, though expressing loyalty to the Union, averred that it was the President's duty " to set his foot firmly upon abolitionism and crush it to pieces, and then the soldiers would fight unembarrassed, and victory must soon sit upon the National banners." Declarations of this kind were generally received with enthusiasm in both halls.

At times, however, under the sting of severe public

---

[6] *Proceedings of the Board of Aldermen,* Vol. LXXXI, pp. 25–26.
[7] This regiment was the Forty-second New York Infantry. Kennedy died a few days after the arrival in Washington, and was succeeded by a regular army officer. The Forty-second took part in thirty-six battles and engagements. Its record stood: killed 92; wounded, 328; missing, 298.

criticism, Tammany Hall made haste to assert its fealty
to the Union cause. In September, 1861, Elijah F.
Purdy, chairman of its general committee, issued a statement that " Tammany Hall had maintained an unswerv-
ing position upon this great question from the time the
first gun was fired to the present hour. It has been
zealously devoted to the Union, in favor of upholding it
with the utmost resources of the nation, and opposed to
any action calculated to embarrass the Government or
to prevent all loyal men from standing together in solid
column for the country." Tammany put forth the claim
that " three-fourths of the volunteer soldiers enlisted in
this city and at the seat of war, are Democrats attached
to Tammany Hall "; and on October 3, 1861, resolved
that with a deep sense of the peril in which the Union
and the Constitution were involved by the reckless war
being waged for their destruction by armed traitors, it
(Tammany Hall) held it to be the first and most sacred
duty of every man who loved his country to support the
Government.

The war, which so engaged and diverted the popular
mind, served as a cover for the continued manipulation
of primaries and conventions, and the consummation of
huge schemes of public plunder. Wood himself pointed
out that from 1850 to 1860 the expenses of the city
government had increased from over $3,200,000 to
$9,758,000, yet his tenure of office from 1860 to 1862
was characterized by even worse corruption than had
flourished so signally in his previous terms. After his
installation, in 1860, it was charged that he had sold the
office of City Inspector to Samuel Downes, a man of
wealth, for $20,000; that Downes had paid $10,000 to
certain confederates of Wood, and that he had afterward been cheated out of the office. Another charge,
the facts of which were related in a presentment by the
Grand Jury, accused Wood of robbing the taxpayers
of $420,000. The Common Council had awarded a five-

years' street-cleaning contract to Andrew J. Hackley, at $279,000 a year, notwithstanding the fact that one among other responsible persons had bid $84,000 a year less. Afraid to submit the contract to the ordeal of public opinion, which might give rise to injunctions, the Common Council sped it through both boards on the same night. Waiting in his office until nearly midnight for the express purpose of signing it, the Mayor hastily affixed his signature the moment it reached him. The Grand Jury found that the sum of $40,000 in bribes had been raised and paid for the passage of the contract. It was asserted that the equivalent Wood received for signing the bill was one-fourth the amount of the contract, or $69,750 a year, for five years, free of any other consideration than his signature, the other beneficiaries of the contract supplying all the money needed to protect the fraud. Spurred on by public opinion, the police — when the work was not done in compliance with the contract — had reported to the Controller, who had refused to pay the monthly bills. Then the contractors reduced the pay of their laborers from $1.25 to 95 cents a day in order to make good their payments to Wood.[8]

Hiram Ketchum, in November, 1861, publicly accused Wood of promising two men — Woodruff and Hoffman — Mozart Hall nominations for Judgeships, upon which they each paid $5,000 in checks to Wood's account for " election expenses." Pocketing the money, Wood then made an agreement with Tammany to unite on two other men — Monell and Barbour — for Judges, on condition that Tammany should not unite with the Republicans against him in the December Mayoralty election.

S. B. Chittenden, a citizen of wealth and standing,

---

[8] Hackley, in fact, received $279,000 for only six months' work. During the two years " for which he received full pay he has not done more than one year's actual work in cleaning the city, as the returns in this department abundantly prove." *Documents of the Board of Aldermen,* 1863, part 1, No. 4.

charged, in Cooper Institute, November 26, 1861, that the signature of the Street Cleaning Commissioner necessary for certain documents could be bought for $2,500, and intimated that Wood was not dissociated from the procedure.

Wood had spent an enormous amount in his political schemes. He himself admitted, according to the testimony of A. W. Craven, Chief Engineer of the Croton Aqueduct Department, before a committee of Aldermen, " that his object in removing heads of departments was to get control of the departments, so that he could put in those who would cooperate with him and, also, could pay off his obligations." [9]

It is possible to give only an outline of the " jobs " stealthily put through the Common Council. Newspaper criticism was, in a measure, silenced by appropriations of from $10,000 to $20,000 a year for " advertising," though occasional exposures were made in spite of this. One of these related to the appropriation of $105,000 in July, 1860, for a few days' entertainment of the Japanese Embassy in New York. Of this sum only a few thousand dollars were used for the purpose, the rest being stolen.[10]

Never more than now was patriotism shown to be the last refuge of scoundrels. Taking advantage of the war excitement, the most audacious designs on the city treasury were executed under color of acts of the purest patriotism. At a special meeting of the Common Council, on August 21, 1861, called ostensibly to help the families of the poor volunteers, a measure providing for

[9] *Documents of the Board of Aldermen*, 1860–61, Vol. XXVII, No. 18.

[10] The original.appropriation had been $30,000. The joint Council committee, of which Francis I. A. Boole was the head, submitted bills for alleged expenditures aggregating $125,000. Boole explained that his colleagues considered this sum excessive, and would therefore " knock off " $20,000. *Documents of the Board of Aldermen*, 1861, No. 17.

the appointment of twenty-two Street Opening Commissioners was hurriedly passed, upon motion of Alderman Terence Farley, against whom several untried indictments were pending. Without entering into details, it can be said that this action represented a theft of $250,000, in that the Commissioners were superfluous, and their offices were created merely to make more places for a hungry host of political workers.

If the city was a richer prize than ever to the politicians, the Legislature was no less desirable. Alien members of both branches of that body were under the complete domination of political managers. It was notorious that the Democratic and the Republican lobby lords exchanged the votes of their respective legislative vassals, so that it mattered little to either which political party had the ascendency in the Legislature. One celebrated lobbyist declared that it was cheaper to buy, than to elect, a Legislature. The passage of five franchises by the Legislature, on April 17, 1860, over Gov. Morgan's veto, cost the projectors upwards of $250,000 in money and stock.[11]

Apparently hostile, the leaders of Tammany and of Mozart Hall soon saw that it was to their mutual benefit to have a secret understanding as to the division of the spoils. While Mozart had supremacy for the moment, Tammany had superior advantages. It could point to a long record; its organization was perfect; it had a perpetual home, and the thousands of its disappointed ward-workers and voters who had transferred their allegiance to Mozart, in the hope of better reward, would certainly flow back in time. This changing about was an old feature of New York politics. A successful political party was always depleted by thousands of office-seekers who left its ranks because disappointed in their hopes. Most important of all, Tammany had dealt

[11] For this and other instances see *The History of Public Franchises in New York City*, by the author.

the decisive blow to Mozart Hall at the Charleston convention, in 1860, and at the Syracuse convention, in
September, 1861, when its delegation secured the recognition of " regularity."

Hence Mozart Hall, to avoid losing the State offices,
willingly bargained with Tammany, and in the Fall of
1861 the two combined on nominees for the Legislature.
They could not agree on the Mayoralty, Wood determining to stand for re-election. But true to their agreement not to ally themselves with the Republicans, the
Tammany leaders nominated independently, selecting C.
Godfrey Gunther. Once more a non-partizan movement
sprang up to combat the forces of corruption. The
People's Union, composed of Republicans and Democrats, succeeded, despite the usual frauds, in electing
George P. Opdyke, a Republican, by less than 1,000
plurality, he receiving 25,380 votes; Gunther, 24,767;
and Wood 24,167. In violation of the law, returns in
ten districts were held back for evident purposes of
manipulation. When the figures showed Opdyke's election, attempts were made to deprive him of his certificate
on the pretense that the returns as published in the daily
newspapers were inaccurate. After much counting by
the Board of Aldermen, whose attempt at " counting
out " Opdyke was frustrated by the vigilance of his
friends, the latter was declared elected by 613 plurality.

Newspaper accounts described a lively time, quite in
keeping with a long line of precedents, in Tammany
Hall on election night. The crowd was in unpleasant
humor because of Gunther's defeat. When " Jimmy "
Nesbit, a good-natured heeler of the Sixth Ward, was
called upon to preside, he tried to evoke cheers for Gunther. Chafing at the lack of enthusiasm, he swore
fiercely at his hearers. A shout was heard, " Three
cheers for Fernando Wood," whereupon the eminent
chairman lost his equanimity and let fly a pitcher at the
offender's head. He was on the point of heaving another

missile, a large pewter pitcher, but a bystander caught his hand. Cries of "Tammany is not dead yet," were heard, and then Chauncey Shaeffer regaled the crowd with the information that he got his first meal, with liquor thrown in, at Tammany Hall, sixteen years before, and he would never desert her. Shaeffer told the Tammanyites how he had gone to the White House and advised the President to let out the job of putting down the rebellion to Tammany Hall. Cries broke forth of, "You're drunk, Shaeffer!" "You're a disgrace to Tammany Hall." After trying to sing "The Red, White and Blue," Shaeffer stumbled off the platform. Isaiah Rynders then arose, and after denouncing the leaders for not being there, assured his hearers that there were many respectable gentlemen present and some d — d fools. This edifying meeting ended by "the chairman jumping from the platform and chasing a Wood man out of the room."

Though no longer in office, Wood was still a powerful factor, since Mozart Hall, of which he was the head, could poll, or pretend to poll, 25,000 votes. Further overtures were made between him and the leaders of Tammany in 1862, with the result that an understanding was reached to divide the nominations equally. The partition was conducted amicably until the office of Surrogate was reached. Besides this there was an odd member of the Assembly not accounted for. The leaders could not agree as to how these two offices should be disposed of, and on the evening of October 2 the general committee met in the Wigwam to discuss the profound problem. Crowds were gathered inside and outside the hall, in the lobby, bar-room and on the stairs. The excitement was such that a squad of police was sent to the scene to maintain peace.

Their services were needed. Heated discussions had been going on all the evening. Richard B. Connolly had his "party" an hand, eager for the fray. Francis I.

A. Boole mustered his retainers by the score —"fine strapping fellows, with upturned sleeves and significant red shirts that told of former battles and hard-earned laurels." At 11 o'clock the fighting began. It had not progressed far, however, when the police charged, and wielding their clubs right and left, drove the combatants in disorder into the street. The committee was in session nearly all night, but a renewal of the scrimmage was not attempted.

After much haggling, the factions finally agreed. Nominations brought such great sums that the severe contention of the leaders is easily explainable. A hint of the enormous sums wrung from this source was given by Judge Maynard, when addressing a meeting of the "Representative Democracy," in Cooper Union, on October 27, 1863. He stated that one man in Mozart Hall (doubtless referring to Fernando Wood) was the chief of all the "strikers" in New York City, and that this person made from $100,000 to $200,000 every year marketing offices.[12] Nominations and appointments went to the highest bidders, and some of the leaders held as many as thirteen different offices each. At the same meeting W. R. Ranken stated that "the manner in which these two organizations — Tammany and Mozart Hall — have packed their preliminary conventions and organizations, has been of such a character as to bring the blush of shame to every man of principle in the party. No man, were he to poll 10,000 votes, under those primary elections, could be admitted within the precincts of Tammany Hall unless he came with the indorsement of the Election Inspectors who were under the influence of the two or three men who held the reins of power there."[13]

[12] This speech was reprinted in the New York *Herald,* October 28, 1863. The *Herald* was known as Wood's special organ.

[13] In a remarkable report handed down in 1862 by a select committee of the Board of Aldermen, the admission was made that the "primary elections are notoriously and proverbially the scenes of the most disgraceful fraud, chicanery and violence. They are without

The State and Congressional elections in November showed the power of the combined halls. Seymour, for Governor, carried the city by 31,309 plurality. Among the Democratic Congressmen elected was Fernando Wood, who, evidently despairing of again filling the Mayor's chair, had determined to employ his activities in another field.

The city election for minor officers occurred in December, and the two halls again won. The apportionment of the offices, however, caused a number of clashes. One of the offices filled was that of Corporation Counsel, the nomination to which fell to the lot of Mozart Hall. Wood had promised it to John K. Hackett, subsequently Recorder, but gave it to John E. Devlin, a Sachem, supposed to be one of Wood's bitterest opponents. By way of smoothing Hackett's ire, Wood promised to have him appointed Corporation Attorney. This promise was also broken. Hackett went to Wood's house and was shown into his parlor. "Mr. Wood," said Hackett, as soon as the man who had been thrice Mayor of the metropolis of America appeared, "I called to say to you, personally, that you are a scoundrel, a rascal and a perjured villain." Wood threatened to put him out and rang the bell. As the servant was on the point of entering, Hackett drew a revolver from his pocket and went on: "If that man comes between us, I shall blow out his brains and cut off your ears. So you may as well listen. On a certain night, in a room of the Astor House, were four persons, Mr. D., Mr. X., Mr. Y., and yourself. One of these four is a scoundrel, a rascal, a perjured villain and a hound. It is not Mr. D., nor Mr. X., nor Mr. Y. Who he is, I leave you to imagine."

The degraded state of politics, sinking yearly still

legal restraint or regulation, nor can such restraint or regulation be imposed upon them. Peaceable and orderly citizens, almost without exception, refuse to attend these meetings." *Documents of the Board of Aldermen,* 1862, Vol. XXIX, No. 7.

lower, caused unspeakable disgust, but the honest element of the citizenship seemed powerless. The occasional election of a reform Mayor made little difference in the situation, for either through the impotence of his position or his personal incompetency, the spoilsmen managed to prevail. The Common Council was the supreme power, and this body Tammany, or Tammany and Mozart together, generally controlled. The public money was spent as the Aldermen pleased. The Mayor's veto became a legal fiction, for a bare majority [14] sufficed to overcome it, and this could generally be secured through deals and the trading of votes on one another's " jobs." The veto, in the words of a later Mayor, amounted " to nothing more than the publication of his remonstrance in corporation newspapers, to cause a few hours' delay and excite the contempt of the members [of the Common Council] who have determined to carry their measure in spite of his remonstrance." [15]

Public indignation resulted in another anti-Tammany demonstration of strength in 1863. The Wigwam nominated for Mayor, Francis I. A. Boole, generally considered as nauseating a type of the politician as Tammany could bring forth. Independent Democrats and some Republicans thereupon rallied to the support of C. Godfrey Gunther, nominee of a new " reform " organization — the " McKeon Democracy." The Republican organization, however, stood apart, nominating Orison Blunt. Gunther was elected, receiving 29,121 votes, to 22,579 for Boole, and 19,383 for Blunt. At this, as in previous elections, there were unmistakable Wigwam frauds, such as repeating and altering election returns.

Hitherto, in Presidential conventions since Van Buren's time, the Democratic candidates had been nominated

---

[14] The reformers of the city had unsuccessfully sought to incorporate in the charter of 1853, a clause requiring a two-thirds vote to overcome a veto.

[15] *Documents of the Board of Aldermen*, 1865, part 1, No. 1.

against Tammany's resistance, the organization having had each time a candidate of its own whom it sought to force on the convention. In 1864, however, the Wigwam shrewdly anticipated the action of the Chicago convention by recommending McClellan as the Democratic nominee. On the night of McClellan's nomination, Tammany held a ratification meeting in the City Hall Park, denounced " the imbecility of the administration of Abraham Lincoln " in the conduct of the war and " its ruinous financial policy," and declared that it had "forfeited the confidence of the loyal States; usurped powers not granted by the Constitution; endeavored to render the executive, aided by the military, superior to the judicial and legislative branches of the Government, and assumed to destroy life and confiscate property by its unconstitutional proclamations." Again, on November 16, at a meeting of the general committee, George H. Purser, a lobbyist and organization leader, offered a resolution, which was unanimously approved, practically declaring the war a failure.

In this election the Republicans took precautions to prevent repetition of the frauds of preceding years. An investigation disclosed illegal registration on a large scale. To hold the lawless in check, Gen. Benjamin F. Butler was ordered to New York. He brought 6,000 of his own troops, with artillery and a regiment of regulars, which he kept within call outside of the city until after the election, and he established a civilian system of surveillance in every election district. An unusually orderly election was the result, though fraud was not entirely suppressed, and it was charged that both sides were parties to it. McClellan received a majority in the city of 37,023, of the total vote of 110,433.

In 1865 Tammany again nominated Francis I. A. Boole for Mayor. Boole, as City Inspector, was the head of a department which embraced the Street Cleaning and Health Bureaus. Daniel B. Badger testified before the

Senate Investigating Committee of 1865 that in the previous year he had put in a written bid to clean the
streets for $300,000, but when it was opened, Boole an-
nounced loudly that it was $500,000, and gave the con-
tract elsewhere, with the consequence that it cost $800,-
000 to clean the streets in 1864.[16] Many witnesses
swore that they paid various sums, ranging about $200
each, for positions under Boole, only to be suddenly dismissed later.[17] A surprising number of men were on
Boole's payrolls who had other business and who appeared only to draw their salaries.[18] The filthy condition of the city entailed a fearful sacrifice of life, the
average deaths yearly being no less than 33 in 1,000.[19]
Nearly all the 220 Health Wardens and special inspectors under Boole were illiterate and unfit. One of them
testified that he thought " the term ' hygienic ' meant the
odor arising from stagnant water." [20]

Boole, about this time, was engaged in other activities
than the protection of the city's health. In a suit
brought by William Elmer against Robert Milbank in the
Superior Court, in 1867, Milbank testified that he had
called upon Boole to learn how he could secure the passage of an ordinance allowing the People's Gas Light
Company to lay pipes in the streets. Boole referred him
to Charles E. Loew,[21] a clerk in the Common Council,
and later County Clerk, and a noted Tammany figure.

16 Senate Documents, 1865, Vol. II, No. 38, pp. 75–76.
17 Ibid., pp. 166–70, etc.   18 Ibid., pp. 252–56.
19 City Inspector's Report for 1863. The wretched condition of the
city about this time caused the Legislature to establish the Metropolitan Board of Health, to have jurisdiction over the counties of New
York, Kings, Westchester and Richmond and certain other territory. This board's first report declared that the hygienic conditions of the city were disgusting and horrible; that epidemics were
frequent, and that one-third of the deaths occurring in New York and
Brooklyn were due to zymotic diseases. See Report of Metropolitan
Board of Health, 1866, p. 133.
20 Senate Documents, 1865, No. 38.
21 Loew was several times a Sachem, holding that rank as late as
1886.

Milbank gave Loew $20,000 cash [22] and $30,000 in stock, whereupon the Common Council passed the ordinance on the same night.

Public criticism was so caustic that Tammany withdrew Boole and nominated John T. Hoffman, a man of some popularity and considerable ability. The Mozart faction nominated John Hecker, a religious and political enthusiast of narrow views, but acceptable to the Mozart " boys " or " strikers," because of his willingness to supply an abundance of money. Smith Ely, Jr., urged Hecker to withdraw, as his candidacy was hopeless. " Mr. Ely," said Hecker, " you form your opinions in the ordinary way of a business man and politician, but I receive my impressions directly from on High." The Republicans nominated Marshall O. Roberts, and the " McKeon Democracy " renominated Gunther.

Frauds were as common as ever. It was well established that 15,000 persons who had registered could not be found at the places given as their residences. In the disreputable districts, upon which Tammany depended for a large vote, a non-Tammany speaker was in actual danger of his life. Hoffman received 32,820 votes; Roberts, 31,657; Hecker, 10,390, and Gunther, 6,758.

There is little to say of Hoffman's administration. Frauds and thefts of every description continued as before, though it is not possible to connect his name with any of them. His popularity grew. The Tammany Society elected him Grand Sachem, the Democratic State Committee named him for Governor in 1866,[23] and toward the end of his term as Mayor he was renominated for that office. Fernando Wood again came forth as the Mozart Hall nominee, and the Republicans selected William A. Darling. Hoffman swept everything before him

---

[22] See Judgment Roll (1867) in the Superior Court docket and Exhibit A, forming part of the bill of particulars.
[23] He was defeated by Reuben E. Fenton.

(December, 1867), receiving 63,061 votes, to 22,837 for Wood, and 18,483 for Darling.

The total vote was 104,481, an increase of 22,779 in two years. The reasons for this astounding augmentation were no secret to any one. Repeating was one cause, and false registration was another; in one ward alone — the Eighteenth — in this election, 1,500 fraudulent registrations were discovered. But the main cause was illegal naturalization. In the Supreme Court and the Court of Common Pleas, citizens were turned out at the rate, often, of about 1,000 a day. The State census of 1865 gave the city 51,500 native and 77,475 naturalized voters.[24] The figures were doubtless false, probably having been swelled to allow fraudulent totals at the polls to come within the limits of an officially declared total of eligible voters. Nevertheless, the figures are significant of the proportion of aliens to natives. The predominance of the former, moreover, was daily made greater through the connivance of corrupt Judges with the frauds of the politicians. The bulk of these aliens added to the hopelessness of the local situation. With their European ideas and training, and their ignorance of our political problems, they became the easy prey of the ward " bosses " and aided in imposing upon the city a reign of unexampled corruption.

Heretofore the Tammany organization had been held in the control of constantly changing combinations. Duumvirates, triumvirates and cliques of various numbers of men had risen, prospered and passed away. The period is now reached when the power became centralized in one man. Fernando Wood had illustrated the feasibility of the " boss " system; William M. Tweed now appeared to develop it to its highest pitch. The " boss "

---

[24] From 1847 to 1860, 2,671,745 immigrants landed at the Port of New York. *Documents of the Board of Aldermen*, 1861, Vol. XXVIII, No. 5. In 1855 the native voters in New York City had numbered 46,173, and the aliens, 42,704.

was the natural result of the recognized political methods. Where, as in previous times, three or four or half a dozen leaders had put their wits together and dictated and sold nominations, Tweed, astute, unprincipled and thoroughly versed in the most subterranean phases of ward politics, now gathered this power exclusively in his own hands. How he and his followers used it was disclosed in the operations of the extraordinary Tweed, or Tammany " Ring."

CHAPTER XXIII

1867–1870

THE Tweed "Ring" was, in a measure, the outgrowth of the act of 1857 creating the Board of Supervisors. The Whigs, and their successors, the Republicans, had up to that year held the legislative power of the State for the greater part of ten years, during which their chief concern had been the devising of means for keeping down the Democratic majority in New York City. Their legislation was directed to the transferring of as much as they could of the government of the city to State officials, a change generally welcomed by the honest part of the citizenship, on account of the continuous misgovernment inflicted by city officials.

The real result of these transfers, however, was merely to make two strongholds of corruption instead of one. The Republican power in Albany and the Tammany power in New York City found it to their interests to arrange terms for the distribution of patronage and booty. Accordingly, as one means to that end, the Board of Supervisors for New York County was created. It was founded strictly as a State institution. Unlike the Boards of Supervisors of other counties, it had no power to tax. It could only ascertain and levy the taxes decreed by the State Legislature, which was required to pass yearly a special act declaring the amount necessary for the maintenance of the city government. It was to be an elective body, and each side was to have an equal quota of the twelve members. But in the first board convened, this delicate balance was upset, as has been shown, by the buying of a Republican member, which in effect gave Tammany a majority.

William M. Tweed was born in Cherry street in 1823. He spent the usual life of a New York boy. His father was a chairmaker in good circumstances and gave his children a fair education. Fascinated, as were most New York boys of the period, with the life of a volunteer fireman, he became a runner with Engine 12 before he was of age, and in 1849 he was elected foreman of another fire company. Carrying a silver-mounted trumpet, a white fire-coat over his arm and wearing an old-fashioned stiff hat, he led the ropes. So popular was young Tweed that he became a powerful factor in ward politics, and gifted with the qualities that counted most in those circles, he was not slow in utilizing his popularity. The Americus Club, for a long time Tweed's favorite quarters, and at times the place where Tammany politics were determined, was started with him as its foremost luminary.

Though defeated for Assistant Alderman in 1850, he was elected the next year and served in the "Forty Thieves" Board. He was a delegate, in 1852, to the Congressional convention of the Fifth District, composed of two East Side wards of New York City, and Williamsburg. A deadlock ensued, through each of two candidates polling forty-four votes. Finally the Williamsburg delegates "threw over" their favorite and voted for Tweed, who as chairman of the convention, cast the deciding vote for himself, with the statement that "Tweedie never goes back on Tweedie." He was elected, but beaten for reelection, in 1854, by the "Know-Nothings." The latter he fought so persistently that he became known as the champion of the foreign element. He was made a Sachem of the Tammany Society because of his extreme popularity, and in 1857 he was elected to the Board of Supervisors. Selling his business of chairmaking, he thereupon devoted his entire time to politics.

The first " ring " was the Supervisors' " Ring," founded in 1859 by the Democrats in the board for the purpose of procuring the appointment of Inspectors of Election.[1] One member of the board, as already shown, was bribed by a present of $2,500 to stay away from a session when the Inspectors were appointed. Tweed was so well pleased with the success of this scheme that he was inspired to wider efforts. Aided by two men — Walter Roche and John R. Briggs — he began a systematic course of lobbying before the Board of Aldermen in support of excessive bills for supplies. He and his associates collected heavy tribute on every successful bill.

His prestige was not visibly lessened by his defeat for Sheriff, in 1861, by James Lynch, a popular Irishman. In the same year he was elected chairman of the Tammany General Committee. This instantly made him a person of great political importance. But his grasp was yet insecure, since a hostile body of Sachems might at any time declare the general committee " irregular." Recognizing this, he planned to dominate the society by having himself elected Grand Sachem. Holding these two positions, he reckoned that his power would be absolute. For the time, however, he thought it wise to be satisfied with the one; but eventually he succeeded Hoffman as Grand Sachem, and in his dual positions gained

[1] *Documents of the Board of Aldermen,* 1877, part 2, No. 8, pp. 15–16. This document, embodying the full confession of Tweed before a special investigating committee, will be frequently referred to in this and the following chapter. Its value as a support to many of the statements made in the text of this work rests upon the credibility of Tweed's word. The best opinion is that Tweed told the approximate truth. He was not a vengeful man; he was, at the time, old, and broken in power and health; he had no reason for concealment or evasion, and it is unlikely, considering his moral temperament, that he would have made false statements for the purpose of involving innocent men, or of adding to the sum of venality already proved against the guilty.

complete control of the political situation and dictated nominations at will.

The title of " boss " he earned by his despotic action in the general committee. When a question was to be voted upon which he wished to have determined in his favor, he would neglect to call for negative votes and would decide in the affirmative, with a significantly admonishing glance at the opposing side. Soon friends and enemies alike called him " Boss " Tweed, and he did not seem to take the title harshly.

He made short shrift of his antagonists. Once, when chairman of a Tammany nominating convention, he declared the nomination of Michael Ulshoeffer, for Judge, unanimous, amid a storm of protests. On adjournment, thirty delegates remained behind to make a counter-nomination. Tweed blocked their plan by having the gas turned off.

Meanwhile he daily increased his strong personal following. Nominally Deputy Street Commissioner, to which place he was appointed in 1863, he was virtually the head of that department, and could employ, when so inclined, thousands of laborers, who could be used in manipulating ward primaries when the ward leaders showed a spirit of revolt. The Aldermen had to apply to him for jobs for their ward supporters. As a member of the Board of Supervisors at the same time, he was in a position to exercise his mandatory influence respecting the passage of resolutions dealing with expenditures and the giving out of contracts. In 1868 he added a third office to the list — that of State Senator, and was thus enabled to superintend personally the " running " of the Legislature.

The members of the " ring "— Tweed and his subordinates, Peter B. Sweeny, Richard B. Connolly and the rest — were growing rich at a rapid rate. According to the subsequent testimony of James H. Ingersoll, it was in 1867 that the understanding was reached that

persons who supplied the public offices with materials
would be required to increase the percentages given to the
officials, and that all purveyors to the city must comply.
The previous tax had been but 10 per cent., and it had
been somewhat irregularly levied. A few tradesmen refused to pay the advance, but plenty there were to take
their places. Ingersoll was one of these. He was told
to fix his bills so as to " put up 35 per cent.," and he
obligingly complied with the command. Of the 35 per
cent collected, 25 went to Tweed and 10 to Controller
Connolly.

Tweed had become dissatisfied with the old Tammany
Hall building, and a site for a new hall — the present
location on Fourteenth street — was secured. The funds
in hand for the building were insufficient, however, and
had to be augmented by private subscription. It well
illustrates the liberality with which the Tammany chieftains were supplying themselves financially, to note that
when John Kelly, the Grand Sachem, at a meeting of
the society announced that a loan of $250,000 would be
needed, the sum of $175,000 was subscribed on the spot,
fifteen members alone subscribing $10,000 each.[2] A far
more astonishing incident happened in the Fall of 1867,
when Peter B. Sweeny, the City Chamberlain,[3] announced
his determination to give to the city treasury, for the
benefit of the taxpayers, over $200,000 a year, interest
money, which before that had been pocketed by the City
Chamberlain.

While the " ring " was plundering the city and plot-
ting theft on a more gigantic scale, the Sachems, many
of them implicated in the frauds, laid the corner-stone of
the new Tammany Hall building. The ceremony was
marked by the characteristic pronouncement of virtuous-

[2] New York *Herald,* September 10, 1867.
[3] " I heard that Peter B. Sweeny paid $60,000 for his confirmation
as City Chamberlain by the Board of Aldermen "— Tweed's testimony, *Document No. 8,* p. 105.

sounding phrases. "Brothers and friends," rhapsodized Mayor Hoffman, " in the name of the Tammany Society, I proceed to lay the corner-stone of a new hall which will, for the next half century at least, be the headquarters of the Democracy of New York, where the great principles of civil and religious liberty, constitutional law and national unity, which form the great corner-stones of the republic, will always be advocated and maintained. . . ." The " braves " then marched to Irving Hall, where Tweed, Sweeny and Connolly had caused such inscriptions as these to be hung about: " Civil liberty the glory of man "; " The Democratic party — Upon its union and success depends the future of the republic. He who would seek to lower its standard of patriotism and principle, or distract its councils, is an enemy to the country." Gazing approvingly on these inscriptions from the platform sat Tweed, Sweeny and Connolly, A. Oakey Hall and a host of Judges and office-holders of all sorts, while Andrew J. Garvey (who will reappear in these chapters) conducted the invited guests. The building of this hall — an imposing one for the day — in a central part of the city, gave to the Tweed combination an advantage of no inconsiderable significance.

In the new Wigwam, on July 4, 1868, the Democratic national convention was held. Tammany, in fact, forced its candidate, Horatio Seymour, on the convention. The galleries were filled with seasoned Wigwam shouters, cheering vociferously for Seymour. Only persons having tickets were admitted, and these tickets were distributed by an able young Wigwam politician, who saw to it that only the right sort of persons gained entrance. Gaining its point on the nomination, Tammany magnanimously allowed the Southern men to dictate the declaration in the platform that the reconstruction acts were " unconstitutional, revolutionary and void." There was a general suspicion that the organization, hopeless of the election of a Democratic President, had forced Seymour's nomination for the purpose of trading votes for its State and local ticket.

The State convention again named Hoffman for Governor, and preparations began for a lively campaign. Tammany addressed itself to the citizenship as the defender of the interests of the poor, and instanced the candidacy of John A. Griswold for Governor, Edwin D. Morgan for Governor, and " several other millionaires," as a proof of the plutocratic tendencies of the Republican party. On October 19 the general committee, with Tweed in the chair, adopted an address urging the people to stand by Seymour and Blair. Continuing, it said:

> " We are united. We believe in our cause. It is the cause of constitutional liberty, of personal rights, of a fraternity of States, of an economical government, of the financial credit of the nation, of one currency for all men, rich and poor, and of the political supremacy of the white race and protection of American labor. . . . [Hoffman] is the friend of the poor, the sympathizer with the naturalized citizen, and the foe to municipal oppression in the form of odious excise and all other requisitional laws. . . . Is not the pending contest preeminently one of capital against labor, of money against popular rights, and of political power against the struggling interests of the masses? "

Public addresses and pronunciamentos, however, formed but a small part of the Tammany program for 1868. For six weeks the naturalization mills worked with the greatest regularity in the Supreme, Common Pleas and Superior Courts, producing, it was estimated, from 25,000 to 30,000 citizens, of whom not less than 85 per cent voted the Tammany Hall ticket. On October 30 Tweed announced to the general committee that " at 10 o'clock to-morrow the money for electioneering purposes will be distributed " and that those who came first would be served first. The chairman of the executive committee spread forth the glad tidings that there was $1,000 ready for each election district. There being 327 election districts, this made a fund of $327,000 from the general committee alone, exclusive of the sums derived in the districts themselves from the saloonkeepers and the tradesmen, whose fear of inviting reprisals by Tammany officials made them "easy marks" for assessments. Tweed personally suggested to the twenty-four leaders the stuffing of ballot boxes.[4] By fraudulent naturalization, repeating, the buying and trading of votes, and intimidation, Seymour secured a total of 108,316 votes, against 47,762 for Grant. The whole vote of the city was swelled to 156,288, of which, it was conclusively demonstrated, at least 25,000 were fraudulent.[5] Tweed himself confessed, nine years later, that he thought the Inspectors of Elections "lumped" the votes and declared them without counting, in order to overcome the result in the rest of the State and give the electoral vote to Seymour.[6] To prevent the Republicans from getting the use of certain telegraph wires on election night, Tweed sent out long, useless messages, and it was even proposed to telegraph the whole Bible if necessary.[7]

Hoffman was swept into the Governorship on the strength of the frauds. His election left vacant the Mayor's chair, and a special election to fill it was called for the first Tuesday of December.

It was all essential to the "ring" that its candidate, A. Oakey Hall, should be elected. The candidacy of Frederick A. Conkling, the Republican nominee, was not feared, but John Kelly, who controlled a considerable part of the Irish vote, was a threatening factor. Disappointed at not receiving a new post at the close of his term as Sheriff, he had led a revolt against the "ring," and had himself nominated for Mayor at the Masonic

4 *Document No. 8,* p. 225.

5 It was probably at this election that a certain amusing incident in the swearing in of the Election Inspectors occurred. No Bible being at hand, they were sworn on a copy of Ollendorf's *New Method of Learning to Read, Write and Speak French.* The courts subsequently upheld the substitution of Ollendorf for the Bible, deciding that it was not such an act as would vitiate the election. *Documents of the Board of Supervisors,* 1870, Vol. II, No. 12.

6 *Document No. 8,* pp. 133–34.

7 *Document No. 8,* p. 226.

Hall " reform " convention. " Influences " were soon set
at work; and suddenly, after Kelly had appeared before
the nominating convention and accepted the nomination,
he withdrew from the contest, on the score of ill-health.[8]
Hall won, receiving 75,109 votes, to 20,835 for Conkling.
The degree in which Tammany fraudulently increased the
vote at the November election is indicated in the fact that
at the December election, despite a repetition of frauds,
the Tammany vote declined 33,000.

The " ring " nominations, being equivalent to election,
yielded a large price. There was no Democratic opposition, Mozart Hall having practically passed out of
existence, through Wood's resignation of its leadership.
The revenues of the various city offices were constantly
rising, and a keener competition for the places arose.
In 1866, before the really extensive operations of the
" ring " began, it was estimated that the offices of Sheriff
and County Clerk were worth $40,000 a year each.
Several years later it was found that the yearly revenue
of the Register amounted to between $60,000 and
$70,000, partly derived from illegal fees. It was well
known that one Register had received the sum of $80,000
a year.[9] The yearly aggregate of the illegal transactions in the Sheriff's office could not be accurately ascertained; but it was a well-authenticated fact that one
Sheriff, about 1870, drew from the office the sum of
$150,000 the first year of his term. He was a poor man
when elected; upon retiring at the end of the two-years'
term, he did not conceal the fact that he was worth
$250,000, clear of all political assessments and other
deductions.

All nominations for city, county and, too often, State
offices, and notoriously those for Judges, were dictated

[8] Kelly left rather hastily for Europe, where he remained three
years.
[9] Report of the Bar Association Committee on Extortions, March
5, 1872.

by Tweed. He not only controlled all the local departments, but swayed every court below the Court of Appeals.[10] Judges were nominated partly with a view to the amount they could "put up," and partly with a view to their future decisions on political questions. Fernando Wood had frankly presented the latter reason in his speech nominating Albert Cardozo, one of Tweed's most useful puppets, for the Supreme Court.[11] At the Judiciary election of May, 1870, repeating was the order of the day, and the registry was swelled to an enormous extent. In one of the wards, about 1,100 negroes were registered; but when they went to the ballot boxes, they were amazed to learn that white repeaters had already voted upon nearly 500 of their names. Later, when a few of the negroes tried to vote, they were arrested as repeaters. The corrupt means used in selecting the Judiciary, and the hopelessness of securing just verdicts in any of the courts, prompted one writer seriously to discuss, in the pages of a standard magazine, the formation of a vigilance committee modeled upon that of San Francisco.[12]

Tweed had for some time recognized the importance of gaining a seat in the State Senate. That body could at any time create or abolish city departments or offices, or change the laws affecting them. The Tammany officials, realizing its potentialities, had already made terms with it, and the "ring," which subsisted at first between the two factions of partizans in the Board of Supervisors, had grown into a compact "ring" between

[10] Tilden: *The Tweed Ring*, J. Polhemus, 1873.

[11] "The Ermine in the 'Ring,'" *Putnam's Magazine* supplement (about 1869). It happened that a singular suit brought by Wood against the city came before this very Judge, when Wood obtained by his decision a judgment for $180,000 for the rent of premises owned by him, not worth, for any use of the city, over $35,000. The buildings, in great part, were so unfit for use that the city, although paying rent for them for years, established its departments elsewhere. Wood re-leased these unused offices, collecting a double rent.

[12] *Ibid.*

the Republican majority at Albany, the Board of Supervisors and the Democratic officials of New York City. Tweed saw the necessity of being at the center of political bargaining and legislative manipulation, and accordingly had himself elected to the upper house.

Upon taking his seat, in 1868, he at once began to procure legislation increasing his power in New York City. His first measure was the "Adjusted Claims" act, which gave the City Controller power to adjust claims then existing against the city, and to obtain money by the issue of bonds. Payments under this act were first made by the Controller in July, 1868, and were continued to January, 1869. During this time, 55 per cent. of the claims paid were divided among the members of the "ring." In July, 1869, payments under the act were resumed, but the percentage was increased to 60 per cent., and after November, 1869, to 65 per cent.

The conspiring contractors were led by Andrew J. Garvey, Ingersoll & Co. and Keyser & Co. At first, 25 per cent of the spoils went to Tweed, 20 to Connolly and 10 to Sweeny. When the rate was subsequently increased, others were permitted to share in the harvest, and Watson, the County Auditor; Woodward, the clerk of the Board of Supervisors, and the recognized go-betweens for the "ring" members, received 2½ per cent. Five per cent was reserved for "expenses"— in other words, the sums necessary to bribe the requisite members of the Legislature. The division of the spoils was a matter of daily occurrence when Tweed was in town, and took place in the Supervisors' room in the County Court House. After Watson's warrants had been cashed, Garvey would carry Tweed's share of the plunder to the "Boss" at the office of Street Commissioner George W. McLean. On one such visit Garvey found McLean present. In trying to hand the parcel secretly to Tweed, it fell on the floor. Tweed quickly covered it with his foot, and later, with apparent carelessness, picked it up and threw it into a drawer. The too-ingenious Garvey was thereafter instructed to " do business " with Woodward.[13]

Tweed soon reached a position of general control in the State Legislature. But it cost him hundreds of thousands of dollars. Often he had to pay for what he wanted quite as heavily as did the corporations who maintained lobbies there. " It was impossible to do anything there without paying for it," were his own words; " money had to be raised for the passing of bills." [14] A well-known lobbyist of the time stated that for a favorable report on a certain bill before the Senate $5,000 apiece was paid to four members of the committee having it in charge. On the passage of the bill a further $5,000 apiece, with contingent expenses, was to be paid. In another instance, when but one vote was needed to pass a bill, three Republicans put their figures up to $25,000 each. One of them, it is needless to say, was secured. A band of about thirty Republicans and Democrats, shortly afterwards becoming known as the " Black Horse Cavalry," organized themselves under the leadership of an energetic lobbyist, with a mutual pledge to vote as directed.[15] Naturally their action exercised a strong " bull " influence on the market for votes; and the sums paid by Tweed and other " promoters " grew to an enormous aggregate.

Honesty among legislators was at a discount. There were some honest men in both houses who voted for several of the bills alluded to, on their merits. The lobbyists entered these men in their memoranda to their corporations as having been " fixed," put the money in their own pockets and allowed the honest members to suffer

[13] Garvey's testimony, *Tweed Case,* etc., Supreme Court, 1876, Vol. I: pp. 814–16.
[14] *Document No. 8,* p. 29.
[15] *Document No. 8,* pp. 212–13.

under the imputation of having been bribed. Any corporation, however extensive and comprehensive the privileges it asked, and however much oppression it sought to impose upon the people in the line of unjust grants, extortionate rates or monopoly, could convince the Legislature of the righteousness of its requests upon "producing" the proper sum.[16] The testimony before the Select Committee of the New York Senate, appointed April 10, 1868, showed that at least $500,000 was expended to get legislation legalizing fraudulent Erie Railway stock issues.

In 1869 the "ring" opened operations in the Legislature and in the municipal bodies on a greater scale than ever. Tweed began to concern himself in Erie and other railroads, and to compel different corporations to give tribute for laws passed in their interest or for providing against hostile measures. He ordered the passage of the Erie Classification bill, at the suggestion of "Jim" Fisk, Jr., and Jay Gould, who for that service made him a director of the Erie railroad.[17] At this juncture Fisk and Gould were engaged in great stock frauds and in breeding a disastrous panic, which caused widespread ruin and suffering. Tweed abetted their schemes. One of his most servile tools, Judge George G. Barnard, of the Supreme Court, did whatever Tweed directed him, especially in favor of Gould and Fisk. One biographer of Fisk wrote quite innocently: "Jay Gould and Fisk took William M. Tweed into their [Erie] board, and the State Legislature, Tammany Hall and the Erie 'Ring' were fused in interest and have contrived to serve each other faithfully."[18] Once Tweed complained

16 New York *Sun*, February 6, 1871.

17 Q.—"Did you ever receive any money from either Fisk or Gould to be used in bribing the Legislature?"

A.—"I did, sir! They were of frequent occurrence. Not only did I receive money, but I find by an examination of the papers that everybody else who received money from the Erie Railroad charged it to me." Tweed: *Document No. 8*, p. 149.

18 *A Life of James Fisk, Jr.*, New York, 1871.

that a friend "had gone back on him," and when asked in return how it was that he could stand such drains on his check-book, he laughed and showed a slip of paper on which he had calculated his Erie profits for the foregoing three months; they amounted to $650,000.

During the campaign of 1869, for the election of members of the Common Council and certain State officers, a legal question arose as to whether Mayor Hall had been elected for two years or merely for the unexpired year of Hoffman's term. Hall claimed a two-years' term, and the best lawyers supported the claim. But to make sure of the matter, Tammany, in the late days of the campaign, instructed its members and followers to cast ballots for him, and the Police Commissioners distributed special ballot boxes for the Mayoralty vote. As no proclamation on the subject had been issued, the Republicans and other opponents of Tammany Hall had no opportunity to make nominations. Mayor Hall consequently received nearly the entire number of votes cast — 65,568, out of a total of 66,619.

After entering the Board of Supervisors, Tweed had boasted that he would soon be among the largest real-estate owners in the city. He made good the boast. A comparatively poor man in 1864, he was reputed five years later to be worth $12,000,000. This was an exaggeration, for he was not worth anything like that sum at any one time; but he was, nevertheless, an enormously rich man. He had investments in real estate and iron mines; he was interested in every street opening and widening scheme; he had a hand in all city, and in some State, contracts, and he held directorships in many railroad and gas companies and other corporations. Connolly, who some years before had left a position as a book-keeper, at a moderate salary, to engage in politics "as a financial speculation"; Sweeny, and the rest of the "ring," suddenly became millionaires. Many other politicians shared in the sacking of the city.

CHAPTER XXIV

1870–1871

URGED by various motives, a number of Tammany leaders combined against Tweed. Some sought more plunder, others felt that their political aspirations had not been sufficiently recognized, and a number were incensed against Sweeny. They were led by Henry W. Genet, John Fox, John Morrissey, James O'Brien, "Mike" Norton and others, and called themselves the "Young Democracy." Tweed had used these men in building his power; now, combined, they believed they could retire him. The dangerous classes joined them. Heretofore, these had stood by Tweed under a reciprocal agreement valuable to both sides. But the "Boss" had recently yielded to the public indignation over the leniency shown to an influential murderer, and had given orders to the Judges to deal more severely with flagrant criminal cases. This act constituted a virtual breaking of the compact, and the lawbreakers with one accord turned against him. There were at this time in the city, it was charged, about 30,000 professional thieves, 2,000 gambling establishments and 3,000 saloons.[1]

The plan of the Young Democracy leaders was to induce the Legislature to pass a measure known as the Huckleberry charter, the object of which was to abolish the State commissions governing the city and to obtain a

[1] Statement of Rev. Dr. H. W. Billings, in Cooper Union, April 6, 1871.

relegation of their powers to the Board of Aldermen. The disclosure was made, many years later, that Richard Croker and seven other members of the Board of Aldermen had signed an agreement before a notary public, on March 20, 1870, pledging themselves to take no official action on any proposition affecting the city government without first obtaining the consent of Senator Genet and four other Young Democracy leaders.[2] These latter boasted that they would " put the charter through " if it took $200,000 to do it. To save himself, Tweed opened a half-way understanding with the Young Democracy chiefs, by which he was to join them and abandon Sweeny. Tweed even offered — though vainly — one of the most formidable young leaders $200,000 outright if he would swerve the Young Democracy to his interest.

The Young Democracy succeeded in winning over a majority of the general committee, and influenced that majority to call a meeting to be held in the Wigwam, on March 28. But the plotters had overlooked the society, whose Sachems, being either in, or subservient to, the " ring," now exercised the oft-used expedient of shutting out of the hall such persons as happened to be obnoxious to them. When the members of the general committee appeared before Tammany Hall, on the night of March 28, they found to their surprise that the " ring " had caused to be placed a guard of 600 policemen about the building, to prevent their ingress. The gathering convened in Irving Hall, nearby, where by roll call it was found that 187 members of the committee, later increased by about a dozen — a clear majority of the whole number — were present. Fiery speeches were made, and the set purpose of dethroning and repudiating the " ring " Sachems was emphatically declared.

But the Young Democracy failed to distribute among the members of the Legislature the sum promised, and the country members, by way of revenge, voted down

[2] Testimony *Senate Committee on Cities,* 1890, Vol. II, pp. 1711–12.

the Huckleberry charter. Greatly encouraged by his enemies' defeat, the " Boss " went to Albany with a vast sum of money and the draft of a new charter. This charter, supplemented by a number of amendments which Tweed subsequently caused the Legislature to pass, virtually relieved the " ring " of accountability to anybody. The State commissions were abolished, and practically the whole municipal power was placed in the hands of a Board of Special Audit, composed of himself, Connolly and Mayor Hall. No money could be drawn from the city without the permission of this board. The powers of the Board of Aldermen, moreover, were virtually abolished.[3]

The charter, which immediately became known as the " Tweed charter," was passed on April 5. The victory cost every dollar of the sum Tweed took with him. Samuel J. Tilden testified that it was popularly supposed that about $1,000,000 was the amount used.[4] Tweed stated that he gave to one man $600,000 with which to buy votes, this being merely a part of the fund. For his services this lobbyist received a position requiring little or no work and worth from $10,000 to $15,000 a year.[5] Tweed further testified that he bought the votes of five Republican Senators for $40,000 apiece, giving one of them $200,000 in cash to distribute.[6] The vote in the two houses was practically unanimous: in the Senate, 30 to 2, and in the Assembly, 116 to 5. The state of the public conscience in New York City may be judged from the fact that the charter received the support of nearly all classes, " large numbers," according to the Annual

[3] The amendments to the charter of 1857 had abolished the Board of Councilmen and reinstituted the Board of Aldermen and the Board of Assistant Aldermen, the two constituting the Common Council. The " Tweed charter " continued these two boards, legislating the then incumbents out of office, and ordering a new election in May. The " ring," of course, secured a large majority in this new Council.

[4] *The Tweed Case,* etc., Supreme Court, 1876, Vol. II, p. 1212.

[5] *Document No. 8,* p. 73.

[6] *Ibid.,* pp. 84–92.

Cyclopedia for 1871, " of the wealthiest citizens signing
the petition " [for its passage].

Tweed's enemies were now crushed. At the election
(April 18) of the Sachems of the society the opposition
could poll only a paltry 23 votes, against the 242 secured
by Tweed's candidates; and even this minority was a fac-
titious one, Tilden declaring that Tweed had arranged
for it, to furnish the appearance of a contest.

Tweed's organization was wonderfully effective. The
society stood ready at a moment's notice to expel from
the Wigwam any person or group obnoxious to him.
The general committee was now likewise subservient. In
every ward he had a reliable representative — a leader,
whose duty was to see that his particular district should
return its expected majority. Under the leaders there
were sub-leaders, ward clubs and associations, and captains of every election district. The organization covered every block in town with unceasing vigilance, ac-
quainting itself with the politics of every voter. The
moment a leader lost his popularity, or hesitated at scru-
ples of any sort, Tweed dismissed him; only vote-getters
and henchmen were wanted. So large was his personal
following, that he not only caused thousands to be appointed to superfluous offices, but had a number of retainers, to whom he paid in the aggregate probably
$60,000 a year, " letting them think they were being paid
by the city." [7] Opposition he had no difficulty in buying
off, as in the case of one " Citizen's Association," whose
principal men he caused to be appointed to various lucrative positions in the city government.[8]

The Registry law having been virtually repealed at
Tweed's order, election frauds were made easier, and as
a result of the abolition by the " Tweed charter " of the
December city election, and the merging into one day's
polling of national, State and city elections, the " ring "

[7] *Document No. 8*, p. 212.
[8] *Ibid.*, pp. 223–25.

was in a position to resume the old practise of trading candidates, if all other resources failed.

With the passage of the " Tweed charter " and the City and County Tax Levy bill [9] of 1870, the stealing expanded to a colossal degree. At a single sitting — on May 5, 1870 — the Board of Special Audit made out an order for the payment of $6,312,500 on account in building the new County Court House. Of this sum barely a tenth part was realized by the city.[10] From the 65 per cent levied on supplies, at the end of 1869, the rate was swelled to 85 per cent. " Jobs " significant of untold millions lurked in every possible form. Great projects of public improvements were exploited to the last dollar that could be drawn from them. A frequent practise of Tweed was to create on paper a fictitious institution, jot down three or four of his friends as officers, put a large amount for that institution in the tax levy and pocket the money. Asylums, hospitals and dispensaries that were never heard of, and never existed except on paper, were put down as beneficiaries of State and city. The thefts were concealed in the main by means of issues of stocks and bonds and the creation of a floating debt, which the Controller never let appear in his statements.

A new reform movement appeared during the Summer and Fall of 1870. Republicans, independents and disaffected Democrats combined forces and nominated Thomas A. Ledwith for Mayor. The reform ticket was apparently received with great public approval, and hopes began to be entertained of its success at the polls. Tweed, however, had already secured, by ways known

[9] For the passage of this bill Tweed paid " in the neighborhood of $50,000 or $100,000." *Document No. 8*, p. 154.

[10] While this was going on Tweed maintained the most benevolent attitude in public. At the Fourth of July celebration in the Wigwam he "called the vast assemblage to order, and with coolness, but delighting (*sic*) modesty, welcomed brothers and guests." *Celebration at Tammany Hall of the 94th Anniversary, etc., by the Tammany Society or Columbian Order*. Published by order of the Tammany Society, 1870.

best to himself, assurance of Republican assistance; he had large numbers of Republican officials, Election Inspectors, and the like, in his pay, and therefore knew that he had nothing to fear. Besides this, Tammany was united and enthusiastic. Its candidates, Hall, for Mayor, and Hoffman, for Governor, had seemingly lost none of their popularity with the rank and file. A few days before the election a popular demonstration, perhaps the largest in Tammany's history, was held in and about the Wigwam. August Belmont presided, and addresses were made by Seymour, Hoffman, Tweed and Fisk (who had now become a Democrat). All the speakers were received with boisterous enthusiasm.

Tweed won, Hall receiving 71,037 votes, to 46,392 for Ledwith. But the indications were plain that a reaction against the "ring" had begun, for Hoffman's vote exceeded that of Hall by 15,631, while Ledwith's vote exceeded that of Stewart L. Woodford, the Republican candidate for Governor, by nearly 12,000.

Partly to quiet his conscience, it was suspected, and in part to make himself appear in the light of a generously impulsive man, Tweed gave, in the Winter of 1870–71, $1,000 to each of the Aldermen of the various wards to buy coal for the poor. To the needy of his native ward he gave $50,000. By these acts he succeeded in deluding the needier part of the population to the enormity of his crimes. Abstractly, these beneficiaries of his bounty knew he had not amassed his millions by honest means. But when, in the midst of a severe Winter, they were gladdened by presents of coal and provisions, they did not stop to moralize, but blessed the man who could be so good to them. Even persons beyond the range of his bounty have hailed him as a great philanthropist; and the expression, "Well, if Tweed stole, he was at least good to the poor," is still repeated, and furnished, in its tacit exoneration, the prompting for like conduct, both thieving and giving, on the part of his successors.

One of Tweed's schemes was the Viaduct Railroad bill, which virtually allowed a company created by himself to place a railroad on or above the ground, on any city street. The Legislature passed, and Governor Hoffman signed, the bill, early in 1871. One of its provisions authorized and compelled the city to take $5,000,000 of stock; [11] another exempted the company's property from taxes or assessments, while other bills allowed for the benefit of the railroad the widening and the grading of streets, which meant a " job " costing the city from $50,000,000 to $65,000.000.[12] Associated with Tweed and others of the " ring " as directors were some of the foremost financial and business men of the day. The complete consummation of this almost unparalleled steal was prevented only by the general exposure of Tweedism a few months later.

In the Assembly of 1871 party divisions were so even that Tweed, though holding a majority of two votes, had only the exact number (65) required by the constitution as a majority. In April " Jimmy " Irving, one of the city Assemblymen, resigned, to avoid being expelled for having assaulted Smith Weed. But Tweed was equal to the occasion, for the very next day he obtained the vote and services of Orange S. Winans, a Republican creature of the Erie Railroad Company. It was charged publicly that Tweed gave Winans $75,000 in cash, and that the Erie Railroad Company gave him a five-years' tenure of office at $5,000 a year.[13]

Tweed neglected no means whatever to avert popular criticism. A committee composed of six of the leading and richest citizens — Moses Taylor, Marshall O. Rob-

11 *Senate Journal,* 1871, pp. 482–83.
12 See *A History of Public Franchises in New York City,* by Gustavus Myers.
13 Winans was unfortunate in his bargain, for after rendering the service agreed upon, his employers failed to keep their promises. Tweed gave him only one-tenth of the sum promised, and the Erie Railroad Company gave him no office, nor, so far as can be learned, any compensation whatever.

erts, E. D. Brown, J. J. Astor, George K. Sistare and Edward Schell — were induced to make an examination of the Controller's books, and hand in a most eulogistic report, commending Connolly for his honesty and faithfulness to duty. So highly useful a document naturally was used for all it was worth.[14]

But it was in his tender providence over the newspapers that his greatest success in averting public clamor was shown. Both in Albany and in this city he showered largess upon the press. One paper at the Capital received, through his efforts, a legislative appropriation of $207,900 for one year's printing, whereas $10,000 would have overpaid it for the service rendered.[15] The proprietor of an Albany journal which was for many years the Republican organ of the State, made it a practice to submit to Tweed's personal censorship the most violently abusive articles. On the payment of large sums, sometimes as much as $5,000, Tweed was permitted to make such alterations as he chose.[16] Here, in the city, the owner of one subservient newspaper received $80,000 a year for "city advertising," and to some other newspapers large subsidies were paid in the same guise. Under the head of "city contingencies," reporters for the city newspapers, Democratic and Republican, received Christmas presents of $200 each. This particular practice had begun before Tweed's time,[17] but in line with the expansive manner of the "ring," the plan was elaborated by subsidizing six or eight men on nearly all

[14] John Foley stated to the author that the six members of this committee were intimidated into making this report under the threat that the city officials would raise enormously the assessments on their very considerable holdings of real estate.

[15] *Document No. 8*, pp. 215–18.

[16] *Ibid.*

[17] It was city money which the reporters frequenting the City Hall and court buildings received. The Aldermen passed in 1862 a resolution giving them (sixteen in all) $200 apiece, for "services." Mayor Opdyke vetoed the resolution, but it was passed over his veto. (*Proceedings of the Board of Aldermen*, 1862, Vol. LXXXVIII, p. 708.) The grant was made yearly thereafter.

the city newspapers, crediting each of them with $2,000
or $2,500 a year for " services." ¹⁸

The proprietor of the *Sun,* a newspaper that, from
supporting the Young Democracy, veered suddenly to an
enthusiastic devotion to the " Boss," proposed, in March,
1871, the erection of a statue to Tweed. The " Boss's "
adherents jumped at the idea; and an association for
the purpose was formed by Edward J. Shandley, a Police
Justice, and a host of other men of local note, in professional, political and social circles, among whom were
not only ardent friends of Tweed, but also those who,
having opposed him, sought this opportunity of ingratiating themselves into his favor. The statue was to be
" in commemoration of his [Tweed's] services to the com-
monwealth of New York "— so ran the circular letter.

In a few days the association had obtained nearly
$8,000, some politicians giving $1,000 apiece. Other
men pledged themselves to pay any amount from $1,000
to $10,000, and were on the point of making good their
word when a letter from Tweed appeared, discountenanc-
ing the project. It was printed in the *Sun* of March 14,
1871, under the heading:

"A GREAT MAN'S MODESTY.

" THE HON. WILLIAM M. TWEED DECLINES THE SUN'S STATUE — CHARAC-
TERISTIC LETTER FROM THE GREAT NEW YORK PHILANTHROPIST — HE
THINKS THAT VIRTUE SHOULD BE ITS OWN REWARD — THE MOST RE-
MARKABLE LETTER EVER WRITTEN BY THE NOBLE BENEFACTOR OF THE
PEOPLE."

" Statues," wrote Tweed in part, " are not erected to
living men, but to those who have ended their careers,
and where no interest exists to question the partial trib-
utes of friends." Tweed hinted that he was not so defi-
cient in common sense as not to know the bad effect the
toleration of the scheme would have, and, ever open to
suspicion, he broadly asserted that the original statue

¹⁸ Statement of Mr. Foley.

proposition was made either as a joke or with an unfriendly motive.

One of the signers of the circular has assured the author that it was a serious proposal. The attitude of the *Sun* confirms this. On March 15 that newspaper stated editorially that it thought " Mr. Tweed had acted hastily," and inquired whether it was too late " to realize so worthy and so excellent an idea." In the same issue appears an interview with Justice Shandley, who says :

> " We had contemplated eventually making a public proposition that the testimonial finally take the form of the establishment of a grand charitable institution, bearing Mr. Tweed's honored name, and so overcome the prejudices that the statue proposition have engendered, and passing the fame of that statesman, philanthropist and patriot down to future generations. Mr. Tweed has willed otherwise, and we must submit."

A Chicago clergyman, reading of the suggestion, publicly declared that Tweed was " more dangerous than were the ancient robber kings." Copying this expression, the *Sun* urged editorially on May 13 :

> " Now, let the friends of Mr. Tweed combine together and answer this clergyman by erecting and endowing the Tweed Hospital in the Seventh Ward of this city. A great monument of public charity is the best response that can be made to such accusations."

Tweed aimed at a high social place. He had removed from his modest house on Henry street to a pretentious establishment on Fifth Avenue. His daughter's wedding was among the marvels of the day; from her father's personal and political friends she received nearly $100,000 worth of gifts. Among the wedding presents were forty complete sets of silver and fifteen diamond sets, one of which was worth $45,000. Her wedding dress cost $4,000, and the trimmings were worth $1,000.

All of his expenditures showed a like disregard of cost. In the construction of the stables adjoining his Summer place at Greenwich, Conn., money " was absolutely

thrown away." The stalls were built of the finest ma-
hogany. All told, these stables were said to have cost
$100,000.

The Americus Club was his favorite retreat, and there
his satellites followed him. Scores of them were only
too glad to pay the $1,000 initiation fee required, in ad-
dition to the $2,000 or so charged for sumptuously fit-
ting the room to which each was entitled. The grandeur
of their club badges well illustrated their extravagance.
One style of the badges was a solid gold tiger's [19] head in
a belt of blue enamel; the tiger's eyes were rubies, and
above his head sparkled three diamonds of enormous size.
Another style of badge was of solid gold with the tiger's
head in *papier-maché* under rock crystal. It was surrounded by diamonds set in the Americus belt. Above
was a pin with a huge diamond, with two smaller diamonds on either side. This badge was estimated to be
worth $2,000. A third style showed the tiger's head in
frosted gold, with diamond eyes.

Everywhere the prodigal dissipation of the plunder was
visible. Sums of a few thousand dollars Tweed professed to hold in utter contempt. A city creditor once
appealed to him to use his influence with Controller Connolly to have a bill paid. Twenty times he had asked
for it, the creditor said, and could get it only by paying
the 20 per cent. demanded. (This 20 per cent., it should
be explained, was the sum extorted from all city creditors by the officials in the Controller's office as their
portion after the chiefs of the " ring " had taken the
lion's share.) Tweed looked at the man a moment and
then wrote hastily to Connolly:

[19] The tiger as the symbolic representation of Tammany Hall doubtless dates from this time. This animal was the emblem of the Americus Club, and in Mr. Nast's cartoons it frequently appears, with the
word AMERICUS on its collar. In all probability Mr. Nast was responsible for the transference of the symbol from the club to the organization. The author has been unable to find any earlier reference
to the Tammany tiger.

"Dear Dick: For God's sake pay ——'s bill. He tells me your people ask 20 per cent. The whole d——d thing isn't but $1,100. If you don't pay it, I will. Thine. William M. Tweed."

The " Boss's " note being virtually a command, the bill was paid in full.

CHAPTER XXV

THE downfall of the "ring" was inevitable. No such stupendous series of frauds could reasonably be expected to continue, once the proper machinery for their exposure and for the awakening of the dormant public conscience was put in motion. Protests and complaints and even concerted opposition might for the time prove futile, as indeed they did; but the wind had been sown for the reaping of the whirlwind, and it could not be averted. One conspicuous instance of apparently futile criticism of the " ring " was the action of the New York City Council of Political Reform. This body, but recently organized, held a mass-meeting in Cooper Union, April 6, 1871, to consider " the alarming aspects of public affairs generally," and to agree upon means for arousing the public to some remedial action. Speeches were made by Henry Ward Beecher, Judge George C. Barrett, William F. Havemeyer, William Walter Phelps and William M. Evarts. It was pointed out that the city debt had increased from about $36,000,000 in 1868 to over $136,000,000 at the close of 1870. But amazing as were the facts, the meeting produced no direct effect.

The immediate causes of the exposure were fortuitous and accidental. In December, 1870, Watson, who had become one of the chiefs in the Finance Department, was fatally injured while sleigh-riding, and died a week later. In the resultant change, Stephen C. Lyons, Jr., succeeded Watson, and Matthew J. O'Rourke succeeded Lyons as

County Book-Keeper. Mr. O'Rourke gradually came upon the evidence of the enormous robberies. In the meantime some of the evidence had also come into the possession of James O'Brien, one of the Young Democracy leaders. Controller Connolly was on the point of paying out the $5,000,000 called for by the Viaduct Railroad act, as well as other sums, but learning of O'Brien's knowledge of the situation, resolved to defer the payments. In the Summer of 1871 Mr. O'Rourke presented his evidence to the New York *Times*.

This newspaper published the figures in detail, producing fresh disclosures day after day, and showing indisputably that the city had been plundered on a stupendous scale. In two instances alone — in the printing bills and the bills for the erection and repairing of the County Court House — the *Times* averred that over $10,000,000 had been illegally squandered. Tweed had bought an obscure sheet, the *Transcript*, and had made it the official organ for city and county advertising. He had also formed the New York Printing Company, which not only did the city printing, but claimed the custom of many persons and corporations whom he was in a position either to aid or injure. These two properties served as the highly useful *media* with which to extort millions from the city treasury. The *Times* gave the incontestible figures, disclosing that the sum of nearly $3,000,000 was squandered for county printing, stationery and advertising during the years 1869, 1870 and 1871.

But the new County Court House, the *Times* demonstrated, was the chief means of directly robbing the city. All told, so far as could be learned, the sum of $3,500,000 had been spent for " repairs " in thirty-one months — enough, the *Times* said, to have built and furnished five new buildings such as the County Court House. Merely the furnishing, repairing and decorating of this building, it was shown, cost $7,000,000. One firm alone — Ingersoll & Co.— received, in two years, the gigantic sum of

$5,600,000 " for supplying the County Court House with furniture and carpets." In brief, the County Court House, it was set forth specifically, instead of costing between $3,000,000 and $5,000,000, as the " ring " all along had led the public to believe, had actually cost over $12,000,000, the bulk of which was stolen.

The members of the " ring " affected an air of uncon- cern regarding the disclosures. When Tweed was ques- tioned as to the charges, he made his famous reply: " What are you going to do about it? " He professed not to care for newspaper attacks. Yet Thomas Nast's terribly effective cartoons pierced him to the heart. " If those picture papers would only leave me alone," he lamented, " I wouldn't care for all the rest. The people get used to seeing me in stripes, and by and by grow to think I ought to be in prison." Mayor Hall put on an air of jocose indifference, occasionally replying to the charges by references to the alleged frauds in the Fed- eral Government,[1] but oftener by wondrously facetious jests such as: " Counts at Newport are at a discount "; " shocking levity — the light-ship off Savannah has gone astray "; " these warm, yet occasionally breezy days, with charmingly cool mornings and evenings, are an indication that we are likely to have what befell Adam — an early Fall." [2]

The public, however, was at last aroused, and the impu- dent flippancy of Tweed, Hall and others only added to the public indignation. Though the *Times* was but im- perfectly armed with proofs, each day's revelations brought the citizens to a keener realization of the unprec- edented enormity of the thefts, and the resolve was made by leading members of both parties in the city to unite and crush the " ring." A call for a mass-meeting, to be held in Cooper Union, September 4, was met by a tremen- dous outpouring of citizens. William F. Havemeyer, the

1 New York *Times,* August 29, 1871.
2 *Ibid.,* August 30, 1871.

former Mayor, presided, and 227 vice-presidents and 15 secretaries were chosen from among the foremost names in the community.   Among the speakers were Robert B. Roosevelt and Judge Edwards Pierrepont.   Now, for the first time, the public obtained a really definite idea of the magnitude of the sum stolen by the " ring " and its followers.   Resolutions were reported by Joseph H. Choate, stating that the acknowledged funded and bonded debt of the city and county was upward of $113,000,000 — over $63,000,000 more than it was when Mayor Hall took office — and that there was reason to believe that there were floating, contingent or pretended debts and claims against the city and county which would amount to many more millions of dollars, and which would be paid out of the city treasury unless the fiscal officers were removed and their proceedings arrested.   The resolutions concluded by directing the appointment of an Executive Committee of Seventy, to overthrow the " ring," abolish abuses, secure better laws, and by united effort, without reference to party, obtain a good government and honest officers to administer it.

The first move decided upon by the Committee of Seventy was to make a thorough examination of the city's accounts.   A sub-committee was on the point of doing this when, on the morning of September 11, it was reported that the Controller's office, in the City Hall, had been broken into on the previous night and the vouchers, more than 3,500 in all, stolen.   The " ring " confederates pretended that the vouchers had been abstracted from a glass case — an absurd explanation considering that after spending $400,000 for safes the city officials should have chosen such a flimsy receptacle.   Later, the charred remains of these vouchers were discovered in an ash-heap in the City Hall attic.

As if to yield to public opinion, Mayor Hall at once asked Connolly to resign as Controller.   Connolly refused, on the ground that such a step without impeachment and conviction on trial would be equal to a confession of guilt. Secretly, however, fearing that the other members of the " ring " intended to make a scape-goat of him, he was disposed to make terms with the Committee of Seventy to save himself. Upon the advice of Havemeyer, he appointed Andrew H. Green, Deputy Controller. With Mr. Green in that post, the Committee of Seventy could expect a tangible computation of the " ring's " thefts. Alive to their danger, the other members of the " ring " in terror tried to force Connolly to resign, so as to end the powers he had delegated to the new Deputy Controller. Mayor Hall insisted that in making Mr. Green Acting Controller, Connolly's action was equivalent to a resignation, and with much bluster said he would treat it as such.

In October the sub-committee made a hasty examination of such of the city accounts as were available, and were enabled to report that the debt of the city was doubling every two years; that $3,200,000 had been paid for repairs on armories and drill rooms, the actual cost of which was less than $250,000; that over $11,000,000 had been charged for outlays on the unfinished County Court House,[3] the entire cost of building which, on an honest estimate, would be less than $3,000,000; that safes, carpets, furniture, cabinet-work, painting, plumbing, gas and plastering, had cost $7,289,466, the real value of which was found to be only $624,180; that $460,000 had been paid for $48,000 worth of lumber; that the printing, advertising, stationery, etc., of the city and county had cost in two years and eight months, $7,168,212; that a large number of persons were on the payrolls of the city whose services were neither rendered nor needed; and that figures upon warrants and vouchers had been altered fraudulently and payments made repeatedly on forged endorsements.

[3] Later estimates put the expenditures on the Court House at $13,-000,000. The generally accepted figures were over $12,000,000.

These figures, though presenting nothing more than an outline of the immensity of corruption, gave the Committee of Seventy a foundation upon which to proceed legally. It at once obtained an injunction from Judge Barnard, restraining for the time the payment of all moneys out of the city treasury.[4] The order was modified subsequently to permit the necessary payments. The city treasury had been sacked so completely that it was found necessary to borrow nearly a million dollars from the banks to satisfy the more pressing claims.

The Committee of Seventy next presented Mayor Hall before the Grand Jury for indictment. Anticipating this, the "ring" had "packed" the Grand Jury; but such was the public outcry on this fact becoming known, that Judge Barnard was forced to dismiss the jury and order a new panel. The second jury, however, did not indict the Mayor, giving, as a reason, the lack of conclusive evidence. Later, Hall was tried, but the jury disagreed. The Committee of Seventy next procured the appointment of Charles O'Conor as assistant to the Attorney-General, and then engaged, as O'Conor's assistants, William M. Evarts, Wheeler H. Peckham and Judge Emmott, with the express view of driving the "ring" men into prison. Through their energy, Tweed was arrested, on the affidavit of Samuel J. Tilden, on October 26, and held to bail in the sum of $1,000,000.

But Tweed was not yet crushed. In a few days — on November 7 — an election for members of the Legislature, State officers, Judges of the Supreme Court, and Aldermen and Assistant Aldermen, was to be held. Most

---

[4] It was John Foley who procured the injunction. Mr. Foley later informed the author that upon the original injunction being obtained, the "ring" made a great clamor about the thousands of laborers who would be deprived of their wages, and ordered their hired newspaper writers so to incite the workingmen that the chief movers against the "ring" would be mobbed. In fact, were it not for public protection, grudgingly given on demand, it is doubtful whether some of the opponents of the "ring" would have survived the excitement.

of the "ring" men, in the very face of the revelations of
their stupendous thefts, forgery, bribing and election
frauds, came forward as candidates for renomination and
election. Once elected, they reckoned upon their "vindication." The Committee of Seventy naturally aimed at
the defeat of the Tammany candidates, both for political
and moral effect, and placed candidates in the field for all
local, legislative and judicial offices.

As Grand Sachem and chairman of the Tammany
General Committee, Tweed was still "boss." He arranged to win by his oft-used weapons of bribery and
intimidation, if not by violence. The two Republican
Police Commissioners were his hirelings, owing their offices
to him. They could be depended upon to aid their Tammany colleagues into making the police a power for his
benefit. How well, otherwise, the "ring" was fortified,
was shown when the *Times* [5] charged that sixty-nine members of the Republican General Committee, which assumed
to direct the counsels of the Republican party in the city,
were stipendiaries of Tweed and Sweeny. One of them
was quoted as saying, " I go up to headquarters the first
of every month and get a hundred dollars, but I don't hold
no office and don't do no work."

Tammany feigned to regard Tweed as a great benefactor being hounded. Tweed carried out the comedy to his
best. On September 22 a " great Tweed mass-meeting"
assembled in " Tweed Plaza." Resolutions were vociferously adopted, that,

" pleased with his past record and having faith in his future, recognizing his ability and proud of his leadership, believing in his integrity and outraged by the assaults upon it, knowing of his stead-
fastness and commending his courage, admiring his magnanimity
and grateful for his philanthropy, the Democracy of the Fourth
Senatorial District of the State of New York, constituents of the
Hon. William M. Tweed, in mass-meeting assembled, place him in
nomination for re-election, and pledge him their earnest, untiring
and enthusiastic support." [6]

[5] August 19, 1871.
[6] New York *Times*, November 2, 1871.

Despite the public agitation over the frauds, the Tammany nominations were of the worst possible character. Nominees for the State Senate included such " ring " men as Genet, " Mike " Norton, John J. Bradley and Walton; and for the Assembly, " Jim " Hayes, an unscrupulous tool; " Tom " Fields, reputed to be probably the most corrupt man that ever sat in the Legislature; Alexander Frear, who for years had engineered " ring " bills; and " Jimmy " Irving, who had been forced to resign his seat in the Assembly the previous Winter to avoid being expelled for a personal assault on a fellow-member. The innumerable Tammany ward clubs, all bent on securing a share of the " swag," paraded and bellowed for these characters.

The election proved that the people had really awakened. The victory of the Committee of Seventy was sweeping. Of the anti-Tammany candidates, all of the Judges, four of the five Senators, 15 of the 21 Assemblymen, and all but two of the Aldermen were elected, and a majority of the Assistant Aldermen had given pledges for reforms.

The one Tammany candidate for Senator elected was the " Boss " himself, and he won by over 9,000 majority. The frauds in his district were represented by careful observers as enormous. In many precincts it was unsafe to vote against him. Opposing voters were beaten and driven away from the polls, the police helping in the assaults. The reelection of Tweed, good citizens thought, was the crowning disgrace, and measures were soon taken which effectually prevented him from taking his seat.

On November 20 Connolly resigned as Controller, and Andrew H. Green was appointed in his place. On November 25 Connolly was arrested and held in $1,000,000 bail. Unable to furnish it, he was committed to jail. On December 16 Tweed was indicted for felony. While being taken to the Tombs he was snatched away on a writ of *habeas corpus* and haled before Judge Barnard, who released him on the paltry bail of $5,000. A fortnight later, forced by public opinion, Tweed resigned as Commissioner of Public Works, thus giving up his last hold on power.

The careers of the "ring" men after 1871 form a striking contrast to their former splendor. Tweed ceased to be Grand Sachem. Almost every man's hand seemed raised against him. The newspapers which had profited most by his thefts grew rabid in denouncing him and his followers, and urged the fullest punishment for them.

He was tried on January 30, 1873. The jury disagreed. During the next Summer he fled to California. Voluntarily returning to New York City, against the advice of his friends, he was tried a second time, on criminal indictments, on November 19. Found guilty on three-fourths of the 120 counts, Judge Noah Davis sentenced him to twelve years' imprisonment and to pay a fine of $12,000. Upon being taken to Blackwell's Island, the Warden of the Penitentiary asked him the usual questions: "What occupation?" "Statesman!" he replied. "What religion?" "None."

After one year's imprisonment, Tweed was released by a decision of the Court of Appeals, on January 15, 1875, on the ground that owing to a legal technicality the one year was all he was required to serve. Anticipating this decision, Tilden and his associates had secured the passage of an act by the Legislature, expressly authorizing the People to institute a civil suit such as they could not otherwise maintain. New civil suits were then brought against Tweed, and as soon as he was discharged from the Penitentiary he was rearrested and held in $3,000,000 bail.

This bail he could not get, and he lay in prison until December 4, when, while visiting his home, in the custody of two keepers, he escaped. For two days he hid in New Jersey, and later was taken to a farm-house near the Palisades. He disguised himself by shaving his beard and clipping his hair, and wearing a wig and gold spectacles. Fleeing again, he spent a while in a fisherman's hut near the Narrows, visiting Brooklyn and assuming the name of " John Secor." Leaving on a schooner, he landed on the coast of Florida, whence he went to Cuba in a fishing smack, landing near Santiago de Cuba. The fallen " Boss " and a companion were at once arrested as suspicious characters — the Ten Years' War being then in progress — and Tweed was recognized. He, however, smuggled himself on board the Spanish bark *Carmen*, which conveyed him to Vigo, Spain. Upon the request of Hamilton Fish, Secretary of State, he was arrested and turned over to the commander of the United States man-of-war *Franklin*, which brought him back to New York on November 23, 1876.

In one of the civil suits judgment had been given against him for over $6,000,000. Confessing to this, he was put in jail, to be kept there until he satisfied it, a requirement he said he was unable to meet. The city found no personal property upon which to levy. Tweed testified in 1877 that he held about $2,500,000 worth of real estate in 1871, and that at no time in his life was he worth more than from that amount to $3,000,000.[7] He had recklessly parted with a great deal of his money, he stated. He testified also to having lost $600,000 in two years in fitting up the Metropolitan Hotel for one of his sons,[8] and to having paid his lawyers $400,000 between 1872 and 1875. His escape from Ludlow Street Jail had cost him $60,000. It is reasonably certain that he had been blackmailed on all sides, and besides this, as has already been shown, he had been compelled to disgorge a vast share of the plunder to members of the Legislature and others. When his troubles began he transferred his real estate — and, it is supposed, his money — to his son, Richard M. Tweed.

[7] *Document No. 8,* p. 306.   [8] *Document No. 8,* p. 372.

In Ludlow Street Jail he occupied the Warden's parlor, at a cost of $75 a week. As he lay dying, on April 12, 1878, he said to the matron's daughter: "Mary, I have tried to do good to everybody, and if I have not, it is not my fault. I am ready to die, and I know God will receive me." To his physician, Dr. Carnochan, he said: "Doctor, I've tried to do some good, if I haven't had good luck. I am not afraid to die. I believe the guardian angels will protect me." The matron said he never missed reading his Bible. According to S. Foster Dewey, his private secretary, Tweed's last words were: "I have tried to right some great wrongs. I have been forbearing with those who did not deserve it. I forgive all those who have ever done evil to me, and I want all those whom I have harmed to forgive me." Then throwing out his hand to catch that of Luke, his black attendant, he breathed his last.

Only eight carriages followed the plain hearse carrying his remains, and the cortège attracted no attention. "If Tweed had died in 1870," said the cynical Coroner Woltman, one of his former partizans, "Broadway would have been festooned with black, and every military and civic organization in the city would have followed him to Greenwood."

Sweeny settled with the prosecutor for a few hundred thousand dollars and found a haven in Paris, until years later he reappeared in New York. He lived to an old age. The case of the People against him was settled — as the Aldermanic committee appointed in 1877 to investigate the "ring" frauds reported to the Common Council — "in a very curious and somewhat incomprehensible way." [9] The suits were discontinued on Sweeny agreeing to pay the city the sum of $400,000 "from the estate of his deceased brother, James M. Sweeny." What the motive was in adopting this form the committee did not know. The committee styled Sweeny "the most despicable and

[9] *Document No. 8*, p. 29.

dangerous [of the "ring"] because the best educated and most cunning of the entire gang." [10]

Connolly fled abroad with $6,000,000, and died there. Various lesser officials also fled, while a few contractors and officials who remained were tried and sent to prison, chiefly upon the testimony of Garvey, who turned State's evidence, and then went to London. Under the name of "A. Jeffries Garvie," he lived there until his death in 1897.

Of the three Judges most involved — Barnard, Cardozo and McCunn [11]— the first and the last were impeached, while Cardozo resigned in time to save himself from impeachment.

The question remains: How much did the "ring" steal? Henry F. Taintor, the auditor employed in the Finance Department by Andrew H. Green to investigate the controller's books, testified before the special Aldermanic committee, in 1877, that he had estimated the frauds to which the city and county of New York had been subjected, during the three and a half years from 1868 to 1871, at from $45,000,000 to $50,000,000.[12] The special Aldermanic committee, however, evidently thought the thefts amounted to $60,000,000; for it asked Tweed whether they did not approximate that sum, upon which he gave no definite reply. But Mr. Taintor's estimate, as he himself admitted, was far from complete, even for the three and a half years. It is the generally accepted opinion among those who have had the best opportunity for knowing, that the sums distributed among the "ring" and its allies and dependents amounted to over $100,000,-000. Matthew J. O'Rourke, who, since his disclosures, made a further remarkable study of this special period, informed the author that, from 1869 to 1871, the "ring"

[10] *Ibid.*, p. 30.

[11] Barnard and Cardozo were both Sachems. Mr. Foley is the author's authority for the statement that when Barnard died, $1,000,000 in bonds and cash was found among his effects.

[12] *Document No. 8.*

stole about $75,000,000, and that he thought the total
stealings from about 1865 to 1871, counting vast issues
of fraudulent bonds, amounted to $200,000,000. Of the
entire sum stolen from the city only $876,000 was recov-
ered.

The next question is: Where did all this money go?
We have referred to the share that remained to Tweed
and Connolly, but the other members of the great " ring "
and its subordinate " rings " kept their loot, a few of
them returning to the city a small part by way of restitution. When Garvey died in London, his estate was valued
at $600,000.

CHAPTER XXVI

1872-1874

AFTER the disclosures of 1871, the name of Tammany Hall became a by-word throughout the civilized world, and the enemies of corruption assured themselves that the organization was shorn of political power for a long time to come. But the wonderful instinct of self-preservation which had always characterized Tammany, joined with the remarkable sagacity which its chiefs almost invariably displayed in critical times, now conspired to keep the organization alive despite every antagonistic influence. The Tammany Society still had its charter, and while that charter remained intact, Tammany retained strong potentialities for regaining power. The reformers neglected to ask for its annulment — though it is doubtful if they could have obtained it, since the Governor, John T. Hoffman, was a creation of the Tammany organization.

The urgent need of the Wigwam was a leader. In response to the demand, two men, John Kelly and John Morrissey, stepped to the front. Both of them were the product of local politics, and having made a science of their experience, they knew that the Tammany Hall that now lay prostrate and reviled could be raised and again made a political factor, and eventually the ruler of the city. The few men of fair character in the organization were undesirous of appearing too prominently in its councils; but despite the general odium attached to it, Kelly and Morrissey found that a large part of the thoughtless

mass of the Democratic voters were still willing to follow
its leadership.

Kelly had been in Europe from 1868 to late in 1871,
and had not been directly implicated in the Tweed frauds.
He had a strong personality, and was popular among the
largest and most energetic part of the voting population
— the Irish. He was called " Honest John Kelly," and
he took care to strengthen the belief implied in that name,
surrounding himself at all times with a glamour of political probity. Born April 20, 1822, in New York City,
of poor parents, his early life was divided between hard
work and fighting, though he never appeared in the prize-
ring. His trade was that of a grate-setter and mason.
His early education was defective, but he later improved
his natural talents by study at the parochial and evening
schools.

The district in which he lived was the roughest in the
city. Being a man of aggressive ways and popular
enough to control the turbulent elements, the politicians
in 1853 had him elected an Alderman, a post which he
retained during 1854 and 1855. In this body he was
known as a " bench-warmer "— that is, a member who
kept his seat and followed the orders of his political masters without question. Giving satisfaction, he was selected to run for Congress in the district then represented
by " Mike " Walsh — who was regarded in Washington
as the leader of the rowdy element of New York City.
Walsh ran independently, but Kelly beat him by 18 votes
in a total vote of 7,593. It was generally charged then
and long after that Kelly was " counted in."   Later he
was reelected. During his terms in Congress, Kelly controlled most of the Federal patronage in New York City,
and it was through his influence especially that Isaac V.
Fowler — who, as we have mentioned, was afterward
found to have embezzled over $155,000 from the Govern-
ment — was reappointed Postmaster by Buchanan.

In 1863 Kelly, disgruntled at not being appointed a

Police Commissioner, led a portion of the Irish vote from the Wigwam over to the Germans, helping in the election of Gunther as Mayor. Having proved his influence, Tweed, in order to gain him over, gave him the nomination for Sheriff, to which office he was elected. His nomination for Mayor and his sudden withdrawal we have already related.

At the time of his flight to Europe he was a rich man. Mayor Havemeyer charged, in 1874, as we shall see, that some, at least, of Kelly's wealth was obtained by anything but proper methods.

This was the successor of Tweed as the " boss " of Tammany Hall. His coadjutor for a time, John Morrissey, was a professional prize-fighter and gambler, whose boast was that he " had never fought foul nor turned a card." [1] When these men assumed control of the Wigwam, few persons believed it could outlive the " ring " revelations and regain power.

Then occurred an extraordinary happening, though quite in keeping with Tammany shrewdness. At the society's annual election, in April, 1872, Kelly and Augustus Schell (who had been elected Grand Sachem after Tweed was forced to resign) caused to be selected as Sachems some of the identical men who had been most conspicuous in the reform movement, such as Samuel J. Tilden, Charles O'Conor, Horatio Seymour, Sanford E. Church and August Belmont. The best proof that the non-partizan movement of 1871 was already dissolving was the readiness with which these men accepted these elections. Their acceptance may have been due to a mixed desire to make of the organization a real reform body as well as to advance their political fortunes.

The Tammany Society now stood before the public as

[1] In Tweed's confession (1877) Morrissey is mentioned as having introduced a system of repeating from Philadelphia, and also as having acted as paymaster of the fund of $65,000 distributed among the Aldermen to secure the confirmation of Sweeny as Chamberlain.

a reform body, with the boast that all the thieves had been cast out. Next it appointed a reorganization committee to reconstruct the Tammany Hall political organization. Under its direction the general committee was enlarged to nearly five hundred members, and a new general committee, of unquestionably better quality than its predecessor, was elected. In the case of disputing district delegations, the Tammany Society's committee decided by selecting the best men for both.[2] Out of chaos, within a few months of the " ring's " overthrow, Kelly created a strong organization, so deftly composed as to place itself before the people as an entirely distinct set of men from the " ring " thieves — as a really Democratic body, quite as heartily in favor of good government as the most exacting reformer.

Kelly acted with great shrewdness, executive force, knowledge of men, and apparent regard for the public interests and proprieties. He affected extreme modesty, and made it appear that the delegates chose nominees by their own uninfluenced will. At the Judiciary convention in Tammany Hall, in October, 1872, he insisted that each delegate vote; in his speech he said that Tammany should have no more of the times when tickets were made up outside of conventions. Some delegates shouting for the nomination of a man of dubious character, he declared, with the air of a man exerting himself for the good of his party only, that it was time that Tammany Hall should put such a ticket in the field that no man could hold up the finger of scorn at any individual on it. He furthermore caused the appointment of a committee to cooperate in the work of reform with the Bar Association, the Committee of Seventy, the Municipal Taxpayers' Association and the Liberal Republicans.

At Kelly's suggestion the Wigwam, in the Fall of 1872,

[2] The reorganization committee reached the understanding that the society should thereafter keep in the background and that it should not prominently interfere in the organization's affairs.

nominated for Mayor, Abraham R. Lawrence, a member of the Committee of Seventy and its counsel, and for Judges of the Supreme and Superior Courts, men of ability and unimpeachable name. Altogether, Tammany took on such a new guise that thousands of voters returned to its support. But the anti-Tammany movement had not yet dissipated its strength, even though it presented a divided front. One wing of this opposition was the new " reform " organization, the " Apollo Hall Democracy," founded by James O'Brien, who now stood forth as its candidate for Mayor. The other wing, composed of the individuals and associations centering about the Committee of Seventy, nominated William F. Havemeyer.

Tammany had the advantage of a Presidential year, when the obligation of " regularity " could be imposed upon a goodly share of the Democratic voters, and the further advantage of a high order of personal character in its nominees. Nevertheless, Havemeyer won, the vote standing approximately: Havemeyer, 53,806; Lawrence, 45,398; O'Brien, 31,121. The results from several election districts were missing and were never canvassed by the Board of Canvassers. For Horace Greeley, the Democratic Presidential candidate, Tammany Hall carried the city by 23,000 majority.

Mayor Havemeyer's administration differed greatly from most of the " reform " administrations that had preceded it. Never since the year 1800 had the city revenue been distributed with such great care. The utmost regard was paid to the ordinances dealing with public health and security, and the streets were kept cleaner than ever before. The rowdy and criminal classes were deprived of the free sway they had so long enjoyed. The public school system was improved, and the standard of official character was of a higher type than had been known in many a decade. The city expenditures in 1873 were about $32,000,000, as compared with $36,262,589.41 in 1871, and notwithstanding the tremendous legacy of debt left by the Tweed "ring" to be shouldered by later administrations, Mayor Havemeyer's administration reduced the city expenses about $8,000,000 in reality, though the bare figures on their face did not show that result.

Mayor Havemeyer complained, as so many of his predecessors had done, of the perverse interference of the Legislature in city affairs — an interference which constantly embarrassed his plans and set back the cause of reform.

The Mayor was not destined to serve his full term. In September, 1874, a bitter quarrel sprang up between him on the one hand and John Kelly and John Morrissey on the other, apparently over the appointment, at Kelly's request, of Richard Croker to be a Marshal. "When Croker's appointment was announced," wrote the Mayor, "I was overwhelmed with a torrent of indignation." In a public letter addressed to Kelly, Mayor Havemeyer charged that the former, while Sheriff, had obtained $84,482 by fraudulent and illegal receipts, adding this further characterization:

"I think that you were worse than Tweed, except that he was a larger operator. The public knew that Tweed was a bold, reckless man, making no pretensions to purity. You, on the contrary, were always avowing your honesty and wrapped yourself in the mantle of piety. Men who go about with the prefix of 'honest' to their names are often rogues."

Kelly replied that he had acted in the Sheriff's office as had his predecessors, and brought a libel suit against the Mayor, in the answer to which the latter embodied his charges in full. But on the day the suit was to come to trial Havemeyer fell dead of apoplexy in his office.

During the two years (1872–74) various forces combined to restore Tammany to the old power. The two great parties were struggling for partizan advantage for future State and national elections. This brought about the old party alignment, the reform Democrats, as a rule, acting with the Wigwam, and the reform Republicans drifting to the Republican side. The disreputable classes issued forth in greater force than ever to help replace in power the Tammany that meant to them free sway. The panic of 1873, with the consequent " hard times," turned great bodies of voters against the dominant party. The " ring " had so thoroughly looted the city that Havemeyer's administration was forced to practise economy in the public works. The working classes either did not understand the motive of this retrenchment, or did not appreciate it. Out of the 24,500 mechanics in the city during the Winter of 1873–74, 15,000, it was estimated, were unemployed. Tammany now adroitly declared itself in favor of giving public employment to the workers. The Wigwam agents scoured the poorer districts during the campaign of 1874, giving aid to the needy, and gained their support. The agitation against a third term for President Grant; the demand for a low tariff and the denunciation of the Washington " ring," all had their effect, while the impression which naturally might have been expected from Havemeyer's charges against Kelly was entirely lost by the former's slurring allusions to Kelly's humble birth and early occupation — allusions which threw the sympathy and support of the masses strongly to Kelly and his ticket.

The astonishing consequence was that in November, 1874, Tammany Hall which, in 1871, seemed buried beneath obloquy, elected its candidate for Mayor, William H. Wickham (a diamond merchant and an anti-" ring " Democrat and a member of the Committee of Seventy) by nearly 9,000 majority over all, his vote being 70,071, against 24,226 for Oswald Ottendorfer, the Independent Democratic candidate, and 36,953 for Salem H. Wales, the Republican. At the same election, Tilden, who had also contributed to the downfall of the " ring," received the solid support of Tammany, and was elected to the Governorship.

Tammany Hall under the surface was rapidly becoming its old self. Its candidate for Register, " Jim " Hayes, had made, it was charged, $500,000 during the Tweed régime. Fully three-fourths of the office-seekers in this election were connected with the liquor interests ; and as many of these were keepers of low groggeries, they were in constant conflict with the law. Nine of the fifteen Tammany candidates for Aldermen were former creatures or beneficiaries of the " ring," one of them being under two indictments for fraud. Yet the partizan currents at work again swept almost all of them into office.

Well realizing the value of appearances, Kelly lectured the new members of the Common Council,[3] telling them that " there must be no bad measures, no ' rings,' no getting together of a few men for the purpose of making money and controlling patronage." Yet Kelly himself at this time absolutely controlled the strongest and probably the most corrupt political organization in the Union. He dictated State, Judicial, Congressional, Legislative and municipal nominations at will, and continued to be the absolute " boss " until his death in 1886.

[3] Amendments to the charter, passed in 1873, vested local powers in a Board of Aldermen and a Board of Assistant Aldermen — the latter to be abolished on and after January 1, 1875, and the Board of Aldermen to form thenceforth the Common Council. The Common Council was not to pass any measure over the Mayor's veto without the vote of two-thirds of all its members. A part of the former Aldermanic powers was restored to this board by the amendments of 1873 and later years.

CHAPTER XXVII

THE DICTATORSHIP OF JOHN KELLY

1874–1886

THE history of the Tammany Society and of Tammany Hall during the period from 1874 onward embraces a vast and intricate web of influences, activities and consequences. To present this period in the detail proportionate to that employed in the preceding chapters would require an amount of space inconsistent with the projected volume of this work. It will, therefore, be presented in the manner of a COMPREHENSIVE SUMMARY, in which the main movement will be outlined, and particular treatment given only to the more important features and events.

Toward the end of 1874 Kelly's rule had become supreme. Under the form of "requests" he assessed every office-holder, even calling upon men receiving only $1,000 a year to pay as much as $250. To systematize these assessments, he established a regular collectorship, in charge of the society's Wiskinskie, a city employee drawing $1,500 a year for apparent services. Abundant charges, some of which were proved, were made as to corruption in many of the city departments.

During the next year (1875) a number of disaffected Wigwam men formed the "Irving Hall Democracy" and issued an address denouncing the Tammany General Committee as the creature of the society. The effect of this defection and of the charges of public corruption were such that in the local elections Tammany lost many of the minor offices.

The friendship between Kelly and Tilden had already been broken. Kelly organized a bitter opposition to Tilden at the St. Louis national convention, in 1876, but pledged himself to support the nominations, and kept his word.

The Presidential campaign of this year held the municipal struggle within strict party lines. The various Democratic factions united on Smith Ely, electing him Mayor by a majority of 53,517 over John A. Dix, the Republican candidate.

From December, 1876, to December, 1880, Kelly filled the position of City Controller, and was credited with reducing the city debt. Politics, however, rather than fiscal administration for the benefit of the city, continued to be his main business. One of the numerous examples of his superior sagacity in bowing to the general public sentiment was his support, in 1878, of Edward Cooper, an anti-Tammany nominee for Mayor, a man of recognized independence of character, who was elected. Tammany at this time was still largely influenced by the old Tweed conspirators, the assertion being made in 1877 that at least fifty former office-holders under Tweed were to be found in the general committee.[1]

In 1879 occurred the well-known fight of Tammany against the Democrats of the rest of the State. The Democratic State convention had assembled at Syracuse. The roll-call had barely begun when Augustus Schell, spokesman for the Tammany organization, stated that as there was every prospect that Gov. Lucius Robinson would be renominated, the delegates from New York City would withdraw, although they stood ready to support any other name. This "suggestion," as Schell afterwards called it, was unheeded, whereupon the entire Tammany delegation retired. The delegation meeting elsewhere, Kelly, with the specific object of defeating Rob-

[1] *Document No. 8,* p. 102.

inson, caused himself to be nominated for Governor. The quarrel between Robinson and the Tammany chief was personal, arising from the fact that the Governor had removed Henry A. Gumbleton, a prominent Wigwam man, from the office of County Clerk. Such was the discipline to which Kelly had reduced the organization that it obeyed his word without a single protest.

He succeeded in his ulterior object. His 77,566 votes caused the defeat of Robinson, who received 375,790 votes, to 418,567 for Alonzo B. Cornell, the Republican candidate. The significant lesson furnished by Kelly's making good his threat, was one generally heeded thereafter by State and national politicians and candidates, who declined to invite the hostility of so great a power. But for this secession, and the consequent demoralization of the Democratic party in the State, New York's electoral vote, it is generally thought, would have gone to Gen. Hancock in 1880. Mayor Cooper refused to reappoint Kelly to the office of Controller at the expiration of his term, in December, 1880, because of his supposed agency in the defeat of Hancock.

In 1880 the Democrats of the city were divided into the factions of Tammany Hall and Irving Hall, but laying aside differences till after the election, they agreed upon an apportionment of the local offices. The Democratic candidate for Mayor, William R. Grace, was selected by the Tammany committee from a list of names submitted by Irving Hall. Many of the members of the latter organization, however, were prejudiced against Mr. Grace because of his Roman Catholic faith, fearing that in case of his election the public school appropriations would be diverted to sectarian uses. They joined with the Republicans in support of William Dowd. The vote stood: Grace, 101,760; Dowd, 98,715.

Mayor Grace's official power was considerably limited by the action of the Legislature, which had made the tenure of office of executives of departments longer than

his own — a law which in effect put the department heads
in a position independent of the Mayor. In frequent
messages, Mayor Grace expressed himself, as had Mayor
Havemeyer, pointedly, though vainly, on the evils of
legislative interference with the local government.

In December, 1880, a new organization, called the
"New York County Democracy," was formed by Abram
S. Hewitt and others, to oppose both Tammany Hall
and Irving Hall. This body soon had a large enrolled
membership, and was joined later by a number of Democrats who had unsuccessfully attempted to bring about
reform in Tammany. To that end they had made an
effort, at the society's annual election in April, 1881, to
elect their candidates for Sachems, when the ticket headed
by Kelly won by an average majority of 50 in about 775
votes. The fact, or belief, that the result was secured
through repeating and other unfair means, caused a considerable defection from Tammany.

In the State convention of October, 1881, the Tammany delegation was ruled out, and the County Democracy was declared "regular." At an earlier period this
adverse decision might have entailed serious, if not fatal,
consequences to the Wigwam. But now that the organization was in a state of absolute discipline, ruled by
one hard-headed, tireless "boss," with each member understanding that his self-interest required his "standing
by" the organization in times of trouble, as well as in
times of triumph, the blow had no lasting effect.

Holding the balance of power in the Legislature of
1882, the Tammany members resolved to force the "regular" Democracy to make terms with them. To that end
they attended no party caucuses, and refused to support
men nominated by the "regular" Democrats. At Kelly's order they demanded, as the price of their cooperation, certain chairmanships of important committees.
Not getting them, they continued for weeks their stubborn opposition. Finally the two houses were organized,

the Tammany men voting for the Republican candidate for clerk. Charges were freely made of a political bargain between Kelly and Gov. Cornell.

There were three Democratic factions in the city in 1882 — Tammany Hall, Irving Hall and the County Democracy. A movement to obtain non-partizan government caused the independent nomination of Allan Campbell for Mayor. The Republicans indorsed him, but their support was greatly weakened by their nomination of a spoils politician, John J. O'Brien, for County Clerk. The three Democratic factions agreed on Franklin Edson, who was elected by a majority of 21,417, the vote being: Edson, 97,802; Campbell, 76,385.

In the Chicago national convention of 1884 the Tammany delegation bitterly oposed the nomination of Grover Cleveland, its orators virulently assailing his private and public character. Though profesing afterward to support him as the Democratic candidate, the Wigwam refused to unite with other Democratic organizations in any political demonstration. The reason seems to have been Mr. Cleveland's publicly expressed independence of Kelly and his machine. After the ensuing election, Tammany was generally charged with treachery. The Wigwam nominated a separate city and county ticket, naming Hugh J. Grant for Mayor. The County Democracy and Irving Hall agreed upon the nomination of former Mayor William R. Grace, and elected him with the rest of the fusion ticket, the vote being: Grace, 96,288; Grant, 86,361; Frederick S. Gibbs (Republican), 45,386.

In these years the control of the city offices was frequently divided among the various parties and factions. In the Board of Aldermen, as in the departments, were Tammany and County Democracy men and Republicans, so that no one faction or party completely swayed the city. Much of their former power had been restored to

the Aldermen by the charter amendments of 1873, by
the State constitution of 1874 and various legislative
acts. Reports arose from time to time that money was
used to secure confirmation of appointments by the Aldermen, but the nearest approach to detail was the testimony of Patrick H. McCann before the " Fassett Committee " in 1890.

Mr. McCann testified that Richard Croker, a brother-
in-law, came to his store in 1884, with a bag containing
$180,000, which, he said, was to be used in obtaining
Aldermanic votes to secure the confirmation, in case of
his appointment, of Hugh J. Grant as Public Works
Commissioner, and that he (Mr. Croker) was to get ten
cents a barrel on all cement used by that department.[2]
Mr. McCann further testified that Mr. Croker had told
him that $80,000 of this sum was furnished by Mr. Grant,
and the remainder by the organization. Mr. Croker,
according to the same testimony, opened negotiations
through Thomas D. Adams for the purchase of two Republican Aldermen, whose votes were needed. The alleged " deal," however, was not consummated, and the
money was returned. Mr. Croker and Mr. Grant both
swore that these statements were untrue.[3]

But the extraordinary corruption of the Board of
Aldermen of 1884 is a matter of public record. Twenty-
one members — the exceptions among those present and
voting being Aldermen Grant and O'Connor — voted to
give the franchise for a surface railway on Broadway to
the Broadway Surface Railroad Company.[4] The rival
road, the Broadway Railroad Company, sought to bribe
the Aldermen with $750,000, half cash and half bonds,
but the Aldermen thought the bonds might be traced, and
considered it wiser to accept the $500,000 cash offered

2 *Testimony, Senate Committee on Cities,* 1890, Vol. I, pp. 682–98.
3 *Ibid.,* 733, and *Ibid.,* Vol. II, p. 1693.
4 *Proceedings of the Board of Aldermen,* Vol. CLXXV, pp. 237–39.

by the former,[5] each Alderman receiving $22,000.[6] Mayor Edson vetoed the resolution,[7] but it was repassed.

Other street railway franchises were passed by the same board. Mr. McCann testified in 1890 that Mr. Grant had told him that Mr. Croker strongly advised him [Grant] not to have anything to do with " that Broadway matter," as " they [the other Aldermen] would be caught." [8]   Mr. Grant denied having said so.[9] The fact remains that Mr. Grant was the only Tammany Alderman free of suspicion.   Many of the accused Tammany city fathers were members of the organization's executive committee, which was composed almost exclusively of leaders, and which was supposed to direct the Wigwam's affairs.[10]

One Alderman, Henry W. Jaehne, was sentenced to penal servitude at hard labor for the term of nine years and ten months; and another, " Honest " John O'Neill, to four years and a half, and to pay a fine of $2,000; a third, Arthur J. McQuade, was sentenced to seven years and ordered to return $5,000 of the bribe money to the city, but on July 20, 1889, at a new trial at Ballston, he was acquitted.   Six other Aldermen fled to Canada, and three turned State's evidence.   Ten others were indicted, but were never brought to trial.   As Col. John R. Fellows, the District Attorney who tried the cases, stated to the Fassett Committee, convictions could not then (1890) be secured, because public sentiment had changed; the storm had subsided; people had grown tired of the subject, and many former opponents of the franchise

---

[5] Alderman Arthur J. McQuade's testimony before Recorder Smythe, November 19, 1886.

[6] Alderman Fullgraff's additional testimony before Recorder Smythe.

[7] *Proceedings of the Board of Aldermen,* Vol. CLXXVI, pp. 777–84.

[8] *Testimony, Senate Committee on Cities,* 1890, Vol. I, pp. 706–7.

[9] *Ibid.,* Vol. I, p. 752.

[10] *Ibid.,* p. 744.

had come to look upon it as a benefit.[11]   But there were strong hints that political influence had saved many persons from prison.

Though the facts did not come out until the trials in 1886, public indignation and suspicion were so strong in 1884 that Kelly insisted that the Tammany Aldermen who had voted for the franchise should not be renominated.[12]

Kelly broke down with nervous and physical prostration after the Presidential campaign of 1884.   Grover Cleveland's election, which falsified his predictions, deeply disappointed him.   He kept to his house, No. 34 East Sixty-ninth street, but still issued his orders to the Tammany organization.   Towards the end, he could not sleep except by the use of opiates.   He died on June 1, 1886.

Thus passed away the second absolute "boss" of Tammany Hall.   For more than ten years 50,000 voters obeyed his commands, and it was he and not the people to whom a host of office-holders, contractors, and all who profited directly or indirectly from politics, looked as the source of their appointment, employment or emolument.   On more than one occasion Kelly complained of his onerous duty of providing government for New York City.   The secret of his control was the same as that of Tweed and of the previous cliques: he knew that a large part of the voting mass cared nothing for good government, but looked upon politics solely as a means of livelihood; that another large part were satisfied to vote the "regular" ticket under any and all circumstances; and, with a keen understanding of human nature, he knew how to harmonize conflicting interests, to allay personal differences, and to soothe with large promises of future rewards his disaffected followers.   Profiting by Tweed's

[11] *Testimony, Senate Committee on Cities,* 1890, Vol. III, pp. 2667–68.

[12] Testimony of Hugh J. Grant, *Ibid.,* Vol. I, p. 739.

fate, he knew the value of moderation; and he earned the praise, not only of his interested followers, but also of a tolerant and easy-going class in the community, through the fact that under his rule the stealing, compared to that of the Tweed régime, was kept at a comparatively respectable minimum.   It was pointed out to his credit that the fortune he left — reputed to be $500,000 — was very reasonable for one who so long had held real control of a great city.

CHAPTER XXVIII

1886–1897

UPON the death of Kelly, the twenty-four leaders of the Assembly Districts, comprising the executive committee of Tammany Hall, announced individually that there would be no further " boss," and that the organization would be ruled thenceforth by a committee of twenty-four. However, cliques immediately arose, and soon four leaders — Richard Croker, who had been a sort of deputy " boss " under Kelly; Hugh J. Grant, Thomas F. Gilroy and W. Bourke Cockran — arranged a junta for administering the organization's affairs. By securing the support of 17 of the 24 leaders, Mr. Croker began concentrating power in his own hands, and for about fourteen years remained the absolute ' boss ' of both society and organization.

Mr. Croker was born near Cork, Ireland, November 24, 1843. His father was a blacksmith, who emigrated to America in 1846, and settled in a squatter's shanty in what is now the upper portion of Central Park. From his thirteenth to his nineteenth year young Croker worked as a machinist. At a very early age he distinguished himself in the semi-social fist-fights which were a part of the life of the " gang " to which he belonged. He became, tradition has it, the leader of the " Fourth Avenue Tunnel Gang," and fought a number of formal prize-fights, in which he came out victor.

At the beginning of the Tweed régime, according to his testimony before the Fassett Committee, he was an attendant under Judge Barnard and other Judges in the Supreme Court. Upon leaving that place, for some reason not known, he served as an engineer on a Fire Department steamer.[1] In 1868 and 1869 he was elected an Alderman. With a majority of his fellow-members, he sided with the Young Democracy against Tweed, and was accordingly, with the rest of the board, legislated out of office (April, 1870). But he must have made his peace with the " Boss " soon after, for Controller Connolly appointed him Superintendent of Market Fees and Rents. In 1873 he was elected Coroner. On election day, November 3, 1874, during a street row growing out of a political quarrel between Mr. Croker and James O'Brien, John McKenna was shot dead. Bystanders maintained that Mr. Croker fired the shot, and the Grand Jury indicted him for the crime. The trial jury, after being out for seventeen hours, failed to agree. Public opinion at the time was divided, but it is the preponderance of opinion among those who are in a position to know, that Mr. Croker did not fire the fatal shot.

In 1876 he was reelected Coroner. In 1883 he ran for Alderman, with the understanding that if elected, thus establishing the fact of his constituents' approval, Mayor Edson would appoint him a Fire Commissioner. During the canvass, a Police Captain, one of Croker's protégés, was responsible for a brutal clubbing, the feeling over which had the effect of reducing his plurality to about 200. Mayor Edson, however, gave him the appointment, and he was reappointed by Mayor Hewitt. His alleged connection with the fund of $180,000 to be used in behalf of Hugh J. Grant, in 1884, has already been mentioned. In 1885 he caused the nomination of the latter for Sheriff. Mr. Grant, while in that office, according to Mr. McCann's testimony, gave $25,000, in five presents of $5,000 each, to Mr. Croker's two-year-old daughter Flossie.[2]

[1] *Testimony, Senate Committee on Cities,* 1890, Vol. II, pp. 1708–12.
[2] *Testimony, Senate Committee on Cities,* 1890, Vol. I, pp. 707–8.

Neither Mr. Croker nor Mr. Grant denied this transaction, though both declared the sum was $10,000 and
not $25,000.[3]   Mr. Grant furthermore declared that he
gave it in consideration of Flossie being his god-child.

Mr. Croker showed the sagacity common to a long line
of Tammany chiefs in the municipal campaign of 1886.
It was a time of great excitement.   The labor unions,
including the Knights of Labor, had reached the highest
point in organization and in solidarity of feeling ever
attained by them in the history of the city.   Knowing
their strength, they were ripe for independent political
action, and they were rendered all the more ready for it
by the earnest social propaganda carried on at the time
by Single-Taxers, Socialists and social reformers generally.

The conviction of certain members of a union for carrying on a boycott against the Thiess establishment, on
Fourteenth street, proved the one impulse needed for the
massing together of all the various clubs and unions into
one mighty movement.   The convictions were believed to
be illegal, and moreover to have been fraudulently obtained — and Tammany was held responsible.   Before
long the nucleus of an independent political party was
formed.   Henry George, then at the height of his popularity, was looked upon as the logical leader, and he was
asked to become the new party's candidate for Mayor.
To this request he gave an affirmative answer, contingent
upon the securing of 25,000 signatures to his nominating
petition.

Mr. Croker saw the danger, and he took immediate
steps to avert it.   According to the open letter of Henry
George to Abram S. Hewitt, October 17, 1897, Mr.
Croker, in behalf of Tammany Hall and the County
Democracy, tried to buy off George by offering him a
nomination regarded as equivalent to an election.

3 *Ibid.*, pp. 745–50, and *Ibid.*, Vol. II, p. 1701.

George, of course, refused; the 25,000 names, or a great part of them, were secured; a nominating convention was held; George was formally nominated, and the United Labor party was launched. A spirited campaign in George's behalf was at once begun, and was responded to by the masses with remarkable enthusiasm.

Mr. Croker was equal to the crisis. The agitation among the masses must be met by the nomination of a representative of the conservative interests, and a general appeal be made for the " saving of society." Accordingly he chose as the Tammany candidate the County Democracy's choice, Abram S. Hewitt.

The Republicans nominated Theodore Roosevelt. His candidacy, however, was not regarded so seriously as otherwise it might have been, for the contest narrowed down at once to a class struggle between George and Mr. Hewitt. Anarchy and every other social ill were prophesied by the conservatives as the certain results of the former's election, and Republicans were openly urged to support the latter.

The result proved the keenness of Mr. Croker's foresight. The vote stood: Hewitt, 90,552; George, 68,110; Roosevelt, 60,435. Yet it would be difficult to name a time in recent years, if the reiterated statements of reputable eye-witnesses are to be believed, when frauds so glaring and so tremendous in the aggregate have been employed in behalf of any candidate as were committed in behalf of Mr. Hewitt in 1886. There are few living men among the earnest band who supported George's interests at the polls on that election day who do not believe that their candidate was grossly " counted out."

Mayor Hewitt revealed an independence of character that astonished the Wigwam. Before many months he had antagonized its powerful leaders. By 1888 the United Labor party had dwindled into a faction, and there being no such compelling reason, as in 1886, for choosing a candidate outside of the organization, the

chiefs selected one of their own number, Hugh J. Grant.
Mr. Hewitt was nominated by the County Democracy,
Joel B. Erhardt by the Republicans, and James J.
Coogan by the remnant of the United Labor party. The
vote was as follows: Grant, 114,111; Erhardt, 73,037;
Hewitt, 71,979; Coogan, 9,809. For Grover Cleveland,
whom Tammany had this time supported at the nominating convention, the city gave a plurality of 55,831, out of
a total vote of about 270,000.

One of the Tammany men elected was James A. Flack,
Grand Sachem of the society (1888–1889), who assumed
the duties of Sheriff the following January. During the
same year Flack surreptitiously and fraudulently obtained a divorce in order to remarry. His wife was the
ostensible plaintiff, but it was shown that she knew nothing of the suit. Flack and his accomplices were indicted
by the Grand Jury, whereupon he was tried and sentenced
to two months in the Tombs prison, and to pay a fine of
$500. The Supreme Court later affirmed the sentence.
Some others implicated also went to prison. The scandal
was such that Flack was removed from the Sheriff's office,
and was forced to resign as Grand Sachem of the society.

Tammany was now in practically complete control,
and carried things with a high hand. Most of the departments had again become inefficient and corrupt. On
March 21, 1890, the Grand Jury handed down a presentment stating that the Sheriff's office, which for twenty
years had been a hotbed of corruption, had recently been
brought into " public scandal and infamy," through the
growth of notorious abuses; that in 1889 the Sheriff's net
profits had been at least $50,000, not including certain
" extra compensations that could not be ascertained."
Many other abuses, the Grand Jury further recited, were
found to be connected with the management of this office,
and also with the conduct of the Ludlow Street Jail.

At about the same time the State Senate Committee

on Cities, headed by J. Sloat Fassett, a Republican, undertook an investigation. Though subjected to the charges
of lukewarmness and bargaining, this body, popularly
known as the "Fassett Committee," brought out much
valuable information. Part of its testimony has already
been referred to. It is impossible even to summarize the
vast total embodied in the 3,650 printed pages of its report, but some of the more interesting particulars may be
briefly touched upon.

Henry S. Ives and George H. Stayner testified that,
while prisoners at Ludlow Street Jail, they had paid, for
various favors, $10,000 to Warden James P. Keating,
then and later a prominent Tammany leader, and that
previously they had paid other large amounts to certain
Deputy Sheriffs.[4]

John F. B. Smyth testified that when Sheriff Grant
had appointed him Sheriff's auctioneer — the most valuable gift at the Sheriff's disposal — the latter suggested
his having as a partner ex-Alderman Kirk (one of the
Aldermen of 1884 indicted in connection with the Broadway Surface Railroad franchise),[5] saying that the organization insisted on having " one-half of it [the loot] go to
somebody else." In less than a year the gross proceeds
amounted to about $20,000. Of this, $10,000 went to
various Deputy Sheriffs, one of whom was Bernard F.
Martin, frequently Sachem and another noted Tammany
leader.[6]

A copious amount of similar testimony was brought
out implicating many other Tammany leaders, and showing that the Sheriff's known income from the office ranged

[4] *Testimony, Senate Committee on Cities,* 1890, Vol. I, pp. 235–52,
and *Ibid.,* p. 300.

[5] Kirk had been dropped from the Council of Sachems in 1886 owing
to the disclosures.

[6] *Testimony, Senate Committee on Cities,* 1890, Vol. I, pp. 282–87.
Bernard, or "Barney," Martin and two others had been indicted on
the ground of having been bribed, but the indictments were dismissed
in March, 1890, on a technicality which allowed the defendants to fall
back upon the Statute of Limitations.

from $60,000 to $75,000 a year.[7]   Thomas P. Taylor, a lawyer, swore that one of his clients in 1888 had had a claim of about $4,000 in the Sheriff's hands, and that William H. Clark, a Sachem and a powerful Tammany leader, the partner of W. Bourke Cockran, and sometime Corporation Counsel, had asked him (Taylor), "what he would give to get it." Mr. Taylor further testified that he had given nothing, and that he had secured only a few hundred dollars of the amount, after much trouble.[8] Clark denied the charge.[9]

Corruption, favoritism and blackmail were charged against all the other departments controlled by Tammany, though in the Police and Excise departments, Republican and Tammany commissioners alike were shown to have winked at the abuses. Gambling houses had to pay at least $25 a week for protection,[10] and revenue was likewise derived from every place or person capable of being blackmailed. The testimony strongly pointed to the probability that as much as $10,000 had been paid to get a certain saloon license, though there was no absolute verification of the statement.

One interesting fact officially brought out — a fact long generally known, however, and stated heretofore in this work — was that the Wiskinskie of the Tammany Society, nominally a city employee, was the official agent of the organization in collecting assessments, said to vary from 5 to 10 per cent., on the salaries of every Tammany officeholder. In fact, Mr. Croker unhesitatingly admitted before the Fassett Committee, that at that time it cost from $50,000 to $75,000 to run the organization successfully.[11] Considerable sums were likewise derived from assessments on candidates. Mr. Hewitt, it was said, contributed $12,000 in 1886, but Mr. Croker developed a very

7 *Testimony, Senate Committee on Cities,* 1890, Vol. I, p. 344.
8 *Ibid.,* pp. 502–11.
9 *Ibid.,* p. 513.
10 *Ibid.,* Vol. II, p. 1244.
11 *Testimony, Senate Committee on Cities,* Vol. II, p. 1756.

poor memory when questioned about this and contributions from many Judges and other office-holders.[12]

The revelations, as usual, caused the formation of a citizens' movement, and a strong combination of Republicans, Democrats and independents was formed, under the name of the "People's Municipal League," for the purpose of ousting Tammany. Francis M. Scott, a Democrat, was nominated for Mayor, and a vigorous campaign was waged. Tammany minimized the disclosures, and renominated Mr. Grant. A Democratic tidal wave swept the nation in the Fall of 1890, and on this wave the Tammany ticket was carried to victory, the local majority being 23,199.

The effect on the society and the organization of this victory, following so closely upon the Fassett revelations, was to impress the Tammany men with an added sense of security. Accordingly, by tacit understanding, smirches made upon reputations before the Fassett Committee were to constitute no bar to political advancement, and the old condition of things in the departments was to continue. Many of those who had suffered most at the hands of the Senatorial inquisitors were elected during the next four years to places in the society and to public offices. Irving Hall and the County Democracy passed out of existence, and Tammany had full sway. Administrative corruption continued, and frauds at the polls, despite certain improvements in the ballot laws instituted in 1890, developed to a science, reaching their climax in 1893.

In 1892 Tammany fought the nomination of Mr. Cleveland for President, though it supported him after his election. Thomas F. Gilroy, Grand Sachem (1892-94) was nominated for Mayor, the Republicans presenting Edwin Einstein. A Democratic landslide marked the election, and the Tammany candidates won by practically

12 *Ibid.,* pp. 1757–62.

the same majority as that given to Mr. Cleveland, Mr.
Gilroy receiving 173,510, and Mr. Einstein, 97,923 votes.
Frauds were numerous, as usual. The opposition vote in
a number of election districts was practically nothing. A
certain Tammany politician, later State Senator from
the lower end of town, stood in the envious wonder of his
fellows for a whole year following, for having secured for
the ticket all the votes but four in his election district.

The fame of this enterprising worker aroused a determination in the breasts of others to exceed his record.
During the next campaign (1893) the general indignation against the corrupt conduct of Judge Maynard,
brought out a strong opposition to his elevation to the
bench of the Court of Appeals. Senator Hill caused
his nomination, Tammany supported him, and the word
was passed around that he must be elected at all hazards.
As a consequence, frauds of the gravest character were
committed throughout the city. The Tammany leader
of the Second Assembly District, zealous to outdo the
record of the previous year, offered prizes to his election
district captains for the best results. The election over-
turned all known records. The successful competitor
brought in a poll of 369 to 0. In two other precincts
no opposition votes of any kind were counted, despite
the presence of Republican inspectors, and the fact that
Republicans, Socialists, Populists and Prohibitionists afterward swore under oath that they had voted for their
respective candidates. The vote in this assembly district,
nominally 8,000, rose to nearly 13,000.

A committee from the Populist County Committee, the
local branch of the National People's party, immediately
took steps to secure evidence through which to effect the
punishment of the lawbreakers.[13] The evidence secured,

13 The credit for instituting this prosecution has been variously, and
sometimes impudently, claimed. There is no doubt, however, that not
only the first, but the most important evidence, was furnished by this
committee, whose practical head was William A. Ellis, of the Second
Assembly District.

with that afterwards obtained by the Republican County Committee, the City Club, the Good Government clubs, and the Bar Association, was submitted to the Grand Jury, upon which some sixty indictments were handed down. A number of convictions were obtained, and several Tammany and assistant Tammany election officers were sent to prison. The Tammany leader of the Second Assembly District went to California immediately after the agitation began, and remained there until the affair blew over. In the election the following year the vote of this district fell to the old figures of approximately 8,000.

The city had again become scandalously corrupt. The bi-partizan boards, which originally had been established in the hope of applying some check to the general rascality, had merely furnished greater opportunities for deals and political bargaining. Charges of blackmail, extortion, of immunity given to crime, and most other forms of administrative venality, grew so common that again the State Senate sent (April, 1894), a committee to the city to investigate. This was the body commonly known as the "Lexow Committee," from its chairman, Clarence Lexow. Its counsel, John W. Goff, vigorously conducted the investigation, and the result was a mass of information regarding Tammany methods of government such as the public had not known since the exposures of Tweed's time. We can but touch upon the testimony.

It was shown that during each of the years 1891, 1892 and 1893, many thousands of fraudulent ballots had been cast by the active cooperation and connivance of the police; Police Captains were appointed from those members of the force who especially connived at these frauds, the appointments being made by the President of the Board of Police (who was one of the most conspicuous Wigwam leaders) at the instance of the organization. Tammany influences permeated the Police Department to such a degree that the district leaders dictated appointments, and from Captain down almost the entire force

joined the Tammany district associations. Forced contributions were levied upon the members for the benefit of
Wigwam district organizations.

Capt. Creedon confessed to paying $15,000 to secure
a promotion to a Captaincy, and Capt. Schmittberger, to
having secured the appointment of another man as Captain, in consideration of the payment of $12,000. The
average cost of obtaining an appointment as policeman
was $300. The police functionaries recouped themselves
in various ways. Vice and crime were protected openly.
One woman who kept a number of houses of ill-repute
testified that she had paid continuously for protection an
aggregate of $30,000 or more. The system reached such
a perfection in detail that a ratable charge was placed
upon each house according to the number of inmates, the
protection prices ranging from $25 to $50 monthly.
Women of the streets paid patrolmen for permission to
solicit, and divided proceeds. Visitors were robbed systematically, and the plunder was divided with the police.
More than 600 policy shops paid at the monthly rate of
$15, while pool rooms paid $300 a month. It was noted
by the committee, as a remarkable fact, that when public
agitation grew very strong, a private citizen, Richard
Croker, secured the closing of these places practically in a
single day. Every form of gambling had to pay high
prices for immunity. Green goods swindlers were required
to make monthly payments, to subdivide the city into
districts, and additionally, in case the victim " squealed,"
to give one-half of the plunder to either ward or headquarters detectives. Saloons paid $20 monthly, accord-
ing " to the established custom." The police also acted
in collusion with thieves and dishonest pawnbrokers. Almost every branch of trade and commerce was forced to
make monthly payments, and from every possible source
tribute was wrung.

The committee incorporated in its testimony the estimate of Foreman Tabor, of the Grand Jury, in March,

1892, that the annual income derived from blackmailing and different sources of extortion was $7,000,000.[14]   In this estimate there were probably not included the large sums paid by corporations of every kind, and all who sought the favor or feared the power of Tammany Hall.

The two Democratic members of the Police Board at this time were James J. Martin, one of the powerful district leaders, and John C. Sheehan, who became deputy " boss " during Mr. Croker's absence.   No direct evidence was given to establish their complicity in the general extortion, but John McClave, the Republican Commissioner, resigned after a searching and pointed examination.

Mr. Croker did not testify before the Lexow Committee, urgent business demanding his presence in England throughout the investigation.

The public was aroused as it had not been since 1871. An earnest agitation for reform, largely due to the crusade of Rev. Charles H. Parkhurst, and to the work of the City Club and the Good Government clubs, was begun. A Committee of Seventy, composed of representatives of all classes, was formed to carry on a political contest, and an enthusiastic support was given to it by the great mass of the public throughout the campaign.   William L. Strong, a Republican and a prominent dry goods merchant, was nominated by the Seventy for Mayor, and the Republicans indorsed him.   Tammany, after floundering about for several weeks in the vain hope of securing a candidate strong enough to stem the opposing tide, selected at first Nathan Straus, who withdrew, and then Hugh J. Grant, making its campaign largely on the ground that Mr. Grant was the only unsmirched Tammany member of the " Boodle " Board of Aldermen of 1884.   The contest was bitter and determined on both sides, Tammany putting forth its utmost efforts to avert the inevitable disaster. According to a statement of John C. Sheehan, the organ-

[14] *Investigation of the Police Department,* etc., 1894, Vol. V, p. 5734.

ization expended more money in this election than in any election in recent years.

The convictions of the previous year had served to cool the zeal of the Tammany workers for records at the polls. In consequence of this, and of further changes in the manner of balloting, New York enjoyed probably the most fairly conducted election of any since the first organized effort of Tammany men at the polls in 1800. Strong was elected by a majority of 45,187. With his election went nearly the whole of the city patronage, changes in the new constitution (1894) having greatly centralized the city's administrative functions in the Mayor's hands. Tammany was thus thrust out again.

Mayor Strong's administration on the whole was beneficial. The city budget went up to nearly $44,000,000, but for the first time since Mayor Havemeyer's time the streets were kept clean — a result due to the systematic energy of Col. George E. Waring, Jr. Moreover, new schools were built, new parks laid out, streets asphalted, improvements planned and carried out, while administrative corruption was almost unheard of. Not the least of the benefits of this administration was the partial reform of the Police Department, through the efforts of Police Commissioner Theodore Roosevelt, and his fellow Commissioners, Avery D. Andrews, Andrew D. Parker and Frank Moss.

In the mean time Richard Croker spent most of his time in England. From being a comparatively poor man, as he testified in 1890, he became suddenly rich. From April, 1889, to February, 1890, he was City Chamberlain, at a salary of $25,000 a year, but thereafter he held no public office. Within two years, however, he was able, according to common report, to buy an interest in the Belle Meade stock farm for $250,000, paying additionally $109,000 for Longstreet and other race horses. Later, he built a new house, said to cost over $200,000, and lavishly spent money, and displayed the evidences of wealth in other ways.

When in the city he was, for a considerable number of years, in the real estate business. He is popularly credited with having been interested in the passage and development of certain extremely valuable franchises which were obtained from the Legislature and Board of Aldermen for almost nothing. In 1892 he was reputed to dominate the Legislature, as he did the city, and the lobby disappeared. It was related at the time that all applicants for favors or for relief from hostile measures were advised " to see headquarters."

One of the franchises granted during that year was the " Huckleberry franchise," for a street railway in the Annexed District — a grant which was worth at the time fully $2,000,000, and yet was practically given away under circumstances of great scandal.[15] When testifying before the Mazet Committee in 1899, he was asked whether he had owned, in 1892, 800 shares of the stock of this road, but declined to state.[16] Another illustration of Mr. Croker's alleged diversified interests was furnished by a statement said to have been inspired by John C. Sheehan and published on December 23, 1900. Mr. Sheehan asserted that in 1894 he and Mr. Croker were interested in a company formed with a capital of $5,000,000 for the construction of the rapid transit tunnel. Mr. Sheehan, the statement read, forced through the Board of Aldermen a resolution approving the tunnel route which he and Mr. Croker had selected as the most feasible. The statement further set forth that Mr. Croker had $500,000 worth of this company's stock, which came to him gratuitously, and that he and Mr. Sheehan had been also mutually interested in a proposed surety company.

As chairman of the finance committee of Tammany

[15] See *A History of Public Franchises in New York City,* by the author.
[16] Stenographic minutes, p. 699.

Hall (a post Tweed and Kelly had held, and which carried with it the titular leadership of the organization), all the vast funds contributed for Tammany's many campaigns passed through his hands. As he himself testified, the finance committee kept no books.[17]

Whether Mr. Croker was at home or far abroad, his control of the Wigwam was absolute. Long since, he had inaugurated the system of " turning down " any man that disobeyed orders.

At the time of Mr. Bryan's nomination, in 1896, Mr. Croker was in England. His three years' racing experience there cost him, it was reported, between $600,-000 and $700,000. He remained abroad, leaving the organization, as we have mentioned, in charge of John C. Sheehan as a kind of vicegerent. Mr. Sheehan's public record in Buffalo had been severely criticized, and many organization men had protested against his being put in charge. This protest, however, was generally understood at the time to be founded not so much on the matter of Mr. Sheehan's record as on that of his being an interloper from another section of the State. Tammany that year ignored the national Democratic platform. Though ratifying Mr. Bryan's nomination, a general apathy prevailed at the Wigwam throughout the campaign, and the more radical Democrats repeatedly charged the leaders with treachery to the ticket. The result of this apathy and of other influences was that Mr. McKinley carried the city by over 20,000 plurality.

Mr. Croker finally returned home in September, 1897, shortly before the meeting of the Democratic city convention. It was commonly believed that Mr. Sheehan, the deputy " boss," had made preparations to assume the " boss-ship " himself, but Mr. Sheehan emphatically

17 *Testimony, Senate Committee on Cities,* 1890, Vol. II, p. 1755. Mr. Sheehan in the statement cited stated that when, in 1894, Mr. Croker sent an order to the district leaders requiring that district assessments amounting to $35,000 should be paid before March 1, the payments were promptly made.

denied this. Whatever the circumstances were Mr. Croker promptly deprived the former of power, and later succeeded in practically excluding him from the organization.

The " Boss's " supreme control of city politics was illustrated by the nomination for Mayor of Greater New York of Robert C. Van Wyck, who was in no sense the organization's candidate, but represented merely Mr. Croker's choice and dictation. The Citizens' Union nominated Seth Low, who probably would have been elected had the Republicans indorsed him. But the latter nominated Benjamin F. Tracy, thus dividing the opposition, which was still further disintegrated by the action of the Jeffersonian Democrats in nominating Henry George, and later Henry George, Jr., upon the noted economist dying in the heat of the campaign. The canvass was carried on with the greatest vigor, for under the Greater New York charter all the territory now embraced in the city limits was to vote for one Mayor, with a four-years' term, and almost dictatorial power in the matter of appointments and removals. In his statement, heretofore referred to, Mr. Sheehan asserted that during this campaign he personally collected and turned over to John McQuade,[18] the treasurer of Tammany Hall, the sum of $260,000, irrespective of contributions collected by others, and that at the end of the canvass Mr. McQuade had $50,000 in the treasury.[19]

The vote stood: Van Wyck, 233,997; Low, 151,540; Tracy, 101,863; George, 21,693; scattering, 17,464. The Wigwam was beside itself with joy; the victory

[18] Mr. McQuade was associated with Tweed, as a commissioner, in the building of the Harlem Court House. The testimony brought out in the case of Henry A. Smalley vs. The Mayor, etc., before Judge Donohue, in the Supreme Court, January 28, 1878, showed that the value of all the material used in the building was $66,386, but that the Finance Department had paid out for this material $268,580.

[19] Early in 1898 Tammany Hall, with considerable display, disposed of most of this fund, by giving $20,000 for the poor of the city and a like sum for the Cuban cause.

meant absolute control of the greater city's annual budget of over $90,000,000, not to speak of the tens of millions more derived from rents, fees, fines, interest, assessments for street improvements, bond sales and premiums, and from those vast and varied sources of contract juggling, selling of legislative " goods," and all the other avenues, too numerous to enumerate, of which Tammany from early times has availed itself.   It also meant the control of an army of employees, now estimated at 60,000.   The disreputable classes vociferously celebrated the occasion, assured that the town was once more to be " wide open."

CHAPTER XXIX

THE DICTATORSHIP OF RICHARD CROKER *(Concluded)*

1897–1901

NOW that Tammany was reinstalled in almost absolute power, Mr. Croker set about choosing the important city officials to be appointed by the Mayor. He frankly admitted before the Mazet Committee, in 1899, that practically all of them were selected by him or his immediate associates. Requiring a routine assistant in the work of "bossing," Mr. Croker selected John F. Carroll, who thereupon resigned the office of Clerk of the Court of General Sessions, which yielded, it was estimated, about $12,000 a year, to take a post with no apparent salary. Mr. Croker then returned to horse-racing in England.

The public pronouncements of the organization continued to voice the old-time characteristic pretensions of that body's frugality, honesty and submission to the popular will. In October, 1898, the county convention in the Wigwam passed resolutions commending "the wise, honest and economical" Tammany administration of Greater New York, and denouncing the "corruption, extravagance and waste of the infamous mismanagement" by the previous reform administration. Yet at this very moment the Bar Association was protesting against Mr. Croker's refusal to renominate Judge Joseph F. Daly,[1]

[1] Tweed testified in 1877 that Joseph F. Daly, with two others, constituted the sole membership of the "Citizens' Association" of 1870, and that he had placated the three men by giving them offices, Mr. Daly securing a Judgeship of the Court of Common Pleas.

on the ground of his refusing to hand over the patronage of his court. The convention itself, despite its fine words, acted merely as the register of the will of one man, with scarcely the formality of a contest; and the public had again become agitated over the certainty of grave scandals in the public service.

Tammany's election fund this year was generally reputed to be in the neighborhood of $100,000. As much as $500 was spent in each of several hotly contested election districts. Tammany won, but by a margin less than had been expected and, in fact, arranged for. The State Superintendent of Elections, John McCullough, in his annual report (January, 1899) to Gov. Roosevelt, gave good grounds for believing that Tammany had been deprived of a large support on which it had counted. Of 13,104 persons registered from specified lodging houses in certain strong Tammany districts, only 4,034 voted. It was evident that colonization frauds on a large scale had been attempted, and had been frustrated only by the vigilance of Superintendent McCullough.

The state of administrative affairs in the city grew worse and worse, nearly approximating that of 1893–94. The Legislature again determined to investigate, and accordingly sent to the city the special committee of the Assembly, popularly known as the "Mazet Committee." This body's prestige suffered from the charge that its investigation was unduly partizan. Moreover, it was generally felt by the public that its work was inefficiently carried on. Nevertheless, it produced a considerable array of facts showing the existence of gross maladministration.

It was disclosed that every member of the Tammany Society or of the organization's executive committee, held office, or was a favored contractor. Over $700,000 of city orders went to favored contractors without bidding. Various city departments were "characterized by unparalleled ignorance and unfairness." The payrolls in some of the most important departments had increased

$1,500,000 between July 1, 1898, and September 1, 1899, and the employees had increased over 1,000, excluding policemen, firemen and teachers. The testimony proved the increasing inefficiency and demoralization of the Police and Fire Departments. It further proved the existence of a ramified system of corruption similar to that revealed by the Lexow Committee.

The disclosures attracting the greatest public attention were those relating to the Ice Trust, the Ramapo project, and Mr. Croker's relations to the city government. On April 14 the committee exposed a conspiracy between the Ice Trust and the Dock and other departments of the city government, to create and maintain a monopoly of New York's ice supply. Six days after the exposure, Mayor Van Wyck, as he subsequently admitted in his testimony before Judge Gaynor, acquired 5,000 shares, worth $500,-000, of the Ice Trust stock, alleging that he paid $57,000 in cash for them; but although urged to substantiate his statement, did not produce proof that he actually paid anything. It was shown conclusively before the committee that the arrangement between the Ice Trust and the city officials was such as to compel the people to pay 60 cents a hundred pounds, and that the trust had stopped the sale of five-cent pieces of ice, practically cutting off the supply of the very poor. Many other Tammany officials were equally involved. Proceedings were begun some time after, looking to an official investigation of the Ice Trust's affairs, and charges against Mayor Van Wyck were filed with Gov. Roosevelt. The latter were finally dismissed by the Governor in November, 1900.

In August, the committee uncovered the Ramapo scheme. The Ramapo Water Company, with assets " of at least the value of $5,000," sought to foist upon the city a contract calling for payment from the city treasury of an enormous amount in annual installments of about $5,110,000, in return for at least 200,000,000 gallons of water a day, at $70 per million gallons. This was proved to be an attempt toward a most gigantic swindle. Had not Controller Coler exposed and frustrated the scheme, the Tammany members of the Board of Public Improvements would have rushed the contract to passage.

Mr. Croker's testimony threw a flood of light upon his political views and standards as well as his powers and emoluments as " boss." He acknowledged that he had a powerful influence over the Tammany legislators at Albany, whose actions he advised, and that he exercised the same influence upon local officials. He readily conceded that he was the most powerful man he knew of.[2] " We try to have a pretty effective organization," he said; " that is what we are there for." [3]

Mr. Croker also admitted that judicial candidates were assessed in their districts.[4] In fact, some of the Judges themselves named the respective sums to the committee. Judge Pryor testified that he had been asked for $10,000 for his nomination for a vacant half-term in the Supreme Court.[5] Other judicial candidates, it was understood, paid from $10,000 to $25,000 for nominations.[6] Mr. Croker maintained that the organization was entitled to all the judicial, executive, administrative — in brief, all offices — because " that is what the people voted our ticket for." [7] Mr. Croker refused to answer many questions tending to show that he profited by a silent partnership in many companies which benefited directly or indirectly by his power. " The man who is virtual ruler of the city," said Frank Moss and Francis E. Laimbeer, counsel to the committee, in their report, " can insure peace and advantage and business to any concern that takes him and his friends in, and can secure capital here or abroad to float any enterprise, when he guarantees that the city officials will not interfere with it." Mr. Croker was asked

2 *Stenographic minutes*, p. 451.
3 *Ibid.*, p. 465.   4 *Ibid.*, p. 6806.   5 *Ibid.*, p. 523.
6 *Ibid.*, pp. 6891, etc.   7 *Ibid.*, p. 464.

many other questions touching this subject, but gave little information. He declined to answer the question whether $140,000 of the stock of the Auto-Truck Company had been given to him without the payment of a dollar; it was his " private affair." [8]

" We are giving the people pure organization government," he said. He referred to the thoroughness of discipline in the Wigwam, and stated that the only way to succeed was to keep the whip in hand over his henchmen. It took " a lot of time," and he " had to work very hard at it." Tammany was built up, he said, not only upon the political principles it held, but upon the way its members sustained one another in business. " We want the whole business, if we can get it "; " to the party belong the spoils "; " we win, and we expect every one to stand by us "; " I am working for my pocket all the time," were some of Mr. Croker's answers, most of them told in anything but grammatical English.

The general opinion obtained that the committee's work would have been far more effective and free from charges of partizan bias if Thomas C. Platt, the Republican " boss," had been summoned concerning his alleged political connection with the great corporations and financial interests, as Mr. Croker had been.

Apparently the disclosures made no deep impression on the city administration, for matters went along pretty much as before. On March 9, 1900, the New York *Times* published a detailed statement, which it later reiterated, that the sum of $3,095,000 a year was being paid by the gambling-house keepers of the city to the " gambling-house commission," which, it said, was composed of two State Senators, a representative of the pool-room proprietors, and the head of one of the city departments. This commission, the account stated, received and passed upon applications, established the tariff to be paid by the

[8] *Stenographic minutes*, p. 683.

applicants, and supervised the collections. Later, in the same month, the Grand Jury handed down a presentment arraigning the city officials for the sway enjoyed by the criminal and vicious classes.[9]

Neither the Grand Jury's presentment nor the *Times's* detailed statements had the slightest effect on the conduct of the city administration. In November, however, a marked change occurred. For several years certain reform societies and ecclesiastical bodies, particularly the Episcopal Church, had sought to mitigate the open flaunting of immorality in the tenement houses of a particular police district on the East Side. The attempts had been resisted, not only by those living upon the proceeds of this immorality, but by the police themselves; and two ministers who had complained to certain police officials had been grossly insulted.

Immediately after the Presidential election, Bishop Henry C. Potter, of the Episcopal Church, in a stinging letter of complaint, brought the matter to the attention of Mayor Van Wyck. It was the psychologic moment for such an action, and it produced immediate results. Mr. Croker paused in his preparations for his usual trip to England long enough to give orders to put down the immorality complained of, and he appointed a committee of five to carry his mandate into effect, or at least to make some satisfactory show of doing so. He went further than this, for his orders included a general ukase to the lawbreakers of the city to " go slow," or in other words, to observe, until further advices from headquarters, a certain degree of moderation in their infractions of law and their outrages upon decency.

9 On December 22, 1900, Gov. Roosevelt removed Asa Bird Gardiner, the Tammany District Attorney, who was popularly credited with having originated the phrase, " To hell with reform," for having encouraged the turbulent element to open resistance of the law at the election. Eugene A. Philbin, an independent Democrat, was appointed his successor. The latter promptly demanded the resignations of many of Mr. Gardiner's assistants. Before his election Gardiner had long been chairman of the Tammany Hall Legal Committee.

CHAPTER XXX

TAMMANY UNDER ABSENTEE DIRECTION

1901–1902

IN the municipal campaign of 1901 the anti-Tammany forces combined upon the nomination of Seth Low, a Republican, for Mayor, and upon the nominations of various other candidates for city offices. Tammany's candidate for Mayor was Edward M. Shepard. Both Mr. Low and Mr. Shepard were acclaimed by their respective supporters as men of standing, prestige and public character. Mr. Low was a man of wealth who had become president of Columbia University. Mr. Shepard was a lawyer of note, although some critics pointed out that his practise was that of a corporation attorney, serving the great vested interests. It may be remarked that Mr. Shepard was a son of the brilliant Lorenzo B. Shepard, who, as stated in Chapter XVI of this work, became a leader of Tammany Hall at so early an age and was chosen Grand Sachem of the Tammany Society.

The scandals of Mayor Van Wyck's administration were conspicuous issues of the campaign of 1901. But there were two particularly noteworthy features pressed by the reformers in their indictment of Tammany. One of these issues, which made so deep an impression upon the public mind, especially in the densely populous East Side of New York City, was the flagrant immorality under which young girls of the tenderest age were often decoyed into lives of shame. The question thus presented was neither that of the " suppression of vice " nor that of how people could be made virtuous by mandate of law. The question, as put to voters, was whether a system under which a corrupt, money-making combination of vicious lawbreakers with police and other officials should be allowed to continue an abhorrent traffic.

A widely-circulated pamphlet published by the City Club for the Women's Municipal League presented a series of facts as attested by court records, the statements of City Magistrates, the Society for the Prevention of Cruelty to Children and others, and as reported by the Committee of Fifteen, composed of reformers, probing into the question. The pamphlet declared that the facts justified the conclusion that the business of ruining young girls and forcing them into a life of shame, for the money there was in it for the dealers, had recently grown to considerable proportions; that its existence was known to the police; that the police made little or no effort to stop it; that the police, or those for whom they acted, probably derived profit from the traffic; and that a reasonably active and efficient Police Department could stop the traffic of a deliberate merchandizing of the virtue of women, usually young girls. Details were given of numerous cases which had been passed upon in the courts, and a long description of the traffic was included from a statement made on October 21, 1901, by District Attorney Eugene A. Philbin of New York County.[1]

Justice William Travers Jerome, of the Court of Special Sessions, had already made a similar statement. He was quoted in the New York *Times*, of June 27, 1901, as saying:

" People are simply ignorant of conditions on the East Side [of New York City]. If those conditions existed in some other communities there would be a Vigilance Committee speedily organized, and somebody would get lynched. The continued greed and extortion of the Police Captains who charge five hundred dollars for a disorderly resort to open in their precinct, and then collect fifty to a hundred [dollars] per month, has, however, made even vice unprofit-

[1] *Facts for New York Parents,* etc., Published for the Women's Municipal League by the City Club of New York, October, 1901.

able. Details, I know, are revolting and not nice to read, but yet the people ought to know about them. Just yesterday I sentenced to six months in the penitentiary the keepers of one of the most depraved houses of the East Side. I firmly believe that they were merely the agents of the man who owns not one but many of such places. He is well known as a politician in a certain notorious district.

"That house is but one of hundreds within a radius of one mile of this building [the Criminal Court House] where criminals are sometimes brought to justice. I will stake my reputation that there are scores within less than that distance from here in which there are an average of ten or twelve children from thirteen to eighteen years old." [2]

Nominated for District Attorney of New York County by the anti-Tammany forces, Mr. Jerome's speeches on these existing conditions made a keen impression and excited the deepest feeling, especially among the people of the East Side. Intricate questions of taxation and arrays of figures proving an exorbitant budget and the waste of public funds could not make the same appeal to their indignation as the portrayal of conditions menacing their home life and polluting their environment. The facts thus spread forth caused the most intense resentment against Tammany.

In reply Tammany Hall sought to represent that the traffic thus described was largely mythical — and that at all events it was greatly exaggerated. It was no fiction, however, nor was police connivance and corruption a fiction, either. So far as the open flaunting of vicious conditions was concerned, Tammany Hall had itself been forced to recognize them; as a concession to public opinion Mr. Croker had, in November, 1900, appointed an Anti-Vice Committee with orders to investigate vice conditions and " clean up " the " Red Light " district. To impart a tone of good faith to the work of this committee, he had appointed Lewis Nixon, a naval academy graduate and a ship builder, its chairman. It was generally understood that this committee had been created as a clever campaign move to offset in the public mind the growing indignation

2 *Ibid.*

against Tammany, many of the leaders of which, it was notorious, had profited richly from the system of police " protection " of vice.

In respect to the " white slave " traffic, however, it must be said, in justice to Tammany, that the factors attributed were not the only ones responsible, and such a traffic was far from being confined to New York City; it went on in other cities under Republican and Reform as well as Democratic rule.   This was conclusively shown later by the necessity of the passage of a law passed by Congress aimed at the traffic (a law subsequently diverted some-what from its original purpose), and by official investiga-tions and court proceedings.   The large number of prose-cutions in the Federal courts under that law showed the widespread character of the traffic.

Another important issue of the municipal campaign of 1901 was the scandal growing out of the charges that William C. Whitney, Thomas F. Ryan, W. L. Elkins, P. A. B. Widener, Thomas Dolan and associates had looted the stockholders of the Metropolitan Street Rail-way Company of New York City of tens of millions of dollars.   Whitney and Ryan were credited with being among the chief financial powers long controlling " Boss " Croker; and by means of his control of Tammany Hall, and in turn New York City, securing franchises, privi-leges and rights of enormous value.   This control was often equally true of the New York State legislature; subsequent developments, in fact, revealed that in years when the Legislature was dominantly Republican and therefore could not be ordered by Mr. Croker, both Re-publican and Democratic legislators were corrupted by the Metropolitan Street Railway Company, or by agents acting for it.

According to Mr. W. N. Amory,[3] who was thoroughly familiar with the affairs of the Metropolitan Street Rail-

[3] From 1895 to 1900 Mr. Amory was connected in an official capacity with the Third Avenue Railway Company.

way Company, and who exposed its looting, Mr. Jerome knew, in 1901, " that the conduct of Metropolitan affairs was corrupt. We had on numerous occasions discussed that point."

Mr. Jerome made profuse public promises that if he were elected District Attorney he would press investiga-, tion. " Let me tell you," he said at the conclusion of a speech on October 26, 1901, " that if I am elected I shall make it my business to follow the trail of wrongdoing and corruption not only when they lead into tenement houses, but I shall follow them even if they lead into the office of the Metropolitan Street Railway Company." Mr. Jerome added: " No one knows better than I do that when I am attacking the Metropolitan Street Railway Company, I am arraying myself against the most dangerous, the most vindictive and the most powerful influences at work in this community." [4]

Mr. Jerome's denunciations and promises aroused great enthusiasm and large expectations; they had much effect in contributing to the result of the campaign, for it was popularly realized that while Tammany leaders accumulated their millions of dollars, yet back of these leaders, and secretly operating through them, were magnates of great financial power with their tens or hundreds of millions of dollars acquired largely by means of financial and industrial power conferred by legislation, permissory or statute, of various kinds. The electorate well knew that comparatively small grafters were numerous, but now it had the promise that the large spoliators, hitherto immune, would be exposed and prosecuted, if possible.

The result of the election was that Mr. Low was elected Mayor by a plurality of 31,636. Nearly all of the other anti-Tammany candidates for the large offices were also elected, although Tammany's candidate for the Borough of the Bronx — Louis F. Haffen — was successful.

[4] Report of speech in the New York *Herald,* October 27, 1901.

The total vote stood: Low, 296,813; Shepard, 265,177.
For other political parties a small vote was cast: Benja-
min Hanford, candidate for Mayor of the Social Demo-
cratic party, received 9,834 votes; Keinard, Socialist
Labor candidate for Mayor, polled 6,213 votes, and
Manierre, Prohibition candidate for Mayor, 1,264 votes.

That of a total vote of 561,990 votes cast for the two
chief opposing candidates, Tammany and its allied organizations should have polled 265,177 votes, showed
Tammany Hall's enormous strength, even in the face of
a combination of opponents, with all the strength of
definite issues obviously putting Tammany on the defensive.

Realizing that the attacks upon him personally as the
" boss " of Tammany Hall and of the city had been successful in a political sense, Mr. Croker wisely concluded,
immediately after this defeat, to obscure himself and give
an appearance of retiring from active participation in
the affairs of Tammany Hall. Conscious, too, of the
public discredit attaching to Tammany methods and Tammany leaders, he saw that the time had come to inject
some show of an element of respectability and reform into
Tammany Hall. He now underwent the formalities of
an " abdication."

On January 13, 1902, the astonishing news was made
public that he had selected Lewis Nixon as his successor
as the leader of Tammany Hall. Mr. Nixon, at this time,
was forty-one years old; hailing from Leesburg, Virginia,
he had been graduated from the United States Naval
Academy, and had become a naval constructor, later owning his own naval ship plant at Elizabeth, New Jersey.
He was also connected with a number of private corporations. In 1898 he had been appointed by Mayor Van
Wyck to the office of President of the East River Bridge
Commission, and in 1900–1901 had acted, as we have seen,
as Chairman of Mr. Croker's Anti-Vice Committee.

When the educated Mr. Nixon assumed what he styled

the leadership of Tammany Hall, not only seasoned politicians of all grades but also the sophisticated smiled skeptically. Tammany district leaders maintained in public an air of profound gravity and obedient acquiescence which caused general amusement. And when Mr. Nixon solemnly discussed his plans for the improvement of Tammany Hall, he was popularly regarded as an innocent. Even when Mr. Croker, as an apparent token of good faith, made Mr. Nixon chairman of the Tammany Finance Committee, few considered his appointment seriously; he was generally dubbed " the phantom leader." Having attended to Mr. Nixon's installation, Mr. Croker sailed abroad to his estate at Wantage; to all nominal appearances he had severed himself from Tammany politics.

This comedy lasted but a few months. On May 14, 1902, Mr. Nixon sent his resignation as leader to the Tammany Hall Executive Committee. He accompanied his resignation with a speech in which he declared that since he had become chairman of the Tammany Hall Finance Committee, he had found himself so hampered by a " kitchen cabinet " headed by Andrew Freedman (Mr. Croker's business partner) and by the continued interference of the absent Mr. Croker, that he could no longer lead Tammany Hall and retain his self-respect in the circumstances.

" Every important act of mine," Mr. Nixon announced, " has been cabled to England before it became effective. Mr. Freedman and his party interfered with me at every turn, and at last sought to dictate to me whom I ought to place on the Board of Sachems.

" Then a cablegram came from Wantage [Mr. Croker's estate] direct to me to place certain men on the Board of Sachems, and when I rebelled I found that at every turn I would be opposed by this coterie of interferers.

" I found that nearly all my important acts had to be viséd before they became effective. Many of the district leaders would accept my orders, but before carrying them out, they would get advice from Mr. Croker." [5]

With this announcement Mr. Nixon vanished from the scene of Tammany politics.

As a matter of fact, certain Tammany district leaders were already planning to bring about a change of actual leadership.

On May 22, 1902, the Executive Committee of Tammany Hall took steps which tended to sever the relation that Mr. Crocker retained with the organization. It voted to recommend the abolition of the Sub-Committee on Finance which had always been presided over by the various "bosses" of Tammany Hall, thus eliminating from the chairmanship of that committee Andrew Freedman, who was the representative and mouthpiece of the absentee Mr. Croker.

At the same time the Executive Committee chose a triumvirate of leaders to guide the organization. The regency of three thus selected were Charles F. Murphy, Daniel F. McMahon and Louis F. Haffen. All three, of course, were Tammany district leaders. Mr. Murphy's career is described hereafter. Mr. McMahon was chairman of Tammany's Executive Committee and head of the contracting firm of Naughton & Company. It was this company that made a fortune from the contract for changing the motive power of the Third Avenue Railway, regarding which there was so much scandal. With nothing more than powerful political "pull," this concern obtained large contracts. It was charged by John C. Sheehan that Richard Croker secured 50 per cent of the profits of this company, and that he pocketed $1,500,000 from this source; this assertion, however, depended merely upon Mr. Sheehan's word; it was not established in any official investigation. The third member of the trium-

[5] This speech was published in the New York *Sun* and other newspapers on the following day.

virate, Mr. Haffen, was now president of the Borough of the Bronx.

But this triumvirate did not last long. On September 19, 1902, it was effaced, and Charles F. Murphy became the boss of Tammany. This action was taken at a meeting of the Executive Committee. At this meeting former Chief of Police Devery, holding that he had been elected at the primaries, tried to have himself recognized as a district leader, but his claims were speedily disposed of and he was shut out. Mr. Haffen handed in this resolution:

" Whereas, the experiment of the Committee of Three having proved the desirability of individual responsibility in leadership,

" Resolved, That the powers and duties heretofore exercised and performed by the Committee of Three be hereafter exercised and performed by Charles F. Murphy."

Nine Tammany district leaders, headed by John F. Carroll, who evidently aimed at power himself, opposed the resolution, but twenty-seven other district leaders voted it through. One of the leaders immediately sent a cablegram to Mr. Croker announcing the result. Now that Mr. Murphy was chosen leader, he also became the treasurer of Tammany Hall.

CHAPTER XXXI

1902–1903

CHARLES FRANCIS MURPHY, supreme leader of the Tammany organization from 1902 to this present writing, was born in New York City on June 20, 1858. He was a son of Dennis Murphy, an Irishman whose eight children all were born in the same district in New York City, and all of whom obtained the rudiments at least of a public school education. Dennis Murphy, it may be here said, lived to the remarkably hale age of eighty-eight years, dying in 1902.

As a youth, " Charlie " Murphy worked in an East Side shipyard, by no means a genteel schooling for a boy, although affording a forceful kind of experience of much value in his later career. Having to fight his way among rough youths, he developed both physical prowess and a sort of domineering ascendency which gave him marked leadership qualities among the virile youths overrunning what was then a district noted for its gangs. It was a section of the city filled with vacant lots and was long called the " Gas House District "; here it was that the notorious " Gas House Gang " achieved local reputation.

Tradition has it that when a very young man " Charlie " Murphy organized the Sylvan Social Club, a species of Tammany Hall juvenile auxiliary, composed of boys and youths ranging from fifteen to twenty years of age of whom he became the recognized leader. Later, through political influence, he obtained a job as driver on a cross-

town horse car line. In his later career his enemies in-
vidiously related how jobs of that kind were much cov-
eted at the time because of the fact that as there were
no bell punches or car fare registers, the conductors could
easily help themselves to a proportion of the fares and
divide with the drivers. True, this practise was prevalent, but the implication thus cast upon Mr. Murphy has
been simply a gratuitous one, lacking even the elements
of proof; it can therefore be dismissed from consideration.

He was a manly youth noted for his filial care, a
solicitous son, turning in most of his earnings to his
mother; he was, in fact, the main support of the family.
At the same time he put by enough money — said to have
been $500 — to establish himself in the saloon business.

In 1879 he became owner of a diminutive saloon on
Nineteenth street, east of Avenue A. Four years later,
he opened another saloon, larger and better equipped than
the first, at the corner of Twenty-third street and Avenue
A. He was already a pushful, resourceful Tammany
worker in his district, in which he was a district captain.
Of the underground methods and diversified influences of
district politics he had a good knowledge, and no less so
the application of campaign funds in the most effective
ways for producing votes. Shortly before 1886, Mr.
Murphy opened another saloon, this time at Nineteenth
street and First avenue. Subsequently he opened still
another saloon at Twentieth street and Second avenue,
which was the headquarters of the Anawanda Club, the
Tammany district organization. Selling out the original
saloon in which he had started business, he now opened a
saloon at the northwest corner of First avenue and
Twenty-third street. By 1890 he was the owner of four
prosperous saloons. It was said of him that he never tolerated a woman in his saloons, although all of his saloons
were situated in a district where the admission of women
was a commonplace.

In 1892, at the age of thirty-two years, he was chosen Tammany leader of the "Gas-House" district. He was popular with the generality of people there; however reserved was his talk, he was always credited with being generous with his cash; no poor person was turned away empty-handed. It was narrated of him that during the blizzard of 1888 the Tammany General Committee, at his prompting, voted $4,000 for the relief of the poor, and that a large part of it came from Mr. Murphy's own pocket. Of the $4,000, the sum of $1,500 was given to the Rev. Dr. Rainsford's mission for distribution. Such personal acts of human warmth (irrespective of motive) counted more with masses of voters than tons of formal polemics on civic virtue, nor did the recipients care as to what source the funds came from. Even Dr. Rainsford was so impressed that he was moved to say from the pulpit of St. George's Church that if all the Tammany leaders were like the leader of the Eighteenth Assembly District (Mr. Murphy), Tammany would be an admirable organization.

As a district leader, Mr. Murphy carried on politics and saloons systematically as a combined business. One of his brothers had long been on the police force; another brother was an Alderman; still another brother became an Alderman and Councilman.

When Mr. Van Wyck was elected Mayor, Charles F. Murphy was appointed a Dock Commissioner. Report had it that when he went into the Dock Board Mr. Murphy "was worth" perhaps $400,000, accumulated in the saloon business and politics in eighteen years. He had long been known as "Silent Charlie." Within a few years after his appointment as Dock Commissioner, his fortune, it was said, reached at least $1,000,000. When he became Dock Commissioner, Mr. Murphy nominally assigned his four saloons to a brother and three old friends.

Before leaving the office of Dock Commissioner, John J. Murphy (Charles F. Murphy's brother), James E.

Gaffney and Richard J. Crouch (one of Charles F. Murphy's political district lieutenants) had incorporated the New York Contracting and Trucking Company. Gaffney was an Alderman. These three men were credited with holding only five shares each of the hundred shares of the company; just who held the remaining eighty-five shares has never been definitely explained. When quizzed later by a legislative committee, Charles F. Murphy denied that he had any ownership or financial interest in the New York Contracting and Trucking Company, and no records could be found proving that he did have any interest.

One of the transactions of this company was as follows: In July, 1901, the company leased a dock at West Ninety-sixth Street, and it leased another dock at East Seventy-ninth Street, paying the city a total rent of $4,800 a year for the two properties. It would appear from a report subsequently made by Commissioner of Accounts William Hepburn Russell to Mayor Low that the average profit from the two dock properties was $200 a day, making a rate of 5,000 per cent. on the investment. This particular transaction of the New York Contracting and Trucking Company, lucrative as it was, nevertheless was modest compared to the company's subsequent transactions which we shall duly describe.

Certainly by the year 1902, Mr. Murphy showed the most visible evidences of some sizable degree of wealth; he acquired a suburban estate at Good Ground, Long Island, owning, too, in time, among other possessions denoting wealth, a string of automobiles.

This millionaire leader of Tammany Hall was by no means an unpleasant man to meet. He had a certain diffidence and he was not a good talker; his old habit of attentively listening was too strongly fixed. Physically strong, his deep voice and direct, concise manner when he did speak were impressive and always concentrated on the business at hand. He had none of the ordinary vices; he drank liquor occasionally, it was true, but his drinks were sparse and the times far separated. In smoking he did not indulge, neither did he swear, nor gamble at cards, although he was not a stranger to stock market speculations. A communicant of the Epiphany Roman Catholic Church, he attended mass every Sunday, and gave liberal donations to the church. Unlike Mr. Croker, Mr. Murphy never cared to make the Democratic Club his headquarters; every night, when a district leader, Mr. Murphy could be found, from 7:30 to 10 o'clock, leaning against a lamp post at the northwest corner of Twentieth Street and Second Avenue. Everybody in the district knew that he would be there, accessible to anybody who wanted to talk to him. Such were the career and characteristics of the new leader of Tammany Hall — a dictator in fact, yet preserving all of the tokens of democratic accessibility.

Mayor Low's administration failed to make an impression calculated to influence a majority of voters to reelect him. Quite true, most of his appointees to head the various departments were men of character, administrative capacity and sincerity of purpose — radically different types, indeed, from the Tammany district leaders who were usually appointed to those offices under Tammany administrations.

But in appointing Colonel John N. Partridge as commissioner of police, Mayor Low chose a weak and inefficient man. The demoralized condition of the police administration under Tammany had long been the special target of the reformers' attacks, and people had expected a wholesome overhauling of that department under Mayor Low. Colonel Partridge's administration, however, was so disappointing that the City Club was moved to demand his resignation. It criticized Commissioner Partridge for taking no adequate measures to break up the alliance between the police and crime, or to get a proper understanding of the underlying conditions in the police department, and further criticized him for surrounding himself at headquarters with notoriously corrupt officers, one of whom, in fact, was made his principal uniformed adviser.

The City Club's criticism did not charge that Partridge was personally corrupt, but that he was weak and gullible and was ignorant of real conditions. " Commissioner Partridge and his deputies adopted the idea of ruling the police force according to military ideas. The word of a superior officer was accepted absolutely as against that of a subordinate. In a force where the superior officers had, for the most part, secured their promotions by bribery; where the superior officers were the beneficiaries of blackmailing; and where the honest men, as a rule, remained subordinates — the attempt to instil a spirit of respect among the men for their superiors excited only ridicule, and added to the prevalent demoralization. . . ." [1]

True as such a general statement was, it has been equally true, as experience has shown, that various other reform police commissioners have vainly tried " to break the system "; temporary figures, commissioners come and go, but " The System " has remained more or less intact. Even General Francis V. Greene, appointed by Mayor Low January 1, 1903, to succeed Colonel Partridge (who resigned the day before the trustees of the City Club's demand for his resignation was handed in), found this to be a fact, notwithstanding his earnest, conscientious efforts to correct conditions in the police department.

The vote of the body of the police force themselves showed, in 1902, their complete dissatisfaction with conditions. At least 75 per cent. of the police force voted for Low in 1901; a year later fully 90 per cent. voted for Bird S. Coler, Tammany's candidate for Governor.[2]

---

[1] The Police Department of the City of New York — A Statement of Facts, published by the City Club of New York, October, 1903, pp. 52–55, etc.   [2] Ibid., p. 58.

This was only one of many indications of a forthcoming Tammany victory. Even some reformers criticized Mayor Low as at all times ready to denounce the Tammany leader from whom he could expect nothing, while refraining from saying anything against Senator Thomas C. Platt, the Republican " boss " who represented and headed a political machine element not materially different from that of Tammany. Mayor Low, it was also critically pointed out, was not of a type to hold the goodwill of a large body of the proletarian voters; his views, manner and leanings were of an aristocratic order; and in a city where class distinctions were so notoriously and effectively exploited by Tammany Hall, nothing could be more destructive to the endurance of an administration than the popular belief that its head, however honest personally, embodied the interests and smug views of the people of wealth — that he was, in the expressive phrase of politics, " a silk-stocking." Various acts of Mayor Low's were cited against him and deepened this impression in the popular mind.[3]   Mayor Low's supporters pointed out energetically that he had reduced the city's debt by $7,000,000; that he had reformed the system of tax collection; that he had secured for the city adequate payments for public franchise grants; that he had defeated corrupt " jobs "; that he had reformed the public school system — that in every way he had been a thorough reform Mayor. These representations, the election result showed, were in vain.

With conditions favorable to its return to power, Tammany Hall took measures to make its ticket in the municipal campaign of 1903 headed by a candidate whose name stood for prestige and respectability.

Tammany's candidate for Mayor was George B. McClellan, whose father of the same name, after serving as Commanding General in the Union Army during part of

[3] See a long letter from a leading reformer published in the New York *Herald,* April 12, 1903.

the Civil War, had been the Democratic candidate for
President of the United States in 1864. A political protégé of Charles F. Murphy, George B. McClellan had seen
service in Congress and had been selected by Mr. Murphy
as Tammany's candidate for Mayor a considerable time
before the campaign opened. Jealousy antagonistic to
Tammany's domination and assertion of supreme power,
the Brooklyn Democratic organization, then under control
of " Boss " Hugh McLaughlin, opposed McClellan's nomination, but Mr. Murphy carried his point.

To the amazement and chagrin of the Republicans and
Fusionists, Tammany Hall then consummated a bold and
astute political stroke by appropriating two of the three
principal nominees of its opponents' ticket, and nominating them as Tammany candidates. These two men
were Edward M. Grout and Charles V. Fornes, respectively occupying the offices of Controller and President
of the Board of Aldermen under Mayor Low's administration. With Mayor Low they had been renominated.
Thus did Tammany shrewdly weaken the other side and
present itself as having two chief candidates of the same
identity and capacity as those of the reformers. Mayor
Low and his supporters did not accept this unhumorous
situation complacently; they indignantly forced Grout
and Fornes off their ticket. But the effect sought by
Tammany had been produced.

Mr. McClellan was elected Mayor by a plurality of 62,-
696. The vote resulted: McClellan, 314,782; Low,
252,086. Furman, candidate for Mayor of the Social
Democratic party, received 16,596 votes; Hunter, the
Socialist Labor party's candidate for Mayor, 5,205 votes.
For the Prohibition ticket 869 votes were cast. In this
election Tammany also elected its candidates, including
Grout and Fornes, to all of the other important city of-
fices, except the Presidency of the Borough of Richmond.
The results of the election practically gave Tammany
Hall full control of the city.

CHAPTER XXXII

1903–1905

G RAFT of all kinds was rampant, as later official investigation showed, in Tammany-controlled departments, but in the public mind the question of this form of graft was vastly overshadowed by the revelations of the New York legislative committee investigating the great life insurance companies.

The disclosures showed that Republican legislators as well as Democratic were bought; that enormous corruption funds had been contributed to both political parties, and that one political machine was no better than the other.

Bribery expenditures, the committee reported, were classified on the various insurance companies' books as " legal expenses." The committee described the amounts as extraordinarily large. In the year 1904 alone, the Mutual Life Insurance Company thus disbursed $364,-254.95; the Equitable Life Assurance Society, $172,-698.42, and the New York Life Insurance Company, $204,019.25.[1]

Andrew C. Fields, long engaged by the Mutual Life Insurance Company to manipulate legislation at Albany, lived there in a sumptuously furnished house jocosely styled the " House of Mirth." The expenditures were charged to " legal expenses." The Mutual thus expended more than $2,000,000 in " legal expenses " from 1898 to

[1] *Report of the New York Legislative Insurance Committee,* 1906, Vol. X, p. 16.

1904.[2]   And from 1895 to 1904, the total payments
made by the New York Life Insurance Company to Andrew Hamilton, its chief lobbyist at Albany, amounted
to $1,312,197.16, all of which sum was soberly entered
as " legal expenses." [3]   A present of nearly $50,000 was
contributed in 1894 by the New York Life Insurance
Company to the campaign fund of the Republican National
Committee, and similar amounts in 1896 and 1900 to
the same recipient.[4]   All of the large insurance companies
regularly contributed funds not only for national political
campaigns, but for those in the States; the Equitable,
for example, gave $50,000 in 1904 to the Republican
National Committee, and had also, for many years, been
giving $30,000 annually to the New York State Repub-
lican Committee.[5]   The legislative investigating committee found it impossible to trace all of the directions of this
continuous great corruption. " Enormous sums," the
committee stated, " have been expended in a surreptitious
manner."

Under the pressure of public opinion, District Attorney Jerome finally caused the Grand Jury to proceed
against a few of the figureheads involved; the great magnates who had profited so enormously from the huge
frauds, were, so events proved, left untouched. Although
it had been clearly proved by the testimony that the
frauds and corruptions consummated were gigantic, not
a single one of those of great wealth implicated was ever
sent to jail or even incommoded by the formality of a trial.

In the face of such disclosures, the opponents of Tammany could not well point to Tammany corruption as
an exclusive product. It was a time, too, when what was
termed " muckraking " was almost at its height; magazines and newspapers were filled with articles exposing
in detail the corruptions and colossal manipulations and
spoliation done by great corporations and other vested

2 *Ibid.*
3 *Ibid.*, p. 50.

4 *Ibid.*, pp. 62 and 398.
5 *Ibid.*, p. 10.

interests, and the close connection between these and the
" bosses " and machines of both old political parties.
Public attention was concentrated more upon these nation-
wide scandals than upon local graft — petty, indeed, in
some respects, compared to the great extortions of trusts
and other industrial, transportation and financial corporations.

These factors had their influence in developing in New
York City a powerful movement called the Municipal
Ownership League, later passing under the name of the
Independence League. The head of this organization was
William R. Hearst. He had inherited a large fortune
from his father, United States Senator George Hearst.
The estate comprised a San Francisco newspaper; and
William R. Hearst had come to New York, where he
now had a morning and an evening newspaper. Of a sensational order, yet written in popular style, these newspapers had an extensive circulation, and their agitational
matter were in reality the mainstay of his movement.
Two of the local objectives of this agitation were the
scandalous overcrowding of the street car system and
the methods by which the subway system in New York
City, built by the city's credit, had been turned over to
the profit of private interests. At the same time, no
means was neglected to awaken popular resentment against
the " plunderbund " fattening on the people, and to arouse
indignation against the bossism of Tammany Hall. Day
after day effective articles, editorials and cartoons were
published; written in a simple style, understandable by the
crudest intelligence, they produced a great effect among
the voters. Nothing quite like this original kind of political journalism had ever been known in New York City.

The operations of the New York Contracting and
Trucking Company, in particular, supplied facts which
were used effectually by newspapers and civic organizations to show the new methods by which Tammany leaders
were gathering in millions from contracts. This com-

pany, as we have seen, was headed by John J. Murphy, brother of the Tammany Hall chief, and by Alderman James E. Gaffney.

Its transactions revealed the great difference between Tweed's methods and those of the later leaders of Tammany Hall. Under the Tweed régime tens of millions of dollars were stolen outright. The lesson of the overthrow of the Tweed " ring " was not lost on his successors. Mr. Croker refused to countenance such outworn, discarded and dangerous methods of theft. They had resulted disastrously to Tammany in Tweed's day. In place of direct thieving methods of getting rich, indirect methods, surrounded with secrecy and every possible precaution against detection, were developed. Some Tammany district leaders became opulent on blackmail and extortion, the circuitous route of which it was most difficult to trace (in a legal sense) to its final destination. As for Mr. Croker himself, the question was frequently put to him, " Where did you get it? " [6] He could reply that his operations in amassing his wealth were entirely legitimate; " inside " real estate speculations, connections with trust companies and other corporations and stock transactions. Knowing him to be the source of much legislation and administrative favors worth tens, if not hundreds, of millions of dollars to corporations, his opponents were by no means wholly satisfied with such an explanation, but whatever their suspicions they could never prove that he had personally profited from selling legislation. Essentially, however, Mr. Croker never posed as a business man; he was a politician.

But by the period when Charles F. Murphy became " chief," the " business-man " type of leader had evolved. Under this plan — a plan that afforded the most plausible opportunities for explaining the sudden acquisition of wealth — Tammany men became open or secret partners

[6] Mr. Croker, in 1900, had admitted his liability to an English tax on a yearly income of $100,000.

in contracting firms, using the pressure of political power
to have large contracts awarded to their concerns. It
was not necessary for these leaders to know anything of
contracting; they could be ignorant of every detail; their
one aim was to get the contracts; the actual skilled work
could be done by hired professional men. No law penal-
ized such methods, respectable in every appearance. At
the same time, inasmuch as speculating in the stock market was legitimate in law, fortunes could be made in acting
upon advance information of legislative or other official
means concerning certain corporations.

The first large contract obtained by the New York Contracting and Trucking Company was a $2,000,000 con-
tract for excavating the site for the new Pennsylvania
Railroad Station in New York City.

For a long time, notwithstanding reiterated protests
from the press and public organizations, the Board of
Aldermen, controlled by Tammany, had obstinately refused to vote for the franchise giving the Pennsylvania
Railroad power to use streets for its tunnel approaches
and terminal in Manhattan, New York City. Reports
were circulated that the sum of $300,000 had been de-
manded by the Aldermen, and that until that sum was
produced they would not vote for the franchise. It was
noted that it was " Big Jim " Gaffney, " outside man "
for the New York Contracting and Trucking Company
and Alderman from Leader Charles F. Murphy's district,
who, together with " Little Tim " Sullivan, Tammany
leader in the Board of Aldermen, took a leading part in
persuading the Aldermen to hold out against giving the
franchise for the Pennsylvania tunnel. The newspapers
unanimously described the Aldermanic action as a " hold-
up." Likewise, it was also noted that when from some
mysterious quarter orders reached Tammany Aldermen
to vote for the franchise, it was Alderman Gaffney who
took the lead in rallying the Aldermen to vote it through.

This sudden change of front after a protracted " hold-up," puzzled the public exceedingly, and sinister imputations were made. Not until months later did the public begin to see illumination; it was then announced that although the New York Contracting and Trucking Company had not been the lowest bidder (its bid, according to report, was $400,000 more than that of a competitor), nevertheless it had been awarded the $2,000,000 contract for digging the Pennsylvania Railroad site.

In the case of the awarding of a contract covering several million dollars in February, 1905, to the New York Contracting and Trucking Company for the six-track local improvement of the New York, New Haven and Hartford Railroad, the circumstances were much the same.

A franchise had been asked for a project called the New York, Westchester and Boston Railroad Company. At the same time, another company calling itself the New York and Port Chester Railroad Company, made a similar application and opposed the other company. Both companies, as subsequent developments showed, were in fact owned by the New York, New Haven and Hartford Railroad; the opposition of one to the other was evidently for mere effect.

For three years the Board of Aldermen refused to give the franchises, either one of which would give the New York, New Haven and Hartford Railroad its own independent entrance into New York City. Somehow and from somewhere the announcement was now made that unless the Board of Aldermen acted, a law would be passed by the Legislature stripping it of all power of granting franchises. This threat was executed; the Legislature passed an act vesting franchise-granting power in the Board of Estimate and Apportionment. It may here be parenthetically noted that with the great powers increasingly vested in it the Board of Estimate became the most compact and powerful instrument of government that had ever been developed in the government of New York City.

This body is composed of eight officials. Of these, three officials,— the Mayor, the Controller and the President of the Board of Aldermen,— have, by reason of a greater vested plurality of votes, the dominance of power. The other five members are the Borough Presidents.

The first point passed upon by this Board was the question of whether or not the New York, Westchester and Boston Railroad Company was or was not a defunct corporation. On March 30, 1904, Corporation Council Delany (elected by Tammany Hall) reported to the Board of Estimate and Apportionment that the Board had no jurisdiction to examine the legal capacity or incapacity of the company.[7]

On June 24, 1904, the company received its franchise. The company was really an adjunct of the New York, New Haven and Hartford Railroad, and its franchise gave it the right to operate more than sixteen miles of four-track line within New York City; the company secured practically all the available routes for entrance and exit to and from New York City by way of the Bronx. It was the $6,000,000 contract for constructing this railroad improvement that the New York Contracting and Trucking Company secured.

The declaration was made that no other contractor had ventured to compete for this work; and the explanation was offered in some quarters that inasmuch as a large part of the work was located inside the city limits and as an unfriendly city administration might do much to hamper the carrying out of the contract, the New York, New Haven and Hartford officials, with a cautious eye to the railroad's interests, were willing to award the contract to the Tammany firm and pay higher prices. Mr. Gaffney asserted that politics had nothing to do with the obtaining of the contract and that his company " had

---

[7] The company had filed articles of incorporation in 1872, but was charged with being an abortive corporation in that it had never completed the necessary formalities required by law.

bid with other contractors and won out," but politicians did not take this statement seriously. In February, 1907, the New York Contracting and Trucking Company surrendered its contract for a consideration of $500,000 to another company, the Holbrook, Cabot & Daly Company, which had previously done much of the New York, New Haven and Hartford Railroad's construction work. It was not until seven years later that the fact, originally suspected, as to why the contract had been given without competition to the Gaffney-Murphy company, was authoritatively stated. On May 20, 1914, Charles S. Mellen, long president of the New York, New Haven and Hartford Railroad, testified before the Interstate Commerce Commission that the contract had been turned over to that Tammany concern " to avoid friction with the city," meaning that by giving the contract to the Tammany company, city officials would attempt no " hold-up," such as placing obstacles in the way of carrying the construction work through.

Further disclosures strongly indicated that during the time when the Westchester franchise was acquired by the New York, New Haven and Hartford Railroad, certain powers in Tammany Hall " had to be taken care of," and that they benefited financially.

After being looted of large sums in financial jugglery, the New York, New Haven and Hartford Railroad had been thrown on the verge of insolvency. It was revealed in 1913 that a certain $12,000,000 of New York, New Haven and Hartford Railroad money put into the Westchester project had mysteriously vanished in unexplained directions. The Interstate Commerce Commission, in 1914, conducted an investigation to find out specifically, if possible, what became of those missing millions.

On April 24, 1914, Oakley Thorne, a New York banker, who had been the agent of J. P. Morgan & Company in handling the $12,000,000 for the purpose of secretly purchasing the Westchester and the Portchester franchises

for the New York, New Haven and Hartford Railroad,
gave certain testimony before the Interstate Commerce
Commission. He averred that he had burned the books
containing the particulars as to how he had spent at
least $8,000,000; he explained that he therefore could not
give names, amounts and dates. A letter written by Mr.
Thorne in October, 1906, to C. S. Mellen, president of
the New York, New Haven and Hartford Railroad, was
produced. In this letter Thorne wrote that " there are
people in Fourteenth Street who are very strongly in
favor of Westchester and others in favor of Portchester,"
and suggested that " both sides will have to be taken care
of." Asked what the reference to " Fourteenth Street "
meant, Thorne replied, " Why, I believe, Tammany Hall."
Mr. Thorne testified that he could not possibly remember
the names of any individuals in " Fourteenth Street " who
" had to be taken care of," but he admitted that he knew
that " Big Tim " Sullivan was " friendly " to the Westchester " enterprise " and owned stock in it; at the time
this testimony was given Sullivan was dead.

Mr. Thorne asserted that he could not recall definite
particulars, but he could vaguely remember that there
were persons in " Fourteenth Street " who had, at the time,
been " interested in the Westchester City and Contract
Company, the New York Development Company and other
concerns that subsequently formed a part of the Westchester combination turned over to the New Haven [the
New York, New Haven and Hartford Railroad Com-
pany] through Morgan & Company." Certain " persons in Fourteenth Street," Mr. Thorne further testified,
had to be bought off because of their " nuisance value,"
but precisely what was the nature of that " nuisance
value " was not explained. In the disposition of the many
millions of dollars placed in his hands, Mr. Thorne was
not required to make any accounting or give any vouchers.

Further details of later developments were given in the
testimony of Charles S. Mellen, president of the New York,

New Haven and Hartford Railroad during the years when the above franchises were acquired.

On May 14, 1914, Mr. Mellen testified, at a hearing before the Interstate Commerce Commission, that the directors of that railroad set aside a fund of $1,200,000, the value of 8,000 shares of New York, New Haven and Hartfort Railroad stock, which sum was distributed among " people of influence " in the politics of New York City for the procuring of certain much-desired changes in the charter of the New York, Westchester and Boston Railroad Company. Mr. Mellen further testified that Inspector Thomas F. Byrnes, who, for many years, had been head of the New York Police Department (and who was deceased at the time of this hearing) had acted as the go-between in this transaction; that Byrnes agreed to obtain thirteen different modifications or " amendments " to the New York, Westchester and Boston Railroad charter from New York city's officials; and that to bring about these results stock, or its equivalent in cash, to the sum of $1,200,000, was given to Byrnes for distribution among Tammany politicians whose identity Mr. Mellen declared that he did not know. Mr. Mellen's testimony revealed that some of these persons accepted stock made out in the names of dummies, but that the majority demanded and received cash for their " services." All but $50,000 of the $1,200,000 was distributed.

The records of the Board of Estimate in 1908 and 1909 bear out Mr. Mellen's testimony; they show that nearly every request for alterations of the charter or extensions of time made by the New York, New Haven and Hartford Railroad was granted. The Board of Estimate during the years in question consisted of Mayor McClellan; Controller Herman A. Metz; Patrick F. McGowan, President of the Board of Aldermen; John F. Ahearn, President of the Borough of Manhattan; Bird S. Coler, President of the Borough of Brooklyn; Louis F. Haffen, President of the Borough of the Bronx; Lawrence Gresser,

President of the Borough of Queens, and George Cromwell, President of the Borough of Richmond.[8]

Continuing his testimony, Mr. Mellen stated, on May
20, 1914, that upon further recollection he found that the
amount distributed to politicians in connection with securing the Westchester franchise and alterations to the
charter, really totaled $1,500,000 or $1,600,000. Much
of this amount was presented in the form of due bills sent
in by Tammany politicians by means of messengers; Mr.
Mellen personally handed over cash for the due bills, but
the names of the recipients he said he could not remember. " Do you know," Mr. Mellen was asked, " what all
this Westchester and Portchester stock was doing in Tammany Hall? " " I know," he replied, " what it was doing
to me when I took it on. It was costing me lots of
money." " Do you know how all this stock reached Tammany Hall? " " I have not the slightest idea. I could
suppose a lot of things, but I do not know anything
about it."

Submitting, on July 11, 1914, the results of its investigation to the United States Senate, the Interstate Commerce Commission reported that the facts as to the New
York, Westchester and Boston Railway transaction constituted " a story of the profligate waste of corporate
funds." The fullest details are set forth in that report
of the magnitude of the corruption used. Commenting
upon Mr. Mellen's testimony, the report declared: " The
testimony is somewhat occult, but the character of the
transaction is no less certain. This money was used for
corrupt purposes, and the improper expenditures cov-

8 As we shall see later, the political composition of the Board of
Estimate was at this time considerably mixed; during his second term
Mayor McClellan was fighting Mr. Murphy, leader of Tammany Hall,
and had the backing of Senator McCarren and of McCarren's lieutenant, Controller Metz. Mr. McGowan, president of the Board of
Aldermen, was supposed to be a Tammany man, but was not on good
terms with the " Organization " and was credited with being aligned
with McClellan and Metz.

ered up by the transfer to the New Haven [New York, New Haven and Hartford Railroad Company] of these worthless securities. . . . It seems very strange that Mr. Mellen was not able to identify with any particularity any one with whom he had these transactions except the late Thomas F. Byrnes. No comment is necessary to make clear to the mind the corrupt and unlawful nature of this transaction, and it would seem that the amount illegally expended could be recovered from Mr. Mellen and the directors who authorized it. . . ." [9]

There is now pending (1917) a suit in the United States District Court brought by the stockholders against the former directors of the New York, New Haven and Hartford Railroad Company and against the company for the return of $165,000,000 alleged to have been lost to the treasury of that railroad in various ways.

To return, however, to the operations of the New York Contracting and Trucking Company: Another contract secured by that concern was a contract from the Consolidated Gas Company for grading the site for the Astoria gas plant; the franchise for the Astoria " Gas Grab " had been supported by Tammany.

By 1905 it was estimated that the New York Contracting and Trucking Company or its offshoots had received contracts aggregating $15,000,000 — all contracts from corporations and interests benefiting from the city government or depending upon favors from it. Yet two years previously this very company was a nonentity as far as securing large contracts were concerned, and none of its heads had any experience in the contracting business. Now in a certain well-understood field, it was virtually free from competition.

None could now fail to note the great transition from

[9] *Interstate Commerce Commission Report No. 6569*, In re *Financial Transactions of the New York, New Haven and Hartford Railroad Co.*, July 11, 1914, pp. 35, 38, etc. The above are but a few extracts from this comprehensive report.

the Tweed period when Tammany leaders used only the vulgar and criminal methods of stealing money out of the city treasury. Under Murphy's leadership the obvious methods used were those of " honest graft "— the making of millions from contracts with public service corporations, and this was represented as legitimate business. Fully six Tammany district leaders were members of or " interested " in large contracting firms, although the heads of these, often of a nominal character, were not known as Tammany leaders. These concerns employed a total of many thousands of men, all of whom were expected to be useful at the primaries and elections.

At this time there was discernible the beginnings of a growing feeling that reform officials, while prosecuting gamblers and comparatively petty offenders of all stripes, somehow were singularly ineffective in bringing about the prosecution of corporation magnates charged with looting on a large scale. This feeling had not crystallized as yet, but it was felt in some quarters.

Some of District Attorney Jerome's former supporters were impressed by the fact that despite his campaign promises, he had not caused the indictment or other prosecution of the men who had looted the Metropolitan Street Railway Company. James W. Osborne, a noted attorney, had declared in open court in 1903, that the " insiders " had, by means of duplicating of construction accounts, manipulation and in other ways, stolen $30,000,-000. Mr. Amory declared and specified that an additional $60,000,000 had, by various processes of devious manipulation, gone to enrich the " insiders "— a total of $90,000,000.

On April 25, 1903, Mr. Osborne gave out this statement: " We have produced evidence before Magistrate Barlow which shows a crime has been committed, and now it is up to the District Attorney to say whether he will avail himself of that evidence and proceed against those who have committed the crime. We have charged in open court that $30,000,000 has been stolen, and that [state-ment] never has been disproved by the Metropolitan Com-pany or its counsel. I told Mr. Nicoll, counsel for Mr. Vreeland [president of the Metropolitan Street Railway Company] openly he would not be able to disprove my charges."

Mr. Amory openly declared that Mr. Jerome's investi-gation of the matter in 1903 was not undertaken in good faith. " It was," he wrote, " a deliberate whitewash. I have documentary evidence to prove it." Mr. Amory charged that of the twenty-seven distinct written charges filed with Mr. Jerome against the Metropolitan manage-ment, Mr. Jerome's accountant reported on only seven, and these latter were of minor importance, involving chiefly technicalities of accounts and not serious crimes. Yet Mr. Jerome, was Mr. Amory's indignant comment, represented that the accountant's report was " very clear and full and takes up every charge " and that Mr. Jerome had reported that " the specific charges so far as they in-volve criminal wrong-doing are entirely without founda-tion." [10]

While thus declaring that he could find nothing on which to base prosecution of the Metropolitan Street Rail-way Company magnates, District Attorney Jerome showed by other acts, it was complained, that petty criminals would be prosecuted to the limit of the law. He was charged with discriminating between rich and powerful business offenders, on the one side, and on the other, poor and relatively uninfluential violators of the law.

On one occasion Mr. Jerome appeared before labor unions, delivered homilies on the virtues, and warned them that he would make short shrift of labor grafters. This lecture had reference to the case of Sam Parks, a labor leader, charged with grafting on employers and receiv-ing money for prompting or " calling off " strikes. Dis-

[10] *The Truth About Metropolitan,* by W. N. Amory, pp. 60–64.

trict Attorney Jerome waited for no elaborate formal investigation; he immediately started the machinery of his office against Parks and caused him to be convicted. Already a dying consumptive, Parks was sentenced to prison, where he died shortly after. But no action, it was pointed out, was taken against powerful construction companies that had bribed Parks and other labor leaders to declare strikes on buildings for which competitors had the contracts.[11] Another much-discussed incident was the result of a collision of railroad trains in the Park Avenue tunnel — a collision maiming and killing many persons. The obsolete and dangerous condition of this tunnel had long been known. It was commented that District Attorney Jerome did not make the slightest move against the railroad directors; he hurriedly caused the indictment and arrest of Wisker, a railroad engineer, as the sole culprit and proceeded with despatch to his trial. The jury, however, refused to convict the engineer.

Considering that Mr. Jerome was a leading reformer, such contrasts were gradually calculated to make the very mention of reform odious to the observing of the working people. The complaint was generally heard that the big grafters were safe and immune, while petty offenders were dealt with rigorously. Nevertheless, a large number of voters, influenced by a stream of praise from the press, still believed in Mr. Jerome's promises and motives, and his action in 1905 in not securing a renomination from political bosses but procuring it independently by means of a petition circulated among electors, strengthened the old belief that he was sincere and was independent of political and other domination. Much was made

11 In an effective article in *McClure's Magazine*, Mr. Ray Stannard Baker showed how one of these big companies bribed walking delegates to declare strikes on buildings being put up by rival contractors in order that it — the briber — might be able to get a reputation for building within contract time, and thus exclude competitors from getting further contracts.

of the fact of his independent renomination. The Republicans withdrew their candidate for District Attorney and nominated Mr. Jerome, and the press in general enthusiastically supported him. He was reelected. It was not until some years later when the full effects of his administration could be popularly realized in perspective, that Jerome fell into general disfavor with the voters.

As an instance of the methods of contractors under the Tammany régime during this time, it is only necessary to mention the facts, later disclosed in an investigation by John Purroy Mitchel, Commissioner of Accounts, as to how in 1904 defective hose was sold to the Fire Department. The Windsor Fire Appliance Company (of which the president and chief stockholder was Michael F. Loughman, later appointed Deputy Commissioner of Water Supply) sold 25,000 feet of hose to New York City for $23,410.25. Althought this hose did not answer the specifications of the contract, it was accepted. The consequence was that it burst many times at fires, some of them serious. The same was true of equally worthless hose supplied by other contractors.

The municipal election in 1905 was a triangular contest. Tammany Hall did not fear the Republican ticket headed by William M. Ivins for Mayor. But it did have intense uneasiness over the possibility of Mr. Hearst triumphing; his movement was too plainly making inroads among large numbers of voters that ordinarily would have voted the Tammany ticket. Tammany was particularly bent upon winning inasmuch as by the provisions of the revised charter the term of the incoming Mayor and other officials had been changed to a four-year incumbency. Hearst was the Municipal Ownership League's candidate for Mayor, and Tammany renominated Mayor McClellan. So effective were Hearst's onslaughts on " Boss " Murphy and the elements represented by him that during the campaign Mayor McClellan repeatedly made promises that he would thereafter pursue an independent course, should he be reelected.

Mr. Hearst's vote returns came in so heavily after the polls were closed that it looked as though he were certainly elected. That very night there was a strange interruption, lasting about an hour, in the public giving-out of the returns. Then as the returns were resumed, it appeared that although the vote between McClellan and Hearst was extremely close, McClellan had a little the better of it. The next day it was announced that Mayor McClellan was reelected by a close margin. Mr. Hearst and his followers declared that manifest fraud had been committed, and took steps to have a recount. Meantime while this process was dragging along, Mayor McClellan was widely criticized for his action in immediately claiming his reelection, opposing a recount, and not showing faith in the legitimacy of his claims by waiting with dignity until there had been a careful official recount.

The final official recount gave this result: McClellan, 228,407 votes; Hearst, 224,929 votes; Ivins, 137,184 votes. It may be added here that in the very next year — in 1906 — Hearst accepted a Tammany indorsement when he ran for Governor, but he was defeated by Charles E. Hughes, who, as counsel for the Legislative Insurance Committee, had achieved wide popularity for his exposure of the insurance company iniquities.

With the reelection of Mr. McClellan, Tammany Hall confidently looked forward to four more years of unquestioned control of the immense budget and enormous opportunities embodied in the rule of New York City.

CHAPTER XXXIII

WHEN Mayor McClellan, in the campaign of 1905 promised an independent administration, Tammany leaders did not take his words seriously; they considered his promises mere campaign vapor. In this estimate they were mistaken. Mayor McClellan broke relations with Charles F. Murphy in January, 1906, and announced that he would keep every promise made by him " on the stump." His appointment of anti-Murphy men to office had a nettling effect on the leader of Tammany Hall, against whom he began a systematic campaign. Results, still more serious to Tammany leaders, were forthcoming.

The President of the Borough of Manhattan was John A. Ahearn, a noted Tammany district leader. He had been a State Senator from 1889 to 1902, and had been elected president of the Borough of Manhattan in 1903, and reelected in 1905 for a term of four years. It may be explained that the presidency of a borough was a powerful office, having direct appointive and supervisory power over six departments with expenditures of many millions of dollars annually.[1]

---

[1] When Ahearn was elected president of the Borough of Manhattan, it was " Boss " Murphy, with the " advice and consent " of the Tammany Executive Committee, who really chose his appointees to head the Department of Public Work, the Bureau of Highways, the Bureau of Sewers, the Bureau of Buildings, etc. Of course, Tammany district leaders were appointed; they were really responsible to the Tammany Executive Committee.

Charges of misconduct were brought against **Mr.**
Ahearn, in 1906, by the Bureau of City Betterment (later
called the Bureau of Municipal Research). When **Mr.**
Ahearn requested an investigation by the Commissioners
of Accounts, Mayor McClellan accommodated his desire.
The report of these commissioners, handed in to the
Mayor, July 16, 1907, severely arraigned Ahearn's administration, and after specifying particulars, the report
denounced " the inefficiency, neglect, waste and corruption
disclosed in the course of this inquiry." [2]

The investigation showed that in the three years that
Mr. Ahearn had occupied the office of borough president,
he had control of an expenditure totaling $21,994,477.
Of this amount it was shown that $1,608,762 was spent
in the purchase of supplies without public tender being
asked, as required by law. It was proved that many of
the payrolls (amounting to an aggregate of $5,942,187)
were padded with the names of men who never did a day's
work for the department. Even in the expenditures made
under contract — expenditures totaling $14,447,473 in
the three years — it was proved that little effort was
made to compel contractors to observe their obligations.
Fully a third of the total expenditure — the third amounting to $5,400,000 — was lost to the city, it was asserted,
by the manner in which the department was administered.
There were still further losses to the city; and although,
also, there was plenty of money at Mr. Ahearn's disposal
for the repairs of street pavements, that work, it was
held, was considerably neglected. The evidence in the
commissioners' investigation and the evidence presented
by the City Club in subsequent hearings ordered by Gov-

[2] See *A Report on a Special Examination of the Accounts and
Methods of the Office of the President of the Borough of Manhattan,
Directed by Hon. George B. McClellan, Mayor, Commissioners of
Accounts of the City of New York, July 16, 1907.* This report gives
the full findings of the Commissioners of Accounts. The full testimony is embodied in Vols. 1 to 111 of *Testimony, Ahearn Investigation, 1907, Commissioners of Accounts.*

ernor Hughes showed that supply contractors often made profits ranging from 100 to 200 per cent. (and in at least one case 300 to 500 per cent.) more than the regular prices prevailing in the open market.

Among other disclosures the testimony revealed that $144,500 had been paid out for asphalt "fire burns," which in reality were not "fire burns" at all; they were defects that the asphalt companies were obliged to repair without charge. The favorite contractors were such Tammany district leaders as Bartholomew Dunn, Thomas J. Dunn and others.

On December 9, 1907, Governor Hughes removed Mr. Ahearn from office. In his notice of ejection, Governor Hughes said that justice to Mr. Ahearn required that attention should be called to the fact that " it is not shown, and it has not been claimed, that he has converted public money or property to his own use, or has personally profited in an unlawful manner by his official conduct." But Governor Hughes said that he did find that the charges of maladministration, remissness and grave abuses existing under Ahearn's administration had been proved. Mr. Ahearn was, in reality, a victim of the Tammany system. A few days later, the Manhattan Aldermen reelected him — a move that was contested by taking the case to the Court of Appeals, which in November, 1909, sustained his removal and disapproved of his reelection. Meanwhile, he had continued in office.

Another conspicuous Tammany leader removed from office was Louis F. Haffen, president of the Borough of the Bronx. He had held that office since January 1, 1898, and had been last reelected in 1905. Mr. Haffen was, as we have seen, one of the regency of three controlling Tammany Hall immediately previous to Charles F. Murphy's assumption of sole leadership. He was a Sachem of the Tammany Society.

In November, 1908, twenty-two charges were presented to Governor Hughes by John Purroy Mitchel and Ernest

Gallagher, Commissioners of Accounts of New York City, at the instance of Mayor McClellan.[3] The City Club and the Citizens' Union jointly filed charges against Mr. Haffen and prosecuted them. Governor Hughes, basing his findings and action on the report of Wallace Macfarlane, his Commissioner who heard the evidence, found that the following charges had been established:

That Mr. Haffen had greatly abused his discretionary power in failing to enforce more stringently the time clauses of contracts for public improvements, and that the time statements in his certificates to the Finance Department were in many cases untrue; that the public funds were wasted by loading the payrolls of his department with a large number of superfluous employees; that there was political jobbery in the building of the Bronx Borough Court House; the appointed architect was essentially a politician without professional qualifications who had hired others to do the architectural work. The granite contract for this building was awarded to the Buck's Harbor Granite Company, represented in New York by a Bronx Tammany district leader.

Among an array of further charges against Mr. Haffen that were found true was the charge that he was financially interested in the Sound View Land and Improvement Company, " and that his official action in connection with the Clason's Point Road was induced by his desire to increase the value of his own and his associates' holdings in this company, which had acquired a tract of forty-one acres with a frontage of 2,500 feet on the proposed road, with a view to that improvement."

Another charge established against Mr. Haffen was that

[3] See *A Report on a Special Examination of the Accounts and Methods of the President of the Borough of the Bronx, etc., Commissioners of Accounts of New York City, June 16, 1908.* The complete testimony in the Haffen Investigation is set forth in Vols. I to IV, *Testimony, Borough of the Bronx Investigation, 1908, Commissioners of Accounts.* See also Memorandum submitted to Governor Hughes, by the Commissioners of Accounts, 1909.

as borough president and chairman of the local board of
Morrisania, Mr. Haffen had recommended the acquisition
by New York City of certain property at Hunt's Point on
the East River Shore, for use as a public bathing place.
This property, Governor Hughes declared, was utterly un-
suitable for the purpose because of its proximity to a
trunk sewer.

Governor Hughes set forth that the Hunt's Point transaction was " a highly discreditable affair. This shore
property was about five acres in extent, and the assessed
valuation was about $4,300. During the condemnation
proceedings the attorney for the company which owned
it purchased it from his client for about $86,000.[4] It
was then transferred to another company, and was acquired by the city at a cost of about $247,000, the value
fixed by the condemnation commissioners." Thus the
award for the Hunt's Point property was fifty-eight times
the assessed value, and many times the actual value.

Other charges against Mr. Haffen were sustained.
Overtime charges on contracts had been liquidated arbitrarily; on one occasion $70,000 was improperly remitted
to " Bart " Dunn who previously had contributed $1,000
to the Haffen campaign fund.[5] Payments were made to
contractors on absolutely false statements certified from

---

[4] The attorney here referred to was Joseph A. Flannery. Upon
charges preferred by the Bar Association, and after a three years'
investigation, he was disbarred, May 17, 1912, by the Appellate Division of the Supreme Court of the State of New York. He was
found guilty on five of the six charges brought against him, one of
which charges dealt with the notorious Hunt's Point land " job." It
was on record that Flannery personally profited to the sum of $300,000
from various transactions of land sold to the city at fictitious valua-
tions. On June 11, 1914, W. D. Guthrie, representing the New York
Bar Association, reiterated the charges when he argued before the
Court of Appeals at Albany for the confirmation of Mr. Flannery's
disbarment. Flannery's attorney declared that nobody was misled
or labored under a misapprehension as a result of his client's actions;
that the company for which Flannery was attorney knew as much
about the transaction as did Flannery. On October 24, 1914, the
Court of Appeals sanctioned Flannery's disbarment.

[5] *Summary of Findings, A Report on a Special Examination of the*

Mr. Haffen's office. Extravagance in the Bureau of Public Buildings and Offices resulted in an estimated waste of $175,000 of an available $292,000 in six years of Mr. Haffen's administration.[6] Contract juggling was common. Worn-out Belgian blocks were sold by the borough to contractors and then repurchased by the city as new. In cases where contractors were friends of Mr. Haffen, contract specifications were so drawn as to exclude competitors. Streets were laid in irregular routes so as to aid land development schemes in which Tammany men held control. Highway contract specifications were deliberately violated by the contractors. The labors of the maintenance force in the Bureau of Highways were wasted to such an extent that the investigators estimated a loss of 50 per cent in efficiency, or $1,600,000 in money, within six years.[7] A similar waste of $300,-000 was attributed to the Bureau of Sewers in the same period.

Borough President Haffen was ousted by Governor Hughes on August 29, 1909. When removed from office, Haffen complained, " This is a fine reward for twenty-six and a half years of honest, faithful and efficient service to the people. . . ."

Another high city official who went out of office during this time was Joseph Bermel, president of the Borough of Queens. He hastily resigned while under charges.

Mr. Bermel was not, strictly speaking, a Tammany man; he was an auxiliary satrap. His removal from office had been asked for by Attorney-General Jackson and Deputy Attorney-General Nathan Viadiver, of New York State, at the conclusion of an inquiry into Bermel's office.

Bermel was charged by the Attorney General and by the Queen's Borough Property Owners' Association with various acts. He was accused of conspiring with others

Office of the President of the Borough of the Bronx, etc. Commissioners of Accounts, June 16, 1908, p. 1.
  [6] *Ibid.,* p. 3.   [7] *Ibid.,* p. 3.

to defraud New York City in the purchase or sale of
land to New York City; he was charged with accepting
money from persons interested in the sale of such lands,
and was further charged with selling and using his influence in the land purchases in question. He was accused
of failing to aid the Grand Jury in its investigations into
these transactions, and was further charged with block-
ing the procedure of that body with his influence and
money in refusing to testify in certain matters, and in
other cases testifying falsely and removing his books from
the Grand Jury's jurisdiction. Another charge was that
he swore falsely concerning his bank deposits, which evidence he sought to corroborate by the testimony of a witness who presented apparent confirmation in the shape of
a written paper, which paper upon investigation was
proved to be a false and fraudulent document.

Still further, Mr. Bermel was charged with receiving
money for granting special privileges to contractors; with
neglecting pavements and permitting material of a lower
grade than specified to be used in contract work; with
purchasing supplies for public buildings at exorbitant
prices and with allowing the same high prices to be
charged for repairs to public buildings. Additional
charges were that he appointed incompetent subordinates
and permitted persons who did no work to draw salaries.
Close upon the announcement from Albany that Governor
Hughes had appointed Samuel H. Ordway as Commissioner to take testimony, Bermel on April 29, 1908, resigned from office.[8]

The Aldermen on April 30, 1908, elected Lawrence
Gresser to fill Mr. Bermel's unexpired term as President
of the Borough of Queens, and on November 2, 1909, Mr.
Gresser was elected by the people to that office for the

---

[8] He had been elected Borough President of Queens in 1905, after a
fight upon "Joe" Cassidy, long Democratic "boss" of Queens, in
which campaign Bermel ran as an "Independent Democrat" and had
violently denounced "Cassidyism and public graft."

four ensuing years. In 1911 charges were preferred by citizens of Queens County against Gresser. A number of these charges were sustained by Samuel H. Ordway, the Commissioner appointed by the Governor to take testimony and report. Commissioner Ordway, however, explained in his report made June 16, 1911: " Of those [charges] that are sustained, none, in my opinion, establishes corruption or dishonesty on the part of Mr. Gresser. I believe that he is an honest man and would not be a party to any corrupt acts either for his own benefit or that of his associates. But I am of the opinion that he has been inefficient and incompetent, and has been neglectful of his duty to protect the city and the Borough of Queens against fraud and corruption on the part of his subordinates." [9] After an argument made by Robert S. Binkerd, Secretary of the City Club, asking for Mr. Gresser's removal, Governor Dix removed Gresser from office.

But Tammany men were not the only officials against whom charges were brought. It had long been a subject of increasing general comment that District Attorney Jerome, much noted as such a leading reformer, who had been so conspicuously active in sending petty offenders to prison, had failed to bring about the conviction of any high insurance officials and had not brought about the indictment of a single traction system manipulator.

On September 8, 1907, a voluminous petition was sent by various New York business men and other citizens to Governor Hughes. This petition recited in detail the specific transactions thus complained of, made a scathing criticism of District Attorney Jerome for having failed to prosecute those responsible, and demanded that the Attorney General of New York State be forthwith directed to bring prosecution.

[9] *In the Matter of Charges Preferred against Lawrence Gresser, President of the Borough of Queens, City of New York, Report of Commissioner Samuel H. Ordway, 1911,* p. 91.

Evidence submitted, on December 1, 1907, to the
Grand Jury in General Sessions showed that Thomas F.
Ryan and associates had bought in 1902 from Anthony
N. Brady for $250,000 the franchise of a company called
the Wall and Cortland Street Ferries Railroad Company,
a corporation having a dormant franchise for a road
that had never been built.[10]   They had then sold this
franchise to a dummy corporation, called the Metropolitan Securities Company, for $965,607.19.   Part of this
sum went to the syndicate's brokers; the precise amount
of funds divided among Ryan, Widener, Dolan and the estates of William C. Whitney and William L. Elkins was
$692,292.82.[11]   The surviving members of this group
subsequently settled the transaction by making restitution
of this sum soon after the facts had been made public and
after charges had been made against Jerome.   On the
very day that Mr. Ryan and associates had bought the
non-existent Wall and Cortlandt Street Ferries Railroad,
they had also bought, for $1,600,000, the People's Trac-
tion Company, owning a paper road never built, and the
New York, Westchester and Connecticut Traction Company, a small railway, which a short time previously had
been sold in bankruptcy proceedings for $15,000.[12]   It
was charged that in this transaction also, there was another grand division of funds.

These particular transactions, however, were in reality
insignificant compared to the disappearance of $16,000,-
000 from the treasury of the Third avenue Railway,[13]

[10] In a signed statement in the New York *Evening Call*, February
27, 1909, Col. Amory declared that when this matter was originally
exposed in the hearing before the Public Service Commission, the full
facts were not brought out; that one of the ten original owners had
recently informed him (Amory) that the price paid by Ryan and
Brady was in reality only $25,000.

[11] See *Investigation of the Interborough Metropolitan Company,
etc., 1907, Public Service Commission, First District,* Vol. IV, pp.
1613–1618, etc.

[12] *Ibid.*

[13] After this company had been forced into bankruptcy in 1908, the

and vaster total transactions charged, aggregating, as we have previously noted, about $90,000,000. The fact was brought out in the investigation by the Public Service Commission that all the books of the Metropolitan Street Railway Company in which its affairs from 1891 onward to 1902 were recorded, had been sold to a purchaser who promised to destroy them.[14] Street car lines bought for a few hundred thousand dollars were, it was charged, capitalized at ten or twenty times that sum, and then followed a process by which vast amounts were charged in duplication of construction accounts.

Lemuel Ely Quigg (who for six years had been a member of Congress) admitted that in the four years preceding 1907 he had received $217,000 from the Metropolitan Street Railway Company.[15] This was charged to a construction fund, part of which was another sum of $798,000 paid to different persons whose names were concealed. Further facts in a legislative investigation in 1910 (to which we shall hereafter refer) supplied certain other missing links.

No criminal proceedings, however, were brought against Mr. Ryan. In a statement published on May 26, 1909, Col. Amory averred that when a Grand Jury was called in 1907 to investigate the acts of Ryan and associates of the Metropolitan Street Railway Company, the foreman of the Grand Jury was a director in Mr. Ryan's

above sum was the estimate as stated by Receiver Whitridge. See also Col. Amory's remarks, June 29, 1910, *Third Avenue Company — Plan of Reorganization, Public Service Commission, First District, Stenographic Minutes*, p. 2417.

[14] *Investigation of Interborough Metropolitan Company, etc., 1907, Public Service Commission, First District*, Vol. II, pp. 774–775. D. C. Moorehead, Secretary and Treasurer of the Metropolitan Street Railway Company, further testified that District Attorney Jerome had investigated these books in 1903, and that they were disposed of in 1905 for $117 or so; they were sold, Mr. Moorehead testified, " because of lack of store room." No litigation, he said, was in progress at the time they were sold.

[15] *Investigation of Interborough Metropolitan Company, etc., 1907,* Vol. III, p. 1395, etc.

Equitable Life Assurance Society. Col. Amory also made the accusation that in April, 1903, Daniel Mason, Mr. Jerome's former law partner, and William H. Page, Jr., another of the Metropolitan's lawyers, had attempted to bribe him (Amory) while a State's witness, with $200,000, to withdraw the charges that Amory had filed with Jerome against the Metropolitan Street Railway Company. On January 27, 1908, Judge Rosalsky, in the Court of General Sessions, severely arraigned District Attorney Jerome, declaring that Jerome had so conducted the examination of Thomas F. Ryan before the Grand Jury as probably to invalidate any indictments which that body might have found against Ryan. Paul D. Cravath, Governor Hughes's former law partner, was now Ryan's astute attorney.

Governor Hughes appointed a Commissioner to hear the evidence upon which the charges against Mr. Jerome were made. Jerome admitted that when Ryan, Brady and Vreeland were before the Grand Jury he had put leading questions to them. Further he testified that he had not asked the Grand Jury to indict Ryan in the matter of the Wall Street and Cortlandt Street Ferries Railway transactions. Interrogated as to a certain contribution made to his campaign fund by Samuel Untermeyer, counsel for Mr. Hyde of the Equitable Life Assurance Society, Mr. Jerome denied that any ulterior purpose was behind it. Mr. Ryan admitted on the witness stand that he (Ryan) had contributed heavily to the national fund of the Democratic party in 1900.

The Commissioner's report exonerated Jerome, and Governor Hughes dismissed the charges, saying, " Nothing has been presented which furnishes any just ground for impeaching the good faith of the District Attorney in connection with any of the transactions set forth, nor has anything been shown which would justify his removal from office." The outcome was severely criticized by some of the very newspapers which had once enthusiastically supported Mr. Jerome. Col. Amory wrote that there were other bribes than money bribes, and that he did not believe Mr. Jerome capable of doing a corrupt act for money.[16] Whatever the fundamental facts, the consequences were clear: great sums of money had undeniably vanished, a group of magnates had become additionally enriched, the street railway system was wrecked and thrown into bankruptcy, the statute of limitations had meanwhile been interposed, and nobody had been prosecuted.

These were the essential facts, and they were facts that, after all explanations, could not be evaded. Mr. Jerome himself was forced to recognize them in his own defense; in his public speeches he took great pains to assure his hearers that acts might be wrong and yet not criminal, but it was an explanation not favorably received in general. The great change in public opinion was forcibly shown, when, at a meeting in Cooper Union, on May 26, 1909, Mr. Jerome was badly heckled and asked the most pointed questions as to why he had not prosecuted the traction magnates.

The city finances during these years were in a bewilderingly deplorable state. On December 31, 1907, the total amount remaining uncollected from the tax levies covering the years 1899 to 1907, inclusive, was $90,545,000. In addition, a sum of $12,289,000 remained uncollected from the tax levies prior to the year 1899.[17] Notwithstanding these actual enormous deficiencies, the amounts placed in the tax levies, from the years 1899 to 1905 inclusive, to provide for possible deficiencies in tax collections, was only $11,719,000. During that very period the amounts in discounts, remissions and cancelations amounted to $12,477,000, which was more than $758,000

[16] *Truth About Metropolitan,* p. 2.
[17] *Report of the Joint Committee of the Senate and Assembly of the State of New York, Appointed to Investigate the Finances of the State of New York. March 1, 1909,* p. 10.

in excess of the amount placed in the tax levies to provide for deficiencies in collections. " In other words," reported a Select Legislative Committee, " the amounts placed in the tax levies during those years to provide for deficiencies in collections, did not even equal the discounts, cancelations and remissions, and made no provision whatever for failure or inability to collect taxes levied." [18]

By October 31, 1908, uncollected taxes due the city (including $9,324,000 personal taxes for years previous to 1898, which had been written off as uncollectable), amounted to $84,506,000. Despite the fact that this huge sum had not been collected, the city officials spent the greater part of it as though it had been collected; of the $84,506,000 uncollected, the sum of $76,266,000 had, by October 31, 1908, been expended by the city in appropriations included in budgets which, in reality, ought to have been defrayed by these uncollected taxes.[19]

Basing their action on these uncollected taxes, the city officials had issued, from time to time, large amounts in revenue bonds with which to get money to pay the appropriations in the yearly budgets. On October 31, 1908, there was outstanding against these arrears of taxes $40,606,000 of revenue bonds. This left a balance of $35,660,000 which had been expended by the city for current expenses, but which had neither been collected nor procured by revenue bonds.[20] The Select Legislative Committee commented upon the fact that although the evidence proved conclusively that not more than 65 per cent of personal taxes were collectable, yet the city budget had nearly equaled the entire levy in each year.[21] Furthermore, the sum of $24,521,000 in special franchise taxes had not been collected by December 31, 1907.

The sources of a certain $33,000,000 which had been spent by the city puzzled the Select Legislative Commit-

18 *Ibid.*, p. 11.
19 *Ibid.*

20 *Ibid.*
21 *Ibid.*

tee. Just how this money was obtained the Committee
was not able to ascertain.

But, the Committee added, it was shown that the as-
sessment account for local improvements was depleted
to the amount of $1,900,000. There should have been
a sum of $600,000 comprising trust funds, various be-
quests, intestate estates, etc., but it could not be found.
Also, there should have been in the city treasury $3,800,-
000 more as a special account including deposits made with
the city against contractors' liability for restoring and re-
paving streets and the unliquidated balance of the Brooklyn fund. But this $3,800,000 " did not exist." The ac-
counts of the various boroughs revealed a shortage of
$1,500,000; excise funds were short $5,100,000; the account of unexpended proceeds of the bond account disclosed a shortage of $7,200,000, and the account of that
part of the unexpended bond accounts which had not been
allotted was short $8,250,000.[22]

" The Controller's office," the Select Legislative Committee reported, " was unable within any reasonable time
to determine from what funds the remaining $4,000,000
had been taken, making up the total shortage of $33,-
000,000. But the net result is certain, that for the payment of running expenses over a long period of years,
the City has taken the total amount of $29,000,000 from
specific funds set apart for other purposes, shifting the
resulting deficits from one fund to another as occasion required." [23]

Large issues of corporate stock were also made for
other than permanent improvements.[24]

The city budget appropriations had grown enormously.
In 1898 the amount was $70,175,896. By 1909 it had
mounted to $156,545,148, an increase of more than $86,-
000,000, or approximately 123 per cent. Yet the increase in population had been only about 39.4 per cent.[25]

22 *Ibid.*, p. 13.
23 *Ibid.*, p. 13.
24 *Ibid.*, pp. 14–15.
25 *Ibid.*, p. 16.

Vast sums were squandered in the purchasing of city supplies and in a multitude of other ways. Condemnation proceedings were a source of great scandal. There was the Catskill reservoir and aqueduct to supply New York with water, the estimated cost of which undertaking was $162,000,000. "Rings" of politicians bought land which they sold to the city at high prices. For the one item of advertising "public notices" of condemnation proceedings, the cost already had approximated $800,000.[26] In three years the fees paid to certain Catskill reservoir and aqueduct commissioners appointed to condemn land, aggregated $169,490, and this amount did not include the fees of commissioners who had not yet reported.[27] During the same period the fees paid to commissioners in New York City street and park opening proceedings totalled more than $384,000, while fees paid in other condemnation proceedings (exclusive of the Dock Department) aggregated more than $300,000.[28]

Large as these sums were, they were but a fraction of the total amounts pocketed by all of the beneficiaries.

The city payroll was padded with an extraordinarily large number of superfluous employees. In a separate memorandum to the Legislative Committee report, Mr. William M. Bennet, a member of that committee, quoted Controller Metz's statement in 1909 that from 25 to 50 per cent of New York City's payroll, then totalling $80,-000,000 a year, was "useless."[29] At this time (in 1909) New York City's actual debt reached $800,000,000.[30] In many directions "Organization" men were faring richly. Even though Mayor McClellan was fighting Leader Murphy, Tammany held sway in many administrative and court departments, not included in the Mayor's jurisdiction, and he had certain reasons for placating some Tammany district leaders.

[26] *Ibid.*, p. 26.
[27] *Ibid.*, p. 28.
[28] *Ibid.*

[29] *Ibid.*, p. 115.
[30] *Ibid.*, pp. 112–113.

After declaring his independence of " Boss " Murphy,
Mayor McClellan, supported by Senator McCarren, of
Brooklyn, had begun a contest — futile enough, as it
turned out — to get control of Tammany Hall.   According to a magazine article [31] written by General Theodore
A. Bingham, Police Commissioner during Mayor McClellan's second administration, Mayor McClellan " knew
full well that the most effective weapon was the power and
patronage at his disposal, by virtue of his office.   When
he tried to use the police I objected."   Dismissed by
Mayor McClellan from the office of Police Commissioner,
Mr. Bingham soon after set forth his experiences in the
published article in question.

" In all election contests," wrote General Bingham further,

"whether it be a primary election, a municipal election, or a State
or a National election, the police are a factor.   The district leader
who can control the majority of the uniformed men on duty in his
bailiwick is not apt to have much trouble in fighting off rival candidates.   He has a most influential body of men working for him 365
days in the year.

" The baneful influence of the ordinary Tammany district leader
in a single precinct station house is far-reaching.   When he can do
favors, or persuade the men that he can do them, his influence is
something beyond belief.   Some leaders have had more authority
in some police stations than the executive head of the department.
They have been looked upon as the men from whom to take orders.
They have often visited the station not only to give bail for unlucky
constituents, but to give orders to the captains and lieutenants.

" Policemen as a whole are the most gullible persons in the entire
City Government when it comes to the question of the power of the
political 'boss.'   This is not surprising.   Experience has taught
them that if they displease the local powers they are apt to be transferred to a distant precinct.   Therefore, they fear to take a chance.
The wily leader takes advantage of this weakness.   He uses his power
at every opportunity, and when he meets with opposition he is
prompt with his threats.   Suppose, in the course of time, the offending policeman is shifted as a matter of routine.   Then the leader
struts about telling this offender's fellow officers that he, the leader,
had the man transferred."   And if a policeman showed independence, Mr. Bingham asserted, a word from the leader to the superior

[31] *Why I Was Removed,* by Theodore A. Bingham, *Van Norden's
Magazine,* September, 1909.

officers caused "complaints to be made, extra hours of duty, unpleasant details and the like, until the man's life is made miserable."

General Bingham declared that he had labored to stamp out these abuses, but unavailingly. " So bad did this political influence become in some precincts in Manhattan after Mayor McClellan began his contests at the primaries for the leadership of Tammany Hall, that I had to make radical changes in the personnel of those districts."

It was absurdly easy for Mr. Murphy and his Tammany machine leaders to squelch Mayor McClellan's plans for leadership. No auspicious time was it, however, to nominate a " regular Organization man " for Mayor; respectability had to be invoked and a hack politician obviously would not serve the purpose. Besides, there was resistance from Senator McCarren's Brooklyn organization against the nomination of a distinctively Tammany " Organization " creature.

The candidate of Tammany Hall and its allies was William J. Gaynor. A Brooklyn lawyer, he had signalized his early career by causing John Y. McKane, then Democratic " boss " of Coney Island, to be convicted and imprisoned for ballot box frauds and for defying a court injunction. Elected to the State Supreme Court, Gaynor was a member of that body when nominated for Mayor; and by his constant exposures of the tyrannies and abuses committed by the police force he had become widely and favorably known as a man opposed to " The System." Thus, Tammany could depict its candidate as a genuine and proved reformer. But apart from these representations, Gaynor was, in fact, a man of intellect, force and independence of character, deep understanding of public questions and of progressive, even advanced, views. A far different type he was from the usual run of ignorant grafting politicians.

By his strong denunciations of the looting done by surface-railway manipulators and by his emphatic declarations in favor of the building by the city itself of further subways, Gaynor won a large following. He seemed uncommonly sincere when he caustically arraigned the combination of railway promoters and financiers who, he said, were busy at the " old game " of seeking to enrich themselves manifold more by getting additional traction franchises. " My friends," he asserted in a speech in Tammany Hall, on October 19, 1909, " we are going to build the subways. We do not intend that a single subway or a franchise for it shall be passed over to any of these men." He made other pronouncements to the same effect.

The pushful, insistent Mr. Hearst was still backed by a political organization, now passing under the name of the Civic Alliance, but his course in accepting Mr. Murphy's and Tammany's support during his candidacy for Governor after having bitterly assailed them in previous campaigns when he was an independent candidate, had effectually alienated many of his former followers. By reason of the influence of his newspapers, he still, however, had considerable strength. He was the nominee of the Civic Alliance for Mayor. The Republican and Fusion candidate was Otto Bannard, a banker. Edward F. Cassidy was the Socialist Party's candidate. One of the issues put forward by the Fusion campaigners was the continuing abominations of the " white slave " traffic, operated, it was asserted, with the connivance of the police.

Gaynor was elected. The vote resulted: Gaynor, 250,378; Bannard, 177,304; Hearst, 154,187; Cassidy, 11,768; Hunter (Socialist Labor) 1,256; Manierre (Prohibition) 866. Although, however, Gaynor won, yet by the election of many of the Fusion candidates (to the offices of Controller, President of the Board of Aldermen and presidents of boroughs) Tammany lost control of nearly all of the borough presidencies, and in turn of many of the departments and of the powerful Board of Estimate. In this Board Tammany now had only three votes.

CHAPTER XXXIV

1910–1911

IT was only a few months after this election that the investigations of William H. Hotchkiss, State Superintendent of Insurance, followed by that of a New York Legislative committee into the matter of legislative graft, revealed the extensive and variegated corruption of both political parties.

An examination by Mr. Hotchkiss, in October, 1909, of the affairs of the Phœnix Insurance Company of Brooklyn had brought to light a mass of correspondence apparently disclosing an intimate connection between the president of that company and legislative measures, introduced from 1900 to 1910, affecting fire insurance companies. The materials thus unearthed caused Superintendent Hotchkiss to order a full examination of the books and records of other fire insurance companies, which examination was begun in January, 1910.

On January 18, 1910, the New York *Evening Post* published certain facts the purport of which tended to show that State Senator Jotham P. Allds, when Republican leader of the Assembly, in 1901, had been bribed to assist in killing certain legislation to which bridge construction companies objected. The Senate was forced to investigate, and Allds hastily resigned, but the Senate on March 29, 1910, sustained the charge of bribery by a vote of 40 to 9.

It was well understood that this virtuous action was " a sacrifice " and an ostentatious sop to public opinion;

many more legislators than he were implicated in charges of corruption. Meanwhile, Mr. Hotchkiss was persisting in his investigation. In the course of Mr. Hotchkiss' inquiry, on March 22, 1910, testimony developed the fact that for twenty years or more, " firebug " funds had been raised by insurance companies and lavishly distributed among legislators at Albany and that those companies had employed one William H. Buckley to act as " watcher " on " strike bills " introduced in the Legislature at Albany. Buckley admitted that at a time after only three years' admission to the bar, he had received $27,000 from insurance companies for representing them during the sessions of the Legislature.

One of the bills introduced in the Legislature was a measure fathered by Senator Thomas F. Grady, a noted Tammany leader, celebrated as the chief orator of the Tammany organization. This bill, called a re-insurance act, was introduced and passed under such circumstances that Vice-President Correa of the Home Insurance Company referred to it in a contemporary letter as " bought legislation." Mr. Correa also stated in that letter, which was in evidence, that only three re-insured fire insurance companies supported the bill, which gave those three companies a distinct advantage over 209 direct insurance companies doing business in New York State. The bill dealt with the carrying of a reserve where part of a fire risk was re-insured. Senator Grady declared, in a public interview, that this bill was introduced to protect policy holders by compelling the re-insurance company, when a part of a policy was farmed out by the company of the first instance, to keep an adequate reserve against the policy thus taken, but all of the insurance officers examined by Mr. Hotchkiss admitted either wholly or in part, that Grady's interview did not represent a correct conception of what his bill actually provided.[1]

[1] An indication of Senator Grady's large sources of income had come to public notice in 1907 when the District Attorney's force raided

Another conspicuous Tammany leader implicated in the disclosures before Superintendent Hotchkiss was Senator "Big Tim" Sullivan. He had long been one of the really powerful leaders of Tammany Hall, and held direct sovereignty over the teeming East Side below Fourteenth Street.

Beginning life as a bartender, "Big Tim" Sullivan had been given the nick-name "Dry Dollar" Sullivan, because of his habit of carefully wiping the bar before placing change on it. His career in the Assembly and Senate was notorious for the number of bad bills promoted or supported by him. His power in manipulating primaries and swaying elections on the East Side south of Fourteenth Street was recognized as that of a master hand; he knew how to make the "gangs" his obedient servants; not a secret of colonizing voters and carrying elections was unknown to him and his clan; at the same time he was called "the friend of the poor" because of his yearly practise of giving the wastrels of the Bowery and vicinity Thanksgiving and Christmas dinners and presents. By his proved and consistent ability to sway politics in the great and thickly-populated East Side, he had to be recognized as an independent Tammany power; no one could become "boss" of Tammany Hall without his support. His power in Tammany was exceeded only by Mr. Murphy's. In fact, he was one of the actual rulers, not only of Tammany Hall, but of New York City.

George F. Seward, president of the Fidelity and Casualty Company, testified on March 21, 1910, before Superintendent Hotchkiss, that a man representing himself

the poolroom "clearing house" at 112 Fulton street, New York City. Canceled checks and other records found there revealed that a mysterious person designated variously in the syndicate's account books as "Tommy," "T. G.," "T. Grady," and "Sen.," had "raked off" more than $43,000 on the poolroom business in the first two years of the syndicate's existence and had continued to profit from that source up to the very time of the raid. No doubt, however, Grady had his losses, too.

to be an agent of Senator " Big Tim " Sullivan, in 1891 or 1892, offered, in return for a $10,000 bribe, to have a bill inimical to that company's interests killed. Mr. Seward, in response, dictated this telegram to Sullivan: " Mr. Seward says you can go to hell." In reply to a question as to whether this happened when the Republican party or the Democratic party was in power, Mr. Seward replied, " So far as either party is concerned, I don't think it would make very much difference, and I really do not recall." Both parties, Mr. Seward said, were represented in the " Black Horse Cavalry " at Albany. In a public interview Sullivan denounced Mr. Seward's charge as a lie. Recalled as a witness, on March 22, 1910, Seward adhered to the story he had told. It may be remarked here that when Sullivan died in 1913, he left a considerable fortune, originally estimated at two millions of dollars; his friends represented that he had made it from a chain of showhouses in which he was interested; but the inventory showed that he owned large quantities of stock in mining companies, realty companies and other concerns. Many of these shares, however, were listed by the executors of his estate as valueless. The definite value of Sullivan's estate was placed at $1,021,277.33.

On March 24, 1910, certain definite facts were brought out showing how Buckley, lobbyist at Albany for the fire insurance companies, had succeeded in killing, in 1903, various proposed enactments which those companies did not want enacted.

Correspondence produced showed that Buckley had written to George P. Sheldon, president of the Phœnix Insurance Company, that " it was not difficult to tie the matter [insurance bills] up in the committee," and later correspondence held out the assurance that the matter " had been arranged." According to the testimony, Justice Edward E. McCall of the New York State Supreme Court had indorsed a $35,000 check from Sheldon to Buckley. On March 29, 1910, Darwin P. Kingsley, presi-

dent of the New York Life Insurance Company, testified
that Buckley had offered to buy him the votes of six members of the New York State Senate for a certain amount,
and that when he (Kingsley) declined to pay, a certain
insurance measure which Kingsley had favored was withdrawn.

These are but a few of the specific details brought out
in the hearings before Mr. Hotchkiss; it appeared that at
least ten prominent Republican legislators who had ruled
important Senate and Assembly Committees for years had
speculative accounts in the brokerage firm of Ellingwood
& Cunningham of New York City, in which firm G.
Tracy Rogers, keeper of the traction "Yellow Dog"
fund during that period, was a special partner.

On April 8, 1910, State Superintendent of Insurance
Hotchkiss made a full report to Governor Hughes of the
investigation that he had made.   Mr. Hotchkiss reported
that the aggregate of disbursements by fire insurance companies in connection with legislation affecting those companies, from 1901 to 1909, probably exceeded $150,000.

" The moneys so paid," Mr. Hotchkiss reported, " were
disbursed for traveling expenses of individuals and delegations; annual and special retainers of regular counsels;
so-called retainers of legislative lawyers; contributions
to political committees; gifts or payments to men of
political prominence and influence, and entertaining legislators and others, at times in a somewhat lavish manner."

Mr. Hotchkiss further set forth in his report that the
log rolling of " strike " bills in and out of committees was
a regular business, that the books of the stock brokerage
house of Ellingwood & Cunningham, New York City,
" warrant a strong suspicion that such books, to an extent at least, had been a clearing house for financial transactions connected with legislation during the period mentioned," and that G. Tracy Rogers, a special partner in
the firm and long president of the Street Railways Association of the State of New York, seemed up to the time of

the failure of that firm " to have been the legislative representative at Albany of the traction interests." Mr.
Hotchkiss reported that: " Certain of the accounts in
these ledgers show a close connection between G. Tracy
Rogers and the Metropolitan traction interests in New
York City. The character of the securities dealt in [by
legislators] frequently recalls legislation urged or re-
tarded at about the same time." Mr. Hotchkiss urged
further inquiry, and in a special message to the Legislature, on April 11, 1910, Governor Hughes called on that
body to follow, by means of a general investigation, the
trails of legislative corruption laid bare by the Allds bribery trial and the investigation conducted by Superintendent Hotchkiss.

In the face of the exposures already made and the insistent demands for further investigation, the legislative
committee appointed for the purpose could not evade
pressing the inquiry.

The testimony on September 15, 1910, showed that
during a single month in the summer of 1903, the sum of
$40,000 was sent by an agent of the New York City
street railway interests to the firm of Ellingwood &
Cunningham, and that no vouchers or receipts were asked
or given to account for the distribution of the money.
At previous hearings, the fact had been established that
this brokerage house was the firm which served as a
" clearing-house " for the money supplied to members of
the Legislature by G. Tracy Rogers. At the hearing on
September 16, 1910, the evidence showed that Senator
Louis F. Goodsell and Assemblyman Louis Bedell, prominent Republican leaders in the Legislature, had received
large amounts of money from the Metropolitan Street
Railway Company and G. Tracy Rogers from 1900 to
1904; Goodsell had received $24,800, and Bedell $21,750.
Goodsell admitted that he had " bought " stock without
putting up any margin.

At the same hearing, H. H. Vreeland, president of the

Metropolitan Street Railway Company, testified that the Metropolitan Street Railway Company contributed campaign funds, and that it did so to practically every one that ran for office; he remembered $20,000 or $25,000 given to the Republican organization and $17,000 or $18,000 to the Democratic organization; this was in about the year 1902 or 1903. Another method of subsidizing politicians individually, Mr. Vreeland testified, was by carrying stocks on the books of various brokerage houses for them; these individual stock transactions ran from $20,000 to more than $30,000.

Much further testimony was brought out showing the enormous and continuous subsidizing of both old political parties and politicians by corporations wanting certain legislation enacted or smothered. On September 21, 1910, Mr. Vreeland admitted that the Metropolitan Street Railway Company had, prior to 1903, paid out fully $250,000 in " taking up " stocks that legislators and other politicians had been carrying with brokerage houses and which they desired converted into cash; this was one of the indirect methods of influencing political or legislative action in the interest of the company. G. Tracy Rogers testified that he had disbursed $82,475 in three years, and that most of it went to members of the railroad committees of the New York Legislature. In these hearings the names of a number of conspicuous legislators and the amounts received by them were brought out in the testimony.

Testimony, also under oath, on October 19, 1910, purported to show that a legislative corruption fund of $500,000 was raised at a meeting in Delmonico's to defeat anti-race track gambling legislation at Albany in 1908; that Charles H. Hyde,[2] Chamberlain of New York

2 Hyde, on November 29, 1912, was convicted in court on a charge of accepting a bribe, as a public officer, in consideration for depositing public money in certain banks. He was sentenced to two years in State's prison. But the verdict was later reversed by the Appellate Division of the Supreme Court, and he was released from all criminal charges.

City under Mayor Gaynor, attended this meeting, and that State Senator Frank Gardner went to Albany with Hyde because Hyde did not know the ways of legislators and how to approach them " properly."

Hyde's father-in-law was William A. Engeman, owner of the Brighton Beach race track; according to the testimony, Hyde made a subscription for Engeman (who had failed to pay), and later put in a bill for personal expenses covering the amount. The testimony further represented that there was a dispute as to who was to handle the bribery funds, and that $125,000 was given to James E. Gaffney " to take care of three or four members of the Legislature — Tammany men." According further to the testimony, Senator Thomas F. Grady, Democratic leader at Albany and close friend and spokesman of " Boss " Murphy, received only $4,000 of the bribery fund. Two Republican State Senators wanted $25,000 each. The testimony also involved Senator Patrick H. McCarren. Senator McCarren was the Democratic " boss " of Brooklyn; he was an ally of Tammany Hall (for the Democratic organization in Brooklyn retained its autonomy separate from that of Tammany Hall, yet allied with it), and he was the legislative agent of various financial interests and trusts.

It appeared, according to the testimony, that Senator McCarren was angry that the handling of the race track fund was entrusted to others; he objected " to a strange man going up there, expecting to get away with such a proposition," but later he was placated and lent his aid against the bill. When urging Senator Foelker, a Brooklyn Republican, to vote against the bill, McCarren was represented as saying to Foelker: " You need not fear the indignation of your constituents. If you are afraid of possible reelection or have any doubts about election time, I think I can fix it up for you so you can name your own opponent at the coming election." This was the substance of the testimony of Assistant District Attorney

Robert Elder, of Brooklyn, who narrated the facts revealed to him by former State Senator Frank Gardner, under indictment charged with attempting to bribe Foelker. (Here the fact should be noted that when Gardner was tried on this charge he was acquitted on February 23, 1911.) Mr. Foelker himself testified that he was offered $45,000 and then $50,000 to vote against the bill, which offer he refused; the vote on the bill was extremely close, and a single vote meant its passage or defeat.

At further hearings of the Legislative "Graft Hunt" Committee, Senator Eugene M. Travis, of Brooklyn, testified that an ineffectual effort had been made, at a time when the foes of the measure needed only one or two votes, to bribe him with $100,000 to vote against the bill prohibiting horse racing in New York State. Senator Travis specified three other Senators whom they attempted to bribe. August Belmont testified that the $500,000 fund was "mythical and absurd." It was reported that representations made at the hearing on Novemder 30, 1910, were to the effect that one jockey club alone had expended $33,000 while the anti-race track gambling legislation was pending, and that information from reliable sources tended to show that each of the other seven racing associations had expended a similar sum, or perhaps more. Further information, it was given out, was to the effect that each of ninety-three bookmakers had subscribed $3,-000 each. The total of the above stated contributions would have amounted to $543,000 — supposing the fund to have been a fact.

Whatever were the basic facts, pro and con, as to the alleged $500,000 fund for the defeat of the anti-race-track bill, the record shows that it was defeated on April 8, 1908, by a vote of 25 to 25, and that among those voting against it were such Tammany Senators as Grady, Frawley, McManus, Sullivan and other Tammany men and Democrats,— in all seventeen Democrats and eight Republicans. A new State Senator having been elected in a special election in one district, the bill prohibiting gambling at race tracks was subsequently passed.

Nearly all of those involved made vehement denials. Senator McCarren had died on October 23, 1909 — a year before these hearings. Although cooperating with " Boss " Murphy in elections, there was nevertheless considerable animosity between the two, arising, it was generally believed, from a suspicion that Mr. Murphy, inflated by his personal victory in electing McClellan in 1903, was attempting to extend his political territory to Brooklyn. Senator McCarren had openly protested against this " encroachment " and had threatened trouble if it were pushed. It was this jealously vigilant attitude on the part of the bosses of the other boroughs which prevented Tammany Hall from extending its regular organization outside the former city limits.

McCarren himself was a " sporting man " and reputed to be a " thoroughbred " at that. He had his own elaborate racing stable, and it was said of him that he once uncomplainingly lost $30,000 on a bet, although the decision of the racing judges was open to question. In 1908 the failure of the brokerage firm of Ennis & Stoppani revealed the fact that McCarren was " carrying " $250,000 worth of stock, for which he had paid nothing, and which resulted in a loss to him of about $107,000. No demand had been made by the brokers upon McCarren for margins ; in view of this fact he could not have been compelled to pay losses ; it was said of him, however, that he gave a check to the receiver and took the stock. He was a " heavy operator " in real estate and in the stock market, and had personal relations with H. H. Rogers, Anthony N. Brady, William C. Whitney, J. Pierpont Morgan, W. K. Vanderbilt, August Belmont and other Wall Street magnates, of whose interests he was a recognized pusher in the Legislature.

To return, however, to the hearings of the Legislative

" Graft Hunt " Committee: facts brought out showed that the beet sugar interests had also debauched the Legislature and that State Senator John Raines, a leading Republican, received $9,000 in two years for pushing bounty bills to aid beet sugar interests. These facts were admitted by Henry F. Zimmerlin, former vice-president and Albany lobbyist of the Lyons Beet Sugar Refining Company.

The full testimony tended to show that insurance companies, traction companies, construction companies and other interests paid large sums to defeat legislation that they did not want enacted, or were blackmailed into paying other large sums to have " strike bills " suppressed. But the report of the Legislative Investigating Committee, made on February 1, 1911, was harmless as far as specific findings of corruption were concerned. As to the charges of traction and race track corruption, the Committee reported that no definite and substantial charge, verified by knowledge, had been filed with it, and that " in consequence it finds nothing definite in regard to the traction and race track charges that it examined." [3] There were one or two indictments, but no one, either bribers or bribed, had to go prison, although in charges made in a detached subsequent case, one solitary State Senator, Stilwell, was convicted of bribery charges and sentenced to prison; he was a comparatively obscure politician.

Inasmuch as the Legislature for years had been dominantly Republican, these disclosures had a much more injurious political effect upon the Republican organization than upon Tammany, and they were of weight in

[3] The Committee commented: " The investigation shows clearly the extreme difficulty of securing exact information which will disclose the methods by which powerful financial interests seek to control legislative action in matters coming before legislative bodies.

" The crime of bribery is one of the most difficult of all crimes to uncover. All the resources of ingenuity are used to conceal it, and only in exceedingly rare instances are either of the parties to the crime willing to come forward and disclose the facts."

bringing about the election of a Democratic Governor in
the person of John A. Dix, in 1910. This was the first
Democratic Governor of New York State elected in many
years; the result was the enlargement of Tammany's sway,
and more offices and further fields of power and profit for
" the Organization."

At the same time, a Legislature, the majority of which
were Tammany men and Democrats, was elected. The
election of a United States Senator coming up, the chief
aspirant pushed for the place was William F. Sheehan,
an attorney for the traction magnate, Thomas F. Ryan.
Mr. Murphy had his headquarters in Albany directing the
contest; he was said to have given his promise to Mr.
Sheehan, but when he saw that Sheehan could not be
elected, he tried to bring about the election of Daniel F.
Cohalan, his personal attorney and adviser, as United
States Senator. A few years previously, Cohalan was
an obscure lawyer, but as the friend and adviser of
" Boss " Murphy, his practise had grown to large and
lucrative proportions; it was a practise principally deal-
ing with matters concerning municipal affairs. In 1908
Mr. Murphy had caused Mr. Cohalan to be chosen Grand
Sachem of the Tammany Society.

But Mr. Murphy found that it was not possible to put
Cohalan in the United States Senate. Certain "in-
surgent " Democratic legislators elected from various
parts of the State, wanted neither Sheehan, Ryan's attorney, nor Cohalan, Murphy's attorney. Finally Justice James A. O'Gorman (who years previously had been
elected to the New York State Supreme Court by Tammany) was compromised upon as the candidate for United
States Senator and elected.

Then Mr. Murphy decided to make Mr. Cohalan Justice O'Gorman's successor on the Supreme Court Bench.

According to published report, the appointment of Mr.
Cohalan as a Justice of the Supreme Court by Governor
Dix was the result of " a deal " between Dix and Murphy.

Governor Dix wanted the appointment of George C. Van Tuyl, as State Commissioner of Banks, confirmed. The nomination of Van Tuyl was referred to the Senate Finance Committee, of which Senator Frawley, a Tammany district leader, was chairman. A report was prepared recommending that the nomination of Van Tuyl be confirmed, but this report was held up week after week, and the statement was common in the political slang current at Albany that no action could be taken in presenting the report "until the Governor comes across with Cohalan." At last, on May 18, 1911, Senator Frawley suddenly presented the report, moved its confirmation, and the Senate acquiesced. Sixteen minutes later a message appeared from Governor Dix announcing the appointment of Daniel F. Cohalan to succeed James A. O'Gorman as Justice of the Supreme Court for the remainder of O'Gorman's unexpired term.

The session of 1911 was the first time in nineteen years that the Democratic party had control of the Legislature, and Tammany Hall was in control of the Democratic organization in the State. It was at this session that a strong effort was made to enact the Tammany-Gaynor "Ripper" Charter, the provisions of which aroused much scandal. The majority of the Board of Estimate in New York City were at this time Independent Democrats. The proposed charter would have arbitrarily deprived them of many of their most important functions of office. Its aim was to impair the powers of the Board of Estimate in many destructive ways, and to centralize power in the hands of the Mayor. It would have given the Mayor complete domination of the development of transportation facilities in New York City. Such effective opposition was raised that it was defeated by the votes of Independent Democrats in the Assembly. At this session it was, too, that an attempt was made to pass the Sullivan Inferior Criminal Courts "Ripper" bill which, by making city magistrates elective instead of appointive, would have restored the old pernicious, demoralizing system of local political influence. These were but two of a list of other proposed Tammany measures.

Mr. Murphy's habits as leader at this time were in singular contrast with those of years previously when, as a district leader, he had made his hailing place by a lamp post. He now used a luxurious suite of rooms at Delmonico's fashionable restaurant, at Fifth avenue and Forty-fourth street, where, during campaign contests, he held his secret consultations. Here those whom the " Boss " desired to see on terms of great privacy were summoned, nor were they admitted, it was reported, before they had been first scrutinized and received by Mr. Murphy's factotum, " Phil " Donohue, the treasurer of Tammany Hall, who took his stand in an anteroom. During the campaign of 1911, when County and Assembly candidates were to be elected, Mr. Murphy was to be found almost daily at Delmonico's, and, according to published report, Justice Cohalan was there with him frequently. It was at this election that Mr. Cohalan was elected Justice of the Supreme Court for a period of fourteen years.

Veteran politicians who had learned the wisdom of combining the pocketing of millions with the art of simple appearances, shook their heads ominously at what they considered " Boss " Murphy's tactlessness in vaunting his power, surrounded by ostentation and grandiose luxury.

CHAPTER XXXV

1912–1913

MAYOR GAYNOR was by no means pliable to Tammany purposes; he both asserted and exercised his independence of " Chief " Murphy. But although great powers were centralized in his office, there were nevertheless numbers of Tammany men in the various departments, bureaus and courts. Of the 85,000 regular employees of New York City in 1912 (including 10,118 policemen and 4,346 firemen), many were Tammany men, the larger number of them occupying subordinate positions. The entire city payroll at this time aggregated about $89,000,000 — an average outlay of $7,500,000 a month for salaries and wages alone. The city budget for 1913 was $190,411,000.

Despite the appointment of successive Police Commissioners — there had been eight within eleven years — to remedy matters in the Police Department, the state of affairs in that department was still a fruitful cause of scandal. This continuing scandal was brought to a vivid climax by a murder the deliberate audacity of which horrified and aroused the people of the city.

On April 15, 1912, Police Lieutenant Charles Becker went, at the head of his " raiding squad," to the gambling house of Herman Rosenthal on West Forty-fifth street. On July 11, 1912, Rosenthal went to the West Side Police Court to protest against the " oppression " of the police in stationing a uniformed man constantly on duty in his house. Shortly thereafter, Rosenthal made an affidavit,

which was published in the New York *World* on July 14,
1912, swearing that Police Lieutenant Becker had been
his partner in the operation of the gambling house and
had made the raid for certain personal purposes hereafter explained.

If at this time a Tammany district attorney had been
in office, the results might not have been fatal to Rosenthal. But the district attorney, Charles S. Whitman, was
an official noted for his excellent record. It was well realized that when he agreed to listen to Rosenthal's charges
against Becker, he could not be " reached " by any " influence " or intimidated by any threat. The alternative
on the part of somebody vitally interested was to slay
Rosenthal on the principle that " dead men tell no tales,"
and thus prevent important disclosures being made to the
district attorney.

At 2 o'clock on the morning of July 16, 1912, Rosenthal was summoned out from the doorway of the Hotel
Metropole at Broadway and Forty-third street, and shot
to death by four " gunmen " from within an automobile,
which immediately after the shooting sped away with the
murderers.

Arrests of suspects quickly followed. By July 29,
1912, District Attorney Whitman held four men, all of
whom had become informers. These four were " Bald
Jack " Rose, " Bridgie " Webber, Harry Vallon, and Sam
Schepps — two of whom, Rose and Vallon, had volun-
tarily surrendered. On statements made by Rose and
Vallon, the Grand Jury returned an indictment against
Becker charging murder in the first degree. A few days
later, Becker was re-indicted, and indictments were handed
in against the four " gunmen "— Louis Rosenberg, alias
" Lefty Louie," 23 years old; Harry Horowitz, alias
" Gyp the Blood," 26 years old; Jacob Seidenshner, alias
" Whitey Lewis," 26 years old, and Frank Cirofici, alias
" Dago Frank," 29 years old. These " gunmen " were
variously arrested at different places.

Stirred by this brutal murder, a mass meeting of citizens was held at Cooper Union on August 14, 1912. Resolutions were adopted part of which approved a proposal for an appropriation by the city of $25,000 for an investigation into police conditions and a thorough inquiry into the causes and possible remedies of systems of blackmail and graft. A Citizens' Committee was appointed by this mass meeting to report on these conditions.

Of the police force this committee reported on February 26, 1913, that:

"The corruption is so ingrained that the man of ordinary decent character entering the force and not possessed of extraordinary moral fiber may easily succumb. About him are the evidences of graft and the enjoyment of irregular incomes substantially increasing the patrolman's salary. Inadequate condemnation is shown by his associates in the force for such practises; on the contrary, there is much indirect pressure which induces him to break his oath of office; the families of grafting policemen live better than his own, and the urgencies of his family and of his own social needs tempt him to thrive as do his corrupt associates. Such a system makes for too many of the police an organized school of crime. The improvement of recent years — and there is some — is not great enough to satisfy an aroused public.

"But not resting with this general knowledge of the existence of such matters, this Committee has made an intensive examination of the conditions in a number of police precincts. We know that the connection between members of the police force and crime or commercialized vice is continuous, profitable and so much a matter of course that explicit bargains do not have to be made; naturally this "honor among thieves" is occasionally violated, as is customary among thieves, both the keeping and the breaking of faith being determined by these policemen for their own profit.

"Well knowing this police ' system,' grand juries will not on police testimony indict violators of the law, lest they [the grand juries] be lending themselves to police persecution of a selected criminal who had refused tribute, and so be helping the police ' system.' For the same reason petit juries will acquit, and judges will discharge, and crime increases and goes unpunished, while honest policemen are discredited and discouraged.

"Evil thus breeds new maggots of evil. The sums collected by the police excite the greed of certain politicians; they demand their shares, and in their turn they protect the criminal breaches of the law and the police in corruption. The presence of 'politics' brings strength and complexity to the 'system' and makes it harder to break up. The city, we believe, is convinced that it is time for more radical efforts at improvement." [1]

A Committee of the Board of Aldermen, appointed to inquire into matters connected with the Police Department, held eighty public sessions, took 4,800 pages of testimony and records, handed in certain conclusions, and made recommendations for further laws. "We have received shocking evidence of a widespread corrupt alliance between the police and gamblers and disorderly house keepers," this committee reported in part.[2] During the same time, District Attorney Whitman was vigorously prosecuting public offenders. In a single year four police inspectors were convicted of conspiracy and were also under indictment for bribery, one police captain was convicted of extortion, one lieutenant was convicted of extortion, one patrolman of perjury, and two patrolmen were convicted of extortion. In addition, there were various indictments of patrolmen for extortion. Of the convicted, the captain and one patrolman confessed; an attorney and a citizen indicted for bribery in connection with police matters, also confessed.

To return to the trials for the murder of Rosenthal: At Becker's trial Rose testified that his connection with Becker had begun in 1911, after a "raid" on a gambling house kept by him (Rose) on Second Avenue; that the levying of tribute on "unraided" gamblers was systematized; that Rosenthal was brought under this system of "protection"; that Rosenthal and Becker had become partners; and that Rosenthal, in March, 1912, had refused to "give up" $500 for the defense of Becker's press agent who was charged with the killing of a negro in a "raid" on a crap game. According further to Rose's testimony, this refusal brought on strained relations be-

---

[1] *Report of the Citizens' Committee Appointed at the Cooper Union Meeting, August 12, 1912*, pp. 6–7.

[2] *Preliminary Legislative Report of Special Committee of Board of Aldermen*, p. 6.

tween Becker and Rosenthal; and that after the "raid" on Rosenthal's gambling house, on April 15, 1912, when Rosenthal threatened "to squeal," Becker began to plan for the "fixing" of Rosenthal. In June, 1912 — so Rose testified — when "Big Jack" Zelig, an East Side gang leader, was in the City Prison, the plan was determined upon of negotiating with him that, in exchange for his release, some of his "gunmen" should "attend to" Rosenthal. The four "gunmen" arrested, Rose swore, were the tools that committed the murder, and he (Rose) had acted as Becker's agent in arranging matters with them. The testimony further showed that on the afternoon after the murder, the quartet of "gunmen" had received $1,000 as payment, after which they quit the city.

On the testimony of Rose and others, Becker was convicted on October 24, 1913; the conviction of the four young "gunmen" soon followed. All five were sentenced to death. By a decision of the Court of Appeals, on February 24, 1914, Becker was allowed a new trial upon the ground that by reason of hostile rulings his trial had not been fair, but the conviction of the four "gunmen" was affirmed. They were electrocuted at Sing Sing prison on April 13, 1914. Subsequently, after a second trial, Becker was again convicted, and was duly electrocuted.

Another source of quick-ripening trouble to Tammany Hall, turning large numbers of voters against its chief, Mr. Murphy, and against the whole system of the "Organization," was the summary manner in which it impeached and disposed of Governor William Sulzer.

Mr. Sulzer had been a member of Tammany Hall for twenty-five years, and had always been pushed into office by Tammany Hall since the time when, as a young man, he had been one of Mr. Croker's protégés. Elected to the New York State Assembly, he had been made its Speaker at a youthful age. Later he had been repeatedly sent to Congress by Tammany Hall nominations, and it was primarily a Tammany backing that caused his nomination and election as Governor, in 1912. Tammany believed that it had every reason to feel sure that as Governor Mr. Sulzer would continue pliable and docile to the " Organization's " orders and interests.

" Boss " Murphy, however, was soon disillusioned when Governor Sulzer declined dictation.

According to Mr. Sulzer's detailed story,[3] he (Sulzer), immediately prior to going into office as Governor, spent an afternoon with Mr. Murphy at his request in his private room at Delmonico's.

" His attitude," Mr. Sulzer related, " was very friendly and confidential. He said he was my friend; that he knew of my financial condition and wanted to help me out. As he went on, I was amazed at his knowledge of my intimate personal affairs. To my astonishment, he informed me that he knew I was heavily in debt. Then he offered me enough money to pay my debts and have enough left to take things easy while Governor. He said that this was really a party matter and that the money he would give me was party money . . . and that nobody would know anything about it; that I could pay what I owed and go to Albany feeling easy financially. He then asked me how much I needed, to whom I owed it, and other personal questions.

" As I did not want to be tied hard and fast as Governor in advance, I declined Mr. Murphy's offer, saying that I was paying off my debts gradually; that my creditors were friends and would not press me; that I was economical, that I would try to get along on my salary as Governor." Mr. Sulzer asserted that Mr. Murphy repeated the offer, and that when he (Sulzer) again refused, Mr. Murphy said, " If you need money at any time, let me know, and you can have what you want. We cleaned up a lot of money on your campaign. I can afford to let you have what you want and never miss it."

[3] An extended interview published in the New York *Evening Mail*, October 20 and 21, 1913.

Then, according further to Mr. Sulzer's story, Mr. Murphy wanted Governor Sulzer to meet him at the hotel in Albany where Murphy was staying; Sulzer did not go. Subsequently, on the night of February 2, 1913, they met at Justice Edward E. McCall's house in New York City, where Murphy urged the appointment of his friend, John Galvin, to succeed Mr. Willcox as a member of the Public Service Commission in New York City. The Public Service Commission is a body invested with enormous authority in the matter of granting of public franchises and other comprehensive powers; it had been under anti-Tammany control, and it was a body the domination of which was pressingly sought by Tammany; there were vast subway franchises to be awarded, and the powers of that body could be used with almost autocratic effect in certain ways over the entire range of recognized public service corporations. Governor Sulzer would not appoint Galvin, but finally compromised upon the selection of Justice Edward E. McCall as Chairman of the Public Service Commission.

"At this meeting and subsequently," Mr. Sulzer declared, "Mr. Murphy demanded from me pledges regarding legislation and especially concerning appointments to the Public Service Commission, the Health Department, the Labor Department, the State Hospital Commission, the Department of State Prisons and the Department of Highways." Murphy insisted that various Tammany men whom he named should be appointed to those offices. Mr. Murphy, however, favored the retention in office of C. Gordon Reel, State Superintendent of Highways, saying that he was " a good man." " Mr. Murphy added," Mr. Sulzer's statement continued, " that if I wished a new State Superintendent of Highways, 'Jim' Gaffney was the best all-around man for the job."

" When I took office as Governor of the State last January," Mr. Sulzer declared in a signed published statement,

" on the very first day my attention was abruptly called to the fact that during the year just ended there had been spent in the State $34,000,000 WITHOUT A SINGLE AUDIT.

" On the second day that I was in office a messenger presented to me bills amounting to hundreds of thousands of dollars, pointing out to me where I was to sign my name. If I had attached my signature to those bills they would have been immediately paid, and yet the messenger thought that he was telling me nothing unusual when he said that other Governors had signed bills that way, and that one Governor had left a rubber stamp outside his office with the messenger, so that he would not be bothered.

" ' Leave those bills there,' I said, ' and I'll look into them. The rubber stamp period is over.' "

After Mr. Sulzer had become Governor he learned, as his statement read, that the State Architect had expended more than $4,300,000 in the previous year; that this was done practically on the certificate of that official, and that there had been no proper audit; the vouchers had been carried to the trustees of public buildings, composed of the Governor, Lieutenant-Governor and Speaker of the Assembly by a clerk and approved by the use of a regular office stamp. Governor Sulzer also learned, he said, that the appropriation for 1912 had been exceeded by nearly half a million dollars, and that there was no proper supervision. Governor Sulzer appointed John A. Hennessy as Commissioner to investigate reports of graft in these and other departments. At the same time, he appointed George W. Blake as Commissioner to inquire into prison management.

Mr. Hennessy's report disclosed the most widespread graft. In construction work on public buildings, large bills had been submitted for inferior material; the payrolls on the electrical and other contracts had been padded; regular State employees had been displaced as inspectors and timekeepers by political henchmen from Tammany District Leader James J. Hagan's district in Manhattan, from which the State Architect, his secretary, and the foreman on the general work came. At Governor Sulzer's request, Mr. Hennessy asked the State Architect for his resignation, but Senator Frawley, another Tammany district leader, intervened with a protest to Governor Sulzer against any interference with the work on the State Capitol or other State buildings.

" I sent for Hennessy," Mr. Sulzer's narrative went on, " who in my presence related to Senator Frawley the main facts in the case, but Frawley still persisted that nothing should be done with the State Architect's office, at least until there had been further consideration of the case. I told Hennessy to return to the State Architect (Mr. Hoofer) and insist upon his resignation. What happened between these two men I can only tell from Hennessy's recital to me. Hoofer told him that he (Hoofer) was not a free agent, that he had no control over his deputies, that he had no control over his secretary, nor did he have any control over the men who checked up the work. He (Hoofer) said they were all appointed through Tammany Hall. . . . Hoofer said he wanted to consult somebody in New York. While I held the 'phone, I told Hennessy to ask Hoofer the name of the man, and Hennessy responded that Hoofer wanted an opportunity to see Charles F. Murphy and explain certain things."

Governor Sulzer allowed a few days' delay. Shortly before the time limit that Governor Sulzer had set for Hoofer's resignation, " John H. Delaney came to me," Mr. Sulzer's story went on, " and said that he had been talking to ' the Chief ' over the 'phone, and that Murphy wanted Hoofer's resignation to go over until such time as he could discuss the case with me." A little later " Senator Wagner, Senator Frawley and John H. Delaney came into the Executive Chamber and informed me that Murphy was insistent that nothing should be done in the case of Hoofer during that week, and it was a subject that would have to be discussed with the organization." Upon Governor Sulzer's demand that he resign or be immediately removed, Mr. Hoofer wrote his resignation.

The next official removed by Governor Sulzer was C. Gordon Reel, State Superintendent of Highways, following Commissioner Hennessy's investigation and the disclosures of extensive graft in highway contracts in a large number of counties. The amount of this graft has been variously estimated at from $5,000,000 to $9,000,000. That the system of plundering the State in the building of roads was no fiction was shown later in the large number of indictments (followed by many convictions) handed down against politico-contractors and State employes in New York State.

In the most important of the indictments found by the Suffolk County Grand Jury on January 22, 1914, the Grand Jury charged " grand larceny " and " conspiracy " in the construction of a so-called " cementitious Hudson River gravel road " the specifications of which designated a material absolutely controlled by Henry Steers, of the contracting firm of Bradley, Gaffney & Steers, commonly known as " the Tammany Trust."

During an investigation conducted by James W. Osborne, in behalf of New York State, the testimony, on February 17, 1914, indicated that State Superintendent of Highways Reel ordered the use of a patented road for roadways and caused the specifications to be changed so as to favor the Gaffney-Bradley-Steers Company which controlled this particular patented pavement. And when Mr. Sulzer testified, on February 29, 1914, before the Assembly " Graft Hunt " Investigating Committee, he said that an average of 30 per cent. of the money paid for those State roads (which had been investigated by Mr. Hennessy) went into the contract, and that 70 per cent. went into the pockets of politicians and contractors. Mr. Sulzer asserted that about $9,000,000 had been stolen in 1912.

According to Mr. Sulzer, Mr. Reel's appointment as State Commissioner of Highways had been Mr. Murphy's " personal selection." When Governor Sulzer's attitude indicated Reel's removal, Mr. Murphy (so Sulzer stated) pressed forward the appointment of " Jim " Gaffney to succeed Reel. " Mr. Murphy demanded the appointment of Gaffney, and still later a prominent New Yorker came to me in the Executive Mansion bringing the message from Mr. Murphy that it was ' Gaffney or war.' I declined to appoint Gaffney.

" This is the Gaffney who, only a few months afterwards, on September 4, 1913, in undisputed testimony before the Supreme Court of New York, was shown to have demanded and received $30,000 in money (refusing to take a check) from one of the aqueduct contractors, nominally for ' advice.' This is the man who Mr. Murphy demanded should be put in a position where he would superintend and control the spending of sixty-five millions of the money of the State in road contracts."

Mr. Sulzer here referred to the testimony of Harry B. Hanger, aqueduct contractor, who swore that he paid Mr. Gaffney $30,000 for " expert advice on the labor situation " on one contract, and $10,000 for the same services on another contract. Mr. Gaffney later — on March 20, 1914 — himself testified before the Special Grand Jury in New York City as to this transaction.

It was the same Mr. Gaffney, too, whose name was involved in the award of Contract No. 22 for the Catskill Aqueduct. This contract was awarded on March 19, 1909, over two lower bidders to Patterson & Company, a firm of no great capital or experience. James W. Patterson, Jr., head of that firm, subsequently testified before the Grand Jury, in 1914, to his making arrangements to pay 5 per cent. of the contract price ($824,-942.50) as a " contribution to Tammany Hall." John M. Murphy, a Bronx contractor, testified that, as agent for James E. Gaffney, he had arranged to sell the contract, and had received from Mr. Gaffney 10 per cent., or $4,125, as his share of a certain $41,250, after threatening " to kick over the whole deal " if Gaffney did not give the proper " honorarium."

It appeared from the testimony that $41,250 in bills had been deposited in escrow to be handed over by James G. Shaw, the " stakeholder," to a some one designated as Gaffney, on the day after the award of Aqueduct Contract No. 22. Questioned as to whom this $41,250 was given, Mr. Shaw could not remember, which forgetfulness made the fastening of legal proof impossible. The special Grand Jury investigating this matter reported, however, in a presentment to Justice Vernon M. Davis, in the Supreme Court, New York City, on April 21, 1914, that the Grand Jurors were morally satisfied that a crime had been committed in the sale of Contract No. 22 to Patterson & Company, and that this contract could not have been sold and delivered, as it was, in the name of James E. Gaffney, " without the collusion of a member of the Board (of Water Supply) itself." Inasmuch as five years had passed since the transaction, the Statute of Limitations intervened to bar criminal prosecution.

In an inquiry later conducted by District Attorney Whitman, James C. Stewart swore that one " Gaffney " asked him for a contribution of five per cent. upon $3,-000,000 worth of canal work that he (Stewart) was seeking. Stewart refused to make the arrangement; his bid was much the lowest, but he did not then get the contract. Precisely what " Gaffney " it was who proposed the handing over of this $150,000, Stewart averred that he could not tell; he had never seen him previously. When, on January 30, 1914, District Attorney Whitman brought Stewart and James E. Gaffney face to face, Stewart said that he could not identify Mr. Gaffney as the man who demanded the $150,000.

During the course of this same inquiry Mr. Sulzer testified, on January 21, 1914, that on learning that Stewart was to be denied the contracts, he telegraphed on December 18, 1912, to the Canal Board asking it to defer action until he could consult with its members. Whereupon John H. Delaney came to him and excitedly said, "My God, Congressman, what have you done? It angered the Chief more than anything else I have ever known. The Chief is wild." The "Chief," otherwise Charles F. Murphy, demanded an interview with the Governor-elect at once.

In this interview, which was held at Delmonico's, Mr. Sulzer quoted Mr. Murphy as saying to him, "Why did you send that telegram to the Canal Board? You have no right to butt in on things that don't concern you. I'm attending to that matter, and I want you to keep your hands off. If you are going to begin this way, I can see now where you will end as Governor. You do what you are told hereafter, and don't take any action on matters that don't concern you without conferring with me." When Mr. Sulzer said he was going to be Governor, Mr. Murphy (so Sulzer testified) replied: "So that is the way you understand it? Well, if you go along that line, I can see where you will end up damned quick. You are going to be Governor? Like hell you are!"

Mr. Sulzer further testified at this hearing that on the evening of March 3, 1913, at a luncheon in Washington, he told Senator O'Gorman that Mr. Murphy was putting the "screws" on him and bringing to bear all the influence he could to have James E. Gaffney appointed Commissioner of Highways, and that Senator O'Gorman had said: "Governor, if you appoint Jim Gaffney Commissioner of Highways it will be a disgrace to the State of New York and it will ruin your political career as the Governor. Don't you know that Gaffney is Murphy's chief bagman? Don't you know he is the man Murphy sends out to hold up the contractors? Don't you know he is the man that held up my client, James G. Stewart, for over a hundred thousand dollars, and he would have got away with it if Stewart had not come to me, and if

I had not gone to Murphy and read the Riot Act, telling
him that I would not stand for that kind of politics; that
he had to stop Gaffney, and that if he didn't stop Gaffney, so far as my client was concerned, I would expose
him."

Subsequently Mr. Sulzer met Mr. Murphy several
times, and was importuned (so he testified) to appoint
Mr. Gaffney. When Sulzer replied that it was impossible,
Mr. Murphy announced, "Well, it's Gaffney or war."
Mr. Sulzer's testimony went on: "At this conversation,
one of the things Mr. Murphy said to me was, ' If you
don't do this, I will wreck your administration.' It was
not the first time he had threatened me, and I answered,
' I am the Governor, and I am going to be the Governor.'
He said, ' You may be the Governor, but I have got the
Legislature, and the Legislature controls the Governor,
and if you don't do what I tell you to do, I will throw
you out of office.' " After Governor Sulzer had removed
Reel, Mr. Murphy was still pressing Gaffney's appointment.

Of the inquiries into graft carried on by George W.
Blake and John W. Hennessy, Mr. Sulzer testified:
" Their reports staggered me, and believe me, it takes
something to stagger me. There was graft, graft everywhere, nor any man to stop it." Mr. Sulzer testified
that Mr. Murphy had sought to hamper the graft exposure by causing to be cut off — for the first time in the
State's history, he said — the Governor's contingent fund,
and he described how it became necessary to raise money
by private subscription to enable the graft inquiry to
be carried on.

" I have been in office now for six months," wrote Mr.
Sulzer in a signed article later, " and in that time I have
learned enough to be able to say without fear of contra-
diction that in the past three years $50,000,000 of the
people's money has been wasted or stolen."

In a talk, on March 18, 1913, with Mr. Murphy over

appointments to the Supreme Court of New York State, the Tammany chief — so Mr. Sulzer related —" threatented me with public disgrace unless I agreed to his program on legislative matters and appointments. It was at this conference, too, that he talked about the things he ' had on me,' and said that I had better listen to him and not to his enemies up the State; that if I did what he told me I would have things easy and no trouble, and that if I didn't do what he wanted me to, I would have all the trouble I wanted. . . .

" He was very insulting. Then I asked him what he could do to destroy me. And he said: ' Never mind; you will find out in good time. Stand by the organization and you will be all right. If you go against the organization, I will make your administration the laughing stock of the State.' It was at this time that he asked me to call off George Blake, the commissioner who was investigating the prisons. . . . I told him that Blake was an efficient man and that I was going to let him go on with his work, and he said, ' If you do you will be sorry for it. Mark what I am telling you now ! '

" I told him what I had heard about the vileness of things in the Sing Sing and Auburn prisons. I said: ' We certainly ought not to stand for them. I want to get at the facts, and if there is anything wrong, stop it; if there is any graft, eliminate it.' Mr. Murphy told me that he didn't want anything done in connection with Sing Sing prison by Blake or any other man; that the warden there, Mr. Kennedy, was a friend of his and a good man, and he wanted him left alone. This, remember, was the warden whom I afterward removed from his place on charges and who was since indicted by the Westchester grand jury." It may be noted here that later there were a number of prosecutions in prison graft cases. The graft in the prisons reached a total of many millions of dollars in the one item alone of the substitution of bad food for the good food paid for by the State. Extensive grafting was found in other respects.

Mr. Sulzer added that one of the agents through whom Mr. Murphy most frequently communicated with him was Justice Edward E. McCall. " Judge McCall usually spoke of Mr. Murphy as ' the Chief,' and would say to me that ' the Chief ' wished such and such a thing done, or demanded that I follow such and such a course of action. Every Tammany member of either house who approached me from day to day used the same language, saying that ' the Chief ' demanded this or demanded that, or that ' the Chief ' had telephoned to put through such a piece of legislation, or kill some other piece of legislation."

Meanwhile, on March 10, 1913, reports of trouble between Governor Sulzer and Mr. Murphy had become public; when on this date Sulzer removed C. Gordon Reel as State Superintendent of Highways, it was reported in the newspapers that Murphy had asked Governor Sulzer to name James E. Gaffney, his partner in the contracting business, as Reel's successor. On the next day, Mr. Murphy hotly denied that he had asked Gaffney's appointment. From day to day further reports of estrangement were published. In a speech before the Democratic editors of the State, on March 25, Sulzer asserted: " No man, no party, no organization can make me a rubber stamp. I am the Governor. Let no man doubt that."

It appeared that Mr. Murphy had the idea that Sulzer was at heart a Progressive; it may be explained that the Progressive party had polled a large vote and was recognized as a powerful political factor.

It was on the night of April 13, 1913, that Governor Sulzer, according to his interview published later in the New York *Evening Mail*, held his final interview with Mr. Murphy. " I asked him," Mr. Sulzer said, " not to interfere with the trial of Stilwell in the Senate. I said, 'What are you going to do about him?' 'Stand by him, of course,' replied Mr. Murphy. 'Stilwell will be acquitted. It will only be a three-day wonder. How do you expect a Senator to live on $1,500 a year? That is only chicken feed.' . . . Before we parted that night, I warned Mr. Murphy that he would wreck the party and accomplish his own destruction if he persisted in shielding grafters and violating platform pledges. His angry retort was that I was an ingrate, and that he would disgrace and destroy me."

In fact, as Mr. Murphy predicted, Senator Stephen J. Stilwell was voted not guilty of official misconduct, by a vote of 28 to 21 in the Senate, after an investigation by the judiciary committee of charges of bribery made against him by George H. Kendall, president of the New York Bank Note Company. But subsequently Stilwell was indicted in New York County, convicted of bribery upon substantially the same evidence as that upon which a majority of his colleagues in the State Senate had acquitted him, and he was sentenced to a two-year term in prison.

Replying later to Mr. Sulzer's charges, Mr. Murphy definitely denied that he had ever recommended the appointment of James E. Gaffney as Highways Commissioner; that he ever mentioned Gaffney's name to Governor Sulzer for any office; he emphatically denied that he ever made the threats that Sulzer attributed to him or that he ever sent for Mr. Sulzer to come and see him. Mr. Murphy asserted that he never saw Sulzer alone after he became Governor " because I knew he'd do just what he has done — perjure himself."

In April, 1913, Governor Sulzer pushed his Direct Primary Bill, and Tammany members of the Legislature decided in retaliation to defeat all bills favored by him and to " hold up " all of his appointments. On April 24, 1913, Tammany legislators were stirred to anger by his veto of a direct primary bill that they had concocted; a few days later they overwhelmingly voted down his direct primary bill. More retaliation followed on both sides.

It was during this time — in May, 1913 — that the New York *World* published specific charges that in return for a promise made two years previously to get a lucrative post for J. A. Connolly, a personal friend, Justice Cohalan, Murphy's legal and political adviser, had taken a note from Connolly for $4,000. This promise, it was charged, had not been kept. There were, it was also charged, back of this note a series of transactions in the years 1904 to 1906 between Connolly and Cohalan involving the payment of various sums amounting to $3,940.55; Connolly claimed that Cohalan had demanded and obtained from him 55 per cent. of the net profits on all city work that was given to Connolly's firm by means of Cohalan's influence. Connolly further claimed that the payments to Cohalan were calculated on this basis, and that their friendship ceased when Cohalan demanded $1,-500 more than Connolly reckoned was due him. Threatened with an action at law, Cohalan surrendered the $4,-000 note to Connolly's attorney.

These charges were investigated by the Grievance Committee of the Bar Association; the report of that committee confirmed every charge made. Refusing to recognize the jurisdiction of the Bar Association, Justice Cohalan requested Governor Sulzer to have the charges passed upon by the Legislature; this Governor Sulzer did in a special message embodying the report of the Grievance Committee of the Bar Association. The Legislature ordered a trial before the Joint Judiciary Committee. Justice Cohalan admitted on the witness stand that he had made a great mistake in his dealings with Connolly, and that the money he had paid to Connolly was blackmail given in the hope of hushing up the affair for the good of his party. William D. Guthrie, representing the Bar Association, reviewed the case in detail, and demanded

Justice Cohalan's removal. The Joint Judiciary Committee's report recommended that the case against Justice Cohalan be dismissed, which report was upheld by a majority vote of the Legislature. Opponents of Tammany pointed out that this was a characteristic action from a Legislature dominated by Tammany influences.

CHAPTER XXXVI

1913–1914

THE campaign of retaliation against Governor Sulzer soon came to a climax.

On July 15, 1913, a committee called the Frawley Committee (headed by Senator Frawley) was appointed to inquire into Governor Sulzer's receipts and expenditures of campaign funds. After taking testimony, that committee submitted its report with the finding that, following his campaign for Governor, Mr. Sulzer had omitted declaring in his campaign statement $19,000 of contributions to his campaign fund and had purchased, for his personal account, stocks with part of the moneys thus received.

The evidence, according to the committee's report, showed that a total of $109,016 in cash or stock had been in Mr. Sulzer's possession, and that this sum came from campaign contributions. Mr. Sulzer had used both cash and checks to purchase stocks; and as far as could be brought out by the records and testimony, his Wall Street transactions with three brokerage firms covered a total of $72,428.28, dating from January 1, 1912. It appeared that the greater part of these payments were made after he became a candidate for Governor and was elected to that office. Mr. Murphy and other Tammany leaders pointed out that while these very transactions had been going on, Mr. Sulzer had in his public speeches pretended that he was a poor man.

Mr. Sulzer's own version was that if he had made a mistake in signing his campaign statement it was due to haste and carelessness and not to intent to deceive. " But," he added,

"this is not the only explanation of the failure to itemize certain moneys which were received in the campaign. Some of the moneys were not for campaign purposes at all, but were loans. They were given to me by friends who knew I was heavily in debt, and who loaned me the money to pay my debts or to use as I saw fit. These friends wanted nothing, and in case of my election I knew there was nothing they would ask me to do, or that I could do for them. Politics had nothing to do with the matter.

" All the moneys given to me, or sent to me for the campaign, were turned over to the committee, to which reference has been made, or were subsequently given to Mr. Murphy. Whether the latter turned these moneys over to the State Committee or not I cannot say, but an investigation of the report filed by that committee negatives the assumption."

On August 13, 1913, the Assembly, by a vote of 79 to 45, impeached Governor Sulzer on eight articles. Trial by the High Court for the Trial of Impeachments, consisting of the State Senate and the Judges of the Court of Appeals, followed.

Governor Sulzer vigorously fought back, and public opinion was greatly aroused over his charges that the affair was simply a case of the Tammany " Organization " summarily disciplining him for refusing to be its tool. He was convicted on three of the eight articles of impeachment: (1) that he had filed with the Secretary of State a false sworn statement of his campaign receipts and expenditures; (2) perjury in swearing to the truth of the campaign accounting; (3) committing a misdemeanor in suppressing evidence and preventing or seeking to prevent witnesses from appearing before the legislative committee. On October 17, 1913, Governor Sulzer was removed from office by a vote of 43 to 12 by the High Court for the Trial of Impeachments.

It should be noted that Chief Justice Edgar M. Cullen, of the Court of Appeals, who presided at the trial, voted to acquit Mr. Sulzer on every one of the articles. " Never before the present case," said Chief Justice Cullen, " has it been attempted to impeach a public officer for acts committed when he was not an officer of the State. . . ." Chief Justice Cullen held that Mr. Sulzer had committed no offense in failing to state the amounts and sources of his campaign contributions, and that there was no evidence of any deceit or fraud.

Governor Sulzer's supporters set forth the following as the main actual reasons why proceedings for his removal were pushed:

First: Mr. Sulzer's persistent efforts to secure the enactment of the Full Crew legislation to conserve human life on the railroads.

Second: Mr. Sulzer's success in securing the enactment of the laws that he recommended to compel honest dealings on the New York Stock Exchange.

Third: Mr. Sulzer's refusal to approve the McKee Public Schools Bills which would have given control of public schools to a religious denomination.

Fourth: Mr. Sulzer's successful efforts in causing the repeal of the notorious charter of the Long Sault Development Company, by which the State of New York received back its greatest water power and the most valuable of its natural resources.

Fifth: Mr. Sulzer's defiance of the bosses — big and little — and his fight for honest and genuine direct primaries.

Sixth: Mr. Sulzer's determined refusal to be a proxy Governor or " a rubber stamp."

Seventh. Mr. Sulzer's absolute refusal to follow " boss " dictation regarding legislation and appointments, and his blunt refusal to call off Blake and Hennessy, and stop the investigations which were being made, under his direction, to uncover fraud and expose graft in the State Departments.

Eighth: Mr. Sulzer's moral courage, in the performance of public duty, wherein he insisted on the trial and punishment of Senator Stilwell for extortion.

Ninth: Mr. Sulzer's determination to set in motion the machinery of the law, in various counties of the State, to indict the grafters and bring them to justice.

There could be no questioning that the proceedings against Sulzer had an effect upon the public mind the reverse of that expected by " Boss " Murphy and his advisers.

The attempt of Tammany Hall's leaders to pose in this case as the conservers of political virtue met with a sardonic reception and quickly reacted upon them in unmistakable terms. Public opinion in general made no attempt to mitigate Mr. Sulzer's acts, but, with a keen perception of the fundamental facts, it saw that the real reason why Governor Sulzer was so brutally punished was not because of those acts but because he had finally broken away from Tammany dictation and had sought to be somewhat of an independent Governor. Every intelligent person knew that this was his crime in the view of the Tammany organization, and, according to Tammany standards, the worst crime that could be committed. That an organization which had been steeped in corruption and graft should so ostentatiously pretend to be the exposer and punisher of infractions in an official who had defied its power, excited mockery, resentment and indignation. Public sympathy turned toward the deposed Governor, and he was nominated for the Assembly by the Progressives in an East Side district.

As we have seen, one of the chief issues upon which Gaynor had made his Mayoralty campaign in 1909 was for municipally built and operated subways.

After becoming Mayor, he underwent a decided change of mind. The subway rights were awarded to the Interborough Rapid Transit Company and the Brooklyn Rapid Transit Company. The Final Report of the Joint Legislative Committee appointed to investigate the Pub-

lic Service Commissions severely criticizes the policy and
the terms under which the contracts were made by the
Public Service Commission and the Board of Estimate.
On the other hand, defenders of the Board of Estimate's
action point out that the reasons why that Board changed
from city to company subways were that by the co-operation of the companies, the city had the benefit of $150,-
000,000 more in funds than would have been the case
without that co-operation; that the new subway lines instead of being independent, disconnected routes, unrelated
to existing transportation lines, would be built in appropriate extenso of subway facilities already in operation;
and that by this arrangement not only would the service be harmonized and improved but the payment of
double fares would be done away with and an aggregate
of vast sums thus saved to the traveling public. The
circular routes by which the city's transportation problems will be more effectively and constructively solved
were adopted despite Gaynor's favoring the Interborough
Rapid Transit Company's perpendicular routes plan.

One feature of the testimony later before the Joint
Legislative Committee especially attracting public attention was the imputation that in the contract for the third-
tracking of the Interborough Rapid Transit Company's
elevated railroads, a fund of $2,000,000 was surrep-
titiously provided in the form of a commission to John
F. Stevens. Formerly Mr. Stevens had been associated
in the construction of the Panama Canal with Mr. Shonts
who now was president of the Interborough Rapid Transit Company. This company, in the third-tracking
work, wanted exemption from supervision by the Public
Service Commission. According to a memorandum preserved by George W. Young, an Interborough director,
this contract with Mr. Stevens was entered into (so, it
was asserted, Mr. Shonts told Mr. Lane, another director), because " in connection with the securing of the
contract which had been closed between the City of

Greater New York and the Interborough, Mr. Shonts had found it necesary to make certain commitments and incur certain obligations, and that it was by means of the Stevens contract that he expected to meet and pay these commitments and obligations." [1]

The Joint Legislative Committee thus comments on the testimony: "It is perfectly clear that Mr. Shonts did tell Mr. Lane something about commitments and obligations in respect to this strange proposition; it is equally clear that he was not under any business commitment or honorable obligation to Mr. Stevens. He made a request of the Public Service [Commission] Chairman for an exception from the general contract, relieving third tracking from official supervision, and had told the reason for it in his desire to give the contract to Mr. Stevens. He did obtain exemption from supervision, and that applied to to the contractor to whom finally the contract was awarded." [2]

The chairman of the Public Service Commission here referred to was Edward E. McCall. Whatever may be the shadowy implications conveyed in this report, no statement is made that any corruption was used, nor is any proof presented that any official was improperly influenced. The salient fact was that McCall, in an era when corporation activities were more and more rigorously scrutinized by official bodies, should have reverted to bygone standards and graciously allowed a removal of that very supervision which it was expected the Public Service Commission would insist upon exercising.

Tammany Hall's nominee in the municipal campaign of 1913 was this same Edward E. McCall.

When an attorney, Mr. McCall had been connected with certain operations of the New York Life Insurance Company, of which corporation his brother, John A. McCall,

[1] *Final Report of the Joint Legislative Committee Appointed to Investigate the Public Service Commissions,* March, 1917, p. 67.
[2] *Ibid.,* p. 68.

was president. It appeared from the testimony before
the Legislative Insurance Investigating Committee, in
1905, that Edward E. McCall had given notes, totalling
about $10,000, to " Andy " Hamilton, the chief legisla-
tive lobbyist at Albany of that company and distributor
of the " Yellow Dog Fund."

Precisely why Edward E. McCall should have given
those notes was not explained. Hamilton received great
sums in all for legislative purposes; in the transferring of
some of the sums Edward E. McCall figured. Both Edward E. McCall and " Andy " Hamilton received " excessive remuneration " from the New York Life Insurance
Company, apparently for legal services in a certain case,
which sums, according to the report of Charles E. Hughes,
there was no adequate reason for paying. At the same
time that these sums were paid to them, both Edward E.
McCall and Hamilton were under a regular retainer as
attorneys by the New York Life Insurance Company, each
of them receiving $10,000 a year.

Mr. McCall was put upon the Supreme Court Bench in
1902, by Tammany backing, and remained there until his
appointment, in 1913, by Governor Sulzer as Chairman of
the Public Service Commission, First District.

The greatest exertions were made by Tammany to
sway the electorate so as to swing the election in its favor.
Tammany realized that the Sulzer episode would be an
important issue, but it did not anticipate that the summary removal of Governor Sulzer, with all the attendant
circumstances, would make so unpleasant an impression,
driving large numbers of voters to the other side. Tammany thought that it had put Sulzer on the defensive; it
did not quite foresee the effect of revelations which, before
the campaign was over, placed Tammany seriously on the
defensive and its leaders under the necessity of making
explanations.

Moreover, in selecting its candidates and developing

its campaign tactics Tammany did not appreciate the very much altered attitude of a large section of the public toward municipal politics.   There had arisen in New York City an increased public demand for proved administrative capacity.   The old days of public toleration of choosing politicians for "good fellowship " or subservient qualities had about gone.   The emphasis was now placed by Tammany's opponents upon the fact that cities should be not merely governed, but well governed, by men of vision, ability and integrity.

The candidate for Mayor of the Republicans and Fusionists was John Purroy Mitchel, a young Independent Democrat, who was credited with having made a notable record as Commissioner of Accounts.   Later he had been President of the Board of Aldermen, and then Collector of the Port of New York.   Nominated with him were William A. Prendergast, for Comptroller, and George McAneny for President of the Board of Aldermen; all were eulogized by their supporters with having served the city with constructive ability and marked efficiency, and with having opposed and exposed Tammany graft and extravagance.

The Socialist Party's candidate for Mayor was Charles Edward Russell, a writer of note and a man of high personal character.

Full of bitterness was this campaign.   Perhaps the most effective speakers against Tammany Hall were John A. Hennessy and former Governor Sulzer.   Mr. Hennessy in a public speech on October 23, 1913, specifically charged that he held a note for $35,000 that had been signed by a Justice of the Supreme Court who had been Mr. Murphy's alternative candidate for Mayor.   " I do not say that the $35,000 was ever paid to anybody.   I don't suspect him of any vices that would induce him to borrow $35,000. . . . If he has had to pay $35,000 or more for his [Supreme Court] nomination, why he simply followed a tradition in the organization to which he belonged."

Mr. Hennessy charged Mr. McCall with not answering the question of where he got his campaign money, and asked Mr. McCall whether, in 1902 (when McCall was a candidate for the Supreme Court nomination) he, McCall, had not met George W. Plunkett, a Tammany district leader — the originator of the term " honest graft "— in a room in the Hoffman House, and whether Anthony N. Brady was not in another room at the same time. " I want to ask Judge McCall," Mr. Hennessy continued, " whether his sponsor, Charlie Murphy, had not seen Anthony Brady in respect to McCall's nomination in the Hoffman House, and I want to ask Judge McCall if the gentleman who brought him and Plunkett together to discuss that nomination, did not have something to do with Murphy and Mr. Brady in respect of that nomination." Mr. Hennessy charged that one man that Mr. McCall paid was Plunkett, but he (Hennessy) did not know whether he paid Murphy, or whether he paid the amount to somebody who paid Murphy; he (Hennessy) did not undertake to assert that.

The Anthony N. Brady here mentioned was a traction magnate, who, beginning as a clerk in Albany, had by means of legislative manipulation giving richly valuable railway and other franchises, accumulated an estate of $90,000,000.

In several speeches Mr. Hennessy pointedly asserted that James Stewart, a contractor, had paid $25,000 to a former friend of Charles F. Murphy, and inquired whether J. Sergeant Cram (a prominent Tammany light) had not received $5,000, and Norman E. Mack another $5,000.

At a public meeting on October 25, 1913, Mr. Sulzer declared that he had sent to Charles F. Murphy $10,000 that Allan Ryan (Thomas F. Ryan's son), had contributed to his campaign fund, and that Mr. Murphy had never accounted for it.

Mr. Sulzer named John H. Delaney (later State Commissioner of the Department of Efficiency and Economy),

as the messenger who had carried the $10,000 in bills to
Mr. Murphy. This money, Mr. Sulzer asserted, had originally been handed to him (Sulzer) in his New York office by Mr. McGlone, Allan Ryan's secretary, and that
he (Sulzer) gave the $10,000 to Delaney, who took it up-
town and gave it to Murphy. " Late that afternoon,"
Mr. Sulzer continued, " I saw Mr. Murphy at Delmonico's.
During our conversation, I said, ' Did John give you the
ten from Ryan? ' Mr. Murphy replied: ' Yes, that's all
right, but it's only a drop in the bucket. You'll have to
do better than that.' So far as I know," Mr. Sulzer
continued, " and I am pretty well advised, Mr. Murphy
never accounted for that $10,000, any more than he ac-
counted for the Brady $25,000 which I refused and which
he accepted from Judge Beardsley [Brady's legal repre-
sentative]. At all events, I think Mr. Murphy should
tell the voters what he did with the money." Mr. Sulzer
declared that he (Sulzer) was still in debt, and that " I
am a poorer man to-day than I was when I became a candidate for Governor." No one acquainted with Sulzer's
career could doubt that had he been essentially corrupt,
he could have become a millionaire from huckstering of
legislation when he was Speaker of the Assembly; there
was no bribing him, however, with money; he was, in fact,
a poor man.

Mr. Sulzer then declared that Thomas F. Ryan was
" Boss " Murphy's master.

This, in fact, was the very point made by the Socialists: that the political " bosses " were only the tools of the
great financial and industrial magnates; and that where
the political " bosses " gathered in their millions, the magnates accumulated their tens or hundreds of millions of
dollars as their individual fortunes. Why, queried the
Socialists, concentrate attention on the instruments?
Why not, said they, attack the power of the whole social,
political and industrial system of which the political
" boss " was merely one expression? This system, ac-

cording to the Socialist party, was the capitalist system
for the overthrow of which they declared and agitated.
They pointed out that behind Mr. Murphy and Tammany Hall, as well as behind the Republican organization
where it was in power, were traction, railroad, telephone,
electric lighting, industrial and other financial interests
all selfishly utilizing the power embodied in political
" bosses " for their own ends and aggrandizement, and
that these were the real powers that could make and un-
make political " bosses."

Gaffney, Cram and Plunkett had all denied allegations
aimed at them; Murphy and McCall had remained silent.
But on October 26, 1913, McCall and Murphy both issued
statements. Mr. McCall denied the charge that he had
paid $35,000 for the nomination for the Supreme Court
in 1902. Mr. Murphy made public an affidavit in which
he (Murphy) denied that McCall had ever paid him anything at any time, and branding the charge as false. On
the next day Mr. Murphy gave out a long statement making a sweeping denial of Mr. Sulzer's statements; he asserted that he had received the $25,000 from Anthony N.
Brady, but that he had returned the money the next day;
he also denied that he had ever received $10,000 from
Ryan.

Mr. Hennessy returned to the attack. On the same
day he charged that a seat in the United States Senate
(to succeed Senator Root) had been offered to Sulzer
if he would yield to Mr. Murphy, and that it was Mr.
McCall who acted as the intermediary.

In a public speech on the following day, October 28,
1913, Mr. Hennessy demanded the tracing of Mr. Brady's
$25,000, and suggested that it might be well to examine
the executors of Brady's estate and find out whether
Brady had deposited $25,000 two days after Judge Beards-
ley had handed that money to Mr. Murphy. " I knew
Mr. Brady very well," Mr. Hennessy went on. " I have
known Mr. Brady since he was selling groceries in Albany

twenty-five or twenty-six years ago, . . . and I know that he never carried around $25,000 in bills every day in his pocket; so if he got this $25,000 in bills from Mr. Murphy, he undoubtedly deposited it somewhere." Mr. Hennessy chided Mr. Murphy with having been told by his district leaders to answer him, after he (Murphy) had declared that he would not notice the charges, and said that Mr. Murphy was " shoving it off on a dead man."

When, on October 29, 1913, former Judge Beardsley, counsel for the Brady estate, issued a statement asserting that the $25,000 was returned to Brady, Mr. Hennessy in a public speech demanded proof and charged that an alibi was being proved over the body of a dead man. Mr. Hennessy made the charge that in the campaign of 1910 Mr. Murphy had collected fully $150,000 for which he had not accounted in the statement filed with the Secretary of State. " Most of this money," Mr. Hennessy declared, " came from contractors who were clubbed into giving it."

So this exciting campaign drew to a close amid sensational charges, counter charges, denials and reiterations.

Over in Queen's Borough, the Democratic " boss " of that section, " Joe " Cassidy, was in serious difficulties; he had long, with some intermissions, ruled that part of the city; and although he was not a Tammany man, nor did Tammany rule Queens, in the strict sense of the meaning, yet he was an ally of Tammany and had always " consulted " Mr. Murphy.

Local " Boss " Cassidy and one of his lieutenants were under indictment for conspiring in selling a nomination in 1911, to the Supreme Court Bench to William Willett, Jr., and Willett was indicted for being a party to the conspiracy. During his trial later, Cassidy admitted that he was " boss," but asserted his honesty. Questioned as to why he did not deposit a certain sum in bank, he replied, " I was used to carrying money in my pocket. I was lonesome without a roll in my pocket." It may be said here that Willett was convicted, and likewise were Cassidy and one of his lieutenants by a jury on February 2, 1914; Cassidy and Willett were each sentenced to an indeterminate sentence of not less than a year in prison and a fine of $1,000, and Cassidy's lieutenant " go-between," Louis T. Walter, received a sentence of three months and a fine of $1,000. After serving a year in prison Cassidy was released and later (January 19, 1917) was restored to citizenship by Governor Whitman.

Intelligent people contemplated with wonderment the antiquated tactics that Tammany Hall was blindly following. Although the discussion of pressing economic problems was vitally concerning great masses of people, Tammany Hall seemed unaware of their existence. The rapid development of the trusts, the concentration of capitalist power and wealth, the tense unrest among different classes of people, were reflected in various political and industrial movements, but in Tammany Hall no attention was given to them. Oblivious to the great industrial changes and popular agitations and thought, Tammany still adhered to its old semi-feudalistic methods of " carrying its vote "; it concerned itself only with matters of offices, jobs, contracts and interested legislation; it depended upon immense campaign funds and the personal following of its leaders in marshaling the army of voters all of whom by jobs or other such self interest sought to perpetuate its power.

New York City had also grown too vast for the Tammany district leaders to control as they did in the decades when it was smaller and compact. Great numbers of people had moved from Manhattan to other boroughs; and this constant process of migration had much weakened the power of Tammany organization leaders in keeping in touch with the voters. The Jewish vote had grown to enormous proportions, and so had the Italian, but the

Jewish vote was generally a vote racially independent of
Tammany and not particularly sympathetic to the character, racial and religious, of its leaders.

Tammany Hall was overwhelmingly defeated. Mr.
Mitchel's plurality was 124,262. The vote resulted:
Mitchel, 358,181; McCall, 233,919; Russell, 32,057. All
of the anti-Tammany candidates for city offices were
elected by varying pluralities. Mr. Sulzer was trium-
phantly elected to the Assembly. However, Tammany
men could glean some slight consolation in this hour of
disaster; Lieutenant Governor Martin Glynn, who had
succeeded Sulzer as Governor, could be generally depended
upon to appoint some Tammany men to various appointive offices; when his list of appointments was handed
down they were not altogether disappointed. Tammany
was especially jubilant in getting control of the Public
Service Commission, not to mention a firmer hold in various
State departments.

The results of the municipal election cut Tammany off
from city, county and national patronage; in such an ex-
tremity Mr. Murphy had little to offer famishing followers except soothing words which counted for nothing where
practical results were demanded.

The mutterings against Mr. Murphy in certain quarters grew to open rebellion; no longer was he fulsomely
praised as a sagacious political strategist; he was now derisively called a stupid blunderer for his successive actions and particularly for his campaign of reprisal against
Sulzer — a campaign producing so inflaming an effect
against Tammany.

A resolution introduced in the Democratic Club, on
February 2, 1914, demanded that he retire from " all participation in the party's affairs," to which Mr. Murphy
defiantly replied in an interview, " I am the leader of
Tammany Hall. You can add that I am going to remain
the leader of Tammany Hall no matter what some others
might think they have to say about it." Believing that at

least thirty-two of the thirty-four Tammany district leaders would vote to continue him in power, " Boss " Murphy made this announcement with apparent confidence. Indeed, it was reported that the Executive Committee of Tammany Hall had voted to retain his leadership.

A few days later some extracts from a letter written by Richard Croker to John Fox were made public. " Murphy was a big handicap to McCall," Mr. Croker wrote. " The Hall will never win under Murphy's management. I hope some good man will get in and drive all them grafters contractors out." On March 10, 1914, at a meeting of the Democratic Club, Charles F. Murphy, James E. Gaffney, Thomas F. Foley, George W. Plunkett and Thomas Darlington were rudely read out of that club on the nominal ground of non-payment of dues, whereupon Thomas F. Smith, Secretary of Tammany Hall, styled that action " a joke " and declared that " the club has cut no figure locally since 1896."

Mr. Murphy remained " the Chief " of Tammany Hall.

The various official inquiries into the system of graft in State contracts conducted by Special Commissioner James W. Osborne and other officials continued after the election. In January, 1914, Bart Dunn, an associate Tammany leader of the Eighteenth Assembly District and a close friend of Charles F. Murphy, was convicted of conspiracy in highways construction graft, and sentenced to ten months in the penitentiary and to pay a fine of $500; he took an appeal and was let out on bail. Subsequently, however, he was compelled to serve six months in prison.

On February 15, 1914, after he had been summoned to testify again in an investigation by District Attorney Whitman, State Treasurer John J. Kennedy committed suicide. As State Treasurer, Kennedy was ex-officio a member of the State Canal Board which had control of contracts now under investigation; his son was, in conjunction with others, one of whom was under indictment,

in the business of bonding contractors on canal and other
State work.   It was believed that worry arising from the
forthcoming examination as to his son's transactions, was
the cause of Kennedy's suicide.

At a hearing conducted by the District Attorney's office, in New York City, on February 26, 1914, Mr. Sulzer
again related, this time in testimony, the story of the
$25,000 campaign contribution by Anthony N. Brady
and that of $10,000 by Allan Ryan, both of which con-
tributions were made in 1912.   "Once," Mr. Sulzer testified, "in a talk with Murphy, he told me that Ryan had
given a check for $25,000 in 1912.   Murphy said that he
would report that, but not the $10,000.   He said he
would find a dummy for that.   He also found dummies for
Brady's $25,000."   Mr. Sulzer explained that a certain
$25,000 that Mr. Murphy had returned to Brady was not
the $25,000 that Brady had contributed to the campaign
of 1912.   Brady, so Mr. Sulzer testified, had sued Murphy for $40,000 and Murphy had settled the suit for
$25,000; the records would disclose this suit, Mr. Sulzer
said.

Thus far some of the smaller grafters have been convicted and sentenced to jail, but the really powerful politicians involved have not suffered.   After two months'
consideration of the charges of graft and official misconduct brought against C. Gordon Reel, State Engineer
John A. Bensel, Duncan W. Peck, State Superintendent
of Public Works — the three officials forming the highways Commission under the régime of which, it was
charged, the large grafting had been going on — the Albany County Grand Jury, on April 28, 1914, reported
that no indictments had been found against any of these
men, nor against Charles A. Foley, Deputy Superintendent
of Highways.   According to facts disclosed by Mr. Osborne's investigation, many of the 318 repair contracts let
by Foley and passed by Reel, Bensel and Peck, were
awarded only after contractors had contributed to the

Democratic campaign fund.   Numerous of the roads covered by these contracts were so badly constructed that
they went to pieces within a year; and the State, so Mr.
Osborne charged, thereby lost hundreds of thousands of
dollars.

CHAPTER XXXVII

1914–1917

UPON the removal of Governor Sulzer from office, Martin Glynn, as has already been noted, had become Governor of New York State. A Democrat, he consequently appointed men of the party to which he belonged to various offices. Tammany and its auxiliaries now had control of the Public Service Commission, First District.

But this control was abruptly ended by the effect of the disclosures made in the testimony before the (Thompson) Joint Legislative Committee probing into the affairs of the Public Service Commissions. Mr. Glynn was succeeded as Governor by Charles S. Whitman who had done such notable service as District Attorney of New York County. During 1915 the Joint Legislative Committee held many hearings at which much testimony of an upheaving nature was given.

One result of this inquiry was a series of grave charges against Edward E. McCall, Chairman of the Public Service Commission, First District, and, as we have seen, recent candidate of Tammany Hall for Mayor. Accompanied by a request for Mr. McCall's removal from office, these charges were made to Governor Whitman by the Joint Legislative Committee on December 12, 1915, and were supplemented by a bill of particulars, specifying twenty charges, formally filed ten days later.

The charges declared that Mr. McCall's acceptance of his appointment to the Public Service Commission was in

violation of law; that he was at the time the owner of
stock in a corporation subject to the Public Service Commission's supervision; that thereafter he attempted to
transfer this stock to his wife " which attempt was a mere
subterfuge and a clumsy effort to evade the statute ";
and that as Chairman of the Public Service Commission
he participated in the consideration of matters affecting
the value of this stock.

Further, the charges accused Mr. McCall of accepting
a retainer for legal services from a corporation, the chief
owner of the stock of which was commonly reputed to be
a controlling factor in the management of the Interborough Rapid Transit Company; and that in another case
he accepted a retainer in an action then pending in the
Supreme Court " in which action the engineers in the employ of the Public Service Commission will be necessary
as material witnesses." Other charges specified that he
favored the public service corporations to the detriment
of public interests. The sixteenth charge particularized
that in the matter of the third tracking of the elevated
railroads in Manhattan he failed to reserve the power of
supervision to the Commission " and that as a result of
such failure the lessee of the Manhattan Railway Company [the Interborough] has entered into extravagant
and improvident contracts under which its stockholders
and the people of the City of New York have suffered and
will suffer large losses." The seventeenth charge arraigned McCall for having authorized the construction
of connecting lines by the Interborough Rapid Transit
Company " at an extravagant and exorbitant price and
without competition to the disadvantage of the city of
New York and its inhabitants." The eighteenth charge
set forth that in the execution of the dual subway contracts " he permitted the inclusion of a provision under
which the New York Municipal Railway Corporation will
be permitted unwarrantedly to deduct from the earnings
of that company, before the division of the net earnings

between the company and the city can be accomplished, a sum aggregating more than $10,000,000." In brief, the charges declared that McCall showed misconduct in office, favoritism, neglect of duty, and inefficiency.

After consideration of the charges, Governor Whitman, on December 6, 1915, removed Mr. McCall from office as the Chairman of the Public Service Commission, First District. The particular charge substantiated was that McCall violated that section of the Public Service Commissions law forbidding a Commissioner to hold stock in a corporation subject to the Commission's supervision.

McCall, however, was not the only Public Service Commissioner involved in the revelations before the Joint Legislative Committee. At a session on December 16, 1915, Sidney G. Johnson, vice-president of the General Railway Signal Company, testified that Robert Colgate Wood, another Public Service Commissioner, demanded $5,000 from the Union Switch and Signal Company for using his influence as Commissioner to give that company a subway signal system contract. The offer, it was testified, was refused. On January 25, 1916, the Grand Jury in New York County indicted Mr. Wood for the alleged solicitation of a bribe. Meanwhile, on December 27, 1915, George V. S. Williams, another Public Service Commissioner, resigned from office on the plea that for some time he had been contemplating this step, and now that he was no longer " under fire " he could retire in justice to himself.

Serious as these developments were, they did not have the damaging effect upon Tammany that might ordinarily be supposed. Except in certain offices here and there Tammany was out of power, and therefore, not being prominently on the defensive, could not be effectively assailed. Moreover, in view of the results of a recently tried libel suit, it was anything but a propitious time for Tammany's Republican opponents to make capital from such incidents.

This libel action, which conspicuously held public attention, was one brought by William Barnes, Jr., Republican State leader, against Theodore Roosevelt. In a published article, Colonel Roosevelt had practically charged that there was a corrupt alliance between Mr. Barnes and Charles F. Murphy, the Tammany leader, and that Mr. Barnes had worked through a corrupt alliance between crooked business and crooked politics. The article did not charge personal corruption in the sense of bribery, but emphasized the nature of the political methods used. The trial of this action resulted, on May 22, 1915, in the jury finding a verdict in favor of Roosevelt.

The proceedings of this trial directed general notice much more to the workings of the Republican machine system than to Tammany methods. To the initiated it had long been known that the Republican machine, as the power usually controlling the Legislature, was the preferred instrument through which the powerful financial, industrial, utility, commercial and other corporations operated to get the legislation that they wanted. This fact was now confirmed and disseminated by the outcome of the libel suit. Long, too, had it been suspected that between the apparently hostile political machines there often existed secret understandings or alliances cloaked over by pretended political warfare which was merely mock opposition intended for credulous public consumption. The court proceedings and the verdict showed that the stating of this fact was not a libel.

The effect upon public opinion of this libel action was far more injurious to the Republican State organization than to Tammany, a reaction naturally to be expected in judging an organization which had so long found campaign material in strong virtuous denunciations of " Tammany corruption." At the same time public disfavor of the Republican organization was increased by the bad record of the Republican Legislature in 1915 — a record that in many respects was worse than that of a Tammany Legislature. These influences were to Tammany's advantage. Always rushing to excesses when in prosperity, Tammany in times of adversity moderated its action by observing prudence and deferring to public proprieties. Its chief candidates in the 1915 election were men of accredited good character and reputed ability. These conditions, together with the fact that the Republicans and the Progressives did not unite in opposition to Tammany, helped to bring a measure of success to Tammany. For the first time in more than fifteen years Tammany managed to elect a District Attorney in the County of New York in the person of Judge Edward Swann, and it elected Alfred E. Smith to the office of Sheriff.

From the beginning of 1916 Tammany was thus in full control of the criminal machinery of the law in New York County. District Attorney Swann showed such energy in the sustained prosecution of the infamous "white slavers," that the formulating of charges against him came as a surprise to many citizens who had formed a good estimate of his activities in office. These charges, made by Judge James A. Delehanty of the Court of General Sessions, on December 30, 1916, alleged misconduct in office in the matter of certain assault cases resulting from the garment trades strike of 1914.

In the list of charges forwarded to Governor Whitman Judge Delahanty accused District Attorney Swann of having deliberately presented a false recommendation to a Judge of General Sessions on the strength of which he obtained the discharge on bail of more than a score of defendants indicted in March, 1914, on various charges of assault, riots, and injuries to property occurring during the course of labor disputes on the East Side. Judge Delahanty further charged that District Attorney Swann even sought to have the indictments against these men dismissed, although seven of them had offered to plead guilty. Judge Delahanty had been an Assistant District

Attorney when Mr. Whitman was District Attorney, and hence could claim an intimate familiarity with the details of those very cases. Among the characters concerned in the clothing trades strike were such notorious gangsters as " Dopey Benny " Fein, " Waxy " Gordon, " Jew " Murphy and others such widely known for their activities in the section east of the Bowery.

Assistant District Attorney Lucian S. Breckinridge who had had charge of the preparation of many of these cases for trial, had resigned on March 23, 1916, on the ground that District Attorney Swann's action in the cases was " a travesty on justice, and an outrage to decency," and that he (Mr. Breckinridge) did not purpose to acquiesce in that action either actively or by silence. In his letter of resignation Mr. Breckinridge asserted that the investigation of the strike " disclosed a tale of wrong and outrage, and a use of gangsters and thugs in labor troubles unparalleled in the history of this country." On the other hand, Morris Hillquit, chief counsel for the labor unions involved, asserted in an interview that " the indictments were based on evidence furnished by a combinations of notorious lawbreakers, who were known as such to the prosecuting officials." Mr. Hillquit denounced their story as " a most clumsy concoction, bearing evidence of deliberate fabrication."

After the filing of the charges against him, District Attorney Swann declared that the charges were actuated by politics. He made a bitter personal attack upon Mr. Breckinridge, and retaliated later by causing Mr. Breckinridge to be indicted upon the allegation that he had received a bribe from manufacturers. On January 14, 1917, the City Club presented charges to Governor Whitman and asked for District Attorney Swann's removal from office. The first charge included Judge Delehanty's statements, and declared that District Attorney Swann's efforts to procure the dismissal of indictments against labor union men charged with assault constituted an attempt to perpetrate a fraud on the Court of General Sessions, and that its object was to pay a Tammany election debt to East Side labor unionists. The second charge asserted that by various means Mr. Swann had sought to coerce and intimidate Mr. Breckinridge, who was a valuable witness into any inquiry into the charges against the District Attorney.

At this writing (March, 1917), it is not possible to give the outcome of these charges; the determination of them and the decision are still to be forthcoming from Governor Whitman when sufficient time shall have been allowed for adequate inquiry.

By the end of 1916 the municipal administration headed by Mayor John Purroy Mitchel had been in power for three years with another year to serve. Usually in past times after a fusion administration had been in office for a year or two its unwise repressive acts only the more strengthened Tammany, which always put forth the boast that it was the real democratic bulwark against aristocratic property rule and that it was the genuine representative of the masses. On this claim it generally had succeeded in elections for nearly two decades, returning a majority of from 75,000 to 100,000 for the Democratic candidates, especially in State and National elections. In the 1916 election Tammany was able to give Wilson a plurality of only about 40,000 over Hughes. To accept the results of any one particular election would be unsafe. Nevertheless, it would seem to be the case that as compared with its past Tammany is in a moribund condition; its only large hold, the decline of which is relieved by but an occasional victory, is in Manhattan Borough. The population of Manhattan is not growing nearly as rapidly as some of the other boroughs which at the same time show an increasing anti-Tammany or Republican tendency.

While Tammany has been clinging to outworn tactics and aims out of keeping with the rising standards of the times, the anti-Tammany forces have learned much from the experiences of previous movements. Likewise they have proved responsive to the broadening currents of the age. Whatever their minor mistakes they have not regarded New York City as an object of low political tyranny and brutal spoliation. They have, in the main, applied constructive ability to administration, and have evinced a keen sense not merely of the cleanly appearance and well-ordered functions of the great city but of its architectural and other aesthetic values as well, as shown by several measures recently adopted. This is a very different condition from that prevailing during the times when the city's affairs were dictated by ignorant politicians whose sole aim was to enrich themselves quickly and satisfy the predatory desires of their followers.

The anti-Tammany forces have learned, too, that repression only nullifies in the popular mind the good effects of other accomplishments. In the last few years New York City officials have allowed absolute freedom of speech and freedom of assemblage on the public streets, designating certain places for the purpose, and qualifying this liberty only by the salutary proviso that the speakers be held responsible for any unlawful utterances. An instructively different attitude, this, from that in days not so long gone by when assemblages of citizens were forbidden to use streets and were mauled and clubbed by the police, and when they were prohibited from holding discussions in public buildings.

Judged by the performances of many exploiting administrations that have ruled and robbed New York City, Mayor Mitchel's administration has been one of wholesome tendencies and accomplishments. Its opponents have bitterly attacked some of its policies, but however of a debatable nature these may have been or are, the antagonists of this administration have not been able to assail it on the score of endorsed graft and incompetence as has been the case with so many other city administra-

tions. It is not contended that evils have entirely disappeared, but at any rate the base, ignoble practices and
the repellant incompetence characteristic of past " boss "
rule have been much supplanted by improved methods,
expert judgment, technical experience, a higher tone, and
good spirit.

The police department, so long the special canker, has
been placed on a different basis. A recent report of the
Bureau of Social Hygiene, which has closely investigated
that department, does not claim that graft has been entirely eliminated but it points out that " tremendous gains
have been made." The " vice ring," it reports, has been
broken up; the gambling evil has been greatly reduced;
organized graft is no longer the sinister and secure system
that it was. " Collusion between exploiters of vice and
officials in the Police Department has ceased. Petty grafting still occurs. The man on the beat may take a small
bribe to overlook a breach of the law, but protection can
no longer be purchased." The Committee of Fourteen
gives credit for this transformation largely to the
" clean-up " movement started by Police Commissioner
Cropsey under Mayor Gaynor, and continued and elaborated by Police Commissioner Arthur Woods under Mayor
Mitchel's administration. Some survivals of old standards still remain, particularly in the selection of policemen too much for physical capacity and not enough for
technical intelligence as applied to detective work. From
these continuing old standards serious incapacity has
often resulted in the unearthing of crimes.

Had New York City a homogeneous population the
movement for a general elevation of civic standards would
have proceeded faster. But New York City's conglomer-
ate population with its polyglot diversities has naturally
presented great difficulties in the solid formation of a
unity of understanding and purposes. Nevertheless the
progress has been very considerable. In spreading its
educational measures for the conservation of health, the

Health Department of New York City for example, has obviously encountered serious obstacles in dealing with a heterogeneous and in many quarters a congested population. Yet by intelligent perseverance it has succeeded so well that in 1916, notwithstanding an infantile paralysis epidemic, the death rate was only 13.82 per 1000 — lowest death rate in New York City's history. The notable improvements brought about by these and other departments attest ever-increasing proficiency. Where formerly the traditional conception of politics in New York City was one cynically regarding office as a legitimate means of spoils, graft, corruption and corporation pillaging, new traditions have been gradually substituted. The old influences may here and there persist, but they are no longer accepted by masses of voters as a fixed creed. The stage has been passed when the open venality of politics can be successfully flaunted; it is now the subtle influences often seeking surreptitiously to use government for their own invidious ends that require the watching.

The supporters of Mayor Mitchel's administration hold that by eradicating partisan politics it has been able to concentrate its whole attention upon the one duty of providing efficient government for the city. They point out, that contrary to the careless methods of some former administrations, the Mitchel administration has, by prudent supervision of finances reduced the budget annually by several million dollars, and yet has made notable extensions in service. They further call attention to the fact that the Mitchel administration has put a stop to the ruinous practice of mortgaging the credit of the city for generations in advance. For the first time, they also tell, New York City has protested against the old arbitrary practice of making enormous State appropriations for objects in which New York City had no share; that as result of this protest the State has already made partial restitution; and that the program of city relief in this direction should eventually mean an annual reduction of

$12,000,000 in New York City's tax burdens. The Mitchel administration forces emphasize the great increase in the collections from taxes, assessments, water rates, docks, ferries, subway and miscellaneous revenue. These are some of the financial improvements enumerated.

In the line of departmental progress Mayor Mitchel's administration is credited with a large list of reforms and innovations: The transformed morale of the Police Department; the efficiency of the Fire Department in greatly curtailing the number of fires while at the same time that department has cost $200,000 less a year than formerly; the humanizing of the activities of the Charities Department and of the correctional system; the progressive work of the Health, Education and other departments; the enterprise of the Dock Department in adding seven miles of wharfage and vast areas of dock space to New York harbor's piers. This is but the merest synopsis of the abundant details set forth showing what Mayor Mitchel's administration has done.

So attractive is this record that the description may possibly seem open to the suspicion of being one-sided, if not effusive. Recalling how often New York City has suffered from flagrant maladministration, the skeptic may be tempted to regard these attributed deeds as being too good to be true. Besides, campaign documents are to be scrutinized not so much for their assertions as for their omissions.

It is true that the great bulk of the accomplishments of Mayor Mitchel's administration may be justly claimed by his supporters as genuine services which are bound to become fixed standards any overthrow of which will not be easily tolerated by the educated public. These Administration annalists, however, have not separated the reforms essentially enduring from those which by their nature are merely experimental, as, for example, certain educational policies. But experiments have their distinct value; better that they should be tried than inertia should prevail.

One of the few specific charges brought against Mayor Mitchel's administration is the assertion that a coterie of real estate speculators has profited unduly by the sale of park sites and other real estate to the city and State during recent years. In reply the supporters of Mayor Mitchel's administration say that the acquisition of these properties was indispensable to great public improvements planned; that whatever payments have been made have been paid by the regularly determined award of the courts; and that there is not the slightest evidence of collusion on the part of city officials.

Thus far the opponents of Mayor Mitchel's administration have devoted much of their energy to attempts at personal onslaughts. This line of action has called forth the comment that it is because of the very absence of administrative scandals that the administration's adversaries resort to vague personal attacks. From these opponents has come the persistent innuendo that because of Mayor Mitchel's occasional social associations with rich and powerful personages, his official activities must necessarily be influenced by that contact. It is aptly pointed out that the hypocrisy and demagogery of such an aspersion may be properly estimated when it is recalled that the elements mainly concerned in spreading it have been the identical organized forces that year after year were the tools of designing men and corporations that by the adroit use of corrupt politics vested in themselves huge corporate privileges and powers and enormous wealth.

INDEX

A

Abolitionist movement, 122–123
Ackerman, Simon, 24
Adams, John, 5
Adams, John Quincy, 5, 61–65, 70–74, 82
Ætna Fire Insurance Co., 97
Ahearn, John F., 316, 324–326
Aldermanic corruption, 81, 98–99, 103, 105, 132–133, 155, 156, 167–171, 181, 197–198, 252, 263–265
Allds, Jotham P., 342
Allen, Stephen, 57, 60, 88, 89, 106
Alley, Saul, 106
Amory, William N., 293, 320–321, 332, 334–335
Andrews, Avery D., 279
Anti-Masonic party, 83, 87
Anti-Monopolists, 103, 109, 113–114, 119
Apollo Hall Democracy, 254
Arcularius, Philip I., 23
Astor, John Jacob, 232

B

Bailey, Benjamin, 88
Baker, Gardiner, 7
Baker, Ray Stannard, 321
Bank of America, 96, 126
Bank of the Metropolis, 64
Bank of the United States (see U. S. Bank)
Banks, abuses of, 13–14, 18, 79, 96–98, 106–107, 114
Bannard, Otto, 341–342
Bar Association, 253, 276, 284, 373
Barker, Isaac O., 179–180
Barker, Jacob, 13, 31, 44, 48, 49, 66, 70–71

Barker, James W., 174
Barnard, George G., 223, 242, 244, 248, 268
"Barnburners," 140–149, 161
Barnes, William, Jr., 395
Barr, Thomas J., 163, 165, 170
Barrett, George C., 237
Becker, Charles, 356–357, 859–360
Bedell, Louis, 347
Beecher, Henry Ward, 237
Bell, Isaac, Jr., 192
Belmont, August, 230–252; 350–351
Bennet, William M., 338
Bennett, James Gordon, 72, 144
Bermel, Joseph, 329–30
Bensel, John A., 389
Betts, Peter, 96
Biddle, Nicholas, 89
Billings, Rev. H. W., 225
Bingham, John, 24–25
Bingham, Theodore A., 339–340
Binkerd, Robert S., 331
Birney, James G., 137
"Blackbirds," 186
Blake, George W., 363, 369–370, 377
Bleecker, Anthony J., 179–180
Bloodgood, Abraham, 118
Bloodgood, John M., 118, 125, 144
Blunt, Orison, 205
Bogardus, Cornelius, 165
Bogert, John A., 147
Boole, Francis I. A., 199, 202, 203, 205, 206, 208
Bowne, Walter, 42, 81, 82, 88, 89, 98, 121, 127
Breckinridge, Lucian S., 397–398
Bradley, Gaffney & Steers, 365
Brady, Anthony N., 332, 351, 383, 385–386, 390

405

Brady, James T., 144, 194
Brady, William V., 141–142
Briggs, John R., 213
Broadway Railroad Co., 263–264
Broadway Surface Railroad Co., 263–264
Brooklyn Rapid Transit Co., 378
Broome, John L., 16, 50, 60
Brown, E. D., 232
Brownell, J. Sherman, 141
Brush, Jacob, 165
Bryan, William J., 281
Bryant, William Cullen, 100, 116
Buchanan, James, 178, 180, 194, 251
Buckmaster, George, 40, 41, 60
Buckley, William H., 343
Bureau of Municipal Research, 325
Bureau of Social Hygiene, 400
Burr, Aaron, 12, 13, 14, 15, 17, 126
Butler, Benjamin F., 206
Butler, W. O., 143
Byrnes, Thomas F., 316

C

Calhoun, John C., 64
Cambreleng, C. C., 89, 140
Campbell, Allan, 262
Cardozo, Albert, 220, 248
Carroll, John F., 284–298
Cass, Lewis, 87, 143, 157
Cassidy, Edward F., 341–342
Cassidy, Joseph, 330, 386–387
Catholics, feeling against, 30, 134
Cebra, John Y., 95
Chatham Fire Insurance Co., 97
Cheetham, James, 26, 27, 28
Chemical Bank, 96–97
Chittenden, S. B., 197–198
Choate, Joseph H., 240
Church, Sanford E., 252
Cisco, John J., 150
City Club, 278, 291, 303–304, 325, 327, 331
Citizens' Union, 282, 327
City Reform party, 172–174, 178–180

Civic Alliance, 341
Civil War, 49, 194, 196–197, 306
Cleveland, Grover, 262, 265, 271, 274–275
Clark, Aaron, 109, 110, 118, 120, 144
Clark, William H., 273
Clay, Henry, 82, 137, 157
Clinton, DeWitt, 16, 17–19, 26, 28–30, 31–32, 34, 36, 38–40, 45–48, 52, 54–55, 61, 64, 68, 75, 88
Clinton, George, 2, 17–19, 26
Cochran W. Bourke, 267–273
Cochrane, John, 165, 172, 188
Cockroft, William, 168
Coddington, Jonathan I., 134–135
Cohalan, Daniel F., 353–354, 355, 373–374
Colden, Cadwallader D., 8, 47, 48, 51, 52–53, 60
Coler, Bird S., 304, 316
Commercial Bank, 103
Committee of Seventy, 253; 278
Conkling, Frederick A., 218–219
Conner, William C., 192
Connolly, J. A., 373
Connolly, Richard B., 122, 152, 165, 202, 214–215, 221, 227, 235, 240–241, 244, 248, 249
Conover, Daniel D., 182
Cook, Noah, 119
Coogan, James J., 271
Cooper, Edward, 184, 259, 260
Cornell, Alonzo B., 260, 262
Cornell, William H., 273
Corruption, 77, 96–98, 126, 132–133, 153–154, 167–171, 181–182, 191–192, 197–199, 200, 203, 206–207, 212–213, 219–220, 222–223, 227, 229, 232–233, 238, 239, 241, 263–264, 271–273, 277–278, 288–289, 307–308, 317, 318, 328, 342–350, 358–359, 363–371, 372, 386–387
Coulter, James E., 167
Cram, J. Sergeant, 383–385
Cravath, Paul D., 334
Crawford, William H., 61, 63–64
Creek Indians, 6
Croker, Richard, 226, 255, 263–264, 267–270, 278–282, 284, 287–

289, 292, 293, 295–298, 310, 360, 389

Crolius, Clarkson, 86
Cromwell, George, 317
Cullen, Edgar M., 376–377
Cutting, Francis B., 147

D

Darling, William A., 208
Darlington, Thomas, 389
Davies, Thomas E., 168
Davis, Matthew L., 12, 24, 25, 28, 45, 70–71
Davis, William A., 16, 33
Davis, Vernon M., 367
"Dead Rabbits," 186, 189, 191
Debt, imprisonment for, 94–95
Delaney, John H., 364–365, 368, 383
Delavan, Daniel E., 152
Delehanty, James A., 396–397
Democratic Club, 388
Denniston, Isaac, 51
Devlin, Charles, 182, 204
Dix, John A., 259; 331, 353, 354
Dolan Thomas, 293
Douglas, Stephen, 195
Dowd, William, 260
Downes, Samuel, 197
Drake, Ellis G., 141
Dunn, Bartholomew, 326, 328, 389
Dunn, Thomas J., 326
Duryea, Stephen C., 152

E

Eckford, Henry, 70, 71
Edson, Franklin, 262, 264, 268
Edwards, Ogden, 89
Eighth Avenue railroad, 167
Einstein, Edwin, 274–275
Elder, Robert, 350
Election frauds, 73–75, 90–91, 114, 118–122, 135, 137, 147, 158–159, 177–180, 191, 195–196, 203–204, 206, 208–209, 218, 220, 275, 276

Election violence, 73–75, 92, 159, 177–180
Ellingwood & Cunningham, 346–347
Ellis, William A., 275
Elkins, William L., 332
Ely, Smith, Jr., 208, 259
Emmett, Thomas Addis, 46
Empire Club, 136–138
Engeman, William A., 349
Equitable Life Assurance Society, 307–308, 334
Equal Rights party, 93–95, 98, 100–102, 105–108, 110–111, 114
Erhardt, Joel B., 271
Erie Canal, 16, 40, 45, 48, 49, 54, 65–68
Erie Railway corruption, 223, 231
Evarts, William M., 237–242
Exchange Bank, 48, 70

F

Fairlie, James, 72
Farley, Terrence, 200
Fassett Committee, 263–264, 272–274
Fassett, J. Sloat, 272
Federalists, 9, 11, 13–14, 16, 25–26, 29, 34–37, 40–41, 44, 45, 47, 49, 61, 109, 114
Fellows, John R., 264
Fenton, Reuben E., 208
Ferguson, John, 38, 39
Fidelity & Casualty Co., 344
Fields, "Tom," 244
Fillmore, Millard, 80
Fish, Preserved, 101
Fisk, James, Jr., 223, 230
Flack, James A., 271
Flannery, Joseph A., 328
Foley, Charles A., 390
Foley, John, 232, 242
Foley, Thomas F., 389
Fornes, Charles V., 306
Fowler, Isaac V., 146, 165, 190–191, 194
Fowler, John Walker, 195–251
Fox, John, 225; 389
Francis, John W., 4

Franklin, Morris, 134–135
Freedman, Andrew, 296–297
Free Soilers, 161
Fremont, John C., 80
French Revolution, 8, 9
Fulton Bank, 71

G

Gaffney, James E., 302, 310–311, 313, 349, 362, 366–369, 371–372, 385, 389
Gallagher, Ernest, 329–330
"Gangs," 130–132, 185–186, 267, 299
Gardiner, Asa Bird, 289
Garvey, Andrew J., 216, 221–222, 248–249
Gaynor, William J., 340–341, 349, 356, 378–379, 400
General Railway Signal Co., 394
Genet, E. C., 50
Genet, Harry W., 225, 226, 244
George, Henry, 269, 270, 282
George, Henry, Jr., 282
Gibbs, Frederick S., 262
Gilbert, Garrit, 103
Gillroy, Thomas F., 267, 274, 275
Glynn, Martin, 388–392
Goff, John W., 276
Goodsell, Louis F., 347
Gorham, Daniel, 114
Gould, Jay, 223
Grace, William R., 260–261, 262
Grady, Thomas F., 343–34, 349
Grant, Hugh J., 262–264, 265, 267–269, 271–272, 274, 278
Grant, U. S., 218, 256
Greeley, Horace, 115, 117, 188, 254
Green Andrew H., 241, 248
Green, Duff, 87
Greene, Francis V., 304
Gresser, Lawrence, 316, 330–331
Grinnell, Moses H., 119
Griswold, John A., 217
Grout, Edward M., 306
Gumbleton, Henry A., 260
Gunther, C. Godfrey, 189, 201, 205, 208, 252
Guthrie, W. D., 328, 373

H

Hadfelt, Richard, 36
Haff, John P., 13, 51, 60
Haffen, Louis F., 294, 297, 298, 316, 326–329
Hackett, John K., 204
Hackley, Andrew J., 198
Hagan, James J., 363
Haight, D. H., 168
Hall, A. Oakey, 216, 218, 224, 227, 230, 239, 240–242
Halleck, Fritz Greene, 11
Hallett, William Paxen, 95, 124–125
Hamilton, Alexander, 2, 3, 14, 19, 66
Hamilton, Andrew, 308, 381
Hammond, Judah, 1, 10
Hancock, Winfield S., 260
Hanford, Benjamin, 295
Hanger, Harry B., 366
"Hardshells," 161–165, 173, 174–175
Harlem Railroad, 99, 103, 123
Harper, James, 134–136
Harrison, William Henry, 129–130
Hart, Emanuel B., 141, 184
Haskell, Job, 104, 114
Havemeyer, William F., 138–139, 140, 142, 152, 192–193, 237, 239, 241, 252, 254, 255, 256, 261, 279
Hayes, Jacob, 13
Hearst, George, 309
Hearst, William R., 309, 322–323, 341–342
Hennessy, John A., 363–365, 369, 377, 382–386
Herrick, John J., 174–175
Hewitt, Abram S., 268–271, 273
Hill, David B., 275
Hillquit, Morris, 397
Hoffman, John T., 208, 216–218, 224, 230, 250
Hoffman, Josiah Ogden, 7
Holmes, Silas, 96
Home Insurance Co., 343
Hone, Philip, 69
Hotchkiss, William H., 342–347
Houston, Sam, 141

Hoyt, Gould, 41
Hoyt, Jesse, 106, 124
Hubbard, Ruggles, 50, 60
" Huckleberry " railroads franchises, 280
Hudson Insurance Co., 98
Hughes, Charles E., 323, 326–331, 334, 346, 347, 398
Humbert, Jonas, 23, 24, 25, 60
" Hunkers," 140–149, 159, 161
Hunn, John S., 44
Hunt, Wilson G., 174–175
Hyde, Charles H., 348–349

I

Ice Trust, 286
Immigration, 134, 154–155, 209
Immigrants, marshalling in politics, 128–129, 151, 188, 209, 217
Ingersoll, James H., 214–215, 221, 238
Interstate Commerce Commission, 315–318
Interborough Rapid Transit Co., 378–380, 393
Ireland, W. H., 72, 89
Irish, prejudice against, 30, 45
Irish, mob Tammany Hall, 46
Irving Hall, 226
" Irving Hall Democracy," 258, 260–262, 274
Irving, " Jimmy," 244
Ives, Henry S., 272
Ivins, William M., 322–323

J

Jaehne, Henry W., 264
Jackson, Andrew, 5, 52, 61–65, 70, 73–76, 80, 85–89, 90–91, 115, 123, 188
Jacques, Moses, 94, 106, 110
Jefferson, Thomas, 4, 5, 9, 15, 116, 188
Jerome, William Travers, 291–292, 294, 319–322, 331–335
Johnson, Sidney G., 394
Judah, Napthali, 51, 60

K

Keating, James P., 272
Kelly, John, 215, 218–219, 250–257, 258–261, 267, 268
Kendall, George H., 372
Kennedy, John J., 389–390
Kennedy, William D., 196
King, Charles, 41
Kingsland, Ambrose C., 152
Kingsley, Darwin P., 345
Kipp, Solomon, 167
Knights of Labor, 269
Know-Nothings (see also Native Americans), 174, 191

L

Laimbeer, Francis E., 287
Lawrence, Abraham R., 254
Lawrence, Cornelius W., 92, 102
Lawrence, John L., 72
Ledwith, Thomas W., 229–230
Lee, Gideon, 101
Legislative corruption, 77, 96–98, 103–104, 200, 222–223, 227, 244, 342–350, 352, 372
Leggett, William, 100, 110, 116, 122, 123
Lexow, Clarence, 276
Lewis, Morgan, 18
Liberal Republicans, 253
Libby, James S., 177, 179–180
Life & Fire Insurance Co., 71
Lincoln, Abraham, 196, 206
Livingston, Edward, 9, 16
Livingston family, 30
Locofocos, 102, 108, 115
Loew, Charles E., 206–207
Long Sault Development Co., 377
Lovejoy, Reuben, 170
Low, Seth, 282, 290, 294–295, 302, 303–306
Lowber, Robert W., 181
Lotteries, 51, 52
Lynch, John R., 213
Lyons Beet Sugar Refining Co., 352

M

McAneny, George, 382
McCall, Edward E., 345, 362, 371, 380–382, 385, 388, 392–394
McCall, John A., 380–383
McCarren, Patrick H., 317, 339, 349, 351
McCann, Patrick H., 263, 268
McClave, John, 278
McClellan, Gen. George B., 206
McClellan, George B., 305, 316–317, 322–325, 327, 338–340
McCullough, John, 285
McGillivray, Alexander, 6
McGovan, Patrick F., 316, 317
McKane, John Y., 340
"McKeon Democracy," 205, 208
McKeon, John, 141, 152, 184
McLaughlin, Hugh, 306
McLean, George W., 221
McMahon, Daniel F., 297
McQuade, Arthur J., 264
McQuade, John, 282
Mack, Norman E., 383
Madison, James, 5, 32, 33
Manhattan Bank, 13, 14, 18, 37, 126–127
Manning, John J., 147
Marcy, William L., 91, 119
Martin, Bernard F., 272
Martin, James J., 278
Martling, Abraham, 11
Mason, Daniel, 334
Maxwell, Hugh, 36
Mazet Committee, 280, 284–286
Mechanics' Fire Insurance Co., 71
Medical Science lottery swindle, 51
Mellen, Charles S., 314–318
Merchants' Bank, 96, 100
Merritt, Henry W., 125
Metcalfe, Luke, 96
Metropolitan Securities Co., 332
Metropolitan Street Railway Co., 293–294, 319, 320, 333–334, 348
Metz, Herman A., 317, 338
Mickel, Andrew H., 139, 147, 152
Ming, Alexander Jr., 114

Mitchel, John Purroy, 322, 326, 382, 388, 398–403
Monroe, James, 5, 39, 49, 51, 83
Montgomery, General, 52
Mooney, William, 1, 12, 24, 25, 34, 52, 87
Morgan, Edwin D., 27
Morgan, John J., 110
Morgan, J. Pierpont, 351
Morgan, J. P. & Co., 314–315
Morgans, Morgan, 160
Morris Canal & Banking Co., 71
Morris, Robert H., 127, 130, 132, 134
Morrissey, John, 225, 250, 252, 255
Morse, Samuel F. B., 130
Morss, John, 89
Moss, Frank, 279, 287
Mozart Hall, 188, 190, 196, 198, 200–205, 208, 219
Municipal Ownership League, 309, 322
Municipal Taxpayers' Association, 253
Murphy, Charles F., 297–298, 299–303, 306, 310–311, 317, 322, 324, 326, 338–340, 344, 349, 351, 353, 355, 356, 360–364, 369–373, 375–376, 378, 382–386, 388–389, 395
Murphy, John J., 301, 310
Murphy, John M., 366
Mutual Life Insurance Co., 307

N

Nast, Thomas, 235, 239
National Republican party, 85–86; election frauds, 90–91
Native American party, 103, 108, 121, 128, 134–135, 138, 139, 142, 155, 174–175, 179, 187, 191
Naughton & Co., 297
Nestell, Christian, 24
Newcomb, Colin G., 127
New York Contracting & Trucking Co., 302, 309–312, 314, 318
New York County Democracy, 261–262, 269, 274

New York Life Insurance Co., 307–308, 346, 381
New York Municipal Railway Corporation, 393
New York, New Haven & Hartford Railroad Co., 312–318
New York & Portchester Railroad, 312–318
New York Stock Exchange, 377
New York, Westchester & Boston Railroad Co., 312–318
New York, Westchester & Connecticut Traction Co., 332
Nicholl, Francis S., 63
Ninth Avenue Railroad, 167
Nixon, Lewis, 292, 295–296
Noah, M. M., 47, 60–62, 66, 75, 80, 88, 89, 123, 147
Norton " Mike," 225, 244

O

O'Brien, James, 225, 238, 254, 268
O'Brien, John J., 262
O'Conor, Charles, 147, 242, 252
O'Gorman, James A., 353–354
Ogden, Henry, 123
O'Neil, " Honest " John, 264
Opdyke, George P., 170, 192–193, 201
Ordway, Samuel H., 330–331
O'Rourke, Matthew, 237–238, 248
Osborne, James W., 319–320, 365, 389
Owego Lottery, 51
Owen, Robert, 78
Owen, Robert Dale, 78–79

P

Page, William H., Jr., 334
Page, Samuel L., Jr., 24
Panics, 109, 117, 186–187
Parkhurst, Charles H., 278
Parton, James, 117
Partridge, John N., 303–304
Paulding, William, Jr., 47, 60, 69, 127
Parker, Andrew D., 279
Patterson & Co., 366
Peaconic Co., 101

Peck, Duncan W., 390
Peckham, Wheeler H., 242
Pendleton, Nathaniel, 19
Penn, William, 2
People's Gas Light Co., 206
People's Municipal League, 274
People's Traction Co., 332
Perkins, James, 98, 179
Phelps, William Walter, 237
Philbin, Eugene A., 289–291
Phoenix Insurance Co., 342–345
Phoenix, J. Philips, 129
Pierce, Franklin, 157, 159, 194
Pierson, Isaac, 13
Pierrepont, Edwards, 240
Pintard, John, 7
Platt, Thomas C., 288, 305
Plunkett, George W., 383, 385, 389
Polk, James K., 136–137, 141
Populist party, 275
Porter, Peter B., 45, 46
Potter, Henry C., 289
Prendergast, William A., 382
Price, William M., 124
Prince, Benjamin, 41, 60
Prohibitionists, 275
Progressive party, 371, 396
Public Service Commission, 333, 379–380, 388, 392–394
Purdy, Elijah F., 122, 141, 146, 152, 163, 165, 168, 184, 192, 197
Purser, George H., 206

Q

Queens' Borough Property Owners' Ass'n, 329
Quincy, Josiah, 179
Quigg, Lemuel Eli, 333

R

Radcliff, Jacob, 29, 36, 39, 41, 42, 47
Raines, John, 352
Ramapo Water Company, 286
Rathbone, William P., 71
Reel, C. Gordon, 362, 365, 371, 390

Republicans, 161, 187, 191, 212, 217–218, 229–230, 243, 256, 262, 275, 282, 306–308, 346, 351–352, 382, 394–396
Revolution, American, 1, 3, 82
Reynolds, William B., 171
Riker, Richard, 15, 36
Ringgold, Benjamin, 107–108
Riots, 109, 131–132, 162, 182, 184, 185, 191
Roberts, Marshall O., 208, 231
Robinson, Lucius, 259–260
Roche, Walter, 213
Rogers, G. Tracy, 346–348
Rogers, H. H., 351
Romaine, Benjamin, 13, 22, 23, 25, 33, 34, 61, 72
Romaine, ·Samuel B., 77
Roosevelt, Robert B., 240
Roosevelt, J. J., 95
Roosevelt, Theodore, 270, 279, 285, 289, 395
Rosenthal, Herman, 256–257
Russell, Charles E., 382, 388
Russell, William Hepburn, 302
Rutgers, Col., 42
Ryan, Allan, 383–384, 390
Ryan, Thomas F., 293, 332–334, 353, 383–384
Rynders, Isaiah, 136, 138, 157, 195

S

Sanford, Nathan, 33
Savage, J. Y., 176–177
Schell, Augustus, 252–259
Schell, Edward, 232
Schureman, Nicholas, 70
Scott, Francis M., 274
Shandley, Edward J., 233
Seagrist, Nicholas, 188
Seaver, Joel P., 101
Selden, Dudley, 90, 138
Seventh Ward Bank, 97, 123, 124, 179
Seward, George F., 344–345
Seward, William H., 119
Seymour, Horatio, 152, 204, 216, 218, 230, 252
Sharp, George, 99

Sharp, Jacob, 168, 169
Sharpe, John, 44
Sharpe, Peter, 72, 77, 89
Shaw, James G., 367
Sheehan, John C., 278, 280, 281, 297
Sheehan, William F., 353
Shepard, Edward M., 290–295
Shepard, Lorenzo B., 141, 290, 295
Shonts, Theodore, 379–380
Sickles, Daniel E., 144, 158, 189
Single-Taxers, 269
Skidmore, Burtis, 168
Skidmore, William E., 114
Slamm, Levi D., 94–110
Slavery, Tammany's support of, 143–148
Small, Wilson, 176–183
Smith, Alfred E., 396
Smith, Isaac L., 106
Smith, Morgan L., 107–108
Smith, Robert, 133
Smith, Thomas, 389
Smith, Thomas R., 81
Smythe, John F. B., 272
Socialist Labor party, 306
Socialists, 269, 275, 382, 384
"Softshells," 161–165, 173, 174–175
Spencer, Mark, 71
Stagg, Abraham, 24, 25, 72, 77
Stagg, Peter, 72
State Bank, 107
Stayner, George H., 272
Stevens, John F., 379–380
Stewart, James C., 367, 383
Stilwell, Silas M., 80
Stilwell, Stephen J., 352, 372, 378
Stoneall, James C., 107
Strahan, Edward, 141
Straus, Nathan, 278
Strong, Roger, 41, 60
Strong, William L., 278–279
Sulzer, William, 360–373, 375–378, 381–385, 388, 390, 392
Sullivan, "Big Tim," 315, 344–345
Sullivan, "Little Tim," 311
Swann, Edward, 396–398

Swartwout, John 13, 18, 19, 33, 44
Swartwout, Robert, 13, 16, 33, 63, 97, 118
Swartwout, Samuel, 63, 76, 103, 106, 123-124
Sweeny, Peter B., 151, 176-177, 184, 214-215, 224, 247

T

Taintor, Henry F., 248
Tappan, Lewis, 123
Tammany election frauds, 73-75, 90-91, 120, 135, 137, 154, 158, 159, etc.
Tammany Hall, violence in, 63, 113-114, 131, 138, 158, 161-162, 177, 189
Tammany leaders, frauds of, 23-26, 50-51, 70-71, 123-124, 126-127, 152, 167-171, 182, 194-195, 221-249, 263-264, 272-273, 325, 327-328, 326-329, 389
Tammany sachems in elections, 114-115, 162-165, 183-185, 189-190, 226
Tallmadge, Nathaniel P., 87
Tappan, Lewis, 123
Taylor, Douglas, 184-194
Taylor, Gen., 143
Taylor, James B., 168-170
Taylor, Joseph S., 182
Third Avenue surface railway franchise, 167-168
Thompson, Jonathan, 126-127
Thorne, Oakley, 314-315
Tibbits, Elisha, 95
Tiemann, Daniel F., 181, 187, 188, 192
Tilden, Samuel J., 140, 184, 227, 242, 245, 252, 256, 259
Todd, William, 64, 72
Tompkins, Daniel D., 15, 22, 39, 45, 53-54, 96
Tompkins, Minthorne, 140
Tories, 2, 3
Tradesmen's Bank, 71
Tracy, Benjamin F., 282
Travis, Eugene M., 350
Tucker, Gideon J., 195

Tweed, Richard M., 246
Tweed, William M., 151, 156, 167-168, 191-192, 209-210, 211-224, 225-236, 239-247, 255, 259, 265, 281, 310, 318
Tyler, John, 137

U

Ulshoeffer, Michael, 77
Unionist Club, 137
United Labor party, 270, 271
United States Bank, 71, 84, 86, 89-92, 112-114
Untermeyer, Samuel, 334

V

Valentine, Abraham M., 31
VanBuren, Martin, 13, 72, 87, 88, 108, 112-114, 115, 124, 129, 130, 143, 205
Vanderbilt, William K., 351
Vanderpoel, Judge, 129
VanNess, John, 13, 63
VanNess, William P., 13, 15, 19, 65-66
Van Wyck, Robert C., 282, 286, 289, 295, 301
Van Schaick, Myndert, 144, 148
VanTuyl, George C., 354
Varian, Isaac L., 102, 105, 118, 120, 121, 123, 129
Vermilyea, Thomas, 71
Verplanck, Gulian C., 36, 89, 90, 92
Viaduct Railroad, 231
Voorhis, Peter R., 191
Vreeland, H. H., 347-348

W

Wales, Salem H., 256
Waldron, William J., 97
Wall & Cortland St. Ferries Railroad, 332, 334
Wallach, W. D., 145
Walsh, "Mike," 130-131, 144, 157, 251
War of 1812, 32-34, 35, 49
Ward, Jasper, 97

Waring, George E., Jr., 279
Warner, Cornelius, 23
Washington, George, 5, 6, 9, 10
Waterbury, Nelson J., 165, 190, 195–196
Webb, James Watson, 80, 87, 89
Weed, Thurlow, 98
Webster, Daniel, 188
Wendover, Peter, 61
Westervelt, Jacob A., 159–160
Western, Henry M., 146, 160
Wetmore, Prosper M., 107–108
Wetmore, Robert C., 119
Whig frauds, 108, 118–122, 154
Whigs, 92, 101, 103, 108–110, 114, 117–122, 128–129, 133–134, 137–139, 155, 159, 160, 171, 179, 211
White, Campbell P., 126
Whiting, James R., 125, 179
Whitman Charles S., 357, 359, 367, 387, 389, 392, 394, 396, 398
Whitney, William C., 293, 332, 351
Wickham, William H., 256
Widener, P. A. S., 293, 332, 351

Willett, Marinus, 6, 73
Willett, William, Jr., 386–387
Williams, George V. S., 394
Williams, Talcott, 184
Wilson, Woodrow, 398
Women's Municipal League, 291
Wood, Fernando, 122, 146, 148, 149, 150–152, 159, 165, 174–180, 181–193, 196–205, 208–209, 219, 220
Woodford, Stewart, L., 230
Woodhull, Caleb S., 144
Woodruff, Thomas T., 86
Woods, Arthur, 400
Wortman, Tennis, 15, 26, 41, 51, 60

Y

"Young Democracy," 225–226, 238
Young, George W., 379

Z

Zimmerlin, Henry F., 352

A CATALOGUE OF SELECTED DOVER BOOKS
IN ALL FIELDS OF INTEREST

A CATALOGUE OF SELECTED DOVER BOOKS
IN ALL FIELDS OF INTEREST

AMERICA'S OLD MASTERS, James T. Flexner. Four men emerged unexpectedly from provincial 18th century America to leadership in European art: Benjamin West, J. S. Copley, C. R. Peale, Gilbert Stuart. Brilliant coverage of lives and contributions. Revised, 1967 edition. 69 plates. 365pp. of text.
21806-6 Paperbound $3.00

FIRST FLOWERS OF OUR WILDERNESS: AMERICAN PAINTING, THE COLONIAL PERIOD, James T. Flexner. Painters, and regional painting traditions from earliest Colonial times up to the emergence of Copley, West and Peale Sr., Foster, Gustavus Hesselius, Feke, John Smibert and many anonymous painters in the primitive manner. Engaging presentation, with 162 illustrations. xxii + 368pp.
22180-6 Paperbound $3.50

THE LIGHT OF DISTANT SKIES: AMERICAN PAINTING, 1760-1835, James T. Flexner. The great generation of early American painters goes to Europe to learn and to teach: West, Copley, Gilbert Stuart and others. Allston, Trumbull, Morse; also contemporary American painters—primitives, derivatives, academics—who remained in America. 102 illustrations. xiii + 306pp.
22179-2 Paperbound $3.00

A HISTORY OF THE RISE AND PROGRESS OF THE ARTS OF DESIGN IN THE UNITED STATES, William Dunlap. Much the richest mine of information on early American painters, sculptors, architects, engravers, miniaturists, etc. The only source of information for scores of artists, the major primary source for many others. Unabridged reprint of rare original 1834 edition, with new introduction by James T. Flexner, and 394 new illustrations. Edited by Rita Weiss. 6⅝ x 9⅝.
21695-0, 21696-9, 21697-7 Three volumes, Paperbound $13.50

EPOCHS OF CHINESE AND JAPANESE ART, Ernest F. Fenollosa. From primitive Chinese art to the 20th century, thorough history, explanation of every important art period and form, including Japanese woodcuts; main stress on China and Japan, but Tibet, Korea also included. Still unexcelled for its detailed, rich coverage of cultural background, aesthetic elements, diffusion studies, particularly of the historical period. 2nd, 1913 edition. 242 illustrations. lii + 439pp. of text.
20364-6, 20365-4 Two volumes, Paperbound $6.00

THE GENTLE ART OF MAKING ENEMIES, James A. M. Whistler. Greatest wit of his day deflates Oscar Wilde, Ruskin, Swinburne; strikes back at inane critics, exhibitions, art journalism; aesthetics of impressionist revolution in most striking form. Highly readable classic by great painter. Reproduction of edition designed by Whistler. Introduction by Alfred Werner. xxxvi + 334pp.
21875-9 Paperbound $2.50

VISUAL ILLUSIONS: THEIR CAUSES, CHARACTERISTICS, AND APPLICATIONS, Matthew Luckiesh. Thorough description and discussion of optical illusion, geometric and perspective, particularly; size and shape distortions, illusions of color, of motion; natural illusions; use of illusion in art and magic, industry, etc. Most useful today with op art, also for classical art. Scores of effects illustrated. Introduction by William H. Ittleson. 100 illustrations. xxi + 252pp.

21530-X Paperbound $2.00

A HANDBOOK OF ANATOMY FOR ART STUDENTS, Arthur Thomson. Thorough, virtually exhaustive coverage of skeletal structure, musculature, etc. Full text, supplemented by anatomical diagrams and drawings and by photographs of undraped figures. Unique in its comparison of male and female forms, pointing out differences of contour, texture, form. 211 figures, 40 drawings, 86 photographs. xx + 459pp. 5⅜ x 8⅜. 21163-0 Paperbound $3.50

150 MASTERPIECES OF DRAWING, Selected by Anthony Toney. Full page reproductions of drawings from the early 16th to the end of the 18th century, all beautifully reproduced: Rembrandt, Michelangelo, Dürer, Fragonard, Urs, Graf, Wouwerman, many others. First-rate browsing book, model book for artists. xviii + 150pp. 8⅜ x 11¼. 21032-4 Paperbound $2.50

THE LATER WORK OF AUBREY BEARDSLEY, Aubrey Beardsley. Exotic, erotic, ironic masterpieces in full maturity: Comedy Ballet, Venus and Tannhauser, Pierrot, Lysistrata, Rape of the Lock, Savoy material, Ali Baba, Volpone, etc. This material revolutionized the art world, and is still powerful, fresh, brilliant. With *The Early Work*, all Beardsley's finest work. 174 plates, 2 in color. xiv + 176pp. 8⅛ x 11. 21817-1 Paperbound $3.00

DRAWINGS OF REMBRANDT, Rembrandt van Rijn. Complete reproduction of fabulously rare edition by Lippmann and Hofstede de Groot, completely reedited, updated, improved by Prof. Seymour Slive, Fogg Museum. Portraits, Biblical sketches, landscapes, Oriental types, nudes, episodes from classical mythology—All Rembrandt's fertile genius. Also selection of drawings by his pupils and followers. "Stunning volumes," *Saturday Review*. 550 illustrations. lxxviii + 552pp. 9⅛ x 12¼. 21485-0, 21486-9 Two volumes, Paperbound $7.00

THE DISASTERS OF WAR, Francisco Goya. One of the masterpieces of Western civilization—83 etchings that record Goya's shattering, bitter reaction to the Napoleonic war that swept through Spain after the insurrection of 1808 and to war in general. Reprint of the first edition, with three additional plates from Boston's Museum of Fine Arts. All plates facsimile size. Introduction by Philip Hofer, Fogg Museum. v + 97pp. 9⅜ x 8¼. 21872-4 Paperbound $2.00

GRAPHIC WORKS OF ODILON REDON. Largest collection of Redon's graphic works ever assembled: 172 lithographs, 28 etchings and engravings, 9 drawings. These include some of his most famous works. All the plates from *Odilon Redon: oeuvre graphique complet,* plus additional plates. New introduction and caption translations by Alfred Werner. 209 illustrations. xxvii + 209pp. 9⅛ x 12¼. 21966-8 Paperbound $4.00

DESIGN BY ACCIDENT; A BOOK OF "ACCIDENTAL EFFECTS" FOR ARTISTS AND DESIGNERS, James F. O'Brien. Create your own unique, striking, imaginative effects by "controlled accident" interaction of materials: paints and lacquers, oil and water based paints, splatter, crackling materials, shatter, similar items. Everything you do will be different; first book on this limitless art, so useful to both fine artist and commercial artist. Full instructions. 192 plates showing "accidents," 8 in color. viii + 215pp. 8⅜ x 11¼.   21942-9 Paperbound $3.50

THE BOOK OF SIGNS, Rudolf Koch. Famed German type designer draws 493 beautiful symbols: religious, mystical, alchemical, imperial, property marks, runes, etc. Remarkable fusion of traditional and modern. Good for suggestions of timelessness, smartness, modernity. Text. vi + 104pp. 6⅛ x 9¼.
                                                20162-7 Paperbound $1.25

HISTORY OF INDIAN AND INDONESIAN ART, Ananda K. Coomaraswamy. An unabridged republication of one of the finest books by a great scholar in Eastern art. Rich in descriptive material, history, social backgrounds; Sunga reliefs, Rajput paintings, Gupta temples, Burmese frescoes, textiles, jewelry, sculpture, etc. 400 photos. viii + 423pp. 6⅜ x 9¾.   21436-2 Paperbound $4.00

PRIMITIVE ART, Franz Boas. America's foremost anthropologist surveys textiles, ceramics, woodcarving, basketry, metalwork, etc.; patterns, technology, creation of symbols, style origins. All areas of world, but very full on Northwest Coast Indians. More than 350 illustrations of baskets, boxes, totem poles, weapons, etc. 378 pp.
                                                20025-6 Paperbound $3.00

THE GENTLEMAN AND CABINET MAKER'S DIRECTOR, Thomas Chippendale. Full reprint (third edition, 1762) of most influential furniture book of all time, by master cabinetmaker. 200 plates, illustrating chairs, sofas, mirrors, tables, cabinets, plus 24 photographs of surviving pieces. Biographical introduction by N. Bienenstock. vi + 249pp. 9⅞ x 12¾.   21601-2 Paperbound $4.00

AMERICAN ANTIQUE FURNITURE, Edgar G. Miller, Jr. The basic coverage of all American furniture before 1840. Individual chapters cover type of furniture—clocks, tables, sideboards, etc.—chronologically, with inexhaustible wealth of data. More than 2100 photographs, all identified, commented on. Essential to all early American collectors. Introduction by H. E. Keyes. vi + 1106pp. 7⅞ x 10¾.
                    21599-7, 21600-4 Two volumes, Paperbound $11.00

PENNSYLVANIA DUTCH AMERICAN FOLK ART, Henry J. Kauffman. 279 photos, 28 drawings of tulipware, Fraktur script, painted tinware, toys, flowered furniture, quilts, samplers, hex signs, house interiors, etc. Full descriptive text. Excellent for tourist, rewarding for designer, collector. Map. 146pp. 7⅞ x 10¾.
                                                21205-X Paperbound $2.50

EARLY NEW ENGLAND GRAVESTONE RUBBINGS, Edmund V. Gillon, Jr. 43 photographs, 226 carefully reproduced rubbings show heavily symbolic, sometimes macabre early gravestones, up to early 19th century. Remarkable early American primitive art, occasionally strikingly beautiful; always powerful. Text. xxvi + 207pp. 8⅜ x 11¼.   21380-3 Paperbound $3.50

ALPHABETS AND ORNAMENTS, Ernst Lehner. Well-known pictorial source for decorative alphabets, script examples, cartouches, frames, decorative title pages, calligraphic initials, borders, similar material. 14th to 19th century, mostly European. Useful in almost any graphic arts designing, varied styles. 750 illustrations. 256pp. 7 x 10.   21905-4 Paperbound $4.00

PAINTING: A CREATIVE APPROACH, Norman Colquhoun. For the beginner simple guide provides an instructive approach to painting: major stumbling blocks for beginner; overcoming them, technical points; paints and pigments; oil painting; watercolor and other media and color. New section on "plastic" paints. Glossary. Formerly *Paint Your Own Pictures*. 221pp.   22000-1 Paperbound $1.75

THE ENJOYMENT AND USE OF COLOR, Walter Sargent. Explanation of the relations between colors themselves and between colors in nature and art, including hundreds of little-known facts about color values, intensities, effects of high and low illumination, complementary colors. Many practical hints for painters, references to great masters. 7 color plates, 29 illustrations. x + 274pp.
20944-X Paperbound $2.75

THE NOTEBOOKS OF LEONARDO DA VINCI, compiled and edited by Jean Paul Richter. 1566 extracts from original manuscripts reveal the full range of Leonardo's versatile genius: all his writings on painting, sculpture, architecture, anatomy, astronomy, geography, topography, physiology, mining, music, etc., in both Italian and English, with 186 plates of manuscript pages and more than 500 additional drawings. Includes studies for the Last Supper, the lost Sforza monument, and other works. Total of xlvii + 866pp. 7⅞ x 10¾.
22572-0, 22573-9 Two volumes, Paperbound $10.00

MONTGOMERY WARD CATALOGUE OF 1895. Tea gowns, yards of flannel and pillow-case lace, stereoscopes, books of gospel hymns, the New Improved Singer Sewing Machine, side saddles, milk skimmers, straight-edged razors, high-button shoes, spittoons, and on and on . . . listing some 25,000 items, practically all illustrated. Essential to the shoppers of the 1890's, it is our truest record of the spirit of the period. Unaltered reprint of Issue No. 57, Spring and Summer 1895. Introduction by Boris Emmet. Innumerable illustrations. xiii + 624pp. 8½ x 11⅝.
22377-9 Paperbound $6.95

THE CRYSTAL PALACE EXHIBITION ILLUSTRATED CATALOGUE (LONDON, 1851). One of the wonders of the modern world—the Crystal Palace Exhibition in which all the nations of the civilized world exhibited their achievements in the arts and sciences—presented in an equally important illustrated catalogue. More than 1700 items pictured with accompanying text—ceramics, textiles, cast-iron work, carpets, pianos, sleds, razors, wall-papers, billiard tables, beehives, silverware and hundreds of other artifacts—represent the focal point of Victorian culture in the Western World. Probably the largest collection of Victorian decorative art ever assembled— indispensable for antiquarians and designers. Unabridged republication of the Art-Journal Catalogue of the Great Exhibition of 1851, with all terminal essays. New introduction by John Gloag, F.S.A. xxxiv + 426pp. 9 x 12.
22503-8 Paperbound $4.50

A History of Costume, Carl Köhler. Definitive history, based on surviving pieces of clothing primarily, and paintings, statues, etc. secondarily. Highly readable text, supplemented by 594 illustrations of costumes of the ancient Mediterranean peoples, Greece and Rome, the Teutonic prehistoric period; costumes of the Middle Ages, Renaissance, Baroque, 18th and 19th centuries. Clear, measured patterns are provided for many clothing articles. Approach is practical throughout. Enlarged by Emma von Sichart. 464pp.   21030-8 Paperbound $3.50

Oriental Rugs, Antique and Modern, Walter A. Hawley. A complete and authoritative treatise on the Oriental rug—where they are made, by whom and how, designs and symbols, characteristics in detail of the six major groups, how to distinguish them and how to buy them. Detailed technical data is provided on periods, weaves, warps, wefts, textures, sides, ends and knots, although no technical background is required for an understanding. 11 color plates, 80 halftones, 4 maps. vi + 320pp. 6⅛ x 9⅛.   22366-3 Paperbound $5.00

Ten Books on Architecture, Vitruvius. By any standards the most important book on architecture ever written. Early Roman discussion of aesthetics of building, construction methods, orders, sites, and every other aspect of architecture has inspired, instructed architecture for about 2,000 years. Stands behind Palladio, Michelangelo, Bramante, Wren, countless others. Definitive Morris H. Morgan translation. 68 illustrations. xii + 331pp.   20645-9 Paperbound $2.50

The Four Books of Architecture, Andrea Palladio. Translated into every major Western European language in the two centuries following its publication in 1570, this has been one of the most influential books in the history of architecture. Complete reprint of the 1738 Isaac Ware edition. New introduction by Adolf Placzek, Columbia Univ. 216 plates. xxii + 110pp. of text. 9½ x 12¾.
                    21308-0 Clothbound $10.00

Sticks and Stones: A Study of American Architecture and Civilization, Lewis Mumford.One of the great classics of American cultural history. American architecture from the medieval-inspired earliest forms to the early 20th century; evolution of structure and style, and reciprocal influences on environment. 21 photographic illustrations. 238pp.   20202-X Paperbound $2.00

The American Builder's Companion, Asher Benjamin. The most widely used early 19th century architectural style and source book, for colonial up into Greek Revival periods. Extensive development of geometry of carpentering, construction of sashes, frames, doors, stairs; plans and elevations of domestic and other buildings. Hundreds of thousands of houses were built according to this book, now invaluable to historians, architects, restorers, etc. 1827 edition. 59 plates. 114pp. 7⅞ x 10¾.
                    22236-5 Paperbound $3.00

Dutch Houses in the Hudson Valley Before 1776, Helen Wilkinson Reynolds. The standard survey of the Dutch colonial house and outbuildings, with constructional features, decoration, and local history associated with individual homesteads. Introduction by Franklin D. Roosevelt. Map. 150 illustrations. 469pp. 6⅝ x 9¼.   21469-9 Paperbound $4.00

THE ARCHITECTURE OF COUNTRY HOUSES, Andrew J. Downing. Together with Vaux's *Villas and Cottages* this is the basic book for Hudson River Gothic architecture of the middle Victorian period. Full, sound discussions of general aspects of housing, architecture, style, decoration, furnishing, together with scores of detailed house plans, illustrations of specific buildings, accompanied by full text. Perhaps the most influential single American architectural book. 1850 edition. Introduction by J. Stewart Johnson. 321 figures, 34 architectural designs. xvi + 560pp.
22003-6 Paperbound $4.00

LOST EXAMPLES OF COLONIAL ARCHITECTURE, John Mead Howells. Full-page photographs of buildings that have disappeared or been so altered as to be denatured, including many designed by major early American architects. 245 plates. xvii + 248pp. 7⅞ x 10¾. 21143-6 Paperbound $3.50

DOMESTIC ARCHITECTURE OF THE AMERICAN COLONIES AND OF THE EARLY REPUBLIC, Fiske Kimball. Foremost architect and restorer of Williamsburg and Monticello covers nearly 200 homes between 1620-1825. Architectural details, construction, style features, special fixtures, floor plans, etc. Generally considered finest work in its area. 219 illustrations of houses, doorways, windows, capital mantels. xx + 314pp. 7⅞ x 10¾. 21743-4 Paperbound $4.00

EARLY AMERICAN ROOMS: 1650-1858, edited by Russell Hawes Kettell. Tour of 12 rooms, each representative of a different era in American history and each furnished, decorated, designed and occupied in the style of the era. 72 plans and elevations, 8-page color section, etc., show fabrics, wall papers, arrangements, etc. Full descriptive text. xvii + 200pp. of text. 8⅜ x 11¼.
21633-0 Paperbound $5.00

THE FITZWILLIAM VIRGINAL BOOK, edited by J. Fuller Maitland and W. B. Squire. Full modern printing of famous early 17th-century ms. volume of 300 works by Morley, Byrd, Bull, Gibbons, etc. For piano or other modern keyboard instrument; easy to read format. xxxvi + 938pp. 8⅜ x 11.
21068-5, 21069-3 Two volumes, Paperbound $10.00

KEYBOARD MUSIC, Johann Sebastian Bach. Bach Gesellschaft edition. A rich selection of Bach's masterpieces for the harpsichord: the six English Suites, six French Suites, the six Partitas (Clavierübung part I), the Goldberg Variations (Clavierübung part IV), the fifteen Two-Part Inventions and the fifteen Three-Part Sinfonias. Clearly reproduced on large sheets with ample margins; eminently playable. vi + 312pp. 8⅛ x 11. 22360-4 Paperbound $5.00

THE MUSIC OF BACH: AN INTRODUCTION, Charles Sanford Terry. A fine, nontechnical introduction to Bach's music, both instrumental and vocal. Covers organ music, chamber music, passion music, other types. Analyzes themes, developments, innovations. x + 114pp. 21075-8 Paperbound $1.25

BEETHOVEN AND HIS NINE SYMPHONIES, Sir George Grove. Noted British musicologist provides best history, analysis, commentary on symphonies. Very thorough, rigorously accurate; necessary to both advanced student and amateur music lover. 436 musical passages. vii + 407 pp. 20334-4 Paperbound $2.75

JOHANN SEBASTIAN BACH, Philipp Spitta. One of the great classics of musicology, this definitive analysis of Bach's music (and life) has never been surpassed. Lucid, nontechnical analyses of hundreds of pieces (30 pages devoted to St. Matthew Passion, 26 to B Minor Mass). Also includes major analysis of 18th-century music. 450 musical examples. 40-page musical supplement. Total of xx + 1799pp.
(EUK) 22278-0, 22279-9 Two volumes, Clothbound $17.50

MOZART AND HIS PIANO CONCERTOS, Cuthbert Girdlestone. The only full-length study of an important area of Mozart's creativity. Provides detailed analyses of all 23 concertos, traces inspirational sources. 417 musical examples. Second edition. 509pp. (USO) 21271-8 Paperbound $3.50

THE PERFECT WAGNERITE: A COMMENTARY ON THE NIBLUNG'S RING, George Bernard Shaw. Brilliant and still relevant criticism in remarkable essays on Wagner's Ring cycle, Shaw's ideas on political and social ideology behind the plots, role of Leitmotifs, vocal requisites, etc. Prefaces. xxi + 136pp.
21707-8 Paperbound $1.50

DON GIOVANNI, W. A. Mozart. Complete libretto, modern English translation; biographies of composer and librettist; accounts of early performances and critical reaction. Lavishly illustrated. All the material you need to understand and appreciate this great work. Dover Opera Guide and Libretto Series; translated and introduced by Ellen Bleiler. 92 illustrations. 209pp.
21134-7 Paperbound $1:50

HIGH FIDELITY SYSTEMS: A LAYMAN'S GUIDE, Roy F. Allison. All the basic information you need for setting up your own audio system: high fidelity and stereo record players, tape records, F.M. Connections, adjusting tone arm, cartridge, checking needle alignment, positioning speakers, phasing speakers, adjusting hums, trouble-shooting, maintenance, and similar topics. Enlarged 1965 edition. More than 50 charts, diagrams, photos. iv + 91pp. 21514-8 Paperbound $1.25

REPRODUCTION OF SOUND, Edgar Villchur. Thorough coverage for laymen of high fidelity systems, reproducing systems in general, needles, amplifiers, preamps, loudspeakers, feedback, explaining physical background. "A rare talent for making technicalities vividly comprehensible," R. Darrell, *High Fidelity*. 69 figures. iv + 92pp. 21515-6 Paperbound $1.25

HEAR ME TALKIN' TO YA: THE STORY OF JAZZ AS TOLD BY THE MEN WHO MADE IT, Nat Shapiro and Nat Hentoff. Louis Armstrong, Fats Waller, Jo Jones, Clarence Williams, Billy Holiday, Duke Ellington, Jelly Roll Morton and dozens of other jazz greats tell how it was in Chicago's South Side, New Orleans, depression Harlem and the modern West Coast as jazz was born and grew. xvi + 429pp.
21726-4 Paperbound $2.50

FABLES OF AESOP, translated by Sir Roger L'Estrange. A reproduction of the very rare 1931 Paris edition; a selection of the most interesting fables, together with 50 imaginative drawings by Alexander Calder. v + 128pp. 6½x9¼.
21780-9 Paperbound $1.50

AGAINST THE GRAIN (A REBOURS), Joris K. Huysmans. Filled with weird images, evidences of a bizarre imagination, exotic experiments with hallucinatory drugs, rich tastes and smells and the diversions of its sybarite hero Duc Jean des Esseintes, this classic novel pushed 19th-century literary decadence to its limits. Full unabridged edition. Do not confuse this with abridged editions generally sold. Introduction by Havelock Ellis. xlix + 206pp.   22190-3 Paperbound $2.00

VARIORUM SHAKESPEARE: HAMLET. Edited by Horace H. Furness; a landmark of American scholarship. Exhaustive footnotes and appendices treat all doubtful words and phrases, as well as suggested critical emendations throughout the play's history. First volume contains editor's own text, collated with all Quartos and Folios. Second volume contains full first Quarto, translations of Shakespeare's sources (Belleforest, and Saxo Grammaticus), Der Bestrafte Brudermord, and many essays on critical and historical points of interest by major authorities of past and present. Includes details of staging and costuming over the years. By far the best edition available for serious students of Shakespeare. Total of xx + 905pp.
21004-9, 21005-7, 2 volumes, Paperbound $7.00

A LIFE OF WILLIAM SHAKESPEARE, Sir Sidney Lee. This is the standard life of Shakespeare, summarizing everything known about Shakespeare and his plays. Incredibly rich in material, broad in coverage, clear and judicious, it has served thousands as the best introduction to Shakespeare. 1931 edition. 9 plates. xxix + 792pp.   (USO) 21967-4 Paperbound $3.75

MASTERS OF THE DRAMA, John Gassner. Most comprehensive history of the drama in print, covering every tradition from Greeks to modern Europe and America, including India, Far East, etc. Covers more than 800 dramatists, 2000 plays, with biographical material, plot summaries, theatre history, criticism, etc. "Best of its kind in English," *New Republic*. 77 illustrations. xxii + 890pp.
20100-7 Clothbound $8.50

THE EVOLUTION OF THE ENGLISH LANGUAGE, George McKnight. The growth of English, from the 14th century to the present. Unusual, non-technical account presents basic information in very interesting form: sound shifts, change in grammar and syntax, vocabulary growth, similar topics. Abundantly illustrated with quotations. Formerly *Modern English in the Making*. xii + 590pp.
21932-1 Paperbound $3.50

AN ETYMOLOGICAL DICTIONARY OF MODERN ENGLISH, Ernest Weekley. Fullest, richest work of its sort, by foremost British lexicographer. Detailed word histories, including many colloquial and archaic words; extensive quotations. Do not confuse this with the Concise Etymological Dictionary, which is much abridged. Total of xxvii + 830pp. 6½ x 9¼.
21873-2, 21874-0 Two volumes, Paperbound $6.00

FLATLAND: A ROMANCE OF MANY DIMENSIONS, E. A. Abbott. Classic of science-fiction explores ramifications of life in a two-dimensional world, and what happens when a three-dimensional being intrudes. Amusing reading, but also useful as introduction to thought about hyperspace. Introduction by Banesh Hoffmann. 16 illustrations. xx + 103pp.   20001-9 Paperbound $1.00

POEMS OF ANNE BRADSTREET, edited with an introduction by Robert Hutchinson. A new selection of poems by America's first poet and perhaps the first significant woman poet in the English language. 48 poems display her development in works of considerable variety—love poems, domestic poems, religious meditations, formal elegies, "quaternions," etc. Notes, bibliography. viii + 222pp.

22160-1 Paperbound $2.00

THREE GOTHIC NOVELS: THE CASTLE OF OTRANTO BY HORACE WALPOLE; VATHEK BY WILLIAM BECKFORD; THE VAMPYRE BY JOHN POLIDORI, WITH FRAGMENT OF A NOVEL BY LORD BYRON, edited by E. F. Bleiler. The first Gothic novel, by Walpole; the finest Oriental tale in English, by Beckford; powerful Romantic supernatural story in versions by Polidori and Byron. All extremely important in history of literature; all still exciting, packed with supernatural thrills, ghosts, haunted castles, magic, etc. xl + 291pp.

21232-7 Paperbound $2.00

THE BEST TALES OF HOFFMANN, E. T. A. Hoffmann. 10 of Hoffmann's most important stories, in modern re-editings of standard translations: Nutcracker and the King of Mice, Signor Formica, Automata, The Sandman, Rath Krespel, The Golden Flowerpot, Master Martin the Cooper, The Mines of Falun, The King's Betrothed, A New Year's Eve Adventure. 7 illustrations by Hoffmann. Edited by E. F. Bleiler. xxxix + 419pp.

21793-0 Paperbound $2.50

GHOST AND HORROR STORIES OF AMBROSE BIERCE, Ambrose Bierce. 23 strikingly modern stories of the horrors latent in the human mind: The Eyes of the Panther, The Damned Thing, An Occurrence at Owl Creek Bridge, An Inhabitant of Carcosa, etc., plus the dream-essay, Visions of the Night. Edited by E. F. Bleiler. xxii + 199pp.

20767-6 Paperbound $1.50

BEST GHOST STORIES OF J. S. LeFANU, J. Sheridan LeFanu. Finest stories by Victorian master often considered greatest supernatural writer of all. Carmilla, Green Tea, The Haunted Baronet, The Familiar, and 12 others. Most never before available in the U. S. A. Edited by E. F. Bleiler. 8 illustrations from Victorian publications. xvii + 467pp.

20415-4 Paperbound $3.00

THE TIME STREAM, THE GREATEST ADVENTURE, AND THE PURPLE SAPPHIRE— THREE SCIENCE FICTION NOVELS, John Taine (Eric Temple Bell). Great American mathematician was also foremost science fiction novelist of the 1920's. *The Time Stream,* one of all-time classics, uses concepts of circular time; *The Greatest Adventure,* incredibly ancient biological experiments from Antarctica threaten to escape; The *Purple Sapphire,* superscience, lost races in Central Tibet, survivors of the Great Race. 4 illustrations by Frank R. Paul. v + 532pp.

21180-0 Paperbound $3.00

SEVEN SCIENCE FICTION NOVELS, H. G. Wells. The standard collection of the great novels. Complete, unabridged. *First Men in the Moon, Island of Dr. Moreau, War of the Worlds, Food of the Gods, Invisible Man, Time Machine, In the Days of the Comet.* Not only science fiction fans, but every educated person owes it to himself to read these novels. 1015pp.

20264-X Clothbound $5.00

LAST AND FIRST MEN AND STAR MAKER, TWO SCIENCE FICTION NOVELS, Olaf Stapledon. Greatest future histories in science fiction. In the first, human intelligence is the "hero," through strange paths of evolution, interplanetary invasions, incredible technologies, near extinctions and reemergences. Star Maker describes the quest of a band of star rovers for intelligence itself, through time and space: weird inhuman civilizations, crustacean minds, symbiotic worlds, etc. Complete, unabridged. v + 438pp. 21962-3 Paperbound $2.50

THREE PROPHETIC NOVELS, H. G. WELLS. Stages of a consistently planned future for mankind. *When the Sleeper Wakes,* and *A Story of the Days to Come,* anticipate *Brave New World* and *1984,* in the 21st Century; *The Time Machine,* only complete version in print, shows farther future and the end of mankind. All show Wells's greatest gifts as storyteller and novelist. Edited by E. F. Bleiler. x + 335pp. (USO) 20605-X Paperbound $2.25

THE DEVIL'S DICTIONARY, Ambrose Bierce. America's own Oscar Wilde— Ambrose Bierce—offers his barbed iconoclastic wisdom in over 1,000 definitions hailed by H. L. Mencken as "some of the most gorgeous witticisms in the English language." 145pp. 20487-1 Paperbound $1.25

MAX AND MORITZ, Wilhelm Busch. Great children's classic, father of comic strip, of two bad boys, Max and Moritz. Also Ker and Plunk (Plisch und Plumm), Cat and Mouse, Deceitful Henry, Ice-Peter, The Boy and the Pipe, and five other pieces. Original German, with English translation. Edited by H. Arthur Klein; translations by various hands and H. Arthur Klein. vi + 216pp.
20181-3 Paperbound $2.00

PIGS IS PIGS AND OTHER FAVORITES, Ellis Parker Butler. The title story is one of the best humor short stories, as Mike Flannery obfuscates biology and English. Also included, That Pup of Murchison's, The Great American Pie Company, and Perkins of Portland. 14 illustrations. v + 109pp. 21532-6 Paperbound $1.00

THE PETERKIN PAPERS, Lucretia P. Hale. It takes genius to be as stupidly mad as the Peterkins, as they decide to become wise, celebrate the "Fourth," keep a cow, and otherwise strain the resources of the Lady from Philadelphia. Basic book of American humor. 153 illustrations. 219pp. 20794-3 Paperbound $1.50

PERRAULT'S FAIRY TALES, translated by A. E. Johnson and S. R. Littlewood, with 34 full-page illustrations by Gustave Doré. All the original Perrault stories— Cinderella, Sleeping Beauty, Bluebeard, Little Red Riding Hood, Puss in Boots, Tom Thumb, etc.—with their witty verse morals and the magnificent illustrations of Doré. One of the five or six great books of European fairy tales. viii + 117pp. 8⅛ x 11. 22311-6 Paperbound $2.00

OLD HUNGARIAN FAIRY TALES, Baroness Orczy. Favorites translated and adapted by author of the *Scarlet Pimpernel.* Eight fairy tales include "The Suitors of Princess Fire-Fly," "The Twin Hunchbacks," "Mr. Cuttlefish's Love Story," and "The Enchanted Cat." This little volume of magic and adventure will captivate children as it has for generations. 90 drawings by Montagu Barstow. 96pp.
(USO) 22293-4 Paperbound $1.95

THE RED FAIRY BOOK, Andrew Lang. Lang's color fairy books have long been children's favorites. This volume includes Rapunzel, Jack and the Bean-stalk and 35 other stories, familiar and unfamiliar. 4 plates, 93 illustrations x + 367pp.
21673-X Paperbound $2.50

THE BLUE FAIRY BOOK, Andrew Lang. Lang's tales come from all countries and all times. Here are 37 tales from Grimm, the Arabian Nights, Greek Mythology, and other fascinating sources. 8 plates, 130 illustrations. xi + 390pp.
21437-0 Paperbound $2.50

HOUSEHOLD STORIES BY THE BROTHERS GRIMM. Classic English-language edition of the well-known tales — Rumpelstiltskin, Snow White, Hansel and Gretel, The Twelve Brothers, Faithful John, Rapunzel, Tom Thumb (52 stories in all). Translated into simple, straightforward English by Lucy Crane. Ornamented with headpieces, vignettes, elaborate decorative initials and a dozen full-page illustrations by Walter Crane. x + 269pp.
21080-4 Paperbound $2.50

THE MERRY ADVENTURES OF ROBIN HOOD, Howard Pyle. The finest modern versions of the traditional ballads and tales about the great English outlaw. Howard Pyle's complete prose version, with every word, every illustration of the first edition. Do not confuse this facsimile of the original (1883) with modern editions that change text or illustrations. 23 plates plus many page decorations. xxii + 296pp.
22043-5 Paperbound $2.50

THE STORY OF KING ARTHUR AND HIS KNIGHTS, Howard Pyle. The finest children's version of the life of King Arthur; brilliantly retold by Pyle, with 48 of his most imaginative illustrations. xviii + 313pp. 6⅛ x 9¼.
21445-1 Paperbound $2.50

THE WONDERFUL WIZARD OF OZ, L. Frank Baum. America's finest children's book in facsimile of first edition with all Denslow illustrations in full color. The edition a child should have. Introduction by Martin Gardner. 23 color plates, scores of drawings. iv + 267pp.
20691-2 Paperbound $2.25

THE MARVELOUS LAND OF OZ, L. Frank Baum. The second Oz book, every bit as imaginative as the Wizard. The hero is a boy named Tip, but the Scarecrow and the Tin Woodman are back, as is the Oz magic. 16 color plates, 120 drawings by John R. Neill. 287pp.
20692-0 Paperbound $2.50

THE MAGICAL MONARCH OF MO, L. Frank Baum. Remarkable adventures in a land even stranger than Oz. The best of Baum's books not in the Oz series. 15 color plates and dozens of drawings by Frank Verbeck. xviii + 237pp.
21892-9 Paperbound $2.00

THE BAD CHILD'S BOOK OF BEASTS, MORE BEASTS FOR WORSE CHILDREN, A MORAL ALPHABET, Hilaire Belloc. Three complete humor classics in one volume. Be kind to the frog, and do not call him names . . . and 28 other whimsical animals. Familiar favorites and some not so well known. Illustrated by Basil Blackwell. 156pp.
(USO) 20749-8 Paperbound $1.25

EAST O' THE SUN AND WEST O' THE MOON, George W. Dasent. Considered the best of all translations of these Norwegian folk tales, this collection has been enjoyed by generations of children (and folklorists too). Includes True and Untrue, Why the Sea is Salt, East O' the Sun and West O' the Moon, Why the Bear is Stumpy-Tailed, Boots and the Troll, The Cock and the Hen, Rich Peter the Pedlar, and 52 more. The only edition with all 59 tales. 77 illustrations by Erik Werenskiold and Theodor Kittelsen. xv + 418pp. 22521-6 Paperbound $3.00

GOOPS AND HOW TO BE THEM, Gelett Burgess. Classic of tongue-in-cheek humor, masquerading as etiquette book. 87 verses, twice as many cartoons, show mischievous Goops as they demonstrate to children virtues of table manners, neatness, courtesy, etc. Favorite for generations. viii + 88pp. 6½ x 9¼. 22233-0 Paperbound $1.25

ALICE'S ADVENTURES UNDER GROUND, Lewis Carroll. The first version, quite different from the final *Alice in Wonderland,* printed out by Carroll himself with his own illustrations. Complete facsimile of the "million dollar" manuscript Carroll gave to Alice Liddell in 1864. Introduction by Martin Gardner. viii + 96pp. Title and dedication pages in color. 21482-6 Paperbound $1.25

THE BROWNIES, THEIR BOOK, Palmer Cox. Small as mice, cunning as foxes, exuberant and full of mischief, the Brownies go to the zoo, toy shop, seashore, circus, etc., in 24 verse adventures and 266 illustrations. Long a favorite, since their first appearance in St. Nicholas Magazine. xi + 144pp. 6⅝ x 9¼. 21265-3 Paperbound $1.75

SONGS OF CHILDHOOD, Walter De La Mare. Published (under the pseudonym Walter Ramal) when De La Mare was only 29, this charming collection has long been a favorite children's book. A facsimile of the first edition in paper, the 47 poems capture the simplicity of the nursery rhyme and the ballad, including such lyrics as I Met Eve, Tartary, The Silver Penny. vii + 106pp. 21972-0 Paperbound $1.25

THE COMPLETE NONSENSE OF EDWARD LEAR, Edward Lear. The finest 19th-century humorist-cartoonist in full: all nonsense limericks, zany alphabets, Owl and Pussycat, songs, nonsense botany, and more than 500 illustrations by Lear himself. Edited by Holbrook Jackson. xxix + 287pp. (USO) 20167-8 Paperbound $2.00

BILLY WHISKERS: THE AUTOBIOGRAPHY OF A GOAT, Frances Trego Montgomery. A favorite of children since the early 20th century, here are the escapades of that rambunctious, irresistible and mischievous goat—Billy Whiskers. Much in the spirit of *Peck's Bad Boy,* this is a book that children never tire of reading or hearing. All the original familiar illustrations by W. H. Fry are included: 6 color plates, 18 black and white drawings. 159pp. 22345-0 Paperbound $2.00

MOTHER GOOSE MELODIES. Faithful republication of the fabulously rare Munroe and Francis "copyright 1833" Boston edition—the most important Mother Goose collection, usually referred to as the "original." Familiar rhymes plus many rare ones, with wonderful old woodcut illustrations. Edited by E. F. Bleiler. 128pp. 4½ x 6⅜. 22577-1 Paperbound $1.25

TWO LITTLE SAVAGES; BEING THE ADVENTURES OF TWO BOYS WHO LIVED AS INDIANS AND WHAT THEY LEARNED, Ernest Thompson Seton. Great classic of nature and boyhood provides a vast range of woodlore in most palatable form, a genuinely entertaining story. Two farm boys build a teepee in woods and live in it for a month, working out Indian solutions to living problems, star lore, birds and animals, plants, etc. 293 illustrations. vii + 286pp.

20985-7 Paperbound $2.50

PETER PIPER'S PRACTICAL PRINCIPLES OF PLAIN & PERFECT PRONUNCIATION. Alliterative jingles and tongue-twisters of surprising charm, that made their first appearance in America about 1830. Republished in full with the spirited woodcut illustrations from this earliest American edition. 32pp. $4\frac{1}{2}$ x $6\frac{3}{8}$.

22560-7 Paperbound $1.00

SCIENCE EXPERIMENTS AND AMUSEMENTS FOR CHILDREN, Charles Vivian. 73 easy experiments, requiring only materials found at home or easily available, such as candles, coins, steel wool, etc.; illustrate basic phenomena like vacuum, simple chemical reaction, etc. All safe. Modern, well-planned. Formerly *Science Games for Children*. 102 photos, numerous drawings. 96pp. $6\frac{1}{8}$ x $9\frac{1}{4}$.

21856-2 Paperbound $1.25

AN INTRODUCTION TO CHESS MOVES AND TACTICS SIMPLY EXPLAINED, Leonard Barden. Informal intermediate introduction, quite strong in explaining reasons for moves. Covers basic material, tactics, important openings, traps, positional play in middle game, end game. Attempts to isolate patterns and recurrent configurations. Formerly *Chess*. 58 figures. 102pp. (USO) 21210-6 Paperbound $1.25

LASKER'S MANUAL OF CHESS, Dr. Emanuel Lasker. Lasker was not only one of the five great World Champions, he was also one of the ablest expositors, theorists, and analysts. In many ways, his Manual, permeated with his philosophy of battle, filled with keen insights, is one of the greatest works ever written on chess. Filled with analyzed games by the great players. A single-volume library that will profit almost any chess player, beginner or master. 308 diagrams. xli x 349pp.

20640-8 Paperbound $2.75

THE MASTER BOOK OF MATHEMATICAL RECREATIONS, Fred Schuh. In opinion of many the finest work ever prepared on mathematical puzzles, stunts, recreations; exhaustively thorough explanations of mathematics involved, analysis of effects, citation of puzzles and games. Mathematics involved is elementary. Translated by F. Göbel. 194 figures. xxiv + 430pp. 22134-2 Paperbound $3.00

MATHEMATICS, MAGIC AND MYSTERY, Martin Gardner. Puzzle editor for Scientific American explains mathematics behind various mystifying tricks: card tricks, stage "mind reading," coin and match tricks, counting out games, geometric dissections, etc. Probability sets, theory of numbers clearly explained. Also provides more than 400 tricks, guaranteed to work, that you can do. 135 illustrations. xii + 176pp.

20338-2 Paperbound $1.50

MATHEMATICAL PUZZLES FOR BEGINNERS AND ENTHUSIASTS, Geoffrey Mott-Smith. 189 puzzles from easy to difficult—involving arithmetic, logic, algebra, properties of digits, probability, etc.—for enjoyment and mental stimulus. Explanation of mathematical principles behind the puzzles. 135 illustrations. viii + 248pp.
20198-8 Paperbound $1.75

PAPER FOLDING FOR BEGINNERS, William D. Murray and Francis J. Rigney. Easiest book on the market, clearest instructions on making interesting, beautiful origami. Sail boats, cups, roosters, frogs that move legs, bonbon boxes, standing birds, etc. 40 projects; more than 275 diagrams and photographs. 94pp.
20713-7 Paperbound $1.00

TRICKS AND GAMES ON THE POOL TABLE, Fred Herrmann. 79 tricks and games— some solitaires, some for two or more players, some competitive games—to entertain you between formal games. Mystifying shots and throws, unusual caroms, tricks involving such props as cork, coins, a hat, etc. Formerly *Fun on the Pool Table*. 77 figures. 95pp.
21814-7 Paperbound $1.00

HAND SHADOWS TO BE THROWN UPON THE WALL: A SERIES OF NOVEL AND AMUSING FIGURES FORMED BY THE HAND, Henry Bursill. Delightful picturebook from great-grandfather's day shows how to make 18 different hand shadows: a bird that flies, duck that quacks, dog that wags his tail, camel, goose, deer, boy, turtle, etc. Only book of its sort. vi + 33pp. 6½ x 9¼.
21779-5 Paperbound $1.00

WHITTLING AND WOODCARVING, E. J. Tangerman. 18th printing of best book on market. "If you can cut a potato you can carve" toys and puzzles, chains, chessmen, caricatures, masks, frames, woodcut blocks, surface patterns, much more. Information on tools, woods, techniques. Also goes into serious wood sculpture from Middle Ages to present, East and West. 464 photos, figures. x + 293pp.
20965-2 Paperbound $2.00

HISTORY OF PHILOSOPHY, Julián Marías. Possibly the clearest, most easily followed, best planned, most useful one-volume history of philosophy on the market; neither skimpy nor overfull. Full details on system of every major philosopher and dozens of less important thinkers from pre-Socratics up to Existentialism and later. Strong on many European figures usually omitted. Has gone through dozens of editions in Europe. 1966 edition, translated by Stanley Appelbaum and Clarence Strowbridge. xviii + 505pp.
21739-6 Paperbound $3.00

YOGA: A SCIENTIFIC EVALUATION, Kovoor T. Behanan. Scientific but non-technical study of physiological results of yoga exercises; done under auspices of Yale U. Relations to Indian thought, to psychoanalysis, etc. 16 photos. xxiii + 270pp.
20505-3 Paperbound $2.50

Prices subject to change without notice.
Available at your book dealer or write for free catalogue to Dept. GI, Dover Publications, Inc., 180 Varick St., N. Y., N. Y. 10014. Dover publishes more than 150 books each year on science, elementary and advanced mathematics, biology, music, art, literary history, social sciences and other areas.